Spiritual Education

Cul~~~ ~~~~~rences

URY

Spiritual Education

Cultural, Religious and Social Differences

NEW PERSPECTIVES FOR THE 21st CENTURY

Edited by

Jane Erricker, Cathy Ota
and Clive Erricker

sussex
ACADEMIC
PRESS

BRIGHTON • PORTLAND

2 4 6 8 10 9 7 5 3 1

First published in 2001 in Great Britain by
SUSSEX ACADEMIC PRESS
PO Box 2950
Brighton BN2 5SP

and in the United States of America by
SUSSEX ACADEMIC PRESS
5824 N.E. Hassalo St.
Portland, Oregon 97213-3644

British Library Cataloguing in Publication Data
A CIP catalogue record for this book is available from the British Library.

Library of Congress Cataloging-in-Publication Data
Spiritual education : cultural, religious, and social differences : new perspectives for the 21st century / edited by Jane Erricker, Cathy Ota, and Clive Erricker.
p. cm.
Includes bibliographical references and index.
ISBN 1–902210–60–3 (alk. paper) — ISBN 1–902210–61–1 (pbk. : alk. paper)
1. Religious education—Congresses. 2. Children—Religious life—Congresses.
3. Spiritual life—Congresses. I. Erricker, Jane. II. Ota, Cathy. III. Erricker, Clive.
IV. International Conference on Children's Spirituality (1st : 2000 : University College Chichester)
BL42 .S69 2001
291.7′5—dc.21   2001049346

Typeset and designed by G&G Editorial, Brighton
Printed by TJ International, Padstow, Cornwall
This book is printed on acid-free paper

Contents

Introduction

This collected volume has emerged from the First International Conference on Children's Spirituality held at University College Chichester in July 2000. The reason for the conference was the growing interest in debate on spiritual education both within the United Kingdom and internationally. In 1996 the Children and Worldviews Project launched the *International Journal of Children's Spirituality* in order to foster that debate. By 1998 it became clear that, following the success of the journal in attracting international contributions, and with interest in spiritual education proliferating in other refereed journals – notably with contributions from the United States, Australia and Europe – that an international forum was required. The conference provided a forum where a more organized presentation of contributions could take place, and where those involved in this area internationally, nationally and regionally could meet and discuss informally. In other words, it was time we all got together.

One of the most pleasing outcomes of this event was the real concern evident to discuss and share, and to consider how the delegation could promote and facilitate children and young people's spiritual growth. One result of this was that people wanted to go on meeting; thus a second conference took place in Haifa, Israel, in July–August 2001, and more conferences are planned. Delegates expressed the importance of publishing the contributions to the conference, so that they could be shared more widely. The proceedings of the Haifa conference will be published as *Spirituality and Ethics in Education: Philosophical, Theological, and Cultural Perspectives*, edited by Hanan A. Alexander (September 2002). These two volumes comprise the first publications of a series titled *Issues in Spiritual Education*. Contributors intend using the books, which will also be published as student paperbacks, as set texts for courses in children's spirituality

The papers presented at the conference were too numerous to be included in one volume. Also, a publication such as this has to be more than a collection amounting to the proceedings; it has to have design, structure and coherence for a wider readership. In considering this editorially we laid down criteria we considered worthy to create a volume that faithfully reflected the range of debate and quality of contributions, but which would also provide a marker or basis on which international consideration of spiritual education could be developed more fully. These criteria were as follows:

- the research quality of the submission;
- the suitability for this volume and its readership;
- the contribution to breadth and depth of debate in spiritual education;
- the contribution to breadth of international representation;
- the gender balance of authorship.

Whilst this still left a number of contributions we would have liked to include but could not find space for, the selection process ensured, we feel, both high quality and a suitable representation of research and issues pertaining to spiritual education at the present time.

The structure of this book identifies the range of interdisciplinary approaches to the subject. It is divided into three parts:

- Religious and Theological Approaches
- Psychological and Anthropological Approaches
- Pedagogical Approaches

In arriving at this structure we seek to map out the areas of debate and identify those disciplinary areas from which significant contributions are being made. There is, inevitably, some overlap. But this is largely because of the interdisciplinary nature of the dialogue. This we perceive as a healthy sign. Nevertheless, there are clear disciplinary characteristics in the approaches used in the different offerings; and it was on this basis that the sectional divisions were made. For example, in Part I the orientation of the contributions is from a religious or theological perspective. Part II employs either a psychological or a (socio) anthropological perspective. In Part III the main concern is with pedagogical issues, whether they are being approached from within a religious/theological or humanistic context. With contributions that ranged across these divisions, for example theological and pedagogical, we placed them where they seemed to be most suitably situated in relation to their affinity with other chapters in these sections. The conclusion identifies a number of significant issues raised throughout the book and classifies them.

The delight in editing this volume is that we believe it marks out spiritual education as a discrete academic and educational area of study. It sits alongside values education, religious education and citizenship but is not subsumed within any of them. The reason for this becomes clear in reading the chapters. There is a concern with notions of spiritual well-being at an individual, societal and global level. These concerns relate to the spiritual health of religion, on the one hand, and the spiritual health of the world and its societies, on the other. Thus, the character-ization of spirituality that pervades the observations and analyses of the researchers included is open, inclusive and accepting of diversity. It is not exclusive and doctrinaire. There is a clear concern with political and economic issues related to globalization and corporatism. Authors address the impact of cultural plurality, postmodernity and post-colonialism from the emergent perspectives of spiritual education. Human rights, and the marginalization of individuals and minority groups, are reflected upon in relation to the experiences of, and influ-ences upon, young people in the modern world. There is evidence of real attempts to engage with and listen to young people's experiences and converse with them. There are signs of hope and conviction, even dissent, in the face of the materialist preoccupations of late capitalism. Above all, spiritual education is beginning to find a voice and language with which to address the modern world and its education systems. A key term to emerge from this debate, threading its way through this volume, is "relationality". It refers, in different ways, to the idea that the spiritual health of the modern world can only be recaptured and sustained if we understand and prioritize the importance of relation-ships. Whilst such a term is ubiquitously used within the rhetoric of political and moral pronouncements, and as a result may appear facile, the contributions to this debate have taken it seriously and evidence that such a priority challenges prevalent assumptions within society and education. Spiritual education, we may say, is beginning to offer a radical challenge to our contemporary values.

Part I

Religious and Theological Approaches

RELIGIOUS and theological approaches to spiritual education might seem the most obvious areas of interest in the subject. In a world increasingly beset by secularization, as far as religious institutional affiliation is concerned, a religious and theological commitment would appear to be the most obvious place for spiritual growth and nurture. However, as these contributions show, there is a complexity to be addressed regarding whether traditional religious institutions and theological thinking can adequately meet the needs of the modern child. Perhaps the latter necessarily questions tradition and asks it to consider its purpose in the modern world if it is to be of relevance to young people's spiritual needs and questing. A sense of spiritual identity requires something more in a culturally plural age than mere religious affiliation. The writers in Part I offer challenges and insights as to what is required of theology and religion if they are to provide a spiritual education that matches the spiritual needs and requirements of young people.

Jerome Berryman argues that spirituality is not part of our verbal communication system and therefore it cannot be reduced to the "constraints of symbolic communication". Thus, when he asks: "Why do we know 'spirituality' when we meet it, but can't define it?" he points to it being non-verbal. Turning to Wittgenstein, he refers to the latter's observation that "everything of significance can only be shown and not said". Thus, spirituality is not a philosophical problem. Rather, spiritual matters are existential ones more directly communicated by such "calls" as laughing, crying and silence. Taking laughing and crying as particular connected examples he indicates how different types of laughing and crying "calls" alert us to differing spiritual states which have significant effects on the spiritual nurture of the young. He warns religious educators of the inherent complexity of non-verbal spirituality, which includes its dark side. He concludes by identifying religious language – when uprooted from its living, non-verbal spiritual source – as having potentially destructive spiritual effects.

Sandy Eisenberg Sasso writes from the perspective of a Jewish Rabbi in the Reform tradition. She is also the author of a number of children's books which tell stories from the Jewish tradition. Her concern is how Jewish children can come to learn Torah. Recognizing the inherent spiritual life of children she affirms them as "builders" rather than passive recipients, and asks "How does Judaism know the voice of the child and how does it see fit to honour that voice and help it speak?" She sees this question being answered by encouraging relationship and dialogue. In practice this means encouraging children to ask questions and to respond by telling stories, so encouraging the spirit of wonder. In this children are encouraged to be seekers "yearning for someone to tell them their story". Using the seder meal as a primary example she suggests that stories come to life in the relationship between reader and audience, and that without the presence of children both story and tradition are incomplete. In this relationship the adult becomes the friend and partner to the child on a spiritual journey to discover Torah which "begins with the child's first breath".

Hanan Alexander and Miriam Ben-Peretz call for "a conception of curriculum grounded in ethics and theology". Writing from a Jewish perspective, but also using enlightenment and post-enlightenment thinking, they argue that a curriculum needs an ethical and theological rather than an epistemological basis. The latter, they suggest, is a result of modernist emphasis on objectivity and universality.

Whilst acknowledging Dewey's child-centredness and Lyotard's view that there should be no privileging of epistemological doctrines they reject a thoroughgoing relativism by introducing an appeal to the concept of transcendence and the view that ethics precedes epistemology. Goodness is the primary aim of education and conceptions of the good are based on transcendent ideals. Critically examining this claim results in asking, "What is most worth teaching and learning". In turn, implicit in this question is the concern with identity in community. This approach, they argue, constitutes the basis of a "constitutive curriculum"; one which serves the community and which is addressed by the community through an examination of, and response to, its narratives. They term this a "pedagogy of the sacred" with spiritual and ethical concerns at its heart.

Cynthia Dixon "explores the role of Christianity and its advocates for children's spirituality, and some of the distortions that have caused alienation". Her historical survey marks out the contrasts in the way different civilizations have understood and practised the nurture of the young. She argues that Jesus' attitude to and teaching about children was revolutionary, but that his approach was not sustained as a model either within or beyond the Christian Church. She writes, "rarely have children come first as an array of agendas for them to unfold down through history" and that "A theological rationale for severe coercion as the antidote to sinful nature provided a distortion of the Christian scriptures". She advocates that it is now timely to recognize that the nurturing of spirituality demands acknowledging children's worth and sharing with them creatively.

Mark Chater asks how religious traditions should react to the impact of postmodernism and the demise of certainty. He suggests that what has replaced this certainty is exploration and, in terms of research into children's spirituality, an increasing acceptance of the authority of the child's voice and interpretation of experience, rather than prioritizing religious or spiritual instruction. Focusing on Christianity he reviews the range of responses to this situation. He argues that there is a symbiotic relationship between modernity and postmodernity and that this ensures that the religious traditions have a continuing place in the contemporary world; but that the relationship will require of them "a new evolution in thought and practice" which, in the Christian case, he refers to as a return to "Nicene radicalism" involve a "partnership with the poor and the religious other . . . a radical openness to others". This requires a theology of love within which the nurture of children's spirituality can be contextualized.

Elaine Champagne begins by asking the question "Can we learn from children's spirituality?" Her answer is to engage in a process of listening that amounts to theological reflection – a process of mutual enrichment. Listening is a way to "hear the unpredictable". She illustrates this by relating her experience, in a pastoral role, of laughter and grief and the everydayness of spiritual experience as it reveals itself in the questions, observations and conversation of children. Champagne speaks of listening to explicit expressions of children's spirituality and listening for the spiritual underlying their everyday life. In analyses of the underlying meaning within children's expressions she finds "relational intuitions" that, from a Christian theological perspective, point to a call to relate to a "God of promise who turns man towards an unscripted future".

David Tacey's concern is with how established forms of religion can adapt to the spiritual appetite of the young. Working out from his own students' judgements that the "old cultural order", within which are subsumed the traditional forms of religion, "is already dead", he denies that this judgement evidences an anarchic attitude of present-day youth. Instead, he identifies a questing for spirituality that is continually put down by mainstream society. He observes that "some leave the junkyard of the West, turning to the East for enchantment". Affirming that this "turning to the East" evidences a metaphysical vacuum he argues that what is required is a reaction to the profane and secular values of Western Society, which Western youth are already reacting against. Such a reaction requires a replacement of a "fixed, formal, revealed religious ideology" by "a fluid, flexible, processual understanding of faith". He sees this new understanding of faith being achieved by a new emphasis on the God within, and by turning to a more hopeful and creation-centred theology which takes seriously the "care of the soul".

Chapter 1

The Nonverbal Nature of Spirituality and Religious Language

JEROME W. BERRYMAN

WHY do we know "spirituality" when we meet it, but can't define it? Why do our explanations fail to satisfy? Perhaps, the answer is that spirituality is part of our non-verbal communication system. If this is so we cannot hope to make a point-to-point translation from its way of communicating into symbols. This chapter, then, can only gesture towards the non-verbal nature of spirituality to better understand religious language, which refers to it.

Gesturing towards spirituality's non-verbal nature is useful for four reasons. First, spiritual directors (including religious educators and those charged with the responsibility for worship) need to be more aware of spirituality's non-verbal nature to be better guides. Secondly, those who help children make the transition from non-verbal spirituality to religious language need to find ways for this powerful language to be constructively rooted in the non-verbal. Thirdly, we all need to be better informed about spirituality's dark side, so the misuse of religious language can be detected and remedied. Finally, researchers need a way to describe the non-verbal aspect of spirituality to test this hypothesis about its nature.

I shall begin by clarifying the difference between verbal and non-verbal communication in terms of "referencing". Secondly, the method of modes and vectors for depicting spirituality will be described. Thirdly, the mode-and-vector method will be applied and elaborated. The fourth step will be to examine the primary, non-verbal "calls" used to express spirituality. I shall then turn to spirituality's dark side. A synthesis will then be made in terms of complexity emerging out of chaos. Finally, the four reasons why this speculation is useful will be revisited and fundamental conclusions about spirituality and religious language will be drawn.

Referencing and Spirituality

The basis for the following discussion of language and spirituality is Terrence W. Deacon's *The Symbolic Species: The Co-Evolution of Language and the Brain* (Deacon 1997). Deacon's work has been chosen because it deals with the co-evolution of the brain and language in terms of what Deacon calls "referencing". He follows Charles Sanders Peirce to distinguish three categories of referential associations.

Many great philosophers of the mind have used such categories to describe the fundamental forms of knowing, but what Peirce did was reframe the problem of "mind" as a problem of communication, i.e., sign production and interpretation. The three kinds of referencing are termed iconic, indexical and symbolic.

Iconic referencing can be shown by thinking about a bird searching for food in the bark of a tree. The bird registers only "bark" and "not-bark". If a moth is the same texture and colour as the bark and the bird is not attentive, then the interpretation will be "bark" and the meal will be missed. If the moth moves and this is interpreted as not-bark then the moth is eaten. No language is necessary for such interpretations.

Indexical referencing links memories. Suppose a dog is prompted by nature to chase the small furry creatures we call "cats". The "cat" or "not-cat" interpretation is complicated when a small, black and white, furry creature that looks like a cat is encountered. This cat-like creature stands instead of running, raises its tail, and sprays one with an unforgettable, foul, stinging, vapour. The two iconic references of "cat" and "not-cat" and this "not-cat" and "aversion" are coupled in the dog's memory to make an indexical reference. The next time a small, furry, black and white creature stops and raises its tail the dog will link these memories and retreat. No language is involved here either.

Both iconic and indexical referencing relies on relatively stable physical correlations. There is no *necessary* mental linkage. If a parrot stops being fed when it squawks "Wanna cracker!" it probably will stop producing the sound. This is not true of human language. The symbols chosen to carry specific meanings do so as long as the community continues to use them in a particular way.

Our non-verbal system developed independently and alongside language and uses different parts of the brain. The smiles, grimaces, laughs, sobs, hugs, kisses, and all the rest of our non-linguistic communication system are, therefore, not "words without syntax". This is because gestures and vocalizations cannot explain, describe, command or ask. You can neither argue, disagree, bargain, gossip, persuade or change tense with non-verbal communication. Still, calls, grunts, gestures, social grooming, etc. are needed to understand our symbolic referencing. The referencing of symbols is completely different from non-verbal referencing. It takes a shift in learning strategy to move from indexical to symbolic referencing. This difference must be "discovered". It is a "restructuring event". We must make an effort to suppress one set of associative responses, the indexical, for another strategy derived from symbols. Referencing is also hierarchical. If I fail to grasp the symbolic reference for any reason I could still interpret the indexical or iconic relationship, as many of our pets do when we talk to them.

To summarize, then, iconic referencing is an interpretation based on form. Indexical referencing is based on correlation. Symbolic referencing relies on a socially agreed upon set of relationships among symbols. (A wedding ring references a marriage agreement in some cultures but not in others.) This is why we can only hope to gesture in symbols towards the realm of indexical and iconic referencing and yet our symbols owe some of their meaning to the non-verbal context.

Gesturing towards the Non-verbal by Connotation

A definition of spirituality cannot be as clear and distinct as we might like. This task is not like defining a triangle. Instead of verbal precision we need to apply as much connotation as possible to show the non-verbal nature of spirituality. This is because vestiges of the non-verbal can be found in the verbal by noticing such connotations. There are two groups of human beings which are especially sensitive to connotation. One group is adult artists. They retain a special interest in their iconic and indexical referencing and are adept at playing with words, movement, stone, colour, sounds, numbers, social situations, and other media. The second group is children. They have no choice but to be in tune with their non-verbal system of communication, since their symbolic referencing is just developing. I will use the work of Howard Gardner (1994) to develop this idea.

Connotation is rooted in our pre-object-formation way of knowing and continues to influence our language all our lives. It communicates by what Gardner calls modes and vectors, a kind of deep body knowing. This probably begins in a global way and then develops more specificity at canters of sensitivity such as the mouth. A summary follows (Gardner 1994: 101):

Zones	Characteristic Modes	Vectoral Properties
Lips & Tongue	Passive and Active incorporation – take in, or bite, grasp, investigate	Speed – quick or slow Time – regular or irregular Space – wide or narrow & curved or angular
Sphincter	Retention – hold onto Expulsion – let go, release, push out	Facility – ease or strain Repletion – hollow or full
Penis–Vagina	Intrusion – stick into, go into Inclusion – take into, envelop	Density – thick or thin Boundness – open or closed Also: directionality, force, depth, comfort and texture

Gardner's work is based on that of Erik Erikson (Erikson 1963: 72–97), who attempted to bridge the gap between the child's physiological functioning and psychological processes by describing the psychological implications of organ modes and zones, building on his psychoanalytic background. Gardner then applied this connection to the transition from non-verbal into symbolic, placing the roots of connotation in the non-verbal. This is why our definition of spirituality uses connotation as a pairing of related axes of modes and vectors to show the non-verbal nature of spirituality. The resulting pictures of spirituality are detailed below.

Picturing Spirituality

I shall begin by considering a physical operation not spoken about by Gardner. It is the rhythm of life, our breathing in and out. The connection between life and breath is this reflex. It is one of the few we come equipped with at birth. Babies fight for their air. Their bodies know its importance. The Bible begins by God breathing life into us. The Hebrew term *ruach* has deep connotations in our cultural memory, as do the words "animate" and "inanimate". They entered English from the Latin *animare*, which means to fill with breath.

A second experience we are in tune with before language is being globally full and empty. If we are full we are happy. If we are empty we cry to be filled. (Later this global sense will be distinguished from specific zones of fullness and the need to empty them.) One axis for our basic picture of spirituality, then, is the polarity of being full and empty. The other polarity is being animate or inanimate.

The relationship between the two pairs of polarities shows us by the directional force of the vectors pushing towards one or the other pole that sometimes people who are alive can be empty of spirituality. This is shown in the lower-left quadrant of the figure 1.1. By contrast we find that people who are almost dead can be full of spirituality. This is shown by the upper-right quadrant (figure 1.1):

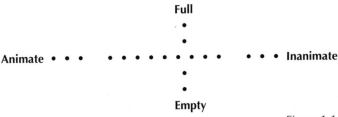

Figure 1.1

To further develop our view of spirituality, let us now examine the vertical spectrum of full and empty more closely. There are different qualities of being globally full and empty. This intuition also has been coded in English with a Latin heritage. *Anima* refers to a current of air, to wind, to breath, and to the soul as a vital principle of life. When the Latin noun becomes masculine, however, as *animus*, the dark side of the polarity becomes evident. *Animus* also refers to the soul, but in contrast to *anima* it points towards intellect and reason. It is also about thought, memory, consciousness and self-possession. There is in addition a hint of character, courage, heart and spirit in its Latin usage, but when the Latin term for spirit becomes masculine it adds the qualities of haughtiness, arrogance, pride, passion, vehemence and wrath. It is this sense, which is the origin of our English word, "animus", which means a feeling of animosity. "Animosity" is the feeling of bitter hostility or hatred towards another person.

There is another breath-related term in Latin for spirit. It is *spiritus*. It refers to breath, air, breeze, spirit, soul, mind, inspiration and courage, but it also refers to haughtiness and pride. It is no wonder that *spiritus* needs to be qualified by the adjective *sanctus* to give it an unqualified sense of the sacred – that which is inviolable, venerable, august, divine, virtuous, holy, pious, innocent, pure, chaste and just.

The polarity of *anima* and *animus* is used to show the quality of spirituality we are full or empty of. The second and related polarity pair shows action in relation to *anima* and *animus*. It ranges from movement towards, to movement away from, another's spirituality. If one moves towards another in a positive way there is pleasure and connectedness. If one moves with *anima* away from such pleasure and connectedness there is loss and sadness. On the other hand, if one moves towards another with animosity the movement is aggressive and unpleasant. Moving away can also be negative if it is done with haughtiness and pride. To capture this complex sense of spirituality the following pairs of modes and vectors are proposed:

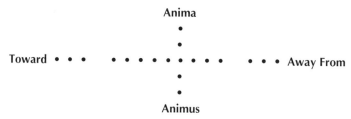

Figure 1.2

I shall now attempt to fill out the meaning of spirituality beyond the above two pictures. A third aspect of spirituality involves an awareness of one's personal life and death. This is spirituality's existential dimension. Existential awareness allows the edge of our knowing and being to come into our consciousness. Such boundary awareness is complicated by a breakdown of language's ordinary usage. Let us take four limit cases to illustrate this. They are existential aloneness (not mere loneliness), freedom, death and the need for meaning.

Let us imagine that these four ultimate issues define the "space" in which we live. These boundaries limit and yet define us and, in addition, all four sides (and there are probably more nuances of our ultimate issues than these four) are related. As we approach any one of the boundaries there is also a kind of oscillation that can be felt between being consumed (thus disappearing and being out of control) and consuming (taking the boundary into one and controlling it).

The consuming aspect of this paradox involves both passive and active incorporation. Passive incorporation involves being taken in. Active incorporation involves biting, grasping and investigating. Other physical connotations jostle us at these boundaries. There are the physical aspects of retention (holding onto) and expulsion (letting go, releasing, pushing out). From the next stage of development there are physical memories of intrusion (stick into, go into) and inclusion (take into, envelop). All of these experiences, felt before we had language or just as it was developing, provide the physical connotation for our words about the above existential issues.

When our ordinary use of language breaks down into the equivocation of existential paradox we stutter and stammer since what we have to say is part of our non-verbal communication system. Some examples will help clarify this. The first example is the case of existential aloneness. I sense that I am alone and crave joining others, but if they begin to incorporate me I oscillate back to aloneness in which I soon begin to crave company again. A second example is our need for meaning. If I create meaning I am comforted by it until I realize that I am the one who created it. It can't define me, since I defined it. We oscillate between seeking and rejecting the meaning we make. With respect to death we rest and then, fearing death, become active, only to rest again. The case of freedom is our fourth example. Freedom is craved by those who are not free until they realize that they *are* free. They then flee to the safety of limitations to avoid taking responsibility for their actions and because of being overwhelmed by the formlessness. Such equivocation is likely to continue all of one's life.

The oscillation described above is entailed in the consuming –consumed axis of figure 1.3, which gestures towards the existential aspect of spirituality. The other axis is the spectrum between the polarities of control and letting go. This is how we often attempt to deal with the consuming-consumed aspect of spirituality.

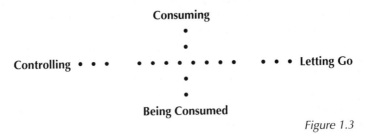

Figure 1.3

With the above three diagrams of spirituality in mind we turn now to three fundamental calls, which alert us further to the complexity of human spirituality. They are laughing, crying and silence.

The Calls of Human Spirituality

In this section we will look at three of the calls used by human beings to signal aspects of their spirituality. They are laughing, crying and silence. By a call I do not mean a simple language without words, because such calls convey very important and complex information. They also have an echo effect, which has benefits as well as dangers. To give an example of a danger related to the mimic effect of laughter, let us suppose children grow up hearing only sarcastic, put-down laughter from living people and the electronic media. They are likely to mimic this sarcastic sound which stimulates the state it references. If their repertoire of laughter does not include the laughter of delight, which references creativity, their creativity is likely to atrophy. If creativity disappears among *Homo sapiens* the ability to adapt is lost and the whole species is in danger of extinction.

The warning call of the vervet monkeys is a further example of audible but non-verbal communication and its echo effect. Once the call is sounded the whole troop picks it up and continues until long after the danger is past. There are three such calls. One signals the danger of eagles and sends the monkeys racing down from upper regions of the trees. The second call sounds the danger of leopards, which sends the troop scampering into the small branches in the upper parts of the trees. The third alarm alerts the monkeys to the danger of snakes. They begin peering into the grass and bushes around them. Such communicating and recruiting arousal is more than predator information. It refers to things in the world and to internal states (Deacon 1997: 59) as language does, but although it grew up alongside language it is independent from it. Despite this, such communication influences our language. For example identical words said with a smile, a sneer, a wink, or tear can mean different things. Our depiction of calls, signalling states of spirituality, will begin by pairing laughing and crying. This is because we sometimes laugh until we cry and cry until we laugh. Both polarities can result in tears. The laughing–crying axis will be related to ecstasy (overwhelming delight) and devastation (overwhelming annihilation). The vague discrimination of these sounds is learned as one grows up, but for researchers and spiritual directors becoming connoisseurs of their nuances it is important to be able to better communicate and monitor the mimic affect.

To give an idea of the kinds of laughter we usually intuit but need to become connoisseurs of are the categories defined for my own Laughter Scale: derision, sardonic, ironic, neutral (from tickling), comic, mirth and delight laughter. Seven such distinctions are about at our limit for ongoing conscious analysis, but Baldasar Castiglione, who counselled one to do everything with *sprezaturra* (graceful ease), identified 35 different kinds of laughter in his *Book of the Courtier* (translated into English in 1528) and illustrated them with jokes taken from Cicero (as referenced by Sanders 1995).

The analysis of tears also invites verbal distinctions, none of which can exhaust the meaning of the non-verbal communication any more than our laughter distinctions can. In *Crying: The Natural and Cultural History of Tears*, Tom Lutz discusses tears of pleasure, theological grace, heroism, mourning, revenge, seduction, escape, empathy and fiction (Lutz 1999). Our relational display is as follows:

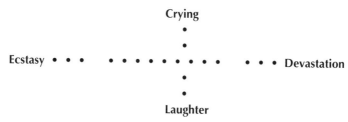

Figure 1.4

When the vectoral force on the horizontal axis of ecstasy and devastation moves one near ecstasy as overwhelming delight we can become "beside ourselves". If the direction of the force moves us towards "devastation", the overwhelming annihilation can also make us beside ourselves. In either case a person may not return from such extreme states. There may be no self to return to. It is no wonder, then, that crying and laughing can become signs of madness when one goes beyond delight and annihilation.

If the force vectors carry us into the upper-left quadrant we find the tears of overflowing fullness. If we are carried into the lower-left quadrant we find the laughter of delight. If we are carried into the upper-right quadrant the tears signal painful loss. Experience in the lower-right quadrant is conveyed by cynical, sarcastic laughter.

We turn now to the third kind of call. It communicates as a call but involves no sound. Silence can signal as well as sounded calls. The clue for its depiction is in the ambiguity of the language we use to refer to silence. In many languages there is a cluster of words which refers to communication without sound. In English they are "stillness", "silence" and "quiet". All three are needed, because no single one contains all that is meant by the whole cluster. Our task, therefore, is to depict this complexity to gain access to its non-verbal nature.

One axis shows stillness, which refers to both movement and sound. For example, when the lake or woods is still, it is not moving. It is also silent. Movement and sound are related. The relationship in terms of physics has to do with movement in the medium of light (waves or quanta) as it stimulates our eyes and in the medium of air as sound waves stimulate our ears.

Figure 1.5

The distinction between quiet and silence is on the basis of motivation. Quiet's motivation is inward while silence is imposed from outside. For example, public silence can be imposed to force an outward calm while at the same time increasing inward agitation.

Discussion of the calls and their references adds to the complexity of spirituality. I turn now to its dark side.

The Dark Side of Spirituality

Each of the above pictures of an aspect of spirituality has a negative as well as positive tone to it. Being Empty (figure 1.1), *Animus* (figure 1.2), Being Consumed (figure 1.3), Devastation (figure 1.4) and imposed silence (figure 1.5) are examples. The religions of the world have built up treasuries of wisdom about how to cope with this dark side. They have also warned followers to be aware that even the positive side of spirituality can be dangerous.

I turn now to a primary polarity of the dark side not yet examined. It deserves special attention, because it comes disguised as play, another aspect of our non-verbal communication system. Play is pleasurable, has no extrinsic goals, is spontaneous, requires engagement, and has formal links to creativity, language learning, and learning social roles. It is an indicator of people who are full of spirituality. Pseudo-play is associated with empty people, who become spirituality sponges. Pseudo-players are parasites. They attract people full of spirituality by their personality or by being so powerful in their social positions that they can compel victims to come close enough to be robbed. Their obsession to control others is motivated by the need to suck their spiritual vitality from them. They are detached, clever and assume disguises for this exploitation. Satan in Milton's *Paradise Lost* is a classic example.

Play and pseudo-play make up one axis to depict this danger. The related polarity is the creation–destruction axis. A few words need to be said about the creative process to show what this polarity is about. The creative process operates on many levels – from biology, to psychology, to sociology, to spirituality. It provides the means to create a menu for supper or articulate one's destiny. It is also the non-verbal process by which the body, mind and spirit carry out their repairs and regenerate.

The creative process at the level of words begins with a disruption of the status quo. This disruption may be a "soft" one that dissolves one's assumptive world by wondering or as-if play. Disruption may also be a "hard", such as the death of a loved one. Once this disruption takes place we begin scanning for a way to repair it by finding a larger meaning to encompass the change. The scanning often takes place in silence and without words. It usually prompts one's preferred way of creating. Gardner has identified at least seven of these ways: words, music, movement, intra-psychic musings, social activity, visual expression such as painting, or mathematics (Gardner 1993).

Insight comes when a new synthesis has taken form. The formation of this synthesis is often felt before it enters consciousness, because the energy shifts from scanning to insight before it is coded in a preferred creative means. The working-out of the insight in terms of one's preferred way of creating is tested by the canons of the particular form. This is as true for mathematics and the scientific method as it is for music, poetry, social action, dance, painting or psychology. Finally, a decision is made to halt the process, which could go on forever, especially if one is a perfectionist. The insight is considered complete enough to furnish one with a new assumption, which then awaits a new disruption.

The reason that this axis has the mode Putting-Together at one end and Taking-Apart at the other is that the creative process always involves both opposing poles. One tears down (or has the status quo broken or dissolved) to build up better, but one might also tear down what is better for the sake of irrational destruction. The diagram of these polarities in reference to each other looks like this:

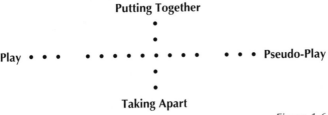

Figure 1.6

I have now presented six figures to show various aspect of spirituality's non-verbal nature, as much as can be shown in symbols and pictures. I now turn to a different kind of presentation, one more dynamic and metaphorical.

The Deep Channel of Living Spirituality

We now need to synthesize the rather static figures above into a dynamic picture of the experience of complexity emerging out of chaos, which makes living systems, human as well as others, "alive". How this feels to human beings is what needs to be conceptualized at this point to guide our recognizing and fostering this positive dynamic in human spirituality.

Complexity emerging in the turbulence of a river is our visual metaphor. On either bank of the river we find the limits for the turbulence, although the river can reshape the banks that give it shape. On both banks we find the collapse of emerging complexity. On one side there is locked-in chaos and on the other bank tightly controlled rigidity.

Laughter/Tears of Madness   **Two-Dimensional Chaos**   **Nothing is Serious**

THE BOUNDARY OF COMEDY IN OPPOSITION TO TRAGEDY

Laughter/   Creativity   Disjunction   Process as Stability   Becoming
Tears of Delight

Serious Laughter/   Complexity   Emerging Game   Comedy–Tragedy   Meaning
Tears of Play   in Interplay

Laughter/   Contemplation   Conjunction   Connection as Stability   Being
Tears of Wonder

THE BOUNDARY OF TRAGEDY IN OPPOSITION TO COMEDY

Laughter/ Tears of Scorn   **Rigidity**   **All is Serious**

Figure 1.7

At one limit is madness, a meaninglessness where nothing matters. On the other bank is the trap of inflexibility where meaning is wound too tightly. The effort to completely control life at this extreme ends in the breaking of the person, heroic as the person may seem. Complexity is found emerging in the interplay of comedy and tragedy, which holds a person in the turbulence of the deep channel. Within the turbulence we can hear the river's sounds. They are the laugher and crying of delight and wonder, which converge into the serious but joyful laugher and tears of play. This is the human sound of complexity as it emerges in the ultimate game, played for the sake of playing without end.

It is in that emerging game within the interplay of comedy and tragedy that we can find our non-verbal meaning for life. It is this dynamic that signals the definition of spirituality at its best, cumbersome and imprecise as the language may be.

Conclusion

The use of the above diagrams will increase the awareness of the non-verbal nature of spirituality for the spiritual director (including religious educators and those charged with the responsibility for worship). They also provide a useful guide for pastoral care. Parents, religious educators and others charged with the responsibility of guiding children from non-verbal spirituality into religious language can find here an appreciation of the child's spiritual complexity, which needs no language. This complexity is important to keep in mind when searching for ways to keep the child's religious language rooted in the creative spirituality they come to us with. We cannot give such spirituality, but we can take it away, even with the best of intentions.

The dark side of spirituality is important for us to know in order to guard against its danger. The traditions of wisdom coded in religious language take on an increased importance when this is understood. It is especially important to be aware of pseudo-play, since it often passes as a way of spiritual direction. Researchers can use the above diagrams to begin to quantify the modes and vectors to make more measurable what is pictured here. Nevertheless, the conceptual work is begun.

It is especially interesting to note the complexity of spirituality shown here. This is one reason why it cannot be translated into a language of spirituality-in-general. It is not an "oblong blur" of good feelings, as is sometimes naively imagined. This means that specific traditions and nuances of religious language are necessary to evoke, guard and nurture our spirituality. Furthermore, since children cannot learn any language-in-general – whether it is the language of mathematics, music, a mother tongue, a way to pray and live, or any other language – we are forced to make compromises. Our non-verbal spirituality must be rendered in specific language traditions despite misunderstanding, misapplication and our inability to translate all that we know, because we are the symbolic species, as Deacon has observed. This is our unique way to make meaning.

Finally, and most importantly, whatever religious tradition of communication we use, we need to ground it in the fullness of a living and creative spirituality. When religious language is uprooted from this source it becomes full of animus and destruction, as all "religious wars" – usually in the name of peace, truth, and love – have shown.

References

Deacon, T. 1997: *The Symbolic Species: The Co-Evolution of Language and the Brain*, New York: W. W. Norton.

Erikson, E. 1963: *Childhood and Society*, New York: W. W. Norton.

Gardner, H. 1993: *Creating Minds: An Anatomy of Creativity Seen Through the Lives of Freud, Einstein, Picasso, Stravinsky, Eliot, Graham and Gandhi*, New York: Basic Books.

—— 1994 [1974]: *The Arts and Human Development*, New York: HarperCollins, Basic Books.

Lutz, T. 1999: *Crying: The Natural and Cultural History of Tears*, New York: W. W. Norton.

Milton, J. 1957: *Paradise Lost*. In M. Hughes, *John Milton: Complete Poems and Major Prose*, New York: Odyssey.

Sanders, B. 1995: *Sudden Glory: Laughter as Subversive History*, Boston: Beacon Press, 1995.

Chapter 2

When Your Children Ask – A Jewish Theology of Childhood

SANDY EISENBERG SASSO

The Taste of Mother's Milk

THE Rabbis of the Talmud tell an extraordinary legend. While a child is still in the womb a light burns above its head. The foetus is able to see from one end of the world to the other. It learns the entire Torah. But as it enters into the air of the world, an angel comes and strikes it directly above the mouth and makes it forget the entire Torah (Niddah 30b). It is said that the groove in the middle of the upper lip (the divine fingerprint) is a reminder of the language we once knew, have lost and yearn to recover. The Latin for this infra-nasal depression is "philtrum" which comes from the Greek root "phileo" which means, "to love". In French the word "philter" means love or magical potion. Set between the nose and mouth, the organs through which we take breath, is a sign of God's love, of our innate spiritual awareness. In Hebrew, the word for breath and soul are the same – *neshama*. The very first act of an infant is to take a breath. So the philtrum may be said to be an outward symbol of the soul.

While the rabbinic legend assumes that the specific content, the religious language of spirituality (as contained in Torah), must be claimed in a life-long process of learning, God's presence is found with each and every breath. Upon birth the infant cries. One might extend the rabbinic *midrash* to say that this results from the angel's strike, the loss of Torah. Milk in the Jewish tradition is a metaphor for Torah. So the first instinct of the child is to nurse, to receive the sweet taste of mother's milk, in other words Torah.

> With whom do you find the cream of Torah? With him who . . . has suckled from his mother's breast. (Berakhot 63b)

To learn Torah then is to engage in an ongoing process of acquiring the sustenance, the ritual and ethics, the narrative and metaphor that provide a way for the soul to speak. In Genesis, the mark on Cain's forehead signifies the human capacity for violence and destruction. In Judaism the narrative paradigm for sin is not Adam and Eve eating from the Tree of Knowledge but Cain's murder of Abel. Cain asks, "Am I my brother's keeper?" His question presupposes a broken universe, where acts are done in isolation of each other, where brother is disconnected from brother. In the rabbinic passage, there is another mark, the "philtrum", the fingerprint of divine love. Rather than teaching of "original sin" Judaism proposes "original virtue", the innate spiritual endowment of the child who perceives the unity of all. The first prayer a Jewish child learns is the *Shema*. It is the central affirmation of the Jewish faith. "Hear, O Israel, the Eternal our God, the Eternal is One." The prayer articulates the oneness experienced in the womb, the "original vision" of childhood.

Children as Builders

Judaism recognizes the inherent spiritual life of children. The tradition welcomes children to the covenant between God and the people of Israel from birth. Ceremoniously, the boy's entry into the covenant is marked during the circumcision ceremony on the eighth day after his birth. In the twentieth century a parallel ceremony (sans the circumcision) has been developed to welcome the girl into the covenant during the naming ritual. The child's place as an integral member of the religious community is affirmed from the very beginnings of life.

A curriculum for formal religious instruction is designated in the *Mishnah*, the earliest post-biblical rabbinic collection of teaching and commentary (which dates from the second pre-Christian century to the early third century of the common era). Children are to learn Scripture at age five, *Mishnah* at age ten, become responsible for the commandments at age thirteen, and are introduced into the study of Talmud at fifteen (Avot 5: 24). But other sources indicate that the spiritual life begins even earlier than formal religious instruction. Abraham is said to have recognized God as Creator at three years of age (Nedarim 32a). Nursing infants, even foetuses, are said to be aware of God's presence: "Out of the mouth of babes and sucklings you have founded strength" (Psalm 8: 3).

Children are neither little adults nor are they empty vessels. A well-known Talmudic passage that finds its way into the synagogue liturgy acknowledges that teaching children about God requires recognition of their religious spirit:

When all your children (*banayich*) shall be taught of the Eternal, great shall be the peace of your children. (Isaiah 54: 13)

Do not call them (*banayich*) your children, but (*bonayich*) your builders. (Berakhot 64a)

One rabbinic interpreter, noting the coincidence of the Hebrew consonants in the words for children, builders and understanding, translates the passage to read: "Do not call them 'your children' but those who have 'true understanding' (root *binah*)" (Shalom 1998: 182). Jewish sources further recognize that children have their own unique understanding of the sacred:

R. Yose bar R. Hanina said: "The Divine Word spoke to each and every person according to his particular capacity (Hebrew – *Koho*). And do not be surprised at this idea. For when manna came down to Israel, each and every person tasted it in keeping with his own capacity – infants in keeping with their capacity, young men in keeping with their capacity, and the elderly in keeping with their capacity. Thus, for the infants . . . the manna tasted like mothers' milk. For it is said 'its taste was like the taste of rich cream' (Numbers 11–18); young men according to their capacity for it is said 'my bread also which I gave you, bread and oil and honey'(Ezekiel 16: 19); and the old men according to their capacity for it is said, 'the taste of it was like wafers made with honey' (Ezekiel 16: 31).

Now what was true about the manna . . . was equally true about the Divine Word. Each and every person heard it according to his own particular capacity. Thus David said, 'The voice of the Lord is in strength' (Psalm 29: 4) – not 'The voice of the Lord is in His strength' (as might be expected from standard Hebrew pronoun usage), but the voice of the Lord is in the strength and capacity of each and every person. Therefore the Holy One said: 'Do not be misled because you hear many voices. Know that I am He who is one and the same: I am the Lord thy God.'" (Pesikta de Rav Kahana 12: 25)

The passage acknowledges that an adult appreciation of the sacred is not better, only different than the child's. Rich cream, bread and honey, wafers and honey are all tasty, albeit not equally so for every age. God speaks in many voices and each voice, including the child's, is but a partial apprehension of the Divine. The more voices one comes to know the closer one comes to understand the One God who includes all voices.

How does Judaism know the voice of the child and how does it see fit to honour that voice and help it to speak? The Jewish text which best answers that question is the *Haggadah*, the book that narrates the experience of the Exodus at the Passover Seder. To be a Jew means to have once been a slave, to have crossed the sea to freedom and to have stood at Sinai. As the death and resurrection of Jesus constitute the core story for Christianity, so Exodus and Sinai contain the central narrative of the Jewish people.

Haggadah – A Pedagogic Model

How striking, then, at the beginning of the *Haggadah*, the child plays a primary role. Early in the Seder the youngest child asks four questions prompted by the differences that appear at this meal. Placing the child at the beginning of the ritual telling of the core event, underscores the centrality of the child in the religious community. The child is not peripheral, someone for whom ancillary activities must be found so as not to disturb the sacred ritual. On the contrary, without the child the ceremony cannot proceed. Not only is the child's spirit honoured, it becomes the starting point of the community's retelling and reliving of its story.

The questions of the *Haggadah* are the beginning of a relationship, a dialogue. To require questions as a liturgical core of the ritual celebration of Passover is to recognize that the spiritual journey is traversed not in isolation but with others. A community's meaning making is embedded in a dialogic process. At the Seder there are two encounters that take place – the meeting of child and family; and the meeting of family and child, with story. In Judaism, the spiritual life is nurtured in the encounter among people and in the people's encounter with sacred narrative or text (Schein 2000).

> Make yourselves into groups to study the Torah, since the knowledge of Torah can be acquired only in association with others . . . Those who sit separately and learn Torah are stupid. (Berakhot 63b)

The traditional method of Jewish study involves two partners and a text. It is from the interaction between individuals and a traditional source of values that learning and spiritual growth occurs. A special name is given to this learning partnership, *hevruta*. It comes from the Hebrew for friendship and derives from the root that means, "bound together". The questions of the *Haggadah* text are meant to provoke a conversation. They are not rote queries; they are born out of wonder. The *Mishnah*, which details the traditional four questions, begins with the observation that (the leader) fills the second cup (of wine) and the child asks his father. If the child does not have knowledge, the *Mishnah* continues, then the father teaches him the four questions (Pesachim10: 4). In a further discussion in the Talmud, the rabbis ask:

> "Why do we remove the table?" (the dishes and seder plate). The school of R. Jannai said: "So that children may perceive (the unusual proceeding)

and inquire (the reasons)". Abaye was sitting before Rabbah, (when) he saw the tray taken up before him. Said he to them: "We have not yet eaten, and they have (already) come (and) removed the tray before us!" Said Rabbah to him: "You have exempted us from reciting, 'Why is this night different?'" (Pesachim 115b)

The Mishnaic and Talmudic passages make it clear that all questions are welcome; the children are not bound to any formulas. The learning environment is so constructed as to invite curiosity. If children do not ask, the appropriate response is not to provide information, which they have not requested, but to pose questions. Spiritual knowledge begins not with the accumulation of facts but with the spirit of inquiry, not with information but discovery. In fact, the four questions might be referred to as the "four wonderments". The usual way of translating the Hebrew of the four questions begins – "Why is this night different . . . " It is also in keeping with the Hebraic formulation to translate – "How different is this night . . . !"

When Your Children Ask – Tell a Story

It might be expected that what follows from the questions that the children ask, their wonderments, are direct answers. But that is not the case. The questions elicit not a single, absolute answer but a story, the story of bondage and freedom. Immediately following the questions, the *Haggadah* reads:

Even if all of us were wise, all of us elders, all of us knowledgeable in the Torah, it would still be incumbent upon us to tell the story of the going out of Egypt. And the more one expands upon the story, the more praiseworthy. (*Haggadah*)

In other words, when your children ask, you should engage in storytelling.

There is a strong storytelling tradition in Judaism. The Torah begins with family narratives and continues through Exodus with the story of a people bound by a covenant, a common text. At the very heart of Sabbath worship is a text, the reading of the Torah. The rabbis, in turn, embellish the stories of the Scripture with *midrashim*. Through *midrash*, a classical method of posing questions and filling in the blank spaces of the sacred narrative, the rabbis bring new meaning to ancient text. Hasidism, which flourished in the eighteenth and nineteenth centuries, added a rich and long folk treasury of story born out of its own unique history. There is an insightful Hasidic story of a wealthy man who had agreed to pay in gold for each and every story the *maggid* (the holy storyteller) could tell him. What he was eager and waiting for years was to hear was his own story. For the great founder of Hasidism, the Baal Shem Tov had once told him, "When someone comes and tells you your story, you will be at peace."

Judaism recognizes storytelling as integral to the spiritual journey. To hear a story it is necessary to quiet the self, to relinquish control. As much as we would like to stop Pharaoh from hardening his heart, God from visiting the tenth plague, we cannot. The characters of the narrative invite the reader into the story not as directors but as witnesses. But if listeners are open enough, silent enough, the soul of the characters touch their own. The spiritual life is precisely about quieting the self, being humble in the face of circumstances beyond control and empathizing with others.

Stories require attention to detail. The time of day or night, the desert or the palace, are all-important to set the stage for the story. It matters if the characters stutter or speak eloquently; travel by horse and chariot or by foot. Stories help readers pay attention to detail, to wonder at what might otherwise be taken for granted.

As characters strive to make sense of their lives, to find a way through difficulty and despair, they pave a path to redemption. They help readers imagine another reality. There should be classrooms in religious institutions, but synagogues, churches, mosques are not only classrooms and their children not only students. Holy places of gathering are gateways and those who enter, especially the young, are seekers yearning for someone to tell them their story.

Jerome Bruner suggests that it is not just the content of stories that is important in education, but also the very structure of narrative. It is how we frame our experiences. He reminds us of how Peter Pan pleads with Wendy to return to Never Never Land to teach the Lost Boys how to tell stories. "If they knew how to tell them, the Lost Boys might be able to grow up" (Bruner 1996: 40).

Different Spiritual Temperaments

Connecting the child's personal story with the larger story of the people of Israel is the purpose of the *Haggadah*. The larger narrative gives meaning to the private story and the personal narrative enlarges the communal story. John Westerhoff tells of four stages of faith – experienced faith, affiliative faith, searching faith and owned faith (Westerhoff 1976). Applying Westerhoff's stages, we discover that what happens in the *Haggadah* is the connection of "my story", experienced faith, with "their story", the community's tradition, in order to arrive at "our story", owned faith. As the narrative of the *Haggadah* proceeds, there is an interlude, reminding the participants that there is more than one way to tell the story. Children are of different spiritual temperaments, at different stages in their development. The *Haggadah* speaks of four children. The wise child asks – "What are the testimonies, the statutes and the laws which the Lord your God commanded us?" (Deuteronomy 6: 20).[1] The wicked child who appears to exclude himself or herself from the community asks – "What does this service mean to you?" (Exodus12: 26). The simple child asks only – "What is this?" (Exodus13: 14). The fourth child is one who does not know how to ask. Once again the four children exemplify Westerhoff's four stages of faith. The child who does not know how to ask is the youngster who is experiencing faith through ritual and celebration, but is not yet able to articulate that experience.

The child who simply asks, "What is this?" seeks a connection with the community's understanding of tradition. The so-called "wicked" or "challenging" child searches for the connection between his or her story and that of the community of faith. Where, in other words, do "I" fit in with them? The wise child (reflective) has found a connection between the two narratives; the faith of the ancestors becomes the faith of the child. In other words, "my story" has found a place in "their story" and has become "our story".

Commentaries on the *Haggadah* have suggested that the text does not refer to four different children, but that something of the characteristics of each child resides in every person (Levitt and Strassfeld 2000). Sometimes children feel comfortable with the community; sometimes they challenge and doubt that their story finds a place in the community's tradition. The four children may also be seen as reflecting different ages and stages of cognitive development or simply be expressions of differing spiritual temperaments. Whatever the explanation, the *Haggadah* includes and addresses all.

The actual telling of the story of the Exodus takes different forms in the *Haggadah* to respond to the different spiritual temperaments at the Seder. An elaboration of Scriptural verse, *midrash*, is reinforced through ritual actions. The story is told and lived out and then celebrated through song. Beginning with questions, with wonderments, proceeding to narrative and then songs of praise, the central event that defines the Jewish people is personally experienced. If one were to ask what is the point of the *Haggadah* the answer, I believe, would be that the story is the point. The story becomes the impetus for action: it provides a narrative for social change because it helps readers imagine an alternative reality.

The Child's Search as Part of the Adult Journey

As the Seder concludes, the child's role again becomes paramount. At the beginning of the Seder, the leader breaks a piece of *matza* into two pieces. The larger piece is wrapped in a cloth and hidden. As the Seder reaches its end, it is customary for the children to search for the hidden *matza*, called the *afikoman*. Until it is found, the Seder cannot conclude. When the *afikoman* is found, the children are rewarded with a small gift, and everyone at the table is required to eat a small piece of this *matza*. In some families, it is the children who try and steal the *afikoman* from the leader and the leader who must encourage the children to return the *matza*. In either case, the ritual points to a crucial understanding of the place of children in the faith community.

The community is not biding its time until the child grows into adulthood. The family's retelling of the ancient story requires the child's story, without which the community is incomplete. Without the child, the community cannot discover what makes it whole. It is the child's questions that open the Seder, and it is the child's search that concludes it.

A Shavuot Ritual

One of the rituals of the Seder is to open the door for the prophet Elijah. It is a custom that developed in the Middle Ages as a way of telling the surrounding community that nothing suspect was going on in Jewish homes on the night of Passover. It was, in part, a response to the accusation of blood libel (which falsely charged Jews of using the blood of Christian children to bake *matza*) that threatened the Jewish community. But the open door was also an invitation to Elijah, the prophet meant to announce the coming of the Messiah, to herald the promise of redemption. How telling then that in some households the custom evolved that the individual chosen to open the door for Elijah is a child. The Passover ritual gives expression to the Jewish understanding of the spiritual nature of the child and models ways to best engage and nurture the child's spiritual endowment.

Other Jewish customs and rituals reinforce this understanding. In a recent study of *Rituals of Childhood – Jewish Acculturation in Medieval Europe*, Ivan Marcus (1996) details an intricate ceremony that marked the child's initiation into study at age five or six. On the morning of *Shavuot*, the festival of the giving of the Torah, the father wrapped his son in a coat or *tallit* (prayer shawl) and carried him to his teacher's house.[2] The child was placed on his teacher's lap. The teacher presented the young boy with tablets of Hebrew letters on which honey had been smeared. Cakes and hard-boiled eggs with Biblical verses were served. The child was invited to lick the honey off the Hebrew letters and after repeating the Biblical verses which the teacher read, to eat the cake and eggs. At the ritual's conclusion, the teacher took the child to a river and told him that his study of Torah would, like the ever-flowing stream, continue forever.

As the Seder is a re-enactment of the Exodus from Egypt, so this Shavuot ritual is a re-enactment of the receiving of Torah at Sinai. Just as the participants in the Seder are to eat bitter herbs and greens dipped in salt water to physically taste the bitterness of enslavement, so the child in this Shavuot ritual is to eat Scriptural verses to symbolize the sweetness of Torah. The Torah enters the child just as the child enters the study of Torah. His learning begins in the lap of the teacher who at that moment imitates God at Sinai. Symbolically, the child is placed in the lap of God, who nourishes him with the milk of Torah. Just as at the Seder the child opens the door to the promise of redemption, so the child studying Torah promises salvation. The rabbis teach: "The world is sustained by the breath of small schoolchildren who study the Torah . . . " (Shabbat 119b).

Like the Seder, the initiation ritual is experiential. Children aren't told the words of Torah are pleasant, they lick the sweet honey off the Hebrew letters of the tablets. Less essential than the content being transferred from teacher to student is the relationship being established. The child sits in the teacher's lap and between them is a text. The image of teacher evoked is that of storyteller. This Shavuot ritual as practiced in thirteenth-century Germany has disappeared, although remnants of it remain a part of Jewish practice. It is still customary to either coat children's first Hebrew letters with honey or to provide sweets. At my congregation we initiate our children into Torah study at *Simhat Torah*, a holiday which marks the conclusion of the year's Torah cycle and the beginning of the next year's. The children are escorted into the sanctuary by their parents. They are covered with a large *tallit* and receive a rabbinic blessing. In addition to a small replica of the Torah, they are rewarded with a sweet chocolate Torah and a prayer that all their learning will be sweet.

Stories for Wandering and Wondering

My own decision to write stories for children, to encourage their spiritual life, is an attempt to reflect some of the insights of the Passover and Medieval initiation ritual. In writing, I create *haggadah*, a story in which the child's imagination is invited to wander and wonder. The narratives

I tell are not meant to provide answers as much as they are intended to provoke questions and invite conversation.

In my first book, *God's Paintbrush* (a series of vignettes that depict the landscapes of children's lives and invite them to imagine God in those places), I provided the questions. Not everyone thought this was a good idea. When after six long years in search of a publisher, I found someone interested; he insisted that I take out the questions. He assured me that parents were afraid of questions and wouldn't buy the book. This was my first book; perhaps I was wrong. I reluctantly consented. In the end, he didn't publish the book. When I sent the books to another publisher, I left out the questions. The publisher enjoyed the manuscript but asked if I wouldn't mind putting in questions! Children tell me what they like most about the book, are the questions! One parent related how her husband read *God's Paintbrush* to their daughter one night. He was in a hurry, so he decided to leave out the questions. "No, dad", she stopped him, "ask the questions!"

In my other books the questions arise out of the stories themselves. Like the broken *matza*, the *afikoman* of the Seder, the story is incomplete without the children. I do not write religious textbooks; I tell stories that address issues of the spirit. When I write, I do not see myself as the child's preacher, but as his or her friend and partner on a spiritual journey. Like the four children of the *Haggadah*, every one approaches the narrative with a different set of experiences and concerns. I view the reader not as a student who I must fill with information but as a guest who I invite to walk along with me, to live in the story for a while. I hope that the children will fill in the blank spaces, find their place in the story, write their own *midrash*. That is what the *Haggadah* does – it invites the readers to walk with their ancestors in their long trek to freedom, to live in the story of the Exodus, to discover what it means to them. It is a drama, not a dissertation on redemption. I. B. Singer has said, "In art, truth that is boring is not truth." The *Haggadah* is art and its truth carries the reader through ten plagues and a raging sea. You can almost feel the hems of your pants or dresses getting wet.

During the Seder the participants get to act out this drama of enslavement and freedom. In a good story, through empathetic imagination, the readers or listeners do exactly that. They try on the role of the characters for a while. The story pulls them inside. They are enabled to look at reality in a new way. Rabbi Menachem Mendel of Kotzk, a leader in Hasidism, said he became a Hasid, a "lover of God", because he met someone who told stories about the righteous. "He told what he knew and I heard what I needed." I write and tell the stories I know and love in the hope that children will hear what they need. In the intersection of story and child the spirit grows.

Sometimes that happens in ways I could not have imagined. When I wrote *In God's Name*, I told of people who called God by different names. They named God out of their own experiences. The farmer called God, Source of Life. The soldier who was tired of too many wars called God, Maker of Peace. The woman who nursed her child called God, Mother. The man who held the hand of his baby called God, Father. The child who was lonely called God, Friend. Each person believed that his or her name for God was the best and that all the others were wrong. The people argued over which was the best name, the only name for God. But in the end, all the people came together and called God, One. After reading the book, a teacher asked her class what they might want to say to the author. A young boy, who was the bully of the class, turned to the picture of the weeping soldier who called God, Maker of Peace – and just ran his hand across the page. When I heard of this, I thought, "the one who does not know how to ask".

I have also used this book with adults and have encouraged them to find the place deep inside them where they name God. After a period of silence, many names come pouring forth. One woman wanted to call God, "an old, warm bathrobe". All those present acknowledged and affirmed her naming but I will admit I thought it a little unusual. One year later, the same woman made a point of telling me how much the exercise meant to her. Her mother had died that past year and she took her old, warm bathrobe and wrapped it around her. She felt the presence of God.

The Blueprint of the Soul

Judaism recognizes the spiritual endowment of children from birth. Their spiritual development is nurtured through experiential ritual, relationship with another, and the imaginative exploration and encounter with a community's story. As God's story is lived in the story of a people, it must be learned in interaction with others. As it is given expression in a narrative, the encounter with that narrative is a focal point of life's sacred pilgrimage.

We began with a legend that said that before a child is born he or she learns the whole Torah and can see from one end of the world to the other. An angel strikes it on the mouth and all is forgotten. The rabbis also imagine that even God looks into the Torah to create the world. According to the *midrash*, the Torah is the blueprint, the story of the world. Life, then, is a journey to discover Torah, the script or blueprint of the individual soul and the soul of the world. It begins with the child's first breath.

Notes

1   While the Biblical text reads, "commanded *you*" many Haggadot follow the
    Jerusalem Talmud in using " . . . commanded *us*" to distinguish the wise
    child from the wicked child.
2   Since formal Torah instruction was, at this time, officially limited to boys,
    this ceremony was limited to sons.

References

Abrams, J. and Abrams, S. 1994: *Jewish Parenting: Rabbinic Insights*, London:
    Jason Aronson.
Bruner, J. 1996: *The Culture of Education*, Cambridge, MA: Harvard University
    Press.
Levitt, J. and Strassfeld, M. (eds) 2000: *A Night of Questions: A Passover Haggadah*,
    Elkins Park: Reconstructionist Press.
Marcus, I. 1996: *Rituals of Childhood Jewish Acculturation Medieval Europe*, New
    Haven: Yale University Press.
Sasso, S. E. 1994: *In God's Name*, Woodstock: Jewish Lights Publishing.
—— 1992: *God's Paintbrush*, Woodstock: Jewish Lights Publishing.
Schein, J. 2000: The Triangle of Text, Teacher and Student. In R. Goodman and
    S. Blumberg (eds), *Teaching God and Spirituality in the Jewish Classroom*, New
    York: ARE Publishing.
Siddur Sim Shalom 1998: The Rabbinical Assembly and The United Synagogue
    of America.
Westeroff, J. 1976: *Will Our Children Have Faith?*, New York: Seabury Press.

Chapter 3

Toward a Pedagogy of the Sacred: Transcendence, Ethics, and the Curriculum

HANAN ALEXANDER AND MIRIAM BEN-PERETZ

THIS essay calls for a conception of curriculum grounded in ethics and theology. Curriculum thought has, for some time, been more concerned with knowledge than ethics. Hutchins (1952, 1953, 1968) placed the transmission of textual knowledge at the centre of curriculum debate while Bobbit (1918, 1924), Charters (1923) and Tyler (1949) focused on "scientific" and technological approaches to the selection knowledge to be learned. Schwab (1978) and Bruner (1960) analyzed the role of structures in the discovery of knowledge, while Apple (1990) and Giroux (1981, 1992) drew attention to its politicization. Eisner (1994) discussed the aesthetics aspects of cognition, and Aronowitz (1988) deconstructed the very idea that we can know anything at all. This epistemological attitude has led to a series of overlapping crises. To address them we follow a path set by Phillip Phenix (1971), David Purpel (1989), Parker Palmer (1993, 1998), Dwayne Heubner (1999) and Philip Wexler (1997) in viewing curriculum as an agent of ethical and theological ideals, rather than epistemological ideals.

We use the term "ethics" in a classical sense that envisages visions of the good associated with life's purposes and meanings, rather than in the modern sense that focuses primarily on the analysis and justification of individual rights and duties (Williams 1985: 6–7). Ethics, in this view, is a teleological enterprise, in which lesser purposes serve greater ones. Theology and religion are important ethical resources because they often give voice to our most cherished ideals.

We use the term "religion" not in a parochial, doctrinal or confessional sense, but rather to capture concepts and practices, such as holiness, ritual and liturgy, that point beyond our circumscribed worldly experience. Some call this natural, as opposed to revealed, theology. Others like to distinguish between spirituality and religion, the former being more universal than the latter. John Dewey (1976: 1–28) used the term "religiosity" as opposed to "religion" to articulate a similar distinction.

Epistemological Crises in Curriculum Thought

Educational thought once placed great emphasis on the cultivation of normative and religious commitments. As modernism took hold, its faith in universal, objective, empirical knowledge and its suspicion of local and parochial custom led to disengagement with ethical and religious discourse in schools. Scientific knowledge – natural, bio-logical, behavioural, social, historical, and even humanistic – is public and attainable. Its application leads to practical outcomes that have technological, economic and social benefit. It belongs, therefore, at the centre of the curriculum. Religion and ethics, on the other hand, are private, often based on unreliable emotions. Since there can be no public agreement about ethical or theological matters, many argued that they ought to remain on the margins of curriculum deliberation (Alexander 2001: 16–22).

This is the view that Bobbit, Charters and Tyler embraced in contra-distinction to curriculum traditionalists such as Hutchins (Kliebard 1987: 209–39). Each successive generation of curriculum critics from Schwab to Aronowitz alluded to the limitations of this modern, positivist con-ception of curriculum. Knowledge growth is so rapid, argued Schwab and the curriculum structuralists, that it has become too vast to be the basis of subject matter. We need to teach students the structure of knowl-edge – substantive and syntactic – so they can inquire on their own. Nor can the behavioural or social sciences be readily translated into peda-gogy. Life in schools is too complex to be captured by any particular theory or discipline. To properly understand curriculum processes, we must examine educational practice eclectically (Schwab 1978).

Yet, according to curriculum reconceptualists such as Apple, the structural turn does not solve the crisis of subject matter, and the arts of eclectic do not resolve the inadequacies of behavioural and social analyses of education (Pinar 1975). All of these forms of "knowledge" are products of ideology rooted in social, economic, cultural, racial or gender interests. The task of subject matter, pedagogy and curriculum inquiry is to empower students to deconstruct what Marx called "false consciousness", to uncover the hidden assumptions in instruction that oppress and enslave (Apple 1993).

Postmodernists such as Aronowitz and Giroux take this analysis further. If "knowledge" is but a reflection of class, culture or gender interest, they ask, by what intellectual or moral right do these groups impose themselves on individuals? Knowledge should not be trans-mitted and cannot be acquired. Each student must construct it according to his or her own needs (Aronowitz and Giroux 1993; Dewey 1909).

And herein lies the latest crisis. The curriculum reconceptualists have done a great service in pointing out the degree to which all "knowledge" is situated and that the selection of what to teach is always a value choice. Their critical program of curriculum deconstruction has in large measure been successful. However, what happens next? If curriculum content is so thoroughly situated, what is left with which to construct subject matter?

If all "knowledge" is relative to ideological interests that are to be deconstructed, what of the reconceptualist claim – stated in the first clause of this sentence – that all "knowledge" is relative to ideological interest? Should we not "deconstruct" this claim as well, recognizing that it represents the interests of radical, feminist, and postmodern theorists? But why should these doctrines be believed, when the likes of Lyotard (1984) argue that the very point of postmodernism is that no doctrines are to be privileged? Indeed, how are individuals to construct subject matter to meet their own needs absent from a context in which to interpret what it means to have a need?

For concepts such as "need" to be meaningful without falling prey to the quagmires of a thoroughgoing relativism, we must assume reference to that which transcends individual or group consciousness (Taylor 1991: 31–41), even if our view is limited by concepts and culture (Kant 1970: 532–49). To make sense of reconceptualist pedagogy, therefore, we are thrown back to ideas that were not only subjected to radical and postmodern critique, but that were abandoned by earlier modernist curriculum theorists as well. We refer, of course, to theological concepts such as transcendence and meaning. Contra Lyotard, we appear required to presuppose that meta-narratives indeed exist – to which our various discourses give voice – that pierce the veils of current circum-stance and grasp transcendent reality. But with Popper (1963: 369–96), we are also compelled to assume that no particular narrative holds the ultimate truth in its pocket.

Transcendence and Ethical Ideals

The postmodernists were not the first to point out the mere customary nature of empirical knowledge. David Hume (1748: 327–33) recognized this fundamental weakness in Enlightenment epistemology. He pointed out that conclusions based on past experience, such as those offered by science, can never be necessary because we cannot know how matters will develop in the future. All scientific conclusions are contingent. They could turn out to be otherwise.

Why, then, believe what science teaches? Hume's response (1748: 337–8) was remarkably similar to those of Horkheimer (1996), Adorno (1973), Lyotard (1984) Foucault (1972) and Derrida (1998) – because we have a psychological interest in doing so. Without adopting customs that enable us to see the world as we do, it would impossible to formulate and enact plans, or to engage in social interactions. It is by means of custom, not reason, that we make our worlds predictable.

Hume's skepticism challenged the very foundations of scientific rationality. Immanuel Kant responded by recognizing the dramatic difference between the world beyond and within consciousness. We can know nothing independent of perception. Knowledge is possible only by virtue of the cognitive structures through which we process experience (Kant 1976). Since we can say nothing directly about the world out there, but only as it appears within, scientific theories can never be more than approximations of the external world. The assumption that there is a reality that transcends experience becomes, in this view, a regulative ideal. It motivates us to strive to improve upon our current approximations while at the same time serving as the ultimate end of inquiry – knowledge, as it were, the way it ought to be.

Thus, the concept of "things in themselves" – the world outside of consciousness – has ethical as well as theoretical significance. The world as it ought to be understood is not only the ideal that scientific reason strives to explain; it is also the sort of existence that moral reasoning teaches us to emulate. The ideals of science and ethics turn out to be the same. Kant called them the Noumenon or the Idea of God (Kant 1970: 532–49).

Karl Marx (1977: 159–91) challenged our ability to interpret such a consciousness-free world independent of socio-economic interests. Fredrich Nietzsche (1966) challenged the very existence of a reality beyond consciousness that could guaranty the possibility of truth. Frankfurt school critical theorists extended Marx's analysis to include cultural biases (Held 1980). And postmodernists built on Nietzsche in arguing that knowledge is utterly without transcendent foundation (Lyotard 1984).

Yet these arguments do not upset the basic distinction upon which Kant's response rested. To be sure, Kant was wrong to assume that all people have a common cognitive structure, free of the influences of class, culture, gender or person history. However, this does not undermine the idea that knowledge is constructed from processing external experiences through internal structures. Nor have these critiques successfully challenged the idea that transcendence is an ethical ideal. A picture that properly considers radical and postmodern arguments suggests, rather, that we construct knowledge through a meeting of consciousness and transcendence, which is influenced but not determined by collective visions of goodness. Ethics, in other words, precedes epistemology! (Alexander 2001: 161).

The Conditions of Ethical Discourse

Yet, if we have no direct access to transcendence other than through the veils that inform the structure of consciousness, how far have we moved from the relativistic idea that goodness and truth are functions of framework? Our response lies in the idea that goodness is an ethical concept that makes no sense absent of certain conditions.

For ethical discourse to be meaningful we must first assume that people are the agents of their actions. Physiological, chemical, genetic, psychological, theological, social, historical and economic considerations – among others – may influence our actions. However, if I have no free will, and my behaviour is determined by external forces, then ethical deliberations would be senseless, since it is not me but some other agent that must be addressed in promoting a particular sort of behaviour. Freedom, then, is the first condition of ethical discourse.

The idea of free choice, however, also entails the presupposition, again within limits, that people have the capacity to understand options and their consequences. To choose one course of action over another I need not be aware of all possible options, or of the complete list of consequences. However, if I understand none of these, there would be no difference between choice and caprice, since the option I selected would be entirely arbitrary. To say that people have free will, therefore, means that they also have the intelligence to distinguish between the value of a number of possible options and their consequences. Intelligence, then, is the second condition of ethical discourse.

In addition to intelligence, the idea of freedom also entails the notion that people can be wrong. To be the agent of my actions, my decisions cannot be the necessary consequence of my nature. Were it impossible for me to do wrong because I was inherently good, there would be no way to distinguish wrong from right. All choices would be necessary and the idea of freedom meaningless. For ethics to make sense, we must assume that moral choices are contingent; they cannot be otherwise. It must be possible for me to be wrong in order to make sense of the claim that I turned out to be right. Fallibility, therefore, is the third condition of ethical discourse (Alexander 2001: 44–9).

To say that ethics precedes epistemology, then, and that all conceptions of the good attempt to give voice to a transcendent ideal that lies beyond the reach of consciousness and experience, does not imply that all ethical visions are equally valid. Education is not about initiation into all putative moral ideals, but only those that embrace the conditions of ethical discourse: freedom, intelligence and fallibility (Alexander 2001: 183–98).

In this connection, critical and postmodern pedagogies are deeply problematic. The former assumes that moral ideals are not chosen but determined by power interests, while the latter presupposes that ideals are completely arbitrary. In either case, there is little room for ethical discourse, and no way to distinguish between education and a-moral ideological indoctrination. Fundamentalist or totalitarian doctrines that claim to have direct access to absolute moral truth fare no better in this regard. By denying the fallibility of their beliefs, they undermine the conditions of intelligence and freedom upon which the meaning of ethical discourse depends (2001: 171–83).

To call for a return to theological and religious language in curriculum thought, therefore, does not entail a flight from criticism. On the contrary, as an educational concept, curriculum thought requires critical thinking which lies at the heart of all ethical deliberations. Criticism of this kind, however, is an ethical, not epistemological, assumption. It is a condition of ethical discourse. Genuine theological and religious deliberations that participate in the promulgation of goodness are necessarily intelligent. Conceiving pedagogy in transcendent terms calls us to expand our conceptions of construct such visions we need to become articulate about norms and identify with ideals. Curriculum, in short, is first an agent of ethics, not epistemology; and identity is a moral rather than an empirical – psychological or socio-logical – category.

The curriculum plays an important role in the construction of identity – cultural, political, intellectual, religious and ethical. It defines the paths students are called to travel in order to be initiated into a community, to identify with its symbols and ideals. Identity refers to the cognitive, affective and behavioural dispositions required for identi-fication with a collective heritage – a community's shared assumptions, conceptions of knowledge, modes of inquiry, means of discourse, customs and practices, and moral and aesthetic values.

Communities educate in different ways, but many use *stories* about group origins, *parables* that communicate important attitudes and beliefs, *rituals* that concretize values and concepts, and *paradigms* that exemplify virtuous behaviour and accepted ways of thinking. We call these stories, parables, rituals and paradigms, when translated into instructional materials, the *constitutive curriculum*. They lead, whether intentionally or not, to the constitution of identity among learners, to the creation of the stories they tell about their lives. We refer to this substantive element as *curriculum narrative*.[1] The process through which identity is constructed involves the cultivation of fundamental commitments and beliefs around which communities are organized. Since these are often called "sacred" commitments, we call this aspect of curriculum thought the *pedagogy of the sacred*.

The *constitutive curriculum* is a tool for curriculum analysis and decision-making – a lens through which to view curriculum deliberations and create curriculum materials that draws attention to the ways instruction reflects the ethical vision of a community and provides material from which identity can be constituted. Consider the century-long battle in American schools over the teaching of evolution. This is not merely a debate concerning how human beings came into existence; it is a struggle over the ideals with which young people will be called to identify.

Creationists emphasize that all people are equal in the eyes of God, regardless of intellectual merit or social status, because all are created in the Divine image. Evolutionists stress the value of truth and free inquiry. The problem raised by this debate is not merely of subject matter but of the sort of people we want our children to become. Viewing the curriculum as contributing to the constitution of identity enables us to articulate alternatives clearly and to make judgements more intentionally and purposefully.

Gail Dorph's study of prospective Jewish educators' beliefs about the nature and teaching of the Hebrew Bible can illustrate the constitutive nature of curriculum. She found that teachers' purposes for teaching the Bible are varied (Droph 1993):

> Let us imagine the teacher of Torah who is about to teach the Cain and Abel narrative (Genesis 4). In teaching Cain and Abel should a teacher emphasize the details of the story? Is it important that students remember that it is Cain who killed Abel or it sufficient for a student to be able to look up such details? Does the teacher think that it is important for students to understand that the account of Cain and Abel is a moral teaching with specific moral lessons? Should the teacher require that students identify only one or several different moral lessons? A list of such lessons could include: the text is teaching us about the inherent value in every human life, the text is teaching us not to kill, or that the text is teaching us to take care of other human beings because we are all brothers. Perhaps the teacher wants students to compare Cain's actions in killing Abel with the actions of Adam and Eve in eating the fruit in the garden by comparing the Hebrew words used to describe the punishments in each of these accounts. In both cases, the "sinner" is told that the earth would be cursed because of his actions. Decisions by a teacher about what to emphasize depend on what the teacher thinks is important for students to learn. In other words, such decisions depend upon the teacher's purposes. (179–80)

This brief section may be understood to reflect what we mean by the "constitutive curriculum", because it entails an examination of decisions concerning what is most worth teaching and learning. These decisions do not relate to the worth of knowledge for the future employment of students. Nor are they conceived as responding to the economic needs of society. These decisions are not determined by notions of the structure of the discipline, or the perceived match with students' interests and inclinations. They are, rather, the outcome of vision, of the good, of ethical deliberations, carried out by teachers or by curriculum developers.

Another illustration of the constitutive curriculum is found in Simone Schweber's study of four high-school Holocaust teachers. For each case Schweber traced the moral and informational dimensions of the Holocaust curricula teachers chose and their transformation by teachers and students. The following excerpt of Schweber's work reflects the intended curriculum of one teacher (Schweber 1998):

> If someone just said, standing on one foot, "what's this curriculum about?" It is an anti-racism, anti-bias curriculum; it is about developing a language about human relations; it is about a specific history, or a couple of, more than one specific history, and how insights from the rigorous study of the history might play out in people's own thinking in their classrooms, in their family lives, in their communities; it's about participatory citizenship; it's about taking responsibility; it's about a lot of things that rarely get spoken about above the level of generality, and it's great to be able to have these kinds of conversations and to have kids have these conversations with each other, and then to have a way to help them construct meaning out of it all . . . we don't just want it to be an encounter group, you know they leave here, they're supposed to feel better because they've had a chance to vent some anger or insecurity. They have to have an opportunity to think about the implications in an intellectual way of what they're-learning and . . . for them to build their own meaning out of it and to share that with other people. It's actually a great vision for what happens when you have community in the classroom and a rigorous, intellectual experience. And one or the other, you can't do without . . . And it's tough to do. You walk a real line between the particular and the universal messages and implications of the history . . . and, um, that's difficult you sort of sculpt the curriculum on a daily basis; it's not a programmed, by – the – numbers, kind of curriculum. (1998: 37)

As in the previous case this teacher's statement may be interpreted as reflecting a constitutive curriculum, not only because it deals with specific and highly important values, like anti-racism, but also because it is "about developing a language about human relations". It is about possible impact of history on people's thinking and acting in their family lives and their communities. In short it is about some of the fundamental beliefs around which communities are organized.

Narrative and Curriculum Content

Curriculum narrative includes the remembrances, stories and expectations we would like our students to discuss about the lives that they choose to live (Connelly and Clandinen, 1995).[2] When the *Haggada* is read on Passover eve, for example, youngsters are initiated into the Jewish people by re-enacting the story of the exodus from Egypt. They come to identify with this community and its traditions by experiencing a narrative, from questions asked and answered, to stories told and interpreted, to foods enjoyed and songs sung (Dorph 1976).

The following excerpt of a transcript of a Bible lesson recorded by Gail Dorph exemplifies what we mean by "curriculum narrative". The lesson is about the Tower of Babel. M.K. is short for the teacher:

M.K.: Remember when we were reading the story of Cain and Abel, I introduced you to a Midrash. A Midrash is a teaching story or explanatory story that the rabbis wrote when they faced a question such as the one we are facing here. We know there is something wrong. But we're not sure what. It's as though something is missing in the story. The rabbis filled in the gap with the following story. This is how they answered the question: what's so bad about building a city with its tower in the sky?

It says in the Torah: all the world had the same language and the same words. The rabbis of the Midrash comment: when everyone had the same language there was peace. But when they began to build the tower, it was such a big project to do that they had to divide the people up. Some were taskmasters and foremen and some were builders. The taskmasters gave the builders very hard work to do.

As the building was being built, if one of the builders fell off and was killed, nobody bothered to turn around and look. But, if a brick which had been hoisted pretty high up fell, then the taskmasters would say, "Oh, this is terrible, how can we ever get another brick up?"

According to the rabbis who wrote this Midrash, what was wrong with building this tower?

JOSH: Nobody cared about life.

ZACK: They cared more about the bricks than the people.

ANNA: They cared more about the materials than the people.

M.K.: Good. The way I had summarized it on my strip was, "it's bad to care more about building a building than about people. It's bad to be or try to reach God. It's bad to care more about building a building than about people. It's bad to think you can make a name for yourself by building a building. It's bad to prevent being scattered when they should fill the earth."

In this class different reasons were given to explain why building the Tower of Babel was a sin. Everyone of these reasons reflects ethical considerations and a vision of the good. The story of the Tower of Babel is an example of the kind of narrative which is part of the culture of a community and has the potential to lead to in-depth ethical discussion about the vision of the good.

Schweber also documents the ways in which narratives – remembrances, stories, and expectations – play a role in the one teacher's pedagogy.

> Like most of his other stories this one exposed a piece of Mr. Zee's personal history to his students. Rather than constructing psychological distance between students and teachers, Mr. Zee immediately put his students at ease by revealing himself to them. I am convinced that part of the distinctiveness of Mr. Zee's classroom evolved from his willingness to share his life with his students. The preponderance of such stories, almost three-quarters of all the stories he told in the first six weeks in fact, accounts for my sub-titling this section of the course, "Getting to Know Mr. Zee". Thus while I was surprised by Mr. Zee's choice of morals for many of these stories, I was nonetheless impressed with the high level of engagement he was able to foster among students by telling them stories garnered from his own life experiences. (Schweber 1998: 48–9)

Mr. Zee's stories are intended to become part of his class's narrative, the stories they tell about themselves out of which they construct their identities. The remembrances he imparted to his students invited them to identify through this group with a vision of a just society that rejects racism and hate for compassion and loving-kindness.

Pedagogy of the Sacred

Pedagogy of the sacred is an instructional concept that engages us in reflection about ritual and liturgical aspects of the curriculum. The term "sacred" usually means set apart for *worship*, worthy of *religious* veneration, or *holy* (Otto 1950). We worship that which merits devotion, usually because of its intrinsic or elevated value. People often express their most cherished ideals in symbolic forms such as ritual or metaphor because they represent deeply felt commitments the intensity of which evades ordinary discourse.

If curriculum decisions rest, as we have argued, on our most cherished commitments, then in an important sense the whole of the curriculum constitutes a pedagogy of the sacred. Indeed, this is why we chose the term for the title of this essay. However, curriculum decisions and substances must also be translated into classroom practice. Hence we also reserve the term for particular instructional methods that emphasize the symbolic expression of our most sacred ideals and beliefs.

The Pledge of Allegiance recited each morning in the American public school, for example, is a ritual – a sacred pedagogy – that initiates students into a story that speaks of "one nation, under God, indivisible, with liberty and justice for all". It speaks to deep feelings about the American self-understanding with which this ritual calls children to identify. Or think of the honour codes of many colleges and universities that students are expected to sign upon registration. The signing of these codes initiates students by means of a public, legalistic ritual to the value of truth and honesty that stand at the heart of the academy.

Gail Dorph's excerpt from the lesson dealing with the Tower of Babel may be interpreted as exemplifying the "pedagogy of the sacred". It focuses on eternal questions concerning the nature of good, and its desire to analyze the reasoning behind the Bible's negative evaluation of the Tower of Babel. The pedagogy in this case entails explication of a sacred text, which according to many interpretations of Jewish tradition is an act of worship (Kadushin 1964). By posing questions to the text and considering alternative interpretations and responses, students are introduced into a way of life deeply rooted in a culture of intelligent engagement with tradition. This mode of instruction reflects the ethical vision of a community and provides material from which identity can be constituted.

Schweber's Mr. Zee also employs components of the "pedagogy of the sacred". For example, he emphasizes connecting the particular to the general, learning to real-world thinking in order "to give more than lip-service to questions about human nature and human behaviour" (1998: 77). Schweber sees Mr. Zee as encouraging philosophizing about morality among his students through both conventional and unconventional means. "By showing videos, reading poems and books and telling stories in which people face complicated moral dilemmas (most often Mr. Zee himself), he considers himself to be relating complex morally rich content" (1998: 77–8).

A pool day planned by Mr. Zee serves as an example of this approach:

> we're not just going swimming on Thursday. There is a reason to do what we're doing . . . They will, semesters from now, be able to articulate something about cultural expectations and how they shape human behaviour, and they may be able to do it on two fronts. One, on a simple, individual front has to do with their own body consciousness, or their own experience of people . . . but on the other hand, that's a vocabulary that serves them well when they think of the unfolding of many different kinds of histories. (1998: 78)

Mr. Zee expresses his ideas about a just and anti-racist society in symbols and experiences because he believes that talking about facts is not sufficient to challenge students to seek social justice. Justice is so crucial to Mr. Zee's vision of the good life, that he seeks to engage students in acting out, role playing, dramatizing and ritualizing their experience so that the will be able to "articulate" it "semesters from now".

Conclusion

In sum, ethics and theology are logically prior to epistemology in curriculum deliberations. In order to decide what knowledge is most worth knowing, and to consider how best to impart or construct it, we must first have a conception of what is worthwhile. This requires that we examine our most fundamental beliefs about the purposes of life and the nature of a good society. These considerations cannot be merely personal. They call us to reach beyond ourselves to the communities in which we live, study and teach, and beyond our communities to transcendent ideals. These ideals constitute the raw material from which identities are constructed in the educational process. They are often preserved in cherished stories, remembrances and texts so as to be retold and re-enacted through ritual, drama and symbolism. Consequently, the design, construction, implementation and evaluation of educational materials can and should be conceived as a sacred task.

Notes

1   Bruner (1986) distinguishes between narrative and theoretical thinking, one relying on humanistic disciplines the other scientific. By using the term narrative, however, we do not preclude the importance of theoretical and scientific deliberations in the curriculum. We mean to suggest, rather, that scientific inquiry is also part of a narrative that people tell about their lives, and that in deciding what science to teach and how to teach it, we need to be articulate about the primacy of these normative dimensions of curriculum deliberation.

2   Connelly and Clandinen (1995) use the term "narrative" in relation to curriculum thought to emphasize the importance of the personal lives of teachers and students in curriculum thought. We embrace this use of the term, but also extend it by underscoring the communal and value-laden context in which these lives are led.

References

Adorno, T. W. 1973: *The Jargon of Authenticity* (Knut Tarnowski and Frederick Will Trans.), Evanston: Northwestern University Press.

Alexander, H. A. 2001: *Reclaiming Goodness: Education and the Spiritual Quest*, Notre Dame: University of Notre Dame Press.

Apple, M. W. 1990: *Ideology and Curriculum*, New York: Routledge.

—— 1993: *Power, Meaning, and Identity: Essays in Critical Educational Studies*, New York: Routledge.

Aronowitz, S. 1988: *Science As Power: Discourse and Ideology in Modern Society*, Minneapolis: University of Minnesota Press.

Aronowitz, S. and Giroux, H. 1993: *Postmodern Education: Politics Culture, and Social Criticism*, Minneapolis: University of Minnesota Press.

Bobbit, F. 1918: *The Curriculum*, Boston: Houghton-Mifflin.

—— 1924: *How to make a curriculum*, Boston: Houghton-Mifflin.

Bruner, J. 1960: *The Process of Education*, Cambridge, MA: Harvard University Press.

—— 1986: *Actual Minds, Possible Worlds*, Cambridge, MA, Harvard University Press.

Charters, W. W. 1923: *Curriculum Construction*, New York: Macmillan.

Connelly, M. and Clandinen, J. D. 1995: *Teacher's Professional Knowledge Landscapes*, New York: Teachers College Press.

Derrida, J. 1998: *Of Grammatology* (trans. G. C. Spivak), Baltimore: Johns Hopkins University Press.

Dewey, J. 1909: *The Child and the Curriculum*, Chicago: University of Chicago Press.

—— 1976: *A Common Faith*, New Haven, Yale University Press.

Dorph, G. Z. 1993: *Conceptions and Perceptions: A Study of Prospective Jewish Educators' Beliefs About Torah*, Doctoral dissertation, New York: The Jewish Theological Seminary of America.

Dorph, S. A. 1976: *A Model for Jewish Education in America*, Doctoral Dissertation, New York: Teachers College, Columbia University.

Eisner, E. W. 1994: *Cognition and Curriculum Reconsidered*, New York: Teacher College Press.

Foucault, M. 1972: *Archaeology of Knowledge* (trans. A. M. Shenden Smith), London: Tavistock.

Giroux, H. 1981: *Ideology, Culture, and the Process of Schooling*, Philadelphia, Temple University Press.

—— 1992: *Border Crossings: Cultural Workers and the Politics of Education*, New York: Routledge.

Held, D. 1980: *Introduction to Critical Theory: Horkheimer to Habermas*, London: Hutchinson.

Heubner, D. E. 1999: *The Lure of the Transcendent*, Mahwah, N.J. : Lawrence Erlbaum Associates.

Horkheimer, M. 1996: *Critique of Instrumental Reason* (trans. M. J. O'Connell,), New York: Continuum.

Hume, D. 1748: *An Enquiry Concerning Human Understanding*, in *The Empiricists*, Garden City, NY: Doubleday.

Hutchins, R. M. 1952: *The Great Conversation*, Chicago: Encyclopedia Britannica.

—— 1953: *The Conflict of Education in a Democratic Society*, New York: Harper and Row.

—— 1968: *The Learning Society*, New York: Fredrick A. Praeger.

Kadushin, M. 1964: *Worship and Ethics: A Study in Rabbinic Judaism*, Evanston: Northwestern University Press.

Kant, I. 1970: *Critique of Pure Reason* (trans. Norman Kemp Smith), New York: Macmillan.

—— 1976: *Prolegomena To Any Future Metaphysics* (trans. Lewis White Beck), Indianapolis: Bobbs-Merrill.

Kliebard, H. M. 1987: *The Struggle for the American Curriculum, 1893–1958*, New York: Routledge & Kegan Paul.

Lyotard, J.-F. 1984: *The Postmodern Condition: A Report on Knowledge* (trans. Goeff Bennington and Brian Massumi), Manchester: Manchester University Press.

Marx, K. 1977: German Ideology. In D. McLellan (ed.), *Karl Marx: Selected Writings*, Oxford: Oxford University Press.

Nietzsche, F. 1966: *Beyond Good and Evil* (trans. Walter Kaufman), New York: Vintage Books.

—— 1966: *Thus spoke Zarathrustra* (trans. Walter Kaufman), New York: Vicking.

Otto, R. 1950: *The Idea of the Holy* (trans. John W. Harvey), Oxford: Oxford University Press.

Palmer, P. 1993: *To Know As We Are Known: Education as a Spiritual Journey*, San Francisco: HarperCollins.

—— 1998: *The Courage To Teach: Exploring the Inner Landscape of a Teachers Life*, San Francisco: Jossey-Bass.

Phenix, P. 1971: *Transcedence and the Curriculum*, Teachers College Record 73, 271–83.

Pinar, W. (ed.) 1975: *Curriculum Theorizing: The Reconceptualists*, Berkeley: McCutchan.

Popper, K. R. 1963: *The Open Society and Its Enemies*, London: Routledge & Kegan Paul.

Purpel, D. E. 1989: *The Moral and Spiritual Crisis in Education*, Granby, MA: Bergin and Garvey.

Schwab, J. 1978: *Science, Curriculum, and Liberal Education*, Ian Westbury and Neil Wilkof (eds), Chicago: University of Chicago Press.

Schweber, S. A. 1998: *Teaching History, Teaching Morality: Holocaust Education in American Public High Schools*, Doctoral dissertation, Stanford University, Stanford: California.

Taylor, C. 1991: *The Ethics of Authenticity*, Cambridge, MA: Harvard University Press.

Tyler, R. 1949: *Basic Principles of Curriculum and Instruction*, Chicago: University of Chicago Press.

Wexler, P. 1997: *Holy Sparks: Social Theory, Education, and Religion*, New York: Macmillan.

Williams, B. 1985: *Ethics and the Limits of Philosophy*, Cambridge, MA: Harvard University Press.

Chapter 4

Who Nurtured the Child?
Without attachment there can be no intimacy

Cynthia K. Dixon

ATTACHMENT – that is, bonding with a carer to foster mutual intimacy and nurture within firm and supportive limits – has been empirically established as core to healthy psychosocial development in children. Research on the nature of children's spirituality offers the definition "relational consciousness" (Hay with Nye 1998), which is essentially a particular experience of attachment and belonging. The history of childhood demonstrates the presence of attachment (Hanawalt 1986; Pollock 1987; Shahar 1990) and of abandonment and coercion (Greven 1990; Stone 1977).

This chapter explores the role of Christianity and its advocates for children's spirituality, and some of the distortions that have caused alienation. Christianity arose within the Jewish community during the height of the Roman Empire. Thus the first Christians came from both pagan Gentile and Jewish backgrounds, bringing with them Graeco-Roman and Hebraic child-rearing and educational practices to be modified in the context of Christianity.

The Classical World

Both warlike Sparta and philosophical Athens viewed children and family life in the context of their political agenda. Sparta's child-rearing aim was preparation for military service and unthinking obedience to the state, achieved by preventing attachment – an approach endorsed by Plato:

as soon as children are born they will be taken in charge by officers . . . these officers will also superintend the nursing of the children. They will bring the mothers to the crèche when their breasts are full while taking every precaution that no mother shall know her own child. (Fildes 1986: 21)

Abandonment on the dungheap to perish or be picked up by some stranger faced the surplus daughter or imperfect child. Boys were trained to be soldiers, sent to boarding school at age seven, where education comprised physical exercising in all kinds of weather. Girls were trained to be the mothers of soldiers.

The more philosophically orientated Athenians believed the world was an ordered cosmos, the analysis of which satisfied both mind and soul. Being irrational, children were regarded as "physically weak, morally incompetent, mentally incapable" (Golden 1990: 5). Training in mind and body to become rational ensured a focus on discipline and control in Greek education. Upper-class Athenian children were raised by their mothers, themselves uneducated, separate from their fathers. The boys, at seven, were taken to school by their slave, who had authority to punish. Childhood and family life held little attraction for Greek men.

The Roman father exerted lifelong absolute power over his family. Choosing to pick up the new-born baby from the floor meant he claimed it as member of the family to be carefully raised by both parents to be a worthy citizen. Otherwise the baby would be placed in the *lactaria*, a public place, for anyone to take. A future of prostitution, slavery, sale or begging lay ahead. Strict fasting or a severe thrashing was regarded as normal practice in a Roman household, although Dixon (1992) notes great physical coercion of children is associated more with teachers than with parents.

The Hebrew World

The Hebrews were a covenant people in relationship with their God, Yahweh. The covenant between Yahweh and His people was with each family, including children who were totally involved in the life of the community and its religious ceremonies through which they learned about the covenant, and their God. Children were called on to honour both their parents, who were responsible for instructing their sons and daughters:

you shall love the Lord your God with all your heart and with all your soul and with all your might. Keep these words that I am commanding

you today in your hearts. Recite them to your children and talk about
them when you are at home and when you are away, when you lie down
and when you rise. (Deuteronomy 6: 4)

By law, Hebrew children belonged to their father and had to be protected from abuse. Child sacrifice was abhorrent to Yahweh. "You shall
not give any of your offspring to sacrifice them to Moloch, and so profane the name of your God" (Leviticus 18: 26). Infanticide and
abandonment played no part in the Hebrew culture. Elementary
schools developed in the synagogues, primarily to study the scriptures. The discipline of children was conceptualized as the bending of
a twig to direct growth. The terse aphorisms of the Book of Proverbs
on discipline have been open to varied interpretations on physical
discipline.

The New Covenant of Christianity

The ancient world would learn that the Christian God cared for children. Jesus "took the children in his arms, put his hands on them and
blessed them" (Mark 10: 16). Jesus welcomed, healed and blessed both
girls and boys, whether the request for help was from a father or a
mother, a Jew or a Gentile. He raised the widow's son and the daughter
of Jairus, a synagogue ruler. He healed a Roman centurion's son, a
Syrophoenician woman's daughter and an epileptic, demon-possessed
boy. The disciples had to learn a new approach when infants were
brought to Jesus for prayer:

> the disciples spoke sternly to those who brought them; but Jesus said,
> "Let the little children come to me, and do not stop them; for it is to
> such as these that the kingdom of heaven belongs". (Matthew 19:13–15)

Children's lack of status and powerlessness in society are the very
credentials to enter the kingdom of heaven. "I tell you, unless you
change and become like little children, you will never enter the kingdom
of heaven" (Matthew 18: 3). Children calling "Hosanna to the Son of
David" enraged the temple authorities, but Jesus replied "Have you
never read, 'Out of the mouths of infants and nursing babies you have
prepared praise for yourself'?" (Matthew 21:16).

Jesus' unique attitude to and teaching about children laid the foundations for the position of children under the new covenant:

> If any of you put a stumbling block before one of these little ones who
> believe in me, it would be better for you if a great millstone were fastened
> around your neck and you were drowned in the depth of the sea.
> (Matthew 18:6–7)

Children continued to be involved in the communal life of the church, called to be obedient, while fathers were warned "Do not provoke your children, or they may lose heart" (Colossians 3: 21). Hoyles (1986) concludes that corporal punishment of children is not and cannot be grounded in words ascribed to Jesus or to Paul.

The Christian church prohibited abortion and infanticide. "Never do away with an unborn child, or destroy it after its birth" urged Barnabas around AD 130 (Lyman 1974: 90). To address the disposal of unwanted children, religious institutions accepted children. Parents could offer their child, an oblatio, to the monastery, a practice soon exploited as Ulrich of Cluny bemoans:

> after they have a houseful, so to speak, of sons and daughters, or if they have any who are lame, or cripple blind, hump-backed or leprous, or who have any defect which would make them less desirable in the secular world, [the parents] offer them as monks with the most pious of vows. (Boswell 1988: 298)

While Christian nurture took place within the home and the worshipping community, Christian children attended pagan schools to learn the morally neutral secular skills of reading, writing and oratory. The increasing numbers in schools led to flogging becoming the standard method of punishment for academic lapses as well as discipline for all schoolchildren, regardless of rank or age (Stone 1977).

Around AD 400 Augustine published an account of his childhood, *The Confessions*. His continuing struggle with his imperfections, despite his Christian commitment, led him to analyze the secular habits which had gradually moulded his personality, including his parents' secular values in terms of his education and career ambitions, and his own desire for status and peer acceptance. Augustine traced how God's grace, rather than any human power to act properly, had brought him where he was. Augustine saw children's shortcomings as serious as adults but grace, provided by baptism, took away the guilt of original sin from the infant. Aware that sin would inevitably reappear as the children grew up he wondered how the developing child could grow in grace? He concluded that just as the state punished adults, so the father should physically punish the child, despite his own memories of fear and dislike of the beatings characteristic of the Graeco-Roman world that he had hated (Wiedemann 1989) and despite his analogy that "a child's fear of beating is analogous to an adult's fear of torture" (Clark 1994: 22). Augustine provided a theological rationale for the pagan tradition of severe physical coercion.

John Chrystosom, Augustine's contemporary, who enjoyed a less punitive upbringing, proposed a less stringent model of child-rearing. Addressing parents in Antioch in AD 388 on rearing children, he notes the malleable nature of children and the need for balanced discipline (Lyman 1974: 87). While education was considered vital to counteract the fallen-ness of human nature, both Chrystosom and Jerome were concerned to prevent children from corrupting influences while being educated.

Renaissance and Reformation

The Renaissance and the Reformation saw the sixteenth century reclaiming the past in reaction to the decadence of the church. Renaissance humanists, led by devout Desiderius Erasmus, sought to produce a society where individuals would act with godly self-discipline for the good of family life, education and poor relief:

> the need to understand the Bible contextually drew them to the study of ancient history; the need for a purified text of the Scriptures impelled them to pursue knowledge of Greek and Hebrew and of classical writing. (Todd 1987: 23)

Erasmus' dream for a Christian social order on the basis of education was not to be. His works were banned by his Church, its power threatened if individuals could read the Scriptures and be personally responsible. Humanism would now cut its Christian roots. Reason alone would reign in the subsequent philosophical movement of the Enlightenment.

The Reformation led by Martin Luther saw changes in family life, which the growth of celibacy as a mark of superior spirituality had denigrated. Luther's marriage and enthusiasm for his large family, including adopted children, set the pattern for Protestant family life. The family was valued as a gift from God. In 1542 Luther, on the death of his eight- month daughter Elizabeth, wrote "I so lamented her death that I was exquisitely sick, my heart rendered soft and weak: never had I thought a father's heart could be so broken for his children's sake" (Ozment 1983: 168).

Luther, once whipped fifteen times before noon for failing to decline and conjugate what he had not yet learned, considered appropriate education vital for boys and girls. He promoted literature and music as essential contributions to theology and worship.

The Puritan Response

Elizabethan England saw renewed emphasis on a restrictive patriarchal model of family life reflecting the authority of the absolute monarch.

The Puritans, seeking a "purer" church, practiced a covenantal theology of grace within the family, to be in relationship with God and with one another. They believed the family was the foundational unit of a godly society. Children belonged to God, children of the covenant entrusted to parents as their stewards. Parents were enjoined to set a good example, and attend first to their children's physical needs. Mothers were encouraged to look after their own children, particularly to breast-feed them. Puritans believed that physical punishment was a last resort, and that discipline should be adapted to the child's temperament, seeking to guide a middle course between being over strict and being over indulgent. "For although there is a Corrupt Nature in every Child in its Infancy . . . yet Care and Education will much prevail to keep under that corrupt principle, and promote better inclinations in them" (Morgan 1966: 94).

Simon D'Ewes, on the death of his son, nearly two years old, in 1636 wrote:

> we both found the sorrow for the loss of this child, on whom we had bestowed so much care and affection, and whose delicate favour and bright grey eyes were so firmly imprinted in our hearts, far to surpass our grief for the decease of his three elder brothers, who, dying almost as soon as they were born, were not so endeared to us as this was. (Pollock 1987: 123)

Romanticism and Revival

In 1689, philosopher and physician John Locke challenged the view that the authority of the king defined in terms of absolute power in the state was analogous to the authority of the father in the family. Locke sought to articulate the form of political order that would ensure a balance between freedom and authority, aware of the potential for evil in human nature, and a model of child-rearing and education to fit that order. He opposed the tight control of swaddling and encouraged breastfeeding. He was adamant that flogging as a means of moral or intellectual improvement was wholly ineffective and that physical punishment at school was counterproductive. Locke (1693) advised that children be educated at home rather than at school, with its possibility of moral contamination, but reproved parents for aloofness towards their children.

Jean Jacques Rousseau (1762) outlined his ideal education from birth to maturity of a boy, Emile, with his tutor. Beginning "The Author of Nature makes all things good: man meddles", he proposed that children were naturally pure, then corrupted by their experience in society. While experiments based on Rousseau's approach of the "noble savage" resulted in uncontrollable children, his tracts, despite his own abysmal failure at parenting, fed into the Romantic era as it turned away from civilization and turned to nature. Glorification of children was their main symbol of beneficent nature (Grylls 1978).

Concurrently religious revival was generated by George Whitefield and John Wesley, defying Church law to preach the gospel to great crowds in the fields, in response to the pleas of the labouring poor for someone to take an interest in them. The plight of children moved them to provide schools and orphanages. "Strolling and vagabond orphans, poor and helpless, without purse and without friend, he [Whitefield] seeks out, picks up, and adopts into his family" (Pollock 1973). They sought to provide those children with knowledge and the capacity to earn a living, thus rescuing them from destitution, hence the emphasis on work and discouragement of play (Brown 1983).

In 1789, slave champion William Wilberforce visited the magnificent Cheddar Gorge near Bristol. Horrified at the impoverishment he had seen in the villages he exclaimed to his hostess, Hannah More, "Miss Hannah More. Something must be done for Cheddar. If you will be at the trouble I will be at the expense" (Collingwood 1990: 73). Thus began Hannah's life-long task of striving to provide Christian-based education and practical care to the exploited. Educated and a prolific author, Hannah opened schools and employed teachers to provide agricultural, industrial or domestic training to the village boys and girls. She travelled ceaselessly by carriage in rugged conditions to teach the children creatively that God loved them. The visible transformation of the ragged and unruly children convinced Hannah that children "brought into the world a corrupt nature and evil disposition, which it should be the great end of education to rectify".

> when they seem to get a little tired, we change the scene; and by standing up and singing a hymn, their attention is relieved. I have never tried the system of terror, because I have found that kindness produces a better end by better means. (Collingwood 1990: 135)

The Industrial Revolution

Industrialization in Victorian Britain produced an affluent middle class and a large wage-earning working class, relocated from rural areas, which dramatically restructured family life. In the agricultural context, the home had been the centre of work, a community where production took place. Family roles were well defined. Men now worked outside the home as production moved to factories. Separate spheres for men and women developed, becoming particularly exaggerated for middle-class women, who, confined to the home, deprived of education and career opportunities, came to be idealized as pure and pious. Benjamin Disraeli claimed the home was revered and the hearth sacred. For John Ruskin, the home was "a sacred place, a vestal temple, a temple of the hearth watched over by Household Gods" (Himmelfarb 1995: 56). Religion was to be located in the private sphere, the responsibility of women, who now became responsible for the morality of family members. This separate sphere ideology of public male and private female domains was thus given religious sanction, as if ordained by God. G. K. Chesterton challenged this development, describing Victorians as the first generation that asked its children to "worship the hearth without the altar" (Briggs 1983: 240), a domestication of the church more in common with the household gods of the early Romans than Christianity (Clapp 1993).

Most restricted were middle-class girls, typified by Virginia Woolf, daughter of leading agnostic and literary critic Sir Leslie Stephen:

> Girls were in a state of suspeded animation in the cocoon of the Victorian family, immobilized, frozen, unable to experience life directly but forced to see it through the thick web of protection which surrounded them. (DeSalvo 1989: 293)

Preoccupation with manners, etiquette and formality, maintaining strict social and class boundaries was accompanied by the addition of the emotionally damaging punishments of solitary confinement, deprivation of food, shaming and ridicule. Brutality and bullying had been endemic in public schools. Thomas Arnold, headmaster of Rugby, introduced what was intended to be a new civilizing Christian influence, but repeats rather the Roman model. He firmly believed in corporal punishment of children because they were inferior to adults (Gibson 1978). His son, Matthew Arnold, hated the flogging his father described. "As for rioting, the old Roman way of dealing with that is always the right one; flog the rank and file, and fling the ringleaders from the Tarpeian Rock" (Wilson 1932: 203).

The children of the working classes and the poor, meanwhile, were appallingly exploited. Destructive labour and being orphaned were the scourges of working-class children. Children had virtually no legal rights and could be bought, sold or otherwise disposed of by their parents. Free, compulsory education as a solution was resisted both as a violation of the father's absolute rights and a fear of social unrest.

The Sunday School Movement initiated free basic education, but even this came under suspicion in times of political unrest, William Pitt contemplating introducing a bill to suppress Sunday Schools. In 1851 three-quarters of the population of working-class children were enrolled. Laqueur (1976) demonstrates that Sunday schools helped to keep the soul alive in a population living under degrading conditions. For Alice Moody it offered "an atmosphere of love, peace and joy, with teachers of good education and children like ourselves. Lovely, lovely Elm Grove Sunday School. Every hour I spent in its walls was a fore-taste of heaven" (Burnett 1982: 143).

Free elementary education for working-class children came in 1870. It was often harsh and substandard, and much legislation to improve conditions had to be fought for. Lord Shaftsbury believed "children should be freed from the tyranny of industry and educated nobly to take their place as intelligent, useful, healthy and happy citizens in a Christian state" (Inchley 1986: 40). His Acts of Parliament freed women and children from virtual slavery in British mines, factories, chimney sweeping, and in rural areas. He founded schools and orphanages. George Muller, trusting God to provide, housed thousands of children in Bristol. William Quarrier opened family-style orphan homes in Scotland, inspiring Dr Barnardo to provide "little ivy-clad cottages each presided over by a kindly Christian woman who would be the Mother" where "anything approaching institutionalism would be scrupulously excluded" (Pinchbeck and Hewitt 1973: 527).

It is not surprising that, confronted by appalling misery, Barnardo and others longed to find ways to offer the slum children a healthier environment. So they participated in a scheme which saw the migration of thousands of children, some as young as four, transported to the colonies -- a scheme which proved to have an agenda less altruistic than that of these Christian advocates:

> throughout the entire period, child emigration was justified on economic grounds and never more so than during the second half of the nineteenth century. The surplus of destitute, homeless and unemployable children in Victorian Britain's urban centres was matched by the need in the Dominions for labour. (Wagner 1982)

Personal accounts of the disruption of the children's personal ties and their experience of abandonment as they were sent overseas, un-accompanied and separated from siblings, are heart-rending (Bean and Melville 1989; Gill 1997). Child migration was meant to be in the best interests of the children, but the children never came first.

Literature as an Advocate for Children

As the promised better world of the Enlightenment deteriorated into war and revolution there was a new sense of urgency to make religion vital. Mrs. Sherwood as an army wife in India had been greatly moved by the neglect of children within the closed ranks of the barracks.

Wherever they were posted she set up school, cared for orphans and wrote, meanwhile grieving the death of her own two children. *The Story of Little Henry and his Bearer* (1814) described the conversion of an orphan boy. A bestseller, it ensured her success as a Christian writer for children back in England. She linked spiritual issues with everyday domestic life. *The History of the Fairchild Family* became core family reading. The Fairchild children were industrious and obedient, yet frequently naughty displaying jealousy, anger, greed and fear. The parents were warm, affectionate and available, strict, but explaining the reason for any punishment and inviting questions. Obedience was demanded, not for parental convenience, but as a prerequisite to faith. Parents had to be a good example, and repent of their wrongdoings. "Her influence upon the domestic order of the Victorian life can hardly be overestimated. No writer made it clearer to her readers that the child who is dutiful within his family is blessed in the sight of God" (Cutt 1974: 41).

Even her critics admitted that Mrs. Sherwood was an excellent and natural storyteller, vigorous and cheerful, who understood how children felt. With the rise of a prosperous middle class, and power shifted to businessmen, abridgments appeared in republications. Any reference to wickedness and sin disappeared or became naughtiness. Lost was her challenge to parents, that they too had wicked hearts, and should confess and repent, "For when sin dwindled into naughtiness, an offended God was replaced by a vexed Papa or a hurt Mama" (Cutt 1974: 81). The parent, not God, became the ultimate authority. A family-based morality became the defining feature of the Victorian age, and as a result mid-Victorian England was "more moral, more proper, and more law-abiding than any other society in recent history" (Wilson 1993: 216), although religious affiliation was actually dropping.

Charles Dickens introduced children as fully developed characters central to his novels. They include the fatherless or motherless, the neglected, abandoned and handicapped. Parents were depicted as miserable failures and irresponsible, often warping their children's minds, while callous and despotic fathers treated their children as personal property. Children were victims "of commerce, of industry, of organized religion, of family authority, of stingy poor relief, and of urban indifference" (Sommerville 1982: 171). Dickens took particular care to share the Jesus story with his sons, writing *The Life of Our Lord* especially for them. "My Dear Children, I am very anxious that you should know something about the History of Jesus Christ, for everybody ought to know about Him" (Dickens [1849] 1934).

In 1847, American clergyman Horace Bushnell published *Christian Nurture*, which addressed children's spiritual capacity. In the revival context of the era Bushnell questioned the prevalent notion that children were outside God's grace until they were old enough for an adult conversion experience. Bushnell indignantly asked why it was assumed that children were not expected to turn to God. He encouraged parents to bring up children in a carefully disciplined, loving and Christian way such that they need not become rebellious and react against God, but should love Him from the start. In a positive environment the child could""grow up a Christian and never know himself as being otherwise" (Bushnell [1861] 1979).

Psychology of the Twentieth Century

Modern "man" had come of age according to Enlightenment philosophy, divesting himself of dependence on God. But the twentieth century ushered in unprecedented wars, a major economic depression and social upheaval. Psychology appropriated the role of guiding and controlling society, establishing norms and measurement of what constituted "normal", the large numbers in schools, asylums, prisons, and factories ideal as experimental subjects. "Normal" was defined in the context of theories of the nature of pathology, good government, economics, eugenics, evolution and heredity. The agenda of scientists who first studied young children was often to underpin their own particular view of human origins and nature. Psychology became society's gatekeeper, often a sterner master than any Victorian moralist (Morss 1990; Rose 1985; Shotter 1984).

The 1920s child-rearing was officially more repressive that in any nineteenth-century decade (Hardyment 1983). Beekman (1977) demonstrates an obsession with control and routine, reflected in feeding schedules, amount of food allowed, and in bowel habits. With strong medical endorsement, advice included a preoccupation with enemas, restrictive physical devices such as braces for posture, and mechanical devices to inhibit the "moral vices" of thumb sucking and masturbation.

In his 1928 child-rearing bestseller, behaviorist John Watson, holding there was no tangible evidence either for consciousness or for the existence of a soul, outlined his ideal – a totally compliant child, trained through control of the environment to be as free as possible from the family situation and from sensitivity to other people. Watson sought to eliminate the love factor claiming that physical affection corrupted the child, making it weak willed. Promoting his strict regime he stated, "You will be utterly ashamed of the mawkish sentimental way you have been handling it" (Hardyment 1983).

Behaviourist B. F. Skinner's desire for a world of cooperation with smooth social coordination made him preoccupied with the technology required to control behaviour, and willing to sacrifice freedom. In his cult novel *Walden Two* (1948) infants were housed in cubicles, watched over by attendants, and free of parental attachment.

Cognitivist Jean Piaget, believing a better world could be based on reason triumphing over emotion, focused on children's logic. The Piagetian image of the lone little scientist constructing concepts spontaneously through enquiry would be replaced by a more relational model when Margaret Donaldson (1978) demonstrated that children's thinking and language develop best when embedded in a familiar context. Guided participation by adults in ongoing cultural activities was identified by Rogoff (1990) as crucial for children to be active participants in their own development, thus emphasizing the importance of relationships.

It would take psychoanalyst Donald Winnicott (1964) to describe the "good enough mother" and to insist that the desired "good, compliant, clean" children of the manuals would be achieved only within positive interpersonal relationships, and the pioneering breakthrough of John Bowlby (1965) to demonstrate the crucial role of attachment for healthy development. The consequent emphasis on relationships, attachment and a secure family environment would transform childcare.

Conclusion

Children have rarely come first in the array of agendas for them identified down through history. The classical model of education and coercive child discipline constantly exerted the attraction of control in contrast to the radical gift of grace and forgiveness offered by Christianity. A theological rationale for severe coercion as the antidote to sinful nature provided a distortion of the Christian scriptures. It is customary to attribute to those whose understanding of evil implies a basic potential for evil in human nature, "original sin", an endorsement of such coercion. Yet the evidence is that the Puritans, Locke, Erasmus, Luther, Wesley and More all held an approach of thoughtful Christian education and measured discipline in the context of positive interpersonal relationships. Coercion was a last resort, seen as a failure on the part of the parents or teachers.

Who bears the blame in secular circles? Justification of punitive methods of control is explained by former psychoanalyst Alice Miller (1984). Aghast at the abusive indoctrination and coercion of Hitler youth, she examined German child-rearing practices and the issues of child abuse, repressive parenting, and the roots of violence. She concluded that much suffering is inflicted on children by parents, teachers and policy-makers passing on the abusive methods perpetrated on them, albeit unconsciously. The battle for control has a psychological rather than theological justification. How do we nurture children to foster essential attachment and the consequent capacity for intimacy? The core of Christianity is relationship. It is about belonging to God and one another, loving one another, forgiving thus fostering the attachment, intimacy and appropriate limits characteristic of psycho-social, intellectual and spiritual well-being. Christianity offered a difference to children, sometimes fulfilled, but frequently eroded for some personal or political agenda, often laced in theological rational-ization. Now seems timely in the postmodern array of options, to reclaim for children Christianity's original offer of individual worth and acceptance and of relationship with God, by sharing with them positively and creatively the invitation to belong and thus be nurtured spiritually.

References

Augustine of Hippo 400 AD: *The Confessions of St Augustine*, translated by Sir Tobie Matthew, revised by Dom Roger Hudleston, London: Collins Fontana Books 1957.

Bean, P. and Melville. J. 1989: *Lost Children of the Empire*, London: Hyman.

Beekman, D. 1977: *The Mechanical Baby: a popular history of the theory and practice of child raising*, Westport, CT: Lawrence Hill & Co.

Boswell, J. 1988: *The Kindness of Strangers: the abandonment of children in Western Europe from late antiquity to the Renaissance*, New York: Vintage Books, Random House.

Bowlby, J. 1965: *Child Care and the Growth of Love*, Harmondsworth: Pelican.

Briggs, A. 1983: *Social History of England*, New York: Weidenfeld and Nicholson.

Brown, E. K. 1983: *Women of Mr Wesley's Methodism*, New York: Edwin Mellen Press.

Burnett, J. 1982: *Destiny Obscure: autobiographies of childhood, education and family from the 1820s to the 1920s*, Harmondsworth: Penguin.

Bushnell, H. 1861 [1979]: *Christian Nurture, Grand Rapids Michigan*, Baker House.

Clapp, R. 1993: *Families at the Crossroads*, Downers Grove: IVP.

Clark, G. 1994: The Fathers and the Children. In *The Church and Childhood*, D. Wood (ed.), Oxford: Blackwell, 1–27.

Collingwood, J. and M. 1990: *Hannah More*, Oxford: Lion Publishing.

Cutt, N. 1974: *Mrs. Sherwood and her books for children*, Oxford: Oxford University Press.

DeSalvo, L. 1989: *Virginia Woolf: the impact of childhood sexual abuse on her life and work*, New York: Ballantine Books.

Dickens, C. [1849] 1934: *The Life of Our Lord*, London: Associated Newspapers.

Dixon, S. 1992: *The Roman Family*, Baltimore: John Hopkins University.

Donaldson, M. 1978: *Children's Minds*, Glasgow: Collins/Fontana.

Fildes, V. 1986: Breast, *Bottles and Babies: a history of infant feeding*, Edinburgh: Edinburgh University Press.

Gibson, I. 1978: *The English Vice*, London: Duckworth.

Gill, A. 1997: *Orphans of the Empire*, Alexandria, Australia: Millenium Books.

Golden, M. 1990: *Children and Childhood in Classical Athens*, Baltimore: John Hopkins University Press.

Greven, P. 1990: *Spare the Child*, New York: Alfred A. Knopf.

Grylls, D. 1978: *Guardians and Angels: parents and children in 19th century literature*, London: Faber and Faber.

Hanawalt, B. 1986: *The Ties that Bound Peasant. Families in Medieval England*, Oxford: Oxford University Press.

Hardyment, C. 1983: *Dream Babies: child care from Locke to Spock*, London: Jonathan Cape.

Hay, D. with Nye, R. 1998: *The Spirit of the Child*, London: Fount.

Himmelfarb, G. 1995: *The De-moralization of Society: from Victorian virtues to modern values*, New York: Alfred A. Knopf.

Hoyles, J. 1986: *Punishment in the Bible*, London: Epworth Press.

Inchley, J. 1986: *The Realities of Childhood*, London: Scripture Union.

Laqueur, T. 1976: *Religion and Respectability: Sunday Schools and Working Class Culture 1780–1850*, London: Yale University.

Locke, J. 1693: *Some Thoughts Concerning Education*, London: Churchill.

Lyman, R. 1974: Barbarism and Religion:Late Roman and Medieval Childhood. In *History of Childhood*, L. deMause (ed.) London: Souvenir Press, 75–100.

Miller, A: 1984. *Thou Shall Not Be Aware; society's betrayal of the child*, London: Virago.

Morgan, E. 1966: *The Puritan Family*, New York: Harper.

Morss, J. 1990: *The Biologising of Childhood: Developmental Psychology and the Darwinian Myth*, Hove: Sussex.

Ozment, S. 1983: *When Fathers Ruled – Family Life in Reformation Europe*, Cambridge, MA: Harvard University Press.

Pinchbeck, I. and Hewitt, M. 1973: *Children in English Society: Volume II*, London: Routledge Kegan Paul.

Pollock, J. 1973: *George Whitefield and the Great Awakening*, London: Hodder and Stoughton.

Pollock, L. 1987: *A Lasting Relationship. Parents and Children over Three Centuries*, London: Fourth Estate.

Rogoff, B. 1990: *Apprenticeship in Thinking: cognitive development in a sociocultural context*, Oxford: Oxford University Press.

Rose, N. 1985: *The Psychological Complex: psychology, politics and society in England 1869–1918*, London: Routledge.

Rousseau, J-J. 1762: *Emile*, Paris: La Renaissance du livre.

Shotter, J. 1984: *Social Accountability and Selfhood*, Oxford: Blackwell.

Sommerville, J. 1982: *The Rise and Fall of Childhood*, Beverly Hills, CA: Sage.

Stone, L. 1977: *The Family, Sex and Marriage in England 1500–1800*, New York: Harper and Row.

The Holy Bible 1989: *New Revised Standard Version*, Nashville: Thomas Nelson.

Todd, M. 1987: *Humanism and the Christian Social Order*, Cambridge: Cambridge University Press.

Wagner, G. 1982: *Children of the Empire*, London: Weidenfeld and Nicolson.

Watson, J. 1928: *Psychological Care of the Infant*, New York: Allen and Unwin.

Wiedemann, T. 1989: *Adults and Children in the Roman Empire*, London: Routledge.

Wilson, J. 1993: *The Moral Sense*, New York: Free Press.

Wilson, J. D. (ed.) 1932 [1869]: *Culture and Anarchy*, London: Cambridge University Press.

Winnicott, D. 1964: *The Child, the Family and the Outside World*, Harmondsworth: Pelican.

Chapter 5

Children, Doorposts and Hearts: How can and should the religious traditions respond to spirituality in a postmodern setting?

MARK CHATER

Hear, O Israel: The Lord our God is one Lord: And thou shalt love the Lord thy God . . . And these words, which I command thee this day, shall be in thine heart: And thou shalt teach them diligently unto thy children . . . And thou shalt write them upon the posts of thy house, and on thy gates. (Deuteronomy 6: 4–9)

I sometimes think about if there is one God and there is . . . everybody, well . . . most people believe in one God and um . . . there's um . . . different people believe in different gods. Which God's real? Um . . . I just can't figure that out . . . I can never . . . get the right answer or even get near it . . . you just wonder. ("Tim", a ten-year old interviewed in Hay with Nye 1998: 97)

IN the community of those concerned with spiritual education these two texts may be said to exercise polar opposing forces. Differences between the texts in terms of their origin, age and tone amount to a great deal. Deuteronomy is magisterial and prescriptive; "Tim", in his touching hesitancy, is symbolic of a universal human search for, and awareness of, meaning. We have become familiar with the ever wider and always interesting reportage of children's theological exploration (Erricker *et al.* 1997). We have placed more weight on the children's discourse; we have pointed to it as evidence, or perhaps illustration, of children's spirituality; we have used it as paradigm both for the nature of spirituality and for appropriate methodological responses to concerns about spiritual development. In this way "Tim" and his fellow theologians have become equal in authority to the Deuteronomist.

The hegemonic consensus of what might be called the school of Tim may be said to consist of the following points. Spiritual awareness is a biological given, emerging in the human species and observable through social anthropology (Hay and Nye 1998: 9ff). Though lodged at a basic level of consciousness, spirituality can be obscured by cultural forces (1998: 21ff) or given a heightened expression in classical religious sources (1998: 19). However, it remains free of doctrinal constructs; its evolution is personal, and its best expression is narrative rather than propositional. The consensus is intensely pluralist, defending every and any spiritual path as valid for the individual. Specific religious nurture may make either a positive or a negative difference to a child's spirituality (Erricker *et al.* 1997: 114ff). Particular forms of experience and opportunity can deepen or develop the child's spirituality, but these need not be overtly religious (Ofsted 1994; SCAA 1996). While these points have not gone uncontested (Thatcher 1996) they form a set of basic assumptions adopted by most of those concerned with spiritual education.

Embedded in the assumptions are values of individuality and diversity, and this allows spirituality to sit easily in a postmodern setting. But there can be no legitimate naming of the characteristics of "postmodern spiritualities" before certain problems of definition are faced. Uncertainty lingers around the term postmodern, which according to Richard Rorty has become "too fuzzy to convey anything . . . too equivocal for profitable use" (Rorty 1999: 262). The same could truthfully be said of the word spirituality. The hydra-like nature of postmodernity, spirituality and postmodern spirituality can be illustrated in a game with simple but appropriately malleable rules. In figure below, string together as many phrases from the lists of words. Start by taking the three columns in order and when you exhaust the possibilities, use the mixers. After that, columns may be taken in different orders or omitted. Several words can be transformed from adjectives to nouns, or vice versa, e.g., revisionist can become revisionism, millennium can become millennial, colonialism can become colonialist, etc.

Prefix	Infix	Suffix	Mixers
Post	Capitalist	Shopping	
Virtual	Community	Sex	
Revisionist	e	Enterprise	without
Cyber	Culture	Narrative	
New	Conscious	Millennium	after
Eco	Globalization	Colonialism	
Relational	Diversity	Program	

What we can learn from this game is that there is an enjoyable and widely-played-out vogue for sticking words and phrases together to create new lifestyles, new realities: a Baudrillardian universe in which all reality is reduced to a simulacrum, all action to abstraction (Baudrillard 1995). In the midst of this explosion of "realities" we may begin to see that flying beyond the gravitational pull of definition is at least part of the purpose of the game.

Postmodernity

Nevertheless, some locating of spirituality in postmodernity must be attempted if we are to understand what the religions are confronted with. It is worth mentioning that the term "postmodernity" is used here, while some might expect the term "postmodernism". For me, "modernity" and "postmodernity" are words to describe political and philosophical backdrops of ideas. In the case of the former those ideas were associated with rationalism and progress; in the case of the latter, the ideas focus on the questioning, deconstruction and dissolution of rationalism and progress. "Modernism" and "postmodernism", on the other hand, I interpret as literary and artistic movements of those times, occupying the foreground in front of the backdrop of ideas. Since this chapter is a discussion of how to respond to the wide backdrop, "post-modernity" is used. I accept, however, that for some there is interchangeability between the terms. The phrase "postmodern con-dition", also in use, is full of possibility: it gets us away from the idea that we are dealing with philosophical or artistic eras, itself an idea reflecting the rigidities of modernity. Instead we can begin to explore postmodernity as a mood or as a dimension of human existence.

Attempts at definition usually begin by identifying modernity and adding that postmodernity is a reaction to it. Thus if modernity is the rational, problem-solving faith in technology and technocracy, post-modernity questions it, laughs at it, is revolted by it. If modernity is the latest of a series of uniform truth-claims, postmodernity puts an end to all truth claims. If modernity is a flowering of personal freedom, post-modernity moves randomly between freedom, convention, fashion and servitude, asking, "what's the difference?" If modernity attempts to locate the spiritual in the familiar, postmodernity calls the familiar strange, and celebrates all forms of diversity, awkwardness and rejec-tion. Yet postmodernity is more than simply the attitude-striking of the young; its healthy skepticism and irresponsibility are to be seen in all ages.

The Christian theologian Hans Kung offers a critique of modernity. A continuation of the project which brought us linear progress, social optimism, technocracy and rationalism will, he believes, end in barbarism – indeed, is already doing so (Kung 1995: 773ff). A useful illustration of this belief might be that famous black and white photograph of the railway lines leading to the gate of Auschwitz: we see the mechanical perfection, the inevitability of the destination and its horror; we read the blind, inhumanly optimistic words above the gate; we ask how such heights of organizational skill could become divorced from compassion and dignity. Any form of religious discourse which continues to make concessions to modernist certainties is confronted with some severe questions of ethics and of the human spirit. Those who make and use doctrinal constructs might be willing to tarry in traditionalism or adapt to modernity, but the breakdown of both impels them forward to postmodernity.

It is useful to note that Kung believes real postmodernity not yet born. He perceives a late flourishing of modernity, a "radical pluralism" which he paints as

> arbitrariness, colorfulness, a mix of anything and everything, an anarchy of thoughts and styles, a principle of aesthetic and literary collage, a methodological "anything goes". (Kung 1995: 771)

This phenomenon is sometimes known as ultramodernity or hypermodernity. Confusingly, Kung's vivid word-portrait is precisely what some people understand as postmodernity or dismiss as "pick and mix spirituality". The latter phrase is unhelpful, especially when aimed at the young, as it asks no questions about why arbitrariness of choice might be attractiveness, and leaves no doors open except for a defeatist return to premodern or modern certainty.

Kung's arbitrary, colourful mix is playful and potentially destructive. It throws off traditional restraints, first in dogma, then ethics, then aesthetics. How does this state evolve into postmodernity? Kung is not sure; perhaps when the vulnerability, which goes with all of that late modern throwing-off of constraints, is realized; perhaps when the cold wind blows in the garden of doctrinal and ethical nakedness; when the same questions reappear in different and more insistent guises; or when the recognition that progress is no progress, development no development, and choice no choice, really begins to bewilder; perhaps then does the real fun of postmodernity begin.

The heroine of Linda Grant's novel *When I Lived in Modern Times* (Grant 2000) is a displaced European Jew in 1946 who comes to live in modernist Tel Aviv. In this world the past has been entirely wiped way: she can only survive by pretending, performing, loving and betraying. Thus she becomes a paradigm of the postmodern wandering away from certainties. Just as she wanders, so does spirituality: away from certainty about religious and other forms of truth (Derrida and Vattimo 1998) towards a default position of accepting and relativizing all personal truth, even of fragmenting the person into different and competing truths; away from faith in language (Barthes 1994) towards a suspicion of religious texts or, sometimes, a preference for silence; away from technocracy and the supremacy of science and information systems (Lyotard 1984) towards the priority of experience, the systematic suspicion of hierarchies and, for some, the spirituality of *Gaia*. Sometimes the wandering away is prelude to an attack: Muhammad, having left Mecca, returns at the head of an army. But now the citadels are many – capitalism, religion, medicine, management, equal opportunities – the weaponry is relentless irony and the tactic is the endless shifting and reconfiguring of terms, provocative twists and turns of interpretation, playful but deliberate re-coinings of words. Thus we see in Lyotard's *Postmodern Fables* (Lyotard 1999) a deconstruction of history including the gulf war.

Sometimes all this deconstructionist playing seems good entertainment, but every so often it turns into a sense of panic. The apocalyptic strain in postmodernity is evident in its exploration of the end of history or the end of time (Fukuyama 1993), and its celebration of the notion of a radical revolution in civilization (Foucault 1990; Fukuyama 2000).

The spiritualities which reside in postmodernity defy umbrella definitions. Children's spirituality enjoys unprecedented freedoms to wander, experiment, reject, attack and create. Exploration produces delight, uncovers ultimate questions and may sharpen mental and emotional skill, even while it bewilders and frightens. In this context, how are the religious traditions to respond? What is expected of them, and what options are open to them?

Response of the Religious Traditions

The confrontation with postmodern spiritualities will, in time, befall all traditions; but at present my discussion must focus on a specific tradition, Christianity, where my own knowledge, experience and belief reside. What Christianity learns about its encounter with postmodernity may well prove useful for its fellow traditions.

We have already glimpsed the non-viability of modernity; for Christians neither a continuation of the modernist project nor a reaction into premodernist traditionalism can serve usefully as paradigms of Christian response. The sterility of those two options is forcefully brought home by Sean O'Conaill in *Scattering the Proud: Christianity Beyond 2000* (O'Conaill 1999). He explores the liberal–conservative dualism, and points to it, and the assumptions about its irreplacability as a framework for direction of the church, as the major problem in itself.

What other responses are available? We might be tempted, as religionists have been, to criticize postmodernity as anarchic, trivial, consumer-driven (for every new lifestyle there is a niche market), or as indiscriminate, socially irresponsible or politically reactionary (we may doubt the reality of the Gulf War or the debt all we like, but out there people are still maimed and starving) (Huws 1999: 29ff). We may regret the arrival of postmodern ways, and wish to return to nineteenth-century social optimism as "the noblest imaginative creation of which we have record" (Rorty 1999: 277). We may want to call on post-modernity to take account of human beings, "in all their rounded, messy, vulnerable materiality" (Huws 1999: 52), in their social relations and their historical contexts – a good old-fashioned dose of Marxist materialism, with which Christianity has been in creative dialogue. Or we may require the advocates of postmodernity to cease their frenetic bout of deconstructing and instead to construct new rules and roles, new safety and stability – the job that Plato set himself after Socrates. These various responses may well have some attractive nobility to them; they will appeal to theological themes and texts; but they are all, to varying extents, calls for a return to modern or premodern frameworks, and as such they will not catch the spirit of postmodernity.

What else is there? If the spirit remains wandering, it remains free, but vulnerable, bewildered, fragmented. The fate of the religious tra-ditions, it is then argued, will be to share that vulnerability and fragmentation felt by everybody else. Churches will be one lifestyle option among thousands of others: they will be pure, prophetic, marginal, doubt-filled, provisional; they will survive not on their money, not on their constitutional position, nor even on popular membership, but on the breath of God. Followers will resemble Dennis Potter's *Son of Man* more than Robert Powell's *Jesus of Nazareth*; they will be more attuned to the disruptive religious agonies of a *Crow* (Hughes 1974: 35) than to the thoughtful religious reconstructionism of an Elizabeth Jennings (Jennings 1985: 17, 58). In this utter vulnerability both the churches and their members will experience bewilderment, but will at least be authentic and at last be on equal terms with the other belief systems and lifestyles they have condemned for so long. That is a future the churches must entertain, because evidence suggests it is possible. Some religionists have thought it to be deserved (Amos 8: 11–12); others believe that marginal vulnerability to be the place where God wants to send the church. Attractive though this may be, there are two objections to this vision of a vulnerable religious response to post-modernity. The first concerns the nature of postmodernity, and the second is moral.

It is significant that so many clustered movements of thought give themselves names referring to that which went before, inviting us to ask how they follow it; modernity – follow that. Post-Christians such as Mary Daly and Daphne Hampson define their belief in relation to a religious tradition they reject as irredeemably patriarchal. Post-structuralists are exponents of the death of the author, and of the genre; they live in attack mode against the conventions of literary creation and interpretation (Barthes 1966; Derrida and Caputo 1997). A post-indus-trial society is one which knows it has lost its powerful manufacturing base and has classified large numbers of people as economically useless, but cannot (yet) name what will power its present and future economy. The post-war period oriented itself, in its mores, education, gender roles and comic strip books to the seismic events of 1939–45, finding in those years a set of values and a self-definition even though knowing the moment had passed. Perhaps all movements beginning with "post" define themselves in relation to some recent moment, something they were but are no longer.

What is the nature of that relationship to the recent moment? I suggest a mix, a paradoxical cocktail – composed of what? Satire and outright rejection, certainly; also familial resemblance and nostalgia. Rorty draws our attention to the "philosophical pluralism" of post-modernity, by which he means the doctrine that there is an infinite number of equally valid ways to lead a human life: there is not, and cannot be, one true account of how things are (Rorty 1999: 268ff). Even while applauding this new diversity, he talks of a sense of the loss of unity and certainty which he detects in most meanings of post-modernity (Rorty 1999: 262). Like other "posts", postmodernity looks back with mixed feelings. It seems that there can be no adventure in deconstruction without solid edifices to attack; no fun in satire unless the objects of ridicule were or are held in high regard; no wincing pleasure in the ironic use of phrases before their unironic use; in short, no postmodernity without modernity. Postmodernity may storm out of the modern house vowing never to come back, but it still carries with it the features of the modernist parents it so loves to hate. If this is true, postmodernity needs modernity and the religious traditions for its own survival; this need will continue indefinitely, and postmodernity will take steps to ensure that they do not die out.

A second objection to a vision of total vulnerability for the traditions is moral. For the starkest possible portrait of ejection from power we can look at Lear: hounded and maddened, humiliated in battle and now a captive with his daughter Cordelia (his own vulnerability, his pride); in his soliloquy ("Come, let's away to prison") (King Lear V: iii) he seems to reach a momentary island of grace in his acceptance of defeat; a sense that his loss of power will bring him peace; a vision of kneeling for forgiveness and laughing at those on the ladder of court ambition; a desire to

... take upon's the mystery of things
As if we were God's spies. (King Lear V: iii)

A parallel in Christian theology is provided by Sean O'Conaill, who proposes that we see in Jesus' life and death

> a deliberate reversal of the human "heroic" journey to adulation and influence, which has caused violence, tyranny and injustice in all epochs ... (he denounces) the upward journey of the church and of the world (which) leads to "pyramids of esteem" and "hierarchies of respect" (O'Conaill 1999: back cover)

which glorify individuals and elites. Instead, the future of Christianity lies in its willingness to abandon this upward journey and return to the counter-cultural stance of Jesus in the gospels.

One is reminded of the work of Jean Vanier, whose emphasis on humility, littleness and simplicity has been so understated and eloquent. Striking a personal note, Vanier says:

> The poor and the weak have revealed to me the great secret of Jesus. If you wish to follow him you must not try to climb the ladder of success and power, becoming more and more important. Instead, you must walk down the ladder, to meet and walk with people who are broken and in pain. The light is there, shining in the darkness. (Vanier 1988: 72)

When writ large, this is an attractive version of the ecclesial future, one for which there appears to be powerful attestation both in the Bible and in spiritual life. But religionists should at least be wary of it for moral reasons. If they opt for a rejection of power and an embracing of simplicity, are they opting out of forms of social interaction which could transform the world? The Christian tradition parted company with Gnosticism on this point: it was considered wrong to disengage from the public world (Hall 1991: 59–60; Bettenson 1956: 90). In another context, that of British left politics since 1945, we have twice seen the upsurge of an equivalent choice in the Labour Party (Howard 1990).

Religionists with an interest in becoming marginalized as a response to postmodernity need to test their reasons. If these include strands of self-righteousness, or romantic attachment to weakness as purity, more solid thought is necessary. Humiliation and marginalization are not, at root, graced situations to any greater extent than positions of relative power. They are powerless, yet they have as much potential for games-playing, manipulation and dishonesty as situations at the middle or the top of the heap.

It might be possible to let the marginalization idea evolve, and here the work of another Christian theologian (O'Leary 1999) looks at the issue through the lens of the Roman Catholic church's crisis. O'Leary

argues for a transformation in church leadership, which needs to rediscover its mystical heart, its divine belief in the goodness of all creation,
and so transcend its suspicions of the world. He also argues for a transformation in spirituality, because a change in leadership can only
happen when the original, dynamic and fearless passion of Jesus for the
equality of all his father's creation is re-adopted by his followers.

O'Leary illustrates this transformation of leadership and of spirituality with a skin analogy (O'Leary 1999: 218). When the religions are
strong, their hearts are strong and their skin is thin and transparent.
They talk together about common tasks and challenges, and work to
achieve them. We could develop the analogy by adding that thin skin
means they are open and easily hurt; they can be seen inside from
outside; they have an inner strength which communicates itself through
the skin and affects the surrounding environment; their inner life is
strong and their effect is strong.

When the religions are weak, their hearts are weak and their skins are
thick. They build walls to sit behind, and cogitate narrow self-imposed
tasks. Again, we could also add that they cannot be hurt by the outside
world; they are immune to it; but neither can they feel its presence, nor
affect how it feels.

The central idea in the "skin" analogy is that a religion should have
porous borders, not rigid barriers, between itself, the world, and other
religions. O'Leary credits John Hull with the idea for this analogy
(O'Leary 1999: 218). There is no printed original source available for this,
but Hull has used it in conversation and in lectures. It reflects his belief
that there is a Christian argument to be made for critical openness (Hull
1984: 212ff; Hull 1991).

This choice of a thin-skinned or a thick-skinned relationship with the
postmodern world has two external tests, for O'Leary: two respondents
outside the churches whose reactions and attitudes are an indicator as
to the thickness of the Christian skin. The two are the poor and the
religious other, both of whom turn their backs on, and deplore, the thick-
skinned approach. The poor do so because they are economically
excluded. With limited or non-existent monetary power, they cannot
call in any recognition. They will, therefore, not be interested in churches
whose skins are as thick, whose values are as excluding and inflexible,
as the commercial world. The religious other are theologically excluded.
We might include, in one or both of these categories, women and those
excluded by ability, ethnicity or sexual orientation. The two groupings
are united in certain key ways: for a thick-skinned organization, weak
in its own beliefs and strong in its defenses, these two groups are
economically or theologically useless, strange, threatening. It is therefore appropriate to say that the poor and the religious other will be the
test of the churches' heart condition. A church strong in heart will have

a thin skin towards the poor and the religious other. The porosity of the skin will enable these two groups to move in and out of the body freely, frequently and creatively. In doing so they will change themselves and their relationship, and they will change the body too.

What is interesting about this vision is that it implicitly changes the plot. The denouement is neither an implosion into traditionalism nor a frantic pursuit of late modernity. It is a future in which core doctrines and narratives are reaffirmed with a strong heart, and this is done in partnership with, and for the sake of, the poor and the religious other. This program has been described as Nicene radicalism.

The tradition, too, exists for the sake of humanity. Just as Buddhism is a raft, to be discarded when one has crossed the river, so the Christian tradition too is finite. If the traditions continue, humbly and without the arrogance which divides and makes dualism, sharing their doctrine and their sacraments, this will make a difference. Particularly, the churches need to overcome dualistic thinking of the sort which divides people into groups of familiar and other, and ideas into categories of right and wrong. In being this open, churches and other traditions implicitly accept that they change. The argument of Karen Armstrong in *A History of God* (Armstrong 1993: 377ff) that the concept of God changes to meet the needs of ages, and therefore that the entire character of a religious tradition may be – to use the skins analogy again – porous, or flexible and fluid, ends by offering real hope that traditions will overcome fundamentalism and will evolve new focuses of meaning.

This can be summed up and generalized as urging the Christian tradition – and it can be extended to the others – into a new evolution in thought and practice. The new evolution draws on the tradition but is not traditionalist; the evolution will lead the tradition to overcome the faults and dualisms which have caused so many to reject it, but will not be modernist; the tradition will live on with a radical openness to others, especially including the poor and the religious other, but with its core beliefs still confidently held and its practices continued. Implicit in this vision is a hope that the religions will end their futile competition with each other and begin standing up to the common enemy, the destroyer of life, the destroyer of meaning, the consumer of the poor and vulnerable.

Untidy Postscript On Love

Perhaps a Christian theology of love is key in understanding how that tradition might live in postmodernity. This is not because of any naïve belief in the all-conquering power of love, or that we can save ourselves through loving service or activism – it isn't as simple as that; but more because a Christian understanding of love within the Godhead, between God and humanity, and amongst people in differing relationship, all these loves which are so different yet go by the same name, might serve as a model of how Christians and others might live with their traditions in a condition of postmodernity.

Sean O'Conaill offers the experience of the Trinity – model of the church and of human relations – as a model for Christians living through the pain or re-evaluating their position. For him,

> experience of the Father begins often with a time of great pain when we are forced to evaluate our lives, then turn prayerfully to the Son in his pain, and when we remember it is always the Father who sends us the Son, which is also the solidarity of the creator with all of his creation, we will receive the Spirit . . . a life in union with the Trinity. (O'Conaill 1999: 95)

This is the same Trinity who is known as Lover, Beloved and Love for Augustine (*De Trinitate* 6:7, 8:14 and 15:29), and who becomes Mother, Lover, Friend for Sallie McFague (McFague 1987) – a community of love, a model for just and loving communities, a Godhead in whom divine love is given and received. It is the same Trinity, and yet it is not, for the language and the models change as the tradition flows.

That same love is shown to humanity by and through the Son, who also loves the church as his bride (Revelation 21: 2), a metaphor which – freed of the sexist connotations of mastery and ownership associated with the opponents of women's priesthood – might now be creatively re-quarried.

I think that between believers and the tradition there can be a relationship analogously described as mature love. Just as lovers begin by believing they cannot live without each other, so people coming freshly to a community of faith may believe they cannot live without it, nor it without them. If they successfully move into mature love, they manage to ask themselves how they can live with each other even while contemplating the possibility of leaving or losing. Even if parting doesn't happen, they face the possibility that it might. The question, "How could I live without you?" takes on a more realistic meaning. They move from dependency to chosenness. So too believers, in relationship with their tradition, must ask themselves "How do we and others live outside this?" This question may take many forms: the chestnut, "How did people achieve salvation before Christ, or before the missionaries came?" is one of the earliest and most elementary forms. Others are the attempt to account for secularization and other religious traditions; the thought that their own personal journey might take them away from the tradition; the realization, like waking up with a partner who seems both familiar and new, that they are seeing their tradition in a different light; the asking, "What do you need me for?" and "What do I need you for?"; the envisaging of a time when they might need each other in a different way, at different times, or not at all. This is how a relationship with a religious tradition moves beyond fundamentalism to chosenness, and from traditional or modern models to postmodern fluidity. In short, if postmodernity spells the end of all absolute truth claims, the new game is not to resort to old truth claims in the old way, nor to create new ones and relate to them in the old way. Postmodernity calls us, instead, to relate to the old truths in a new way.

How, then, do we greet the choices that others make in the kaleido-scope of postmodernity? The love choices that our siblings, friends and children make are their choices; we accept, we include new partnerships in our social circles, we allow friendships to wax and wane. If we can, we celebrate and support other people's choices of love even while saying that we prefer to stay with our own. The many different forms of human love may well enrich our own if we let them. This is only a metaphor, but we can usefully note how hard it is for the churches to be relaxed about choices in sexuality and love, and we can draw the in-ference that love seems to be at the very least a test of the ability to live openly, creatively and faithfully in postmodernity.

And where is all this going? In heaven, people neither give nor are given in marriage (Matthew 22: 30); we may take this to mean a heaven of new configurations of love and fidelity. The resurrected state is perhaps a little like the postmodern condition, in that it has both a con-tinuity and a discontinuity with the known, the modern. It is surprising, contradictory, celebratory, unbound. It gives these characteristics to the imperfect loves we have now. It is certainly ironic towards what we have now. If the Christian tradition avoids the twin temptations of triumphalism and romantic marginalization, and orients itself to that surprisingly postmodern condition of resurrection, it has little to fear, and much to offer to those who search.

References

Armstrong, K. 1993: *A History of God*, New York: Ballantine Books.
Barthes, R. 1966: *Introduction to the Structural*, Birmingham: Birmingham University Press.
Barthes, R. 1994: *The Semiotic Challenge*, Berkeley: University of California Press (English translation).
Baudrillard, J. 1995: *Simulacra and Simulation*, Chicago: University of Michigan Press (English translation).
Bettenson, H. (ed.) 1956: *The Early Christian Fathers*, Oxford: Oxford University Press.
Derrida, J. and Caputo, J. 1997: *Deconstruction in a Nutshell: A Conversation with Jacques Derrida*, New York: Fordham University Press.
Derrida, J. and Vattimo, G. 1998: *Religion*, London: Polity Press.

Erricker, C., Erricker, J., Ota, C., Sullivan, D., and Fletcher, M. 1997: *The Education of the Whole Child*, London: Cassell.

Foucault, M. 1990: *The Order of Things*, London: Routledge.

Fukuyama, F. 1993: *The End of History and the Last Man*, Harmondsworth: Penguin.

—— 2000: *The Great Disruption*, London: Profile Books.

Grant, L. 2000: *When I Lived in Modern Times*, London: Granta Books.

Hall, S. 1991: *Doctrine and Practice in the Early Church*, London: SPCK.

Hay, D. with Nye, R. 1998: *The Spirit of the Child*, London: Fount.

Howard, A. 1990: *Crossman: The Pursuit of Power*, London: Jonathan Cape.

Hughes, T. 1974: *Crow: From the Life and Songs of the Crow*, London: Faber and Faber.

Hull, J. 1984: *Studies in Religion and Education*, Lewes: Falmer Press.

—— 1991: *Mishmash: Religious Education in Multi-cultural Britain: A Study in Metaphor*, Birmingham: Christian Education Movement.

Huws, U. 1999: Material world: the myth of the weightless economy. In L. Panitch and C. Leys (eds), *Global Capitalism Versus Democracy*, London: Merlin Press, 29–55.

Jennings, E. 1985: *Selected Poems*, Manchester: Carcanet Press.

Kung, H. (Eng trans.) 1995: *The Religious Situation of our Time: Christianity*, London: SCM.

Lyotard, J-F. 1984: *The Postmodern Condition*, Manchester: Manchester University Press.

—— 1999: *Postmodern Fables*, University of Minnesota Press.

McFague, S. 1987: *Models of God: Theology for an Ecological Nuclear Age*, London: SCM.

O'Conaill, S. 1999: *Scattering the Proud: Christianity Beyond 2000*, Dublin: Columba Press.

O'Leary, D. 1999: *Lost Soul? The Catholic Church Today*, Dublin: Columba Press.

Ofsted (Office for Standards in Education) 1994: *Spiritual, Moral, Social and Cultural Development: A Discussion Paper*, London: Ofsted.

Rorty, R. 1999: *Philosophy and Social Hope*, London: Penguin Books.

SCAA (Schools Curriculum and Assessment Authority, now Qualifications and Curriculum Authority) 1996: *Education for Adult Life: The Spiritual and Moral Development of Young People*, London: SCAA.

Thatcher, A. 1996: Policing the sublime: a wholly (holy?) ironic approach to the spiritual development of children. In J. Astley and L. Francis (eds), *Christian Theology and Religious Education*, London: SPCK, 117–39.

Vanier, J. 1988: *The Broken Body*, London: Darton, Longman and Todd.

Chapter 6

Listening to . . . listening for . . . : A Theological Reflection on Spirituality in Early Childhood

ELAINE CHAMPAGNE

C AN we learn from children's spirituality? In entering the ongoing dialogue of the true, although still unveiled richness, of children's spirituality, I am inviting you along a path, for a journey that might sound quite unusual at first sight. I am referring to what will be recognized as theological reflection. I intend to say a few words on the process of this reflection, and give you an example of its functioning. We will then listen to Arielle, Nicolas and Katie, and listen for the spiritual they might have expressed in three daily life events. Our theological reflection will take roots from what we will capture from these short experiences. It will clearly be incomplete and might raise more questions than provide answers. It might also bring new insights about our way of understanding and experiencing spirituality. My wish would be that this process simply invites you to pursue its momentum by listening to children, and listening for their spirituality. I believe a mutual enrichment resides there, both for the children, for ourselves, and for our understanding of spirituality.

In order to access more easily the reality of the spiritual, I would like to invite you to listen first, in order to be led by the unexpected, in order to hear the unpredictable. Questions, theories and concepts will be introduced later in the presentation.

Since 1994, I have had the privilege of ministering as a chaplain at the Montreal Children's Hospital. As a team there, the pastoral services have as their mission to offer emotional and spiritual support to families and staff, especially in critical situations involving children facing serious injuries or illness, facing the threat of death or even death itself.

Let me tell you about a family I encountered a few years ago. Being with families like this one made me realize more and more a very precious richness pointed out by the children themselves, within the memories they left. This treasure was often remembered as a gesture, an attitude, a trait or a sentence which can be understood as a metaphor of the children's essence, as a key to their spiritual life. The story I am going to tell you will also offer an example of the method I will be using more directly with children in the further examples.

NATHAN

Nathan, a four-year-old little boy was running to his dad as he was returning from work at the end of the day. The child was fatally hit by a car. In the family room of our emergency department, both parents were completely overcome with sorrow and pain. After long periods of holding the body of their child, after long periods of heavy silence and loud laments, I tried to offer them a discreet pastoral presence. I remember them slowly starting to tell me about Nathan, about the lovely boy he was, about what he enjoyed. While hearing their story, I could picture the child, now lying in their arms, playing around with his sister, being stubborn at times, or simply acting like all other children his age, although being his unique self. Nathan was not just a child among many. He was theirs. I remember them gathering memories, entering very gradually into the process of looking for the whys of this cruel accident, searching for a meaning for his short visit in their lives, yet searching for the indelible mark he had left on them . . . The mother said, in tears, "he was laughing so heartily all the time!" Softly, I replied, "like the Little Prince in the stars". *The Little Prince*, from Antoine de Saint-Exupéry, is a character from a very famous French story carrying wisdom for all ages. *The Little Prince* is a young child who, through his journey on earth, learns the secrets of the heart and teaches them to his new adult friend. He liked to laugh. On his departure, he offered his laughter to his friend for him to remember whenever he looked at the stars. Nathan liked to laugh. And I saw a tiny star twinkle in the mother's eyes.

As Nathan's mother searched for whatever he had left within her, she seized upon his laughter as significant, as potentially containing the very essence of his life. Accompanying this mother required that I be attentive to this inner door she was discovering, and to search for the pictures, images, stories, or symbols she might use as keys for her to enter an open space, a space where she would be able to journey through her grief not only on a psychological level, but also on a spiritual level.

Pastoral presence involved not only *listening to* explicit expressions of her spirituality, but also *listening for* the spirituality underlying her daily life experience with her son. Trying to put into words what is being expressed might reveal the spiritual pearl hidden in the shell of the day-to-day living. This very effort to find meaning and life in what is offered to us in encounters of this kind is what I call theological reflection, or theological interpretation.

I would now like to share with you some of the questions children have left me with. *Listening to* explicit expressions of children's spirituality and *listening for* the spiritual underlying their daily life challenged me to put into words the spiritual in children that might pass unnoticed but which, I believe, contributes to our keen and spontaneous attraction to their genuine liveliness. I take seriously into account Hay's suggestion to researchers "to focus on the perceptions, awareness and response of children to those ordinary activities which can act as what Peter Berger calls 'signals of transcendence'" (Hay with Nye 1998: 54).

I now wish to introduce Arielle, Nicolas and Katie. We will listen to them and listen for the spirituality potentially present in these snapshots taken from their daily lives. The following theological reflection will raise certain questions concerning our understanding of what is spirituality.

Arielle

Arielle, a little three and a half year-old child, was at the supermarket on a summer day, when I overheard her conversation with her father. She was sitting in a stroller, in front of him; he was carrying a few groceries, waiting in line at the checkout counter. The conversation was in French. It went like this:

> Dad, when is your birthday?
> Oh! Not soon . . .
> Dad, when is your birthday?
> In a long time . . .
> Dad, when is your birthday?
> Tomorrow is your mom's birthday.
> Ah . . . Dad, is your birthday also tomorrow?
> No. My birthday is in a long time . . .
> When is your birthday?
> In September.
> When is my birthday?
> In June.

Then, Arielle continued to play quietly. Her persistence and his patience both drew my attention.

What was going on in this conversation? It is not necessary here to talk at length of Arielle's cognitive development from a psychological point of view. However, let us keep in mind a few observations:

- Arielle is repeating the same question to her father, over and over again, "When is . . . ?" She keeps asking about her father's birthday

until she gets the answer whose birthday is on the next day.
* Arielle is asking specifically about birthdays, about the birthdays of each and every member of her family.

A short analysis leads us to state a little more. Arielle's father was certainly attentive in offering her short answers she could understand; while varying his answer to the same question, he could find out what she was looking for. Arielle was confident enough in him to be persistent in questioning him. This says a lot about the quality of their relationship. On the spiritual level, Arielle's conversation brings three main ideas to mind: her family relationships, rituals and time.

Relationships are very basic to spirituality. There is a long tradition in Christian churches of awakening the individual to the three folds of spirituality: relation to self, relation to others, relation to God. In a multifaith context, God could rather be called any of the names one could attribute to this transcendent reality. It is also well known that these relationships are tightly connected in one's life. The way one relates to oneself impacts on his or her way of relating to others and vice versa. The Great Religions also make it clear one cannot separate one's prayer to God from one's actions towards one's neighbour.

The birthdays Arielle is evoking can very spontaneously be associated with rituals. Rituals are not only found in liturgy but also in daily life. They have an impact on our lives as individuals and as part of a larger community.[1] Rituals have to do with time. And this is more specifically what struck me with Arielle. Let us pay more attention to the dimension of time in her conversation.

Arielle is not simply asking for information. When talking to her father, she is not only relating to her father and her family. While she states her question, while she waits for an answer, she experiences time. In this sense, she becomes more aware of time. Arielle is discovering not only her present time, but the continuum of time. While asking her questions, she is actively:

* Waiting
* Exploring time
* Ordering time
* Anticipating time.

Arielle is actively finding out where she belongs in time. Her time was finally named as well. In Arielle's short conversation with her father, family relationships, rituals and time are interwoven.

Time flows. Time lasts. Time is "unseizable". Rituals make us experience a different time. In rituals, we commemorate a special event of the past: in this case, Arielle's birth, the time of her entering time, that is, her beginning of time. This event happened once, and can't be repeated. It is unique. Rituals celebrate a commemorated event made present in time. Birthdays celebrate the very value of one's unique and ongoing life. In that sense, rituals make the future possible, accessible. They put us in the movement of what has been, what is, and what will be. A new individual came to life one day, and this coming into life continues its movement in time towards the future. Rituals are essential to one's existence. They act like signposts, which make us notice time. Those signposts mark out our history, they give consistency to our existence. In a sense, rituals stop time so that we may experience it.

Arielle certainly can't reflect in these terms. But she somehow has a sense that birthdays are very special. There is a time for each birthday. And all of her family have value so everybody has a birthday, which they celebrate together. Life, the very existence of every one surrounding her, has that intrinsic value, highlighted by the birthday ritual.

NICOLAS

Let us now turn to Nicolas. I was working at the hospital, when one morning, a cute little four-year-old took the elevator with his mother. There were certainly five or six other adults in the elevator, smiling with amusement at him. Nicolas was trying to stretch enough to reach the elevator buttons. He could not. While his mother pressed for the eleventh or twelfth floor, he asked his mother, "Mom, are we going way, way, way, way, way, way, way up?" How high this ride appeared to be to Nicolas! Like Arielle, Nicolas used the repetition of a few words to express his inner experience. Like Arielle, he is asking a question to a parent, in this case, to his mother.

As many children their age, both Arielle and Nicolas are open to newness, keen to discover, and actively exploring their universe. Arielle was experiencing time. Nicolas is inhabiting space, moving in space, going up in order to grow up. His question carries his movement in space. I like the English way of expressing this: Nicolas is *raising a question*. A child's eye view of the world is caught by what is up there. If we could borrow their eyes, we might experience their sense of the *grandeur* of the world.

In his own way, maybe Nicolas could relate to what the ancients would have said: God elevated man's forehead and ordered him to contemplate the stars (Nouwen 1974).

Arielle and Nicolas bring to our attention the very challenge of recognizing what, in our daily experience, has the potential of being an open door to spirituality. They can help us discover where spirituality can be found. The challenge resides in our adult ability to share, even to participate in those basic life experiences, which are the very substance of spirituality. The challenge of listening to and listening for children's spirituality is double. It holds the challenge of listening to children, and the challenge of recognising spirituality.

Toddlers are people of few words. And spirituality can't appropriately be expressed in any words. As Simon mentioned:

> Concepts and words can only grope towards expressing the inexpressible . . . What they hide are untold depths of mystery which cannot be spoken in human language or confined to human concepts. (Simon 1993: 17)

Consequently, respecting the truthfulness of a child's spiritual experience in daily life or at any time prompts us to recognize it as it is: a mystery.

KATIE

Katie is a beautiful example of this encounter with mystery. Madeleine Simon describes her story:

> two friends of mine were sitting on the sand at Whitley Bay while Katie, the two-and-a-half-year old daughter of one of them, occupied herself nearby. Having found a gull's feather she spent a long time looking at it, feeling it and turning it every way. She then rested it on the water and watched it being carried a little way away and then being brought back on a wave. She picked it up again and continued to play with it like this for the best part of half an hour. The two friends were forcibly struck by the sheer wonder which had taken possession of that child for so long. (1993: 41)

Once again, we observe. There is Katie, a feather, water, a few adults bewildered at what they witness. The action is simple. What is hidden underneath might however catch our eye. What exactly is Katie doing?

- Exploring: once again, exploring, discovering seems very basic in the attitude of little children. They show an openness to their surrounding which reminds us how new is the world to them.
- Wondering: this world Katie and little children are entering in, is not only observed but questioned. They wonder, not always with words, but with their own special grasp, with their whole being . . . They are puzzled and surprised, but they also marvel at what they encounter. Their simple discoveries nurture them spiritually.
- Contemplating: Simon suggests to us that,

> All these experiences relating to the sense of touch – *as well as the other senses* – provide a medium for the development of wonder, and wonder is prayer in embryo. (my italics; 1993: 27–8)

According to the impact Katie had on the adults surrounding her, she was obviously experiencing the feather with intensity. She was absorbed in her activity, without being distracted for a long time for a child this age. Katie was living her present moment very freely, without making haste nor restraining herself. She was simply being herself.

That might be what most impressed the adults who witnessed her exploration. Katie was not only striving to learn something new, mastering a new ability or showing others what she had learned. She was simply communicating the spirit of the moment she was living. Katie was left the opportunity to be fully herself, living fully that moment. And the quality of her experience points to something more than a feather. Some people might call it harmony with her environment, others might evoke a sense of communion with nature, and others might relate this experience to contemplation. From wonder to praise, from praise to awe, from awe to contemplation, the road is rather short, it is only a step. And this step might be, according to one's religious tradition, to hear the name of the unnamed Presence, to recognize the mystery of the sacred in what is.

Spirituality

In Katie's example, the adults did not participate or respond actively to her experience, although they did *listen to* and *listen for* her spirituality. On the other hand, they provided her with the opportunity to be. And Katie led them to the spiritual. Katie, without words, without even intending to, was able to communicate to them her spiritual awareness.

Listening to and *listening for* Arielle, Nicolas and Katie, has led us to explore different paths of spirituality. Many other examples might be found, many other paths explored. The more attentive to spirituality we become, the more we hear and witness it. Becoming aware of spirituality is undoubtedly one good way to foster it. The challenge is to recognize its presence.

What precedes also illustrates a way to develop a theological reflection initiated from the children's everyday self-expressions. At this point, we need to be a little more systematic in what we mean by spirituality. Keeping in mind what was brought to light from the above observations, and relating them to contemporary works in spiritual theology, I believe that new insights might emerge from this dialogue regarding both our understanding of spirituality and that of children.

So what is spirituality? What comes to mind is a mosaic of related elements: interior life, experience, meaning, expression, relatedness, transcendence, immanence, ultimate values, integrity, awareness, etc. Needless to say, spirituality can be listened to in a different language than religious language; spirituality and religion are interdependent rather than equivalent. Many authors offer us as many definitions of spirituality. In addition, the term, at least in North America, is constantly evolving with society's experience of it.[2] So I choose to examine three characteristics or dimensions of spirituality often recurring in the current literature: spirituality as a human experience, spirituality as a quest for unification and integrity, and spirituality as a quality of consciousness.

Human Experience

Above all, spiritual experience is a human experience. There is no spirituality without the human, without a person experiencing it. In every tradition, not only within Christian perspectives, spirituality is rooted in this reality that we are incarnated. In other words, we are not purely spiritual beings. Sandra Schneiders describes this anthropological affirmation in these terms: "spirituality is virtually coextensive with human transformative experience" (Schneiders 1998: 8).

Thus, it is not limited to a simple mind construct, or a brilliant ideology, or a pure sentiment. "No spirituality comes down from heaven in a disembodied or unfleshy state" (Alexander 1980: 251). On the other hand, spirituality is not limited to the tangible, or to what can be sensed materially. Spirituality cannot be dissociated either from the human or from what is beyond the human, in transcendence and in immanence. Spirituality carries universal basic questions concerning human life: the origin, the end, the purpose. It carries the reality of happiness and sorrow. Our example with Nathan showed us spirituality as experienced as a core of being where one spontaneously turns when in crisis.

Arielle's, Nicolas's and Katie's experiences belong to that humanness. They also point to something beyond it. Within certain limits, they contribute to give shape to their own answers to the meaning of their lives.

Unification and Integrity

Again let us listen to Schneiders and Alexander on what is spirituality:

> Spirituality is understood as the unique and personal response of individuals to all that calls them to integrity and transcendence. (Schneiders 1986: 264)

> A second definition at a higher level of abstraction has the word spirituality point to the integration of ultimate concerns and unrestricted values in concrete life. (Alexander 1980: 253)

> Spirituality has something to do with the unification of life by reference
> to something beyond the individual person. (Schneiders 1986: 266)

It is well understood that spirituality has the capacity to help mobilize an individual's inner resources towards a more unified and a better harmonized existence. Spirituality can act as a source of growth towards one's becoming a relational human being. This movement points to what individuals consider, consciously or not, as the ultimate value emerging from their horizon of meaning and being coherent with their beliefs system.

In a Christian context, spirituality cannot only be described as a forward movement but also as a call. The Christian is not only becoming who he or she is, but also relating to the ultimate Other, who is source of Life. God is here perceived as a "God of promise who turns man towards an unscripted future".[3]

Concretely, adults constantly make conscious or unconscious choices that bring them closer to or farther from this Ultimate concern, thus giving them a sense of focus or of chaos. It is well known that unexpected or intense events in life can also provoke a sense of chaos. Then spontaneously, the whys are asked, a need is experienced to make sense, to refocus on the essentials in order to go on. If unification goes along with simplicity, then one grows towards simplicity with age. The promised unprecedented future might be foreseen in a more and more unified reality.

Arielle, Nicolas and Katie apparently present a different perspective. Their openness, their keenness to discover, points to the richer and more complex reality they are relating to. They also try to make sense of the world, whilst mostly surrounded by the unknown and the mysterious. They rely on close and safe adults, while engaging in the world by themselves.

Consciousness

Consciousness appears as a third dimension very present in contemporary attempts to define spirituality. Schneiders describes it as follows:

> Spirituality . . . is the experience of conscious involvement in the project
> of life-integration through self-transcendence towards the ultimate value
> one perceives. (Schneiders 1998: 3)

She nuances here what she had previously written in another article about spirituality as an "experience of consciously striving to integrate one's life" (Schneiders 1986: 266).

Consciousness is here mainly referring to what relates to the capacity of reflecting, the capacity of taking a distance from an experience, and the capacity of abstraction. If we take into account the cognitive development of young children, most of these abilities are not yet available to them. Does that mean that spirituality is not part of their being? Does that mean that spirituality is not accessible to them? Either we agree that what I earlier called children's spirituality is only the embryo of spirituality, or we must revisit our definitions of spirituality. There is a need to deepen our reflection on this matter.

Other attempts to define spirituality in the context of consciousness raise additional major questions. Apparent similarities are found in the definitions offered by Crompton and Pihlainen.

According to Crompton,

> spirituality is awareness of feeling and beliefs which in turn stimulate self-awareness and answers to "why" questions about life. (Crompton 1998: 44)

And according to Pihlainen, from the Baha'i tradition, also quoted by Crompton,

> spiritualization is . . . a process of growth that occurs as new understandings enlighten our beliefs, values, emotions, attitudes and actions. (Pihlainen 1993: 3)

Are awareness and enlightenment referring to something similar in this case? What happens when those beliefs or values are not yet articulated? Does spirituality need its own consciousness in order to be spiritual? And how can we have access to someone else's consciousness of their own spirituality, especially when language is not readily available, or even sufficient to describe what can be held in no words?

In his chapter "A Geography of the Spirit", drawn from *The Spirit of the Child* (Hay with Nye 1998: 57–75), Hay takes a different point of view. He describes, in a very useful and informative way, three main categories of spiritual sensitivity: awareness-sensing, mystery-sensing, value-sensing. Rather than formally defining spirituality, he offers his readers experiential categories pointing to it. Interviewing children then brought his colleague, Nye, to add another category, which appears even more relevant to children's spirituality: relational consciousness.

> They – the children – have relational intuitions at an extraordinarily early age . . . Similarly, very young children are richly aware of, and have an implicit understanding of their relationship to, their environment long before they can name it. (1998: 145)

I believe Arielle, Nicolas and Katie give us clear examples of their relational way of being.

Conclusion

Arielle, Nicolas and Katie have given us opportunities to listen to explicit expressions of their spirituality and to listen for the spiritual underlying their daily lives. They have pointed out to us fundamental dimensions of their journey as children: relationships (especially with their families), rituals, time, space, and mystery. They have been waiting, exploring, ordering, anticipating, questioning, wondering, contemplating, leading others to the spiritual. They have inspired our reflection and have enriched our perspectives. They might have invited us to revisit our own spirituality. But they also made us raise a few questions.

During the last three years of pre-doctoral work, while I have been listening for and reflecting on the spiritual in children's experience, I have realized more and more both this richness and challenge I am facing. The main questions concern the topic in itself: children and spirituality. How can we access or rather witness young children's interior life while preserving their naturalness and spontaneity? How do we take into account children's imaginative creativity as a basic expression of their spirituality? How do we recognize the truly spiritual dimension of what they are expressing, especially when their verbal language is so limited and in itself needs to be translated? And what makes spirituality so different in early childhood? Can everything be spiritual? Or rather, is the spiritual present in everything? Does spirituality need to be conscious of itself in order to be spiritual? It seems a lot still needs to be done.

But maybe the real question is even more fundamental. Are we willing to consider young children capable of making sense of their lives, capable of a creative way of addressing life which would have nothing to do with a mere repetition of what we would have taught them? Can we believe children have something to offer us concerning our spirituality as the roots of our existence, significant enough to be questioning our ways of seeing life? Can we learn from children? Can we learn from children's spirituality?

Acknowledgment

My thanks go to Professor Jean-Marc Gauthier, from the Faculty of Theology, and Professor Margaret Kiely, from the Department of Psychology, at University of Montreal, my co-directors, for their trust, their support, and their passion for the question of spirituality.

Notes

1   See, for example, Chauvet 1993.
2   See, for example, Alexander 1980, Emblen 1992, or Jacques 1999.
3   *Le Dieu de la promesse qui tourne l'homme vers un avenir inédit* (Geffré 1983: 184). The translation is mine.

References

Alexander, J. 1980: What do recent writers mean by spirituality? *Spirituality Today* 32, 247–56.

Chauvet, L.-M. 1993: *Les Sacrements. Parole de Dieu au risque du corps*, Collection Recherches, Paris: Editions Ouvrières.

Crompton, M. 1998: *Children, Spirituality, Religion and Social Work*, Aldershot: Ashgate.

de Saint-Exupery, A. [1946] 1981: *Le Petit Prince*, Collection Folio Junior, Paris, Gallimard.

Emblen, J. 1992: Religion and spirituality defined according to current use in nursing literature, *Journal of Professional Nursing* 8(1), 41–7.

Geffré, C. 1983: *Le christianisme au risque de l'interprétation* Paris: Cerf.

Hay, D. with Nye, R. 1998: *The Spirit of the Child*, London: Harper Collins.

Jacques, R. 1999: Le spirituel et le religieux, *Théologiques* 7(1), 89–106.

Nouwen, H. J. M. 1974: *Reaching Out*, London: Doubleday.

Pihlainen, M. 1993: *Every Child is Potentially the Light of the World: Reflections on Spiritual Citizenship*, Unpublished paper, Plymouth, University of Plymouth Center for Research into Moral, Spiritual & Cultural Understanding and Education.

Schneiders, S. 1986: Theology and Spirituality: Strangers, Rivals or Partners? *Horizon* 13(2), 253–74.

—— 1998: The Study of Christian Spirituality: Contour and Dynamics of a Discipline, *Christian Spirituality Bulletin* 6(1), 1–12.

Simon, M. 1993: *Born Contemplative. Introducing Children to Christian Meditation*, London: Darton, Longman and Todd.

Chapter 7

Youth Spirituality as a Response to Cultural Crisis

DAVID TACEY

WHAT I have to say about youth spirituality is based on my experience as a teacher at La Trobe University in Melbourne, Australia, but I believe that my observations have more than local interest and can be applied to most modern secular societies. Over recent years, I have been teaching courses on the psychology of religion, spirituality, and rites of passage, and some of my research on young adult spirituality has already been published (Tacey 2000).

Youth spirituality is an interesting and important social phenomenon of our time, but much of it has been invisible to mainstream adult society, because our society has not known how to look for it, and therefore has not known how to respond to it. While mainstream Western society has increasingly identified itself as secular, enlightened, rational and progressive, a counter-cultural stream in youth culture has been in search of new enchantments, new beliefs, and new understandings of the world. Some of these so-called new enchantments are very old indeed, and many derive from pagan, Wicca, druidic, Celtic, Nordic, gothic or even Sanskrit sources, but they are "new" to modern society, and thus are so old they are new again. While it is true that a good deal of youth culture appears to adults to be discordant, nihilistic, depressive or even anarchic, many youth are striving to break the conventions and forms of social reality to allow a new spiritual awareness to enter and transform life (Tacey 2001).

How can breaking the past, especially if that past involves sacred and religious traditions, be associated with the idea of "spirituality"? We misread youth culture if we see it in purely destructive terms. In important ways, youth culture is not merely anarchic; it is concerned with the release and realization of spiritual forces from the encumbrances of (what youth perceive as) an old and decrepit cultural order. The spirit of life appears to them to have deserted the past and its hallowed traditions, and so youth often do not display respect or reverence for those traditions, and exhibit few sentimental attachments to them. This deeply disturbs the guardians of traditional religious culture, because they read this behaviour as deliberately mischievous and malign, but the youth who devalue or undermine the past do not see themselves as blaspheming or engaged in evil, since they do not feel the presence of the divine in what they are rejecting. On the contrary, possessed by the spirit of iconoclasm and a desire to break the forms of the past, they frequently see themselves as heroes of a new spiritual dispensation. They sometimes intimate to me that they are God's helpers, helping God to free him, or herself (the gender of God being problematic in our time), from the stifling structures of a deadening cultural order.

Youth seem to believe that the old cultural order is already dead, that it has collapsed. One of my students wrote the following in a class paper on spirituality:

> Like so many of my generation, I have had to walk among the ruins of what was once a stable, mighty spiritual empire; an empire that took millennia to build and only a few hundred years to collapse. It seems as if the collapse has been accelerating in recent times. I don't know anyone today who attends religious services, but only two generations ago people seemed to belong to this or that religious tradition, or so I am told. It is hard, actually, to imagine that our society was governed by religion so recently, because from today's perspective, we seem to be incredibly secular.

This student sees himself as walking among the ruins of Christendom, and later in the paper he expresses a difficult dilemma. He says he cannot embrace a tradition that is dying and collapsing, and yet he has spiritual urges and impulses that seek outward expression. If he turns to Christianity, he says he will be labelled a "Born Again Christian"; if he turns to Buddhism he will be labelled a "New Ager"; and if he turns to nature and the earth for spiritual solace he will be labelled a "Gaia Worshipper". No matter where he turns or what he does with his spiritual longing, mainstream society will have some hurtful tag or reductive label to attach to his activity. This is one of the ways, he says, that secular society expresses its revenge against the spiritual dimension of life, by representing it as aberrant, silly or escapist.

From my own experience, many youth appear to be turning to the East and especially to Indian religions, because there is a terrible, almost sickening feeling that the West is a spent force in religious and metaphysical matters. The East appears to glow with magical possibilities, while the West looks to them like a museum full of dead corpses or stuffed exhibits. But the West can also appear to them as a rubbish dump or junkyard, where absolutely everything is meaningless and

profoundly out of joint. They whistle and kick cans through this junkyard, often paying little regard to the things they see in it, including a
defunct religious system, a collapsed theology, and a church that barely
manages to keep the rumour of God alive.

Perhaps the various styles of "postmodernism" are their attempts to
enjoy or thrive in these appalling and devastating conditions. Contemporary youth are postmodern in the sense that they come after the
so-called modernist movements in art, literature, poetry, music and
philosophy. Each of these modernist traditions set about to destroy
and debunk the certainties of the past, and there has been so much
debunking and so much "exploding" of cultural myths, that youth
culture almost takes for granted the existential condition that we
associate with T. S. Eliot's *The Waste Land*. We are in a long, dark night
of desolation and disenchantment, and it is difficult to discern in this
long winter what the signs of hope or re-enchantment are. Some youth
ask the question: "What is there to celebrate in a collapsed world?" For
those who see no hope beyond the wasteland, there is simply the
expectation of "making do" with what they have been bequeathed by
previous generations of destructive and ruinous activity, a destruction
expressed theologically as the "death of God", culturally as the collapse
of high culture, morally and ethically as the collapse of certainty and
truth, and literally as war, violence and genocide.

In a collapsed or post-Holocaust culture, the major things that appear
to thrive are the weeds and hybrid growths, that is, virulent and uncontrollable forms of capitalism, materialism, consumerism, nihilism
and escapism. Many youth fail to see the signs of hope, or the signs that
God is still alive, and the "death of God" (or the absence of the Good) is
manifest for them in the culture of greed, in heartless economic
rationalism, in accelerated community breakdown, and in various kinds
of social evil, especially depression and despair. Many youth feel themselves to be nothing more than the rugged and street-wise survivors of
the modernist wasteland, and if they prefer grunge to high culture,
punk to high art, heavy metal and techno to the classics, and New Age
spiritual parodies to religious tradition, this is because, from where they
are sitting in the midst of all this chaos and despair, their discordant and
irregular youth culture speaks to them of the rubble and dissonance, the
horror and the terrible beauty, of what lies about them.

The Birth of The New, The Suspicions of The Old

But for many youth, new life stirs in our Western soul. Although some
of them appear fascinated by the continued processes of decadence,
decay and dissolution, there are increasing numbers of youth who speak

about spirituality and re-enchantment. Some leave the junkyard of the West, turning to the East for enchantment. This was especially true for my own generation, for youth culture in the '60s and early '70s, who found enchantment in foreign places and in exotic religions. But for an increasing number of youth, enchantment seems to be emerging from deep sources in the West itself, from beneath T. S. Eliot's "heap of broken images" (Eliot 1922: 63). It is as if that heap has turned into an organic pile of compost, giving off new life and new sacred forms, some of which, admittedly, are eccentric, strange and difficult to comprehend. Nature goes to work in the junkyard of modernity, destructuring, disassembling and dissolving the old, and manufacturing the new. "Nature abhors a vacuum", not only in natural space "out there", but in metaphysical space as well. But the important point is that God and the spirit cannot be stamped out forever. Our intellectual elites may have decided that God is dead and that the world is no longer enchanted, but the people, and especially young people, will nevertheless bear testimony to the rebirth of God in the soul.

As the old forms of God go into cultural decline, new sacred forms will arise, but these forms will not necessarily be noticed or respected by the old religious culture. Many adults within the churches who are aware of this tidal wave of interest in youth spirituality are, perhaps understandably, suspicious of it. I have been told by some priests, religious educators and religious broadcasters, that youth spirituality represents an underground conspiracy against the church, designed to undermine church tradition and attack its authority. The claim is frequently made that spirituality outside the church is part of the New Age movement, but I think the "New Age", as an identifiable subcultural entity, represents only a narrow portion of this unchurched spirituality, which is widespread and universal in youth culture. I don't think we can blame this spiritual revolution on the New Age industry, although the New Age does try to exploit the spiritual hunger of young people, if they can be lured into the expensive technologies and cults that are for sale in this consumerist movement. Here, as elsewhere, I differentiate between a "New Age" exploitative commercial industry, and a "Coming Age" which carries the genuine spirit of the new, of which the New Age is a kind of vulgar parody.

I have also heard some priests say that when youth claim they are interested in spirituality and on a "spiritual journey" that this is a form of code language for saying, "I take drugs and am getting high on drug abuse". This is a serious allegation, but as yet I have not seen much proof to support it. When I fed this view back to some of my students, most of them almost collapsed in fits of laughter. For them, this suspicious view indicates just how out of touch the churches are, since spirituality outside the familiar forms of religion is still not recognized, and is sometimes denied or berated; especially by conservative persons who are quick to dismiss unchurched spirituality as devil worship, ignorance, narcissism or drug culture. For religious conservatives, true spirituality can only exist within the church, and everything outside it is either mad, bad or morbid. But the churches have to face the fact that they no longer hold a monopoly on spirituality, and that this key term "spirituality" has taken on new meaning in the life of the broader community.

In his book *Reclaiming Spirituality*, Diarmuid Ó Murchú, an Irish Catholic priest, strives to identify and name the new spirituality we find in society today, and he points to the amazement and incomprehension that many in the churches feel towards it:

> For many people it is virtually incomprehensible that spiritual yearnings, feelings or values can arise apart from the context of formal belief; in other words, religion is perceived to be the only fountain from which spirituality can spring forth. Fortunately, human experience suggests otherwise and has done so over many millennia . . . It is not a realm of experience that has been researched or studied systematically as has happened in the case of formal religion. Consequently, we rely on anecdotal evidence, which is now becoming so widespread and compelling that we can't afford to ignore it any more. (Ó Murchú 1997: 2)

Like Diarmuid Ó Murchú, I feel convinced that this new spiritual movement is not a deliberate attempt to undermine the authority of the churches, but that it is a spontaneous movement of the spirit in desperate times. The movement could be described as anti-profane or anti-secular, but it is not primarily anti-religion nor targeted against the churches:

> This new spiritual resurgence is not something planned by a specific group of people or by some new organization that is seeking to undermine the significance of churches, religions or the culture of traditional faith and belief. This is a proactive rather than a reactive movement. Many of the people involved in this spiritual reawakening have little or no familiarity with formal religion. These people are not anti-religion and should not be confused with those who denounce religion because of some past hurtful or destructive experience. (Ó Murchú 1997: 12)

This new "outbreak" of spirituality is a desperate attempt by youth culture to counter the advances of the profane and secular society, with its appalling materialism, disillusionment and absence of hope. The widespread and almost incantatory use of the word "spirituality" could well be an urgent measure against the nihilism that has swept through the postmodern generations that have been brought up on television, junk food and Internet pornography. Even by uttering the word "spirituality", young people seem to aim for some magical effect, hoping that some metaphysical reality will protect them from the virus-like spread of consumerism and materialism. Whereas in the past, peasant-folk in Europe would hold up the sign of the Cross to ward off evil, today youth utter the word "spirituality" to similar effect, hoping that some Good will guide them and some hidden reality protect them from debasement, nihilism and despair. It is not up to adults to criticize this spirituality on theological grounds, but to realize its existential urgency and its psychological effectiveness.

Religious leaders and educators may dislike the current use or misuse of this term, but I see it as a return to the radical, original and primitive uses of the word "spirit" in the days of the early Christian church. For St Paul and the first Christians, spirit was at once a term of protest and affirmation. It was a protest against the Jewish religious establishment of the day, which was felt to be degenerate and empty, and it was a protest against the worldly authority of ancient Rome, which imposed upon other countries its own hegemonic and imperial rule. It was also an affirmation of a truth beyond corrupt religious and political institutions, a truth that belongs to a higher order of reality and to a future and greater manifestation of spirit that is always prophetic and teleological, pointing ahead to an as-yet unrealized Coming Age. We must not forget that primitive Christianity must have looked very much like a New Age cult to the Pharisees, scribes and religious authorities of the day, even though that "New Age" cult eventually gave rise to the Coming Ages of Byzantium and High Christendom.

Today's imperial authority is no longer that of the pagan Romans, but rather the political authority of the multinationals and the forces of international oppression that are euphemistically referred to as "globalization". Youth fear the force of globalization, noticing that it sweeps across regions and countries, converting all places into the same anonymous and empty no-place, where the pagan shrines are not those of the Roman gods, but of American fast-food chains and mobile telephone towers.

Can Religion Recognize the Freedom and Direction of The Spirit?

The vital question we have to ask today is this: can old religion learn to understand and respect the new spirituality? If religious tradition wants to play a leadership role and "lead out" the spirit that is already within the people, then it will have to learn to familiarize itself with this spirit. This may prove to be too difficult for religion, because it will have to sacrifice a great deal of its baggage in order to reach the living spirit that currently resides in the human heart and in the *zeitgeist* or spirit of the time. Today, what youth culture finds to be sacred, namely, nature, ecology, the body, sexuality, matter, experience, the inner or "true" self, and the quest for authenticity, will at first conflict with what formal Western religion has deemed to be sacred, namely, the gospels, the Word of God, the Person of Jesus, and the ideas of church tradition. Also, as discussed, the idea of a fixed, formal, revealed religious ideology will need to give way to a fluid, flexible, processual under-standing of faith and of the "stages of faith". The new spirituality today must involve risk, danger, journeying and questing; this appears to be of central importance to the spirit of the time. Again we have to ask ourselves: can religion recognize the freedom of the Holy Spirit, as that spirit is experienced in the human heart today?

The historian of religions, Mircea Eliade, is not especially sanguine about the capabilities of religion in this regard. Writing about the youth culture of the 1960s, Eliade announced that the religious impulse was making a new and genuine appearance in the cultural forms of the day, but that formal religious tradition seemed incapable of recognizing this new sacredness:

> In the most radically secularized societies and among the most icono-clastic contemporary youth movements (such as the hippy movement, for example), there are a number of apparently nonreligious phenomena in which one can decipher new and original recoveries of the sacred – although, admittedly, *they are not recognizable as such from a Judeo-Christian perspective*. (Eliade 1969: iii)

The fact that an old religious tradition fails to recognize another expression of the religious instinct is hardly a recent phenomenon. This occurred at the beginning of our common era, where the time-honoured Jewish tradition failed to respect the new revelation of Christianity, which it denounced as heretical, cultic, dangerous, feral and "New Age". The old religious form often hates and despises the new, not only because the new revelations challenge the authority of the old, but because the old religion thinks of itself as final, absolute and beyond challenge. The old tradition identifies itself so fully with the eternal realm that it thinks of *itself* as eternal, immutable, unchangeable. The old always suffers from a constitutional arrogance and pride, failing to realize that nothing that is human, cultural or historical can claim immutable status, but is always, and necessarily, subject to time and change. The old religion does not see its own arrogance; instead, it charges the new dispensation with arrogance: the arrogance or hubris of daring to claim sacred status for itself.

The old tradition in any cultural era does not fully grasp the fact that if God is alive and active in the world, then God will be creative within the world, beckoning us to new experiences and transformations. The old tradition may in some ways prefer God to be dead, because then the sacred body of God can be laid out, dissected by systematic theologians and pedants, and pinned down in precise and almost scientific ways. But if God is alive, then our experience of the sacred is messy, creative, imprecise, and always full of surprise and astonishment at the creativity of God. That is to say, if God is alive, God will always reveal itself as mysterious, unknowable, and beyond all our best efforts to contain and capture God.

The New–Old Creation Spirituality and Cosmic Sacrality

The post-Christianity of our youth culture seems in many ways to be pre-Christian, archaic and atavistic. It is "new" only in terms of the recent past, but when we look back into ancient history it seems incredibly old. The spirituality of youth culture, for instance, appears cosmic, primal and almost animistic. It is for good reason that youth today are so excited by the religions of Aboriginals, American Indians, Polynesians and Maoris, because their own experience of the spirit is similarly primordial and ancient. The new experience of spirituality is deeply embedded in the mysteries of nature and the wonders of the natural world, and it appears almost innocent of the dualistic vision that has held spirit and nature apart for many centuries. Youth culture today appears uninterested in a personal God, and instead it is more interested in the ancient force that through the green fuse drives the flower. It is unconcerned about a transcendent God in heaven, but instead discovers God on earth, in creation, and in everyday life.

This is an incredible shock to established religion, which sees such a move as regressive, pagan or pantheistic. It is always quick to judge this new religious feeling, and immediately attempts to assert its dominance over it. But Eliade makes it clear that the natural or cosmic religion that is unfolding in youth culture must not be seen as illegitimate and worthless. The most significant religious structure in youth culture, he writes, is:

> the recovery of the religious dimensions of an authentic and meaningful human existence in the Cosmos, including the rediscovery of Nature, the uninhibited sexual mores, the emphasis on "living in the present" and freedom from social "projects" and ambitions. (Eliade 1969: iv)

The values of youth culture, Eliade writes,

> point to a type of cosmic religion that disappeared after the triumph of Christianity, surviving only among the European peasants. Re-discovering the sacredness of Life and Nature does not necessarily

imply a return to "paganism" or "idolatry". Although in the eyes of a
Puritan the cosmic religion of the southeastern European peasants could
have been considered a form of paganism, it was still a "cosmic, Christian
liturgy". (Eliade 1969: iv)

The new religious expression arising in our time is a cosmic Christian
liturgy, which possibly accounts for the widespread popularity of the
Gospel of John, which emphasizes the cosmic rather than the historical
Christ. But in defence of this new–old spiritual vision, we might use the
word *panentheism*, rather than the scarier and more judgmental term of
"paganism". Whereas paganism refers to an experience in which God
is found everywhere, in all things, panentheism means that "every-
thing-is-in-God". This is an altogether more powerful and challenging
idea, removed from the cliché of pantheism, and worthy of considerable
theological study and exegesis. Panentheism is the awareness of the
incarnational presence of the divine in embodied reality. We have had
two thousand years of strong formal emphasis on the sinfulness of the
world and the fallen nature of creation, and now there is need for a
compensatory counter-movement, a movement towards creation spirituality, which has already been foreshadowed by contemporary
Catholic theologians such as Teilhard de Chardin, Thomas Berry and
Bede Griffiths. The awareness of sin and evil must not disappear, but
we have urgent need to resacralize and celebrate the physical world,
including the world of our own bodies and lives.

Historical Christianity has become too narrowly focused on the
human being and his or her personal redemption through prayer, faith
and good works. Along with this anthropocentric focus has gone a
disregard for the sanctity of nature and the sacredness of the ordinary.
Western religion has become too human, too dogmatic, too dualistic, too
transcendental, too institutional, and too known. It seems entirely fitting
that when the spirit goes out of the formal ecclesiastical structures it
reappears as a new dimension of the world. The old bottle marked
"religion" has been broken, and the spirit that was once apparently
inside the bottle now appears to us from all corners of the earth and from
all aspects of daily living. In having our religion broken, we achieve
the paradoxical result of an all-encompassing sacredness. In losing the
church, the world has become our new church.

Instead of the old mass, we have an even older earth-mass or a cosmic
canticle. The great problem with this new religious vision is that we do
not yet know how to cope with it, how to express it, or how to celebrate
it. Instead, we almost feel guilty about having it, especially when
religious conservatives insist that we are ruining our culture by
reverting to animism, paganism or pantheism. I think our major artists
have been working on this new religious vision for the last hundred

years or more, but it is only recently that our theologians have begun to integrate this challenge into the ongoing religious tradition. Until recently, the cosmic religion and the sacrality of the everyday was experienced as a devastating body-blow to the church; now it seems that this same vision can breath new life into the dying institutions, if they can recover from the shock of the new.

The New Mystical Emphasis on the God Within

Another feature of new spirituality, found especially in the young but by no means confined to them, is the experience of God in the indwelling soul, or within the true self. In falling out of its traditional religious containers, God seems to have fallen into the soul, which accounts for the enormous amount of energy invested in psychotherapy, counselling, introspection, reflection and self-exploration. Again, this new kind of cultural activity meets with enormous resistance and misunderstanding from religious conservatives, who cast negative judgement upon it. It is usually claimed that such inward activity is negative, wasteful, indulgent and mere navel-gazing. This would be so if the self were merely as the conservatives imagine it, namely, a den of sin, temptation and iniquity. But in terms of the new creation spirituality, which imagines the world to be graced by the presence of God, our most immediate and personal experience of God is within the depths of the self. Today, the young, and some of the old, are engaged in self-exploration, not just to indulge the personal but to move beyond the personal into the transpersonal, the archetypal, and the numinous. The self can be a legitimate doorway into the sacred, so long as the investigator moves deeply and far enough into the self so that he or she moves beyond it.

In traditional religious ideology, the self and creation are mainly characterized by sinfulness and evil, and so the exploration of self or interiority is not viewed with much enthusiasm. There is always the possibility of Grace, but in traditional religion Grace comes only through the agency of God, through the ritual activity of holy sacraments, and through the authority of the church and priest. The self, by contrast, is viewed as an endless maze of indulgence, as a pitfall for the unwary, and as narcissistic pond of illusion. There has never been any traditional emphasis on the self, since it is felt to lead the individual away from God rather than towards God. The faithful are advised to drop the self and follow the example of Christ, by good works, faith and social service. But today this language and belief system is entirely out of date. The repression or abnegation of self leads to neurosis and emptiness, rather than to spiritual illumination. In employing the old puritan ethic, people today become angry, shallow, anxious and resentful, rather than genuinely religious. The old talk about the wickedness or self-indulgence of the self has become untenable, and if Western religion wants to renew itself it would do well to help people embark on interiority and internal exploration, rather than to shun this activity as bad or wasteful.

The conservative religious position sees the turn to interiority as a turn to Gnosticism. However, the idea of the "God within" is Scriptural and Biblical, not (only) Gnostic. It is simply a repressed or forgotten dimension of the Western religious experience, and because the church has feared it or not supported it historically, it is not encouraged today either. And so we begin to discern a logic or pattern in the clash between old and new enchantments, in which the old enchantment seeks to overrule the new by discrediting it by the application of hurtful or dismissive tags. The term "Gnostic" is used to ward off the new interiority, in the same way that the terms "pagan" or "pantheistic" are used to undermine the new experience of the sacrality of the world. The old religious dispensation employs such terms as potent talismans, to ward off the "evil" spirit of the new, which is seen as evil because it disrupts the established pattern of the old. But again, since the old religious concepts have already been debunked by history and modernity, we cannot blame the postmodern tribes for being wilfully destructive or for turning the canon of the past into "a heap of broken images".

The old pattern of dropping the self and following Christ no longer appeals to modern taste. What does make its appeal today is the notion of dropping the ego and following the true Self, in which Christ or truth may reside. This may seem like a minor adjustment, but it actually makes a world of difference. The old pattern left the believer without many psychological resources; it also left him without the psyche or soul. If the self was to be transcended through religious devotion, then this involved a crucial "leap of faith" into the unknown. Such leaps of faith are no longer made today, because people want to see what they are doing, and fewer and fewer are able to rely on the spiritual authority of the church and its clergy. To drop the ego and explore or follow the Self is a spiritual discipline that actually comes much closer to Buddhism and Eastern religions, which appear to show much more psychological sophistication than our Western religions. But again, the flight to the East is not entirely necessary, in my view. We already have highly developed mystical traditions involving interiority and the exploration of the God within; we have only to draw these traditions from their historical obscurity and into the light of the present. It is only conventional Christianity based on devotional practice and the leap of faith that is coming to an end in our time, but a mystical Christianity based on interiority and the care of the soul is likely to flourish and develop well into the distant future.

References

Eliade, M. 1969: *The Quest: History and Meaning in Religion*, Chicago: The University of Chicago Press.

Eliot, T. S. 1978 [1922]: The Waste Land. In Eliot, T. S., *Collected Poems*, London: Faber.

Ó Murchú, D. 1997: *Reclaiming Spirituality*, Dublin: Gill and Macmillan.

Tacey, D. 2000: Youth Spirituality and Old Religion. In D. Tacey, *ReEnchantment: The New Australian Spirituality*, Sydney: HarperCollins.

—— 2001: *Jung and the New Age*, London and New York: Routledge.

Psychological and Anthropological Approaches

T HE chapters in Part II represent studies that have approached investigating children's and young people's spirituality, or the concept of spiritual education, by drawing on the methods of the social sciences and, in certain cases, also on philosophy. They also represent, in the interface between method and subject, the way in which the disciplines employed are drawn to a more humanistic approach which acknowledges subjectivity, the importance of narrative, and the values systems within which research and education are conducted, and within which notions of the spiritual become characterized and defined.

David Hay's contribution reflects on the concept of "relational consciousness" developed during his research with Rebecca Nye. Building on the work of Alister Hardy and his hypothesis that spirituality is a biologically rooted phenomenon, he speaks of a natural spiritual awareness in children and its relationship to intimacy. He argues that, contrary to his previous assumption that spirituality was solitary in nature, it is relational and underpins all ethics. Further he suggests that within modern societies there are two potentially major constraints on spirituality: literacy and individualism; the first because it lessens immediacy, the second because it damages the social fabric. This being the case spirituality and spiritual education are at once subversive and politically significant because they are counter cultural in their opposition to the dominant mores of the modern age.

Daniel Scott, writing from within a Canadian context, approaches spirituality through narrative and, in particular, the personal narratives of childhood. He rejects reductionist models of investigating spirituality, based on particular epistemologies, and argues that postmodernism may provide the possibility for "spirituality to be understood in more open and flexible ways". Affirming spirituality to extend across all cultures, he advocates the importance of listening as a means to eliciting spiritual narratives that individuals may be afraid to voice for fear of their strangeness. He also proposes that such stories may have multiple functions. In relation to research he suggests a shift is required in the researcher's approach that recognizes the need for "participatory consciousness", involving a suspension of subject-object dualism and of our desire for epistemological certainty.

Eleanor Nesbitt argues that religious experience and, in the case of one of her two individual studies in this chapter, the experience of *Bhakti*, is important in the studies she has researched as a member of the Warwick Religions and Education Research Unit. With reference to Mina, a young woman with a Gujarati Hindu background, and Alice, who has an English Quaker background, she advocates the importance of longitudinal study, rigorous reflexivity on the part of the researcher, and the notion of research interviews being "intersections of the interviewee's and interviewer's spiritual journeys". Additionally she explores the contexts in which spirituality emerges for individuals, in relation to faith community and tradition and "the dynamics of religious continuity and change". Finally, she advocates that ethnographic research, when reflecting on spirituality, must be grounded in an understanding of "faiths" that goes beyond a world religions paradigm, accepts diversity, and is unpejoratively inclusive.

Liam Gearon presents a spirituality of dissent from a postcolonial studies perspective. He argues that any reference to spiritual education must take account of the analyses of postcolonial writings such as those of Fanon and Said. Introducing the United Nations Proclamation on Human Rights as a seminal text he advances a critique of constructs of spiritual education which align themselves with the interests of First World countries and do not proceed from an examination of basic human needs. Gearon's spirituality of dissent is a polemic against modernist interests which covertly depoliticize the notion of spirituality in education for their own political purposes. His concern is that spiritual education undertaken within the context of First World values will effectively desensitize students' political awareness and thus adversely affect the development of a critical values education.

Sandra Bosacki presents a holistic perspective on the spiritual which, from a psychological perspective, concerns itself with the inner world of the child. She examines the lack of communication between developmental cognitive science and holistic education in order to enquire into how these two fields can better mutually learn how to promote children's well-being. Her proposal is that spirituality can provide an interconnection between "theory of mind" and "theory of soul", with the result that children's appetite for learning and life can be better nurtured. She equates spirituality with a sense of self and connectedness. Observing that within the Canadian educational system children, as they grow older, tend to hide or not be asked to express these qualities, despite their cognitive ability, she suggests that more research is required into children's understanding of a "spiritual self", investigating the links between cognitive and emotional development.

Wong Ping Ho pursues the idea that an increasing interest in the spiritual is a result not of increasing spiritual healthiness, but of increasing spiritual desperation. Relating memories of his own childhood experience to the reflections of Immanuel Kant he deduces that one of the prime characteristics of an increasingly technologized and globalized world is the disappearance of space and silence. In relation to the use of mobile phones he states: "With modern technology, there is no need for waiting, whereas it can conceivably be argued that the ability to be patient and wait is a spiritual virtue". Pursuing further ways in which the modern world affects our consciousness he asks what effect this is having on children. In particular he warns against "the reduction of human communication to abstract exchange of disembodied signals and images" by which people's spirituality and humanity will become stunted.

Jack Priestley's contribution argues for a revaluation of the contemporary significance of the psychologist and philosopher William James. At the beginning of the twentieth century James delivered his influential Gifford Lectures, *The Varieties of Religious Experience*. From this point, Priestley marks out James as a prophet for our times. His approach went against mainstream thinking, moving inexorably towards secularism, and he put no store in the religious defences of dogmatic theology. Defending experience against philosophy and the importance of religious propensities for other than rational reasons he used the phrase "spiritual judgement" as a means of recognizing and valuing the subjective experiences of individuals. This, Priestley suggests, is the basis on which we can both value children's experiences as spiritual and, swimming against the modernist tide, utilize James's approach to knowledge. James's approach, he concludes, with its emphasis on narrative, is "very much the idiom of a postmodern age".

Chapter 8

Spirituality versus Individualism: The Challenge of Relational Consciousness

DAVID HAY

───────

We have to fight uphill to rediscover the obvious, to counteract the layers of suppression of the modern moral consciousness. It's a difficult thing to do.

Taylor, *Sources of the Self: the Making of the Modern Identity* 1992

The Primacy of Immediate Experience

Two people are lying sunning themselves in the middle of a field on a hot summer afternoon. One of them says reflectively, "Isn't life strange." The other asks, "Compared with what?"[1]

I think the strangeness is that we emerge from nothingness to find ourselves in the midst of relationship. From the very start we are growing for approximately three-quarters of a year, deep inside the body of another person. For our mother it is a very physical experience, changing her body chemistry and shape as we grow inside her uterus. At a certain stage we make our presence felt by kicks against the walls of her abdomen that are perceptible to an outsider. After about nine months she and we have the experience of our body moving from inside her body cavity and out into the rest of the world.

When we emerged from our mother's body it is highly probable that we were cradled, embraced, stroked, gazed at, washed and fed. This relationship with the newborn infant is not one way, as has been beautifully shown during the last decade by the Hungarian medical scientists Nagy and Molnar (1994) in studies of large numbers of infants ranging from three and a half to forty hours in age. Not only did the infants demonstrate the ability to imitate the gestures of an adult, many of them also initiated gestures that waited for a response. In summary the physical intimacy of relationship both inside and outside the womb is intense and it is immediate. More recent work by Murray and Andrews (Murray 2000) shows that infant communication begins within minutes of birth. It is very obvious that the business of becoming a human being is the extreme antithesis of an isolated, abstract affair.

The psychologist Margaret Donaldson (1992) tells us that this intimate focusing on the "here and now" or as she calls it "the point mode" dominates the awareness of young children until about the age of eighteen months. And of course focusing on what is immediate is also to concentrate directly on the immediacy of relationship, both with the mother and other carers, and also with the physical surroundings that, as we know with infants, are constantly being touched, smelled, tasted, seen or heard.

What I have been saying is well known to all of us. Its significance is that concentration on immediacy is also characteristic of the acts that lie at the core of practical religion. When I pray – genuinely pray that is, not merely mouthing religious platitudes – I place myself, here-and-now, in the presence of God. When undertaking Buddhist *vipassana* meditation, there is a staying aware of the in-breath and the out-breath here-and-now, or of the movements of the feet during walking. Even in the Jesuit Spiritual Exercises, where I allow my imagination the freedom to recreate the Gospel scene, I say with Ignatius to the God who is here-and-now, "place me with your Son". Incidentally, I notice that simply writing about the immediacy of these religious practices in itself shifts my awareness so that I am more physically aware of the experience of being in my study.

Nevertheless, immediacy has to be worked at if it is to be sustained, as everyone knows who has tried to meditate. This is partly because after about the age of a year and a half the dominance of the point mode begins to be replaced more and more by what Donaldson calls the "line mode". Memories of the past and anticipations of the future take up an increasing proportion of consciousness as our life-narrative begins to be constructed from the raw materials provided by the sequence of physical events that happen to us, and the cultural interpretations of the community to which we belong. The immediacy that is the heartland of the religious exercises I mentioned may well become fairly minimal so that it rarely features in our everyday consciousness, except perhaps on those occasions where we formally choose to "de-automatize" (Deikman 1971) our perception. This could be when we enter a state of prayer or meditation, but it could also occur at times of heightened awareness such as happen in appreciating works of art, or during intense concentration in a sporting activity (cf. Csikszentmihalyi 1975).

Or it can happen involuntarily when we are momentarily shocked or intensely moved by a situation.

The Empirical Investigation of Spirituality

I now want to link what I have been saying to the empirical investigations that my colleagues and I have been making over the past twenty-five years into the nature of contemporary religious or spiritual experience. The start point for this work was the conjecture of the Oxford zoologist Alister Hardy (1966) that what he called "religious experience" is biologically natural to us and has evolved through the process of natural selection because it has survival value.

To those of us who have religious belief, and I count myself in that group, I need to make a comment here about perspective. I am talking about a naturalistic basis for spirituality and you may feel that I am taking up a rather familiar reductionist sociobiological stance. In his book *Theology and Social Theory*, John Milbank (1993) mounts a strong attack on the submissiveness of theologians to what he calls "secular reason" in the study of religion. "The pathos of modern theology", says Milbank,

> is its false humility. For theology this must be a fatal disease, because once theology surrenders its claim to be a metadiscourse, it cannot any longer articulate the word of the creator God, but is bound to turn into the oracular voice of some finite idol, such as historical scholarship, humanist psychology, or transcendental philosophy [or he might have added, "evolutionary biology"]. (1993: 1)

I think Milbank is right in so far as scholarship is used in an arrogant way to dismiss religion. But Hardy was not a dismissive critic of religion. He was, if you like, inside the camp, concerned with what it is about our human nature that enables us to be religious or spiritual in the first place. In fact the perspective he adopted can be seen as protecting religion since if he is right it is not possible to dismiss spirituality as "nothing but" cultural construction. If Hardy is right, spirituality has its roots in what we are as biological organisms.

Research so far shows that Hardy's hypothesis is highly resilient when tested against other reductionist naturalistic accounts (Hay 1994). The hypothesis amounts to a claim that religious awareness is "hard-wired" into the human organism. Hence, it cannot be limited to members of any particular religion or indeed religious people in general. Everybody, including people who hold no religious beliefs whatsoever, must be at least potentially in possession of such awareness. There is such a thing as secular spirituality. I therefore propose to replace Hardy's term with "spiritual awareness" to cover all these cases, whilst recognizing that from a religious perspective it is this natural awareness that makes religious experience possible in the first place.

But what is this natural spiritual awareness? To take this a little further I need to remind you of the important work that Rebecca Nye did when she and I were colleagues in Nottingham University (Hay with Nye 1998). The problem that faced us was this. Traditionally in European culture, spirituality has almost always had a strong association with Christianity. Indeed for much of Western history most people have seen the two as synonymous. But the religious history of Britain since at least the eighteenth century has broadly speaking been one of institutional decline, to the point that in this country only a small and dwindling number of people have any kind of formal Christian commitment. The cognitive majority, who have assimilated the secular mores of adult life, are likely to be suspicious of or sceptical about at least the institutional forms of religious belief, and hence of what they understand by the term "spirituality". We know from our research that this means they keep quiet about or perhaps even repress their spiritual awareness. In such circumstances a good place to find it ought to be amongst young children, before they have learned of the critique of religious belief and hence, by association, of spirituality.

Rebecca's work with six-year-old and ten-year-old children in schools in Nottingham and Birmingham involved getting them to talk about spirituality without introducing religious language, unless they themselves chose to introduce it. We worked out a way of doing this by identifying certain categories of ordinary human experience that we believed to be particularly likely to arouse spiritual awareness (Nye and Hay 1996). These were "awareness of the here-and-now", "awareness of mystery" and "awareness of value".

Among the ways that we encouraged the children to talk about these areas of experience, was to show them a set of photographs of children in circumstances where these categories of experience were likely to be in evidence. What I notice in retrospect is that they all show children in isolation (for example, a little girl gazing into the fire in the evening, a boy in his bedroom looking out at the stars, a girl crying because her pet gerbil has died). It fits with a prejudice I had that spirituality is a thoroughly private thing, isolated from social life. I felt I was supported in this view by well-known religious texts, for example Jesus' advice that when we pray we should go to our private room and close the door, or the advice to the yogi in the *Bhagavadgita* to find a lonely place in the forest and meditate there.

It is therefore striking that at the end of an extremely thorough and repeated line by line analysis of hundreds of pages of transcribed conversations with the children, the term that Rebecca came up with, linking all the passages of spiritual talk, was "relational consciousness". In our book, *The Spirit of the Child*, she describes this as having two aspects:

(a)   An unusual level of consciousness or perceptiveness, relative to other passages of conversation spoken by that child;

(b)   Conversation expressed in a context of how the child related to things, other people, him/herself and God.

This was so contrary to my presuppositions about the solitary nature of spirituality that for a time I was rather disorientated, which I suppose is one of the salutary results of empirical research. But of course once I thought about it, it made eminent sense and I began to make the kind of connections I referred to at the beginning of my talk. Relational consciousness is a pretty good name for the natural awareness that Alister Hardy had in mind. It is because we have such awareness that we can be religious in the first place. It allows the possibility of relationship to God, or, if we are non-theists, the possibility of a holistic relation to the Other, however we conceive of it.

I now see the solitude that is so characteristic of much (but not by any means all) prayer and meditation as merely a setting that is particularly conducive to maintaining the here-and-now immediacy that constitutes spiritual awareness. Thus, Jesus makes it quite explicit that the reason one should retire to one's private room for prayer is to get away from the kind of temptations to hypocrisy that happen when we set ourselves up to pray in public, or give to charity with a trumpet blast, and all the other accoutrements of ego-tripping that are mentioned in the Gospel. Privacy here helps us to remain honestly in the immediacy of the prayer relationship.

Once one accepts that relational consciousness is the precursor of spirituality, it also becomes clear that it must be the underpinning of ethics. I know from literally hundreds of conversations with adults about their spirituality, that the typical result of being directly aware of one's immersion in the physical and social matrix is the experience of a shortening of the psychological distance between oneself and one's surroundings. When a person realizes this, it matters much more to them when some aspect of reality is damaged, whether it is another person or a part of the environment, for they are much more likely to experience it as a shared damage; the feeling is "I too am damaged by what has happened to the other". Hence relational consciousness can be seen as the natural source of ethics.

Since making this particular empirical finding I have become interested in the work of the philosopher Emmanuel Levinas, who writes of ethics as "first philosophy" (Levinas 1989). He lays great emphasis on what happens when I gaze on the face of another undefended human being, and how in that gaze I find my sense of responsibility for the other. For him the ethical impulse precedes all social construction, all discursive philosophising, and all law making. In his fine book *Postmodern Ethics*, Zygmunt Bauman (1993) quotes a Talmudic story to illustrate this:

> Ulla bar Koshev was wanted by the government. He fled for asylum to Rabbi Joshua ben Levi at Lod. The government forces came and surrounded the town. They said, "if you do not surrender him to us, we will destroy the town". Rabbi Joshua went up to Ulla bar Koshev and persuaded him to give himself up. Elijah used to appear to Rabbi Joshua, but from that moment on he ceased to do so. Rabbi Joshua fasted many days, and finally Elijah revealed himself to him. "Am I supposed to appear to informers?" he asked. Rabbi Joshua said, "I followed the law". Elijah retorted, "but is the law for saints?" (Bauman 1993: 81)

If the natural antecedent of both religion and morality is relational consciousness, this may help to make sense of the traditional intuition that there is a close link between morals and religion, without insulting the morality of those who happen not to hold conventional theistic belief. From the perspective I have been describing, the opposite of spirituality is not secularity, it is alienation from the immediacy of relational consciousness.

How has the Alienation from Spiritual Awareness Taken Place?

As we have seen, reductionist critics of spiritual or religious awareness wish to assert that it is a socially constructed false consciousness. My assertion is the reverse of this. I say that it is alienation from relational consciousness that is socially constructed, creating a forgetfulness or discarding of spiritual awareness. That is why spiritual education always has an aspect that is counter cultural. This is as much true of the past as today. The outrage of the Old Testament prophet Amos against the unjust practices of his time indicates as much. The political leaders of the nation wanted to get rid of him. They said,

> Go away, seer; get back to the land of Judah; earn your bread there, do your prophesying there. We want no more prophesying in Bethel; this is the royal sanctuary, the national temple. (Amos 7: 12–13)

What angered them was Amos's insistence that spirituality was inseparable from justice:

> listen to this, you who trample on the needy and try to suppress the poor people of the country, you who say, "when will New Moon be over so that

we can sell our corn, and Sabbath, so that we can market our wheat?" Then by lowering the bushel, raising the shekel, by swindling and tampering with the scales, we can buy up the poor for money and the needy for a pair of sandals, and get a price even for the sweepings of the wheat. (Amos 8: 4–6)

Amos adds that the distancing from justice brings with it an estrangement from spiritual awareness:

See what days are coming – it is the Lord who speaks – days when I will bring famine on the country, a famine not of bread, a drought not of water, but of hearing the word of the Lord. They will stagger from sea to sea, wander from north to east, seeking the word of the Lord and failing to find it. (Amos 8: 11–12)

But what are the cultural processes through which this alienation from immediacy comes about? Can we deconstruct them? Here I am forced to be speculative, and in the space available to me I am only able to comment on some issues that seem to be particularly relevant.

Literacy. There is evidence that the acquiring of language in itself has the effect of setting the consciousness apart from immediate awareness (see Jerome Berryman's contribution, chapter 1). An equally important factor in altering the structure of human consciousness is the appearance of literacy. This was particularly vividly demonstrated nearly seventy years ago in the work of the Soviet psychologist Alexander Luria, not published until the decade of the 1970s (Luria 1976). The 1930s were a time of radical social restructuring throughout the Soviet Union. Stalin had begun to introduce the collectivization of agriculture and alongside this there was a national campaign to eliminate illiteracy. Luria set out from the Institute of Psychology at Moscow University to begin a two-year study of illiterate Muslim peasants living in the remote villages and mountain pasturelands of Uzbekistan and Kyrgyzstan. He wanted to use this unique piece of social engineering as a large-scale natural experiment to observe how the arrival of literacy affected the cognitive processes of people who were hitherto illiterate.

The people Luria was investigating were members of a primary oral culture, that is, a culture untouched by literacy. In case you think of this as unusual, let me remark that primary orality is the default position for the human species. The great majority of human beings for most of history have been illiterate. The American literary scholar Walter Ong (1982) tells us that of the tens of thousands of languages that have been spoken by human beings, only 106 have been committed to writing to the degree that they can be said to have a literature. Of the three thousand or so languages spoken today, only seventy-eight have a literature.

Luria discovered that there were indeed radical differences between people belonging to the primary oral culture and those who had begun to be literate. In summary, the thinking of oral people tends to be "situational" rather than abstract. For example, one of the studies Luria made was of colour perception, inviting people to name the colours of a variety of skeins of dyed wool. He found that semi-educated collective farm activists named colours in much the same way as Moscow people would, in terms of category, shades of blue, red, yellow and so on. On the other hand, illiterate peasant women who were expert embroiderers, and therefore perfectly aware of subtle variations of colour, usually named the skeins concretely, with terms like "pig's dung", "a lot of water", "cotton in bloom", "rotten teeth". When asked to classify the colours into groups, the women would say things like "it can't be done, they're not at all alike; this is like calf's dung, this is like a peach". Similarly, when asked to complete syllogisms, illiterate men were unable to break away from practicality. One man being told, "in the north, all bears are white. Novaya Zemblya is in the North", then asked what colour the bears are in Novaya Zemblya, answered, "I don't know. I've seen a black bear. I've never seen any others". People also seemed not to have much conception of themselves as individuals. For example when asked questions such as, "What sort of person would you say you were?" illiterates appeared to be unable to describe themselves and would refer Luria to other people in the village.

Luria realized that such responses were not due to lack of intelligence, but to the structure imposed on thought by illiteracy. Literacy extends memory. It permits us to classify and to generalize; it gives us the ability to move in thought out of the concrete here-and-now and into lengthy abstraction. It permits the possibility of the subtle and cumulatively developing thought that is necessary for scientific and political progress. Most crucially of all literacy also introduces the possibility of a private world, where we can realize ourselves to be individuals rather than simply part of a collective. It permits the development of individuality, the ability to have a personal point of view; in a sense to feel free. No doubt we see this in almost entirely positive terms, especially as we ourselves are part of that literate world. But it has its drawbacks.

The down side of literacy is that it constructs a private world which creates an extreme attenuation of our awareness of our relationship to the here-and-now. Walter Ong offers a simple illustration of the effect of literacy on the sense of relationship. Suppose I am working on some problem with a class of students. We get on well together and there is a sense of communal achievement about our work. Then I ask the class to turn to a page in a textbook. Immediately what was a community a moment before, becomes a set of isolates, separately absorbed in the text they are reading. Think how much reading and writing dominate our lives as literate adults in a technological culture. Add to that the revolution in electronic communication that is happening around us at the moment, documented by John L. Locke recently in his book *The Devoicing of Society* (1998) where he claims that we are becoming a society of strangers. It is not hard to imagine that in adult life the mode of action of our consciousness is very different from that of our non-literate forebears. It is more difficult, less natural, for literate people to enter the immediacy of awareness that is commonplace amongst primary oral peoples. Let me emphasize though, that within literate communities young children, before they have become fully literate, are much more likely to have a consciousness that is like their peers in primary oral cultures.

Individualism. My second point is to do with the rise of European individualism. I have just noted that a potential major constraint upon spiritual awareness is literacy. Nevertheless all large-scale religious cultures have been spread and become sophisticated through reading and writing. We speak of the three great Western monotheisms as religions of the Book. What we also find in all these religions is a vast and extremely sophisticated literature, the literature of meditation, contemplation, prayer and devotion, which is specifically designed to protect that area of human consciousness I have been discussing. It is when that literature becomes discarded or forgotten, that the attenuation of immediacy must be increased.

But European culture has created an ideology that is much more directly contradictory to our spiritual and ethical awareness, and that is Individualism. Even a cursory glance at an introductory text such as Steven Lukes (1973) on *Individualism* shows the complexity of this issue. Once you reach Louis Dumont's *Essays on Individualism* (1986) it becomes clear that we are dealing with a central characteristic of European modernity. This is so important that, in spite of my lack of expertise in the field, I would like to give a couple of illustrations of the ways in which I believe individualism has an impact on relational consciousness, hence on the extreme constriction of spirituality in our Western culture.

Most commentators identify Thomas Hobbes as one of the central figures in the creation of modern individualism. We all know of him because of his masterwork *Leviathan* (1651) where he comes to the conclusion that human life in the state of nature is "nasty, brutish and short". Hobbes was born in 1588 and lived through what historians see as one of the most violent periods of turmoil in European history. In particular the Thirty Years' War ravaged the continent throughout his early adult life. It is perhaps no surprise that he had a sceptical attitude towards the possibility of human benevolence. His materialist interpretation of human nature led him to the view that in the state of nature life is a warfare of all against all. If we cooperate with other people it is only because we see these interactions as in our interest (in this sense he was a precursor of modern biological theorists of reciprocal altruism). His assumption that each of us is in a struggle for power against everyone else is based on a materialist metaphysics that states that "minds never meet, that ideas are never really shared and that each of us is always and finally isolated from every other individual" (Hampton 1988).

This extreme individualism (or political atomism) was attacked in Hobbes's own day. It is perhaps apposite after my opening reference to the intense relationship between mother and child at birth to note that one critical contemporary of Hobbes said that he,

> might as well tell us in plain termes, all the obligation which a child hath to parent, is because he did not take him by the heels and knock out his braines against the walls, so soon as he was born. (Quoted in Hampton 1988: 10)

Though he was writing in the seventeenth century, Hobbes is anything but out-of-date. C. B. MacPherson (1962), one of the most influential modern interpreters of the seventeenth-century English Revolution, charges Hobbes with creating the doctrine on which bourgeois liberal society still operates, or as he calls it "the theory of possessive individualism". Marx identified this individualism in full flood in the masters of nineteenth-century Europe, when he depicted the typical capitalist entrepreneur as unencumbered by any social ties,

> that is, an individual separated from the community, withdrawn into himself, wholly preoccupied with his private interest and acting in accordance with his private caprice ... [for him] the only bond between men is natural necessity, need, and private interest. (quoted by Michael Walzer 1990)

Such people are by no means a dying breed, and the ideal of the unencumbered self is very much alive. I would suggest that the best way to maintain such a lifestyle is by dismissing any intimations of relational consciousness as unrealistic sentimentality.

Let me briefly add that although the materialist Hobbes's contemporary, René Descartes, lies at the other end of the philosophical spectrum, the continuing influence of his philosophy on the construction of our everyday common sense has had the same isolating effect. If I take the view that my most certain knowledge is of myself as thinker (qua Descartes), then other kinds of knowing are secondary. I have, so to speak, to argue to the existence of the outside world. The Scottish philosopher John Macmurray (1995) concludes that the logical endpoint of this Cartesian isolation is atheism:

the adoption of the "I think" as the centre of reference and starting-point of [. . .] philosophy makes it formally impossible to do justice to religious experience. For thought is inherently private; and any philosophy which takes its stand on the primacy of thought, which defines the Self as the Thinker, is committed formally to an extreme logical individualism. It is necessarily egocentric. (1995: 71)

Thus, two of the most powerful intellectual currents in the history of the European Enlightenment have had a hand in obscuring the relational consciousness that underlies spirituality.

The Ethical and Political Importance of Spiritual Education

We have recently seen the end of another century, even more violent than the one that Hobbes knew and felt terrified by. Underneath the economic rivalry, the tribalisms, the religious hostilities and the racial hatreds that have fuelled these conflicts lies the same kind of fear of the Other that motivated Hobbes's reflections. To take only the most recent outrages, I am sure that in the ruins of Rwanda, or Bosnia, or Chechnya or Sierra Leone, there are already young Hobbeses drawing the appropriate conclusion about human nature from the desolation they see around them.

In the relative calm of our Western world, where most of the violence we do is out of sight or safely abroad, the politics of Hobbes may seem somewhat further away. Yet they are symbolized on every street corner of the modern city. Hobbes's giving over of absolute power to the Sovereign has been replaced by the vigilance of the surveillance camera. If our relational consciousness has been sufficiently suppressed so that we truly believe that the nature of human relationship is a thinly disguised warfare of all against all, the ethical fabric that is woven from our relational consciousness becomes very threadbare. In such a situation the only criterion that prevents us from further attacking that fabric if it suits our purposes is the fear of being caught.

The insights that come from relational consciousness are directly opposed to such an understanding of how human beings relate to one another. The error I made in thinking of spirituality as a private matter, cut off from the realities of the political and social world, is a socially constructed error that needs to be deconstructed. It is one that has done and is doing great damage to the social fabric. That is why spiritual education is a profoundly political matter. It is of crucial social importance and not to be hidden away as a sub-section in a Religious Education syllabus. It belongs to every dimension of the school curriculum. The reason there is a temptation to hide it away is because it is implicitly subversive of the individualist assumptions I have been describing. It has a difficult time being taken seriously by those who manage our economy and have to any degree assimilated Adam Smith's view that the first principle of trade is self-interest.

The good news is that whilst the social processes I have been discussing may have obscured it, relational consciousness seems to be indestructible. Formal religion is declining at a great rate in Britain at the moment. Currently about 7 per cent of the population are in church on a Sunday and the majority of those are elderly. According to the *Report on Religious Trends* compiled by Peter Brierley for 1998/99, regular church attendance fell from 4.74 million in 1989 to 3.71 million in 1998, a drop of 20 per cent in less than a decade. On the other hand, in the Centre for the Study of Human Relations at the University of Nottingham we have been monitoring the spiritual experience of the British since 1976. At the time of writing, our most recent national survey (Hay and Hunt, 2000) shows that since 1976 there has been an increase of more than a 110 per cent in the proportion of the general population that feels they have a spiritual or religious dimension to their experience. Over the last decade the proportion of people who are prepared to break the taboo on admitting to such experience has increased by nearly 60 per cent. Currently more than three-quarters of all adults feel able to say they are aware of their spiritual experience.

In my view there has been no sudden increase in spiritual awareness in the population. What does seem to be happening, in tandem with the decline of the religious institution, is the paradoxical breaking of a taboo against admitting to spiritual experience. The emergence of a recognition of the reality of relational consciousness should give us confidence that the task of the teacher in nurturing spirituality is not a hopeless one.

As we have seen, the insights of spirituality are always likely to be counter cultural, so spiritual educators need to have courage, but if I am right, they have the biological nature of the human species on their side. Their task is not to teach children how to be spiritual, still less to indoctrinate. Spirituality in the form of relational consciousness is already there in all children, as Alister Hardy predicted, and as our work in the University of Nottingham has shown. The teacher's task is much more that of nurturing and protecting the natural inheritance of children and enabling them to reflect upon the implications of the spirituality that is within them.

Above all the privatization of relational consciousness needs to be counteracted. Its disappearance into the privacy of the individual psyche means it has the greatest difficulty in being given public articulation. Hence relational consciousness has even more difficulty in

entering into the political and social legislation that is necessary if it is
to be active in promoting genuine human community or what Philip
Selznick (1992) calls the "moral commonwealth". That is why spirituality needs the context of a culture that recognizes its importance and
allows it to "come out". Our task as educators is to reconstruct that
culture.

Note

1   I saw this interchange in a TV comedy sketch some years ago but can't
track down the author.

References

Bauman, Z. 1993: *Postmodern Ethics*, Oxford: Blackwell.
Csikszentmihalyi, M. 1975: *Beyond Boredom and Anxiety*. San Francisco: Jossey-
Bass.
Deikman, A. 1971: Bimodal Consciousness, *Archives of General Psychiatry* 25,
481–9.
Donaldson, M. 1992: *Human Minds*, London: Allen Lane/Penguin Press.
Dumont, L. 1986: *Essays on Individualism*, Chicago: University of Chicago Press.
Hampton, J. 1988: *Hobbes and the Social Contract Tradition*, Cambridge:
Cambridge University Press.
Hardy, A. 1966: *The Divine Flame*, London: Collins.
Hay, D. 1994: "The Biology of God": What is the Current Status of Hardy's
Hypothesis? *International Journal for the Psychology of Religion* 4(1), 1–23.
Hay, D. and Hunt, K. 2000: Is Britain's Soul Waking Up? *The Tablet*, 24 June, 846.
Hay, D. with Nye, R. 1998: *The Spirit of the Child*, London: HarperCollins.
Hobbes, T. 1985 [1651]: *Leviathan* (edited with an introduction by C. B.
MacPherson), London: Penguin Classics.
Levinas, E. 1989: Ethics As First Philosophy. In Seán Hand (ed.), *The Levinas
Reader*, Oxford: Blackwell.
Locke, J. L. 1998: *Why We Don't Talk to Each Other Any More: the Devoicing of
Society*, New York: Simon and Schuster.
Lukes, S. 1973: *Individualism*, Oxford: Basil Blackwell.
Luria, A. 1976: *Cognitive Development: Its Cultural and Social Foundations* (trans.
by Martin Lopez-Morillas and Lynn Solotaroff; edited by Michael Cole),
Cambridge, MA: Harvard University Press.
Macmurray, J. 1995 [1957]: *The Self as Agent* (with an introduction by Stanley M.
Harrison), London: Faber & Faber.
MacPherson, C. B. 1962: *The Political Theory of Possessive Individualism: From
Hobbes to Locke*, Clarendon Press: Oxford.
Milbank, J. 1993: *Theology and Social Theory: Beyond Secular Reason,*. Oxford:
Blackwell.
Murray, L. 2000: *The Social Baby*, The Children's Project Ltd.
Nagy, E. and Molnar, P. 1994: Homo Imitans or Homo Provocans? In Search of
the Mechanism of Inborn Social Competence, *International Journal of
Psychophysiology* 18, 128.

Nye, R. and Hay, D. 1996: Identifying children's spirituality: How do you start without a starting point? *British Journal of Religious Education* 18(3), 144–54.

Ong, W. 1982: *Orality and Literacy: The Technologising of the Word*, London: Routledge.

Selznick, P. 1992: *The Moral Commonwealth: Social Theory and the Promise of Community*, Berkeley, CA: University of California Press.

Taylor, C. 1992: *Sources of the Self: The Making of the Modern Identity*, Cambridge: Cambridge University Press.

Walzer, M. 1990: The Communitarian Critique of Liberalism, *Political Theory* 18(1), 6–23.

Chapter 9

Storytelling, Voice and Qualitative Research: Spirituality as a Site of Ambiguity and Difficulty

DANIEL SCOTT

SPIRITUALITY as a topic for research presents particular difficulties. In the postmodern context, where the transcendent has been bracketed, where the subject has been called into question, and where there is a degree of suspicion about almost everything – except perhaps suspicion itself – the spiritual remains slippery and elusive. It is awkward to define, being altered by context, tradition and culture. I write in the Canadian context, in the shadow of a dominant American culture with its anxiety about all things spiritual being somehow all things religious and therefore needing to be contained and minimized to protect the public forum from its intrusive ideas and potentially dangerous impact on public space. Yet even in North America spirituality persists, arising in unexpected places: from business to philosophy, from education to religion. There is a strange attractor quality to this topic at this time and I have been attracted, drawn into its influence.

My approach to the study of spirituality is through narrative. My attention has moved between the traditional narratives – stories, legends, tales, parables, sagas, epics and so on – used by spiritual traditions to carry their ideas, beliefs and interpretative structures and the personal narratives that adults, adolescents and children tell of their spiritual lived experiences. In this chapter I focus on personal narratives of childhood spiritual experiences, which may or may not be told during childhood.

Working Assumptions

I begin by outlining my working assumptions about spirituality. First, I deliberately tease apart spirituality and religion, assuming that all humans are spiritual and have spiritual experiences marked by a range of characteristics that may or may not be mediated by religious doctrines or institutional frames (Scott 1998; 1998a). These include direct experiences of mystery and wonder (Otto 1936; Caputo 1987); experiences marked by a sense of connectedness or relatedness beyond the self which may include relations with nature, with other creatures, with the Divine and with other humans (called relational consciousness by Hay and Nye 1998); experiences of struggle or crisis in which energy or force, expressed either as resistance or support, seems to arise beyond the self; and experiences of spirits or unfamiliar forces experienced as personalities (Evans 1993; Torrance 1994). These experiences may induce a range of emotions including fear, awe, wonder, disbelief, astonishment, and are sometimes accompanied by a dual sense of uniqueness and significance (through becoming connected), and smallness and insignificance (through becoming differentiated). At stake in many of these experiences are issues of transcendence, identity, authority and control.

Secondly, human spiritual experiences are common across cultures (Evans 1993; Kovel 1991; Ó Murchú 1998; Torrance 1994), and are expressed in a wide range of styles and structures. Torrance sees humans as *"animal quaerens"* – questing animals whose spiritual questing arises from and is reflected in biology, language, psychology and cultural formations. Spiritual experiences range in intensity and impact. For some, they are life shaping (Robinson 1983) while for others they may be slight and go unnoticed (Scott 1998). These experiences arise in the midst of life, that is, they are immanent. They do not depend on prior knowledge, religious content or existing interpretative frameworks to occur, but they will be shaped, interpreted, and understood through the filters of culture (Ermine 1995; Torrance 1994). They can be powerful, sensate, somatic experiences or vague, intuitive inklings. They can involve physically felt sounds, sights, voices and touch or be fleeting, insubstantial yet still powerful insights, intuitions, or understanding.

Thirdly, spiritual experiences need to be understood on their own terms. They are not completely understandable in psychological or emotional terms (Hillman 1996; May 1982). There is need therefore, to develop epistemologies that accept ways of knowing that acknowledge the unencompassable (Caputo 1987) as part of human experience and understand human relations as including connections to o(O)ther in an engaged, interactive, influential way. We need to acknowledge that the spiritual may not be understandable or necessarily traceable in reductionist models of thinking. It may be more appropriately expressed through ambiguity, multiplicity and complexity. Singular conclusions and dualistic interpretations may limit our ability to understand the spiritual as human, immanent, inherent and common to life experience. Part of the challenge of researching the spiritual is forming ways of thinking and understanding that are open to multiplicity, to the ambiguous, the uncertain, and the complex. The de-centring of post-modernism may be an opportunity for spirituality to be understood in more open and flexible ways.

Narratives

Having assumed spirituality as common human experience, I draw on the role of narrative in reporting human experience from Tappan's work in moral development theory:

> whenever it is necessary to report "the way it really happened", . . . the natural impulse is to tell a story, to compose a narrative that recounts the actions and events in some kind of temporal sequence. Such a story, however does more than outline a series of incidents, it also places those incidents in a particular narrative context, thereby giving meaning to the human experience of temporality and personal action (Polkinghorne 1988). Narrative is thus an essential means by which human experience is represented and interpreted. (Tappan 1991: 8)

Personal narrative is one means of expressing spiritual experiences in a form that allows meaning to be constructed. But narrative requires a listening space for this interpretative work to occur. I have written elsewhere (Scott 1998a) about the nature of narrative as an access point for spiritual experience and understanding because of its qualities of indirectness, implication, ambiguity and its suggestive capacity: narrative opens imaginative and indeterminate space in human life and understanding (Bausch 1984; Bruner 1996; Sanders 1997). Narrative also creates an open space for voicing lived experience which is not dependent on external evidence or objective detail. Narrative has an ability to include without enclosing: that is, it offers space for the un-encompassed to remain unencompassed yet for it to be noted, considered, and implicated (Longxi 1992) through the play of language that can mention and indicate without having to define or finalize.

Second, narrative is interpretative. Any telling is already an in-terpretation of an event or experience. Meaning is being made not only because of how we tell the story but also when we tell it, that is, in what context and for what audience. Narratives are claims and remain rich in implication, as hermeneutic sites. Narrative provides a site for the symbolic to be part of personal experience and one's own story and can therefore serve to link humans to one another beyond themselves through shared symbols and a communal sense of meaning.

I live in a culture that neither expects to hear nor is willing to affirm personal narratives of spiritual experiences. Hay and Nye (1998) argue that by the age of ten children have become reluctant to speak of such experiences, having already absorbed the cultural injunction of silence about spirituality.[1] To begin to tell personal spiritual narratives is to act against a strong cultural message. This creates difficulties in both telling and listening to stories of spiritual experiences.

Approaches to Listening

How a story is heard is part of any narrative exchange. The audience for a story is part of the interpretative dynamic, influencing the narration by creating an acceptable or unacceptable space for the story. There is a multitude of ways to hear or frame stories as they are told. There are ways to silence the voice associated with certain perspectives. It is only recently that we have begun to acknowledge that culture can be and has been built to exclude or minorize certain voices based on gender, race, political leaning or sexuality. My contention is that we must now attend to a similar silencing of spiritual voice. The spiritual voice in Western culture has been occluded and as with other silencings, there are long-term implications.

Problems of the silencing of spiritual narratives are evident in the research. Coles (1991), for example, reports within his own research practice, his dismissal of children's attempts to tell him of their spiritual and religious experience and the shift that occurred, provoked by comments of Anna Freud, to re-examine his work to find what he had not heard from children. Robinson's (1983) *The Original Vision*, includes accounts of childhood experiences that were ignored, mocked or minimalized by adults who did not understand what the child was trying to say. Adults who do not expect spiritual insights from children may not be able to comprehend or hear them when they are offered. Adult responses may range from ignorance to disbelief to distain. The cultural message makes stories of personal spiritual experience difficult to tell.

This coincides with my experience of hearing personal spiritual narratives in two ways. First, I have begun to hear more stories from adults who had childhood and adolescent spiritual experiences and made deliberate attempts to report them to peers, to teachers or professors and were told to forget the experience or to put aside the account.

Such stories were framed with shame, with threats of being seen as crazy, or met with discomfort and inappropriate humour. The stories were silenced and, in most cases, hidden for lengthy periods of time.

Secondly, in my work with child and youth care workers and parents, I have been surprised by the number of stories I have heard from adults of their childhood or adolescent spiritual experiences that were told with the claim: "That's the first time I have told that story". There is and has been a clear message that the stories of spiritual experiences are not acceptable and may, in fact, be dangerous for the narrator. I am concerned that we develop ways to listen to personal spiritual narratives that do not restrict their meanings, qualities and implications. In order for researchers to understand how people experience spirituality, how spiritual experience shapes their perspective, how it affects their lives, and how they manage crisis, difficulty, and moral or ethical decisions differently because of their experiences, we have to provide a listening space that is open, flexible, non-judgemental – one which accepts intuitions, feelings and mystical experiences as normative. We also need to accept the multiplicity of meanings, the ambiguity and uncertainty inherent in their stories. And we have to be prepared to bracket our own judgements about their experiences to create an appropriate narrative space.

Brown and Gilligan proposed a way of listening – "Guide to Listening" – that "listens to a person's story *four* different times, listening . . . for different voices of self-telling different narratives of relationship" (Brown and Gilligan 1991: 45). Their concern is to hear the "complex orchestration" and the "psychological and political structure" in a person's story so that "the listener appreciates the intricate structure of a person's experiences of self and relationships". They are aware of the difficulty of "the powerful act of one person interpreting – "naming" – the experience of another" and call for "authentic relationships . . . that are as open and mutual as a possible, in which partially formed thoughts and strong feelings can be expressed and heard" (54). This approach begins to provide the kind of listening space necessary for spiritual narratives. The attention being paid to the relational links declared by the story provides a potential opening for personal spiritual narratives to be heard as accounts of relational experience. Their suggested approach also includes acknowledging the potentially incomplete and still-in-process quality of spiritual narratives. Although their emphasis is political and psychological I believe the multiple listening practice can include an awareness of and attention to the spiritual relationships present in narratives.

I believe there are several additional difficulties with spiritual narratives. First, spiritual experiences may be outside of a person's expected range of events. A person may have been taken beyond him or her self and the narrative account may having embedded in it, a sense of o(O)ther as active. The account may be presented in a passive voice but still not involve the narrator assuming a passive stance but rather presenting him or her self as receiving the experience and being a participant in it. In the context of ego and identity this kind of telling may be problematic. Secondly, the telling of such stories may feel forbidden or suspect to the narrator. The story may have enough strangeness for the narrator that it feels like it cannot be told or that there may be a social reason for which it must not be told. Initial attempts to tell such stories may have met with reactions that make any subsequent attempts more difficult as there may not be a way of telling that feels adequate as well as acceptable. Thirdly, the impact of the experience may be ongoing in the narrator's life so that the experience may be currently active, a site of uncertainty and incomplete process. To create a hospitable narrative space to overcome these difficulties will require careful and multiple listening practices.

I wish to adapt an approach to listening proposed by Melissa Butler (1998), an elementary school teacher working in a Chicago housing project school, as a method for listening to spiritual narratives. She suggests that in listening to children's stories it is necessary to be aware that narration can serve five different functions:

1 to invent what they wished was true (a way of coping);
2 to show off and impress other children (be "cool");
3 to fit into their consistent understandings of the world;
4 to live within the complexities of hyper reality; or
5 to develop goals or practice ideas for empowerment. (1998: 96)

She acknowledges that: "the way students understand their own lives is significant" because "it is the way they come to know their own identities in relation to others and the world" and "the means by which they negotiate their own agencies in places where limits to agency are profound" (1998: 108). She concludes her study by claiming that:

recognizing the depth of their stories is essential. Legitimization of their knowledges affirms their lived experience and encourages their power to examine the world. (1998: 108)

Butler suggests that it is necessary to listen to stories openly and without judgement so that they can be externalized, processed and worked on, acknowledging their multiple uses and meanings. It is critical to listen well and to allow children to engage their world narratively, especially so that they can become active agents in their own lives, understanding their place of living and becoming actors in it. In the community in which Butler works stories play a critical role in creating hope and learning for living. There are day-to-day experiences in the children's lives that are outside of "normal" childhood expectations and require different kinds of responses and processing to be managed. Narrative exchanges provide places to invent, to show off, to sort, to interpret, to normalize and to dream.

Listening to Spiritual Narratives

I am suggesting that a similar practice of listening would provide a way to hear stories of spirituality when told by children (or adults who may be recounting earlier experiences) that might create a similar empowerment that would lead to a spirituality that was active and engaged. To do so, it is necessary to listen for voice and to grant the narrator a degree of respect acknowledging that the story may have multiple functions and may be part of sorting a complex, hyper-real experience.

A lived spiritual experience may carry a person beyond their normal ego boundaries through a mystical encounter or an act of "relational consciousness" and connectedness. The loss of self or the insights generated may seem hyper-real and require interpretation and contextualization. If there has not been a venue to explore childhood experiences, adult reports of earlier events in their lives may be narrated in a voice that is neither practised nor integrated but juvenile in its abilities. The narrative spiritual voice may not have had an opportunity to mature, or to negotiate an understanding of its place in a life view. It may not have developed a sense of agency. The relational implications may not be worked through. Although the experience may still have influence, the voice may be under-developed, more a "work-in-progress" than a formed identity. The narrator may be using a voice that is best met with the generosity of listening proposed by Brown, Gilligan and Butler. It may take multiple listenings to develop a spiritual voice and to hear its implications.

There may be both issues of confidence and credibility at stake. The experience may remain hyper-real for the teller, especially if it has been negated or mocked in first attempts at telling. The experience may still be internally influential but have no social context or testing of its meaning and limits. A first narration (or a first heard narration) may be doing several things:

1   trying to sort/understand the experience and move it into familiar language that can be shared with a trusted listener who can affirm, support, clarify or explore the experience with the narrator;
2   trying to contend with the hyper-reality of it – the experience may not fit into the normal daily round of reality and it may require

being told as a story to contain it in the safe, open-ended space that narrative provides;

3   trying to fit the experience into what they already know and make links to the familiar in their lives or to render the unfamiliar in a familiar form as a way of managing it;

4   trying to tell it in a way that acknowledges its power in them by working to invent some significance for themselves through the story. They may have no explanation for their own experience but realize that, in certain contexts, it can be used to gain personal importance;

5   the experience may continue to have some force in their lives and the telling of a story may be a way to indicate the ongoing influence and residual mystery of the experience.

If we look at Robinson's correspondents they illustrate the richness, intensity and complexity of early spiritual experiences as well as the continuing impact of those experiences on their lives.

> When I was about five I had the experience on which, in a sense, my life has been based. It has always remained real and true for me . . . Although my flash of comprehension was thrilling and transforming, I knew even then that in reality it was no more than a tiny glimmer. And yet, because there was this glimmer of understanding, the door of eternity was already open . . . This inner knowledge was exciting and absorbingly interesting, but it remained unsaid because, even if I could have expressed it, no one would have understood. Once, when I tried, I was told I was morbid. [F. 55][2] (Robinson 1983: 12–13)

> I have had experiences in my childhood and youth which were quite mystical and vivid. As I have grown older, I no longer have these experiences. I may have enjoyed physical ecstasy as an adult but as a young person I enjoyed spiritual ecstasy. My earliest feelings seem natural and right to me now. I was with the clouds of glory, utterly responsive to the wonders of creation, and a part of it. [M. 53] (1983: 53)

> there was yet another feeling that used to come over me which now I can only call a kind of insight. At the time, when I was a child, I only remember the feeling as one of intense reality and knowing, a sort of grown-up feeling when I really saw and knew how things really were underneath appearances . . . This kind of insight, though so difficult to describe, took place in the deepest part of me and seemed to be the least dependent upon the senses. I understood without seeing, and what I saw or heard or touched seemed to be of secondary importance to what I knew. [F. 49] (1983: 29)

> in that moment I knew that I had my own special place, as had all other things, animate and so-called inanimate, and that we were all part of this universal tissue which was both fragile yet immensely strong, and utterly

good and beneficent. The vision has never left me. It is as clear today as fifty years ago, and with it the same intense feeling of love of the world and the certainty of ultimate good . . . Of course, at the early age of four or five I could not have expressed anything of the experience in words I have now used, and perhaps the attempt to convey the absorption of myself into the whole, and the intensity of meaning, sounds merely over-coloured to the reader. But the point is that, by whatever mysterious perception, the whole impression and its total meaning were appre-hended in a single instant. [F. 57] (1983: 32–3)

I have heard similar stories of encounters, insights, of being over-whelmed with a sense of compassion from life, of speaking to or being spoken to by God, of hearing music in the air, and of meeting deceased loved-ones and receiving guidance. I struggle with how to read and respond to these stories. Can I listen for the multiple ways and means that Butler suggests? Can I hear them in different ways and sort for voice and context? How can I respond to the layers of accrued meaning? What do I think of the claims of influence? How are these events important for the person who tells them? Are these events common in other lives and unreported? What are the limits of experience that I can accept and acknowledge and what do I do with someone who is making claims for experience beyond what I know and can understand? What kind of listening allows those experiences to be heard? What is being occluded from life experience by the silencing or denial of these stories? What other issues of psychic and emotional well-being are at stake in these kinds of stories?

There remain critical questions that must also be processed as part of an inquiry into spiritual experience. Are these stories wish fulfilment? Are they attempts to impress or aggrandize? Are they intended to sort hyper-real experience or to align experience with existing understand-ings of the world? Are they ways of moving towards empowerment and valued action in the world? Some of these? All of these? None of these?

Research Issues

Spirituality is a topic that is intensified by religious, social and intel-lectual assumptions that surround it affecting both narrators and researchers. In the contemporary context how might we make sense of spiritual experience? What sort of vocabulary and fluidity of discourse is available where the practice has been that of silencing stories of spiri-tual experiences? Attitudes embedded in research, as Bronfenbrenner (1979) makes clear in his work with children, do alter what is said and how it is said. How can we alter our attitudes for the benefit of our research? What assumptions must we make as researchers to create a listening space for personal spiritual narratives that will lead to them being processed, integrated and offer agency and legitimacy to the narrators?

I am trying to adopt an open stance to listening, which includes spiritual experience as an aspect of human life, and to work with what Heshusius calls a "participatory consciousness" offering a research engagement that is not from the outside with the "knower . . . separate from the known" (Heshusius 1994: 15) but rather one where "participatory consciousness is the awareness of a deeper level of kinship between the knower and the known" (1994: 16). It is "a mode of consciousness" that "requires an attitude of profound openness and receptivity" which "involves identification or merging" (1994: 16). In this approach we will be "groping to somehow decode our responses to our participatory reactions . . . trying to provide verbal analysis of non-verbal experience" (1994: 20).

I am suggesting that spiritual experience requires a shift in understanding for effective research. Spiritual experience may itself be a form of participatory consciousness in which experience occurs at a level of kinship beyond the self, outside of subject–object structural clarity. Spiritual experiences may be forms of "participatory consciousness" based on openness and receptivity and the narration of those experiences may already be a kind of work for the narrator who is trying to decode and verbalize a non-verbal experience. To comprehend such experience may require researchers to engage in a similar participatory manner. I am suggesting that to approach such experiences researchers must be willing to suspend subject–object dualism, listen for multiplicity, accept ambiguity and uncertainty in order to participate with narrators in engaging the experience and its implications, entering into a form of participatory consciousness that acknowledges the need for understanding that is "mutually evolving", that does not, in its demands for academic rigour, "override the recognition of kinship and the centrality of tacit and somatic ways of knowing" (1994: 20). This means also that researchers must be willing "not to be in charge . . . of it, or of the self" but rather willing "to attend to something in its own right" (1994: 20). This is not comfortable territory. It is not about mastering an understanding of spirituality in order to research it but rather opening a space for engagement and for narration of experience that requires participation and shifts in our epistemological certainty.

Such work in a difficult topic area may provide us with a site that will extend the margins of qualitative practice. In my work I hear many more personal spiritual narratives than I anticipated. By taking up the topic in public settings I am providing a site where spirituality is acceptable and stories are being told, acknowledged, taken seriously and can be questioned and worked on. Some of the stories are naïve, some are underdeveloped, some are not integrated. Some come with strong feelings, some with vivid distinct physical experiences. Others include elements of mystery, coincidence, or synchronicity. Because of my work in the area of child and youth care, many are about children and their life struggles or are adults telling of their own childhood experiences. Some are from adults who are wondering how to engage with and support children in the midst of their spiritual experiences. They are all rich with potential, and engage questions of meaning, human significance, life crises. They remain potential sites for inquiry and understanding. They require me to cross out of my own zones of comfort to listen differently. The boundaries of culture for spirituality can, I believe, be moved through the offering of a generous, open, listening space that is an invitation to participatory interaction.

Notes

1   In work with aboriginal and First Nations peoples in the Americas I have been told that one should expect the spiritual voice of children to go silent between the ages of seven and ten years as the child becomes focused on physical issues and the earth. Western theories of development have not attended to spiritual development and therefore we are speculating as to the shape and movement of spiritual formation and process in children.
2   The square bracket indicates the gender and age of the correspondent who submitted the story to Robinson's research project. In this case it is a fifty-five-year-old female who wrote this account.

References

Bausch, W. J. 1984: *Storytelling, Imagination and Faith*, Mystic, CT: Twenty-Third Publications.
Bronfenbrenner, U. 1979: *The Ecology of Human Development: Experiments by Nature and Design*, Cambridge, MA: Harvard University Press.
Brown, L. M. and Gilligan. C. 1991: Listening for voice in narratives of relationship, *New Directions for Child Development* 34, 43–61.
Bruner, J. S. 1996: *The Culture of Education*, Cambridge, MA: Harvard University Press.
Butler, M. A. 1998: Negotiating Place: The Importance of Children's Realities. In S. R. Steinberg and J. L. Kincheloe (eds), *Students as Researchers: Creating Classrooms That Matter*, London, Bristol P. A.: Falmer Press, 94–112.
Caputo, J. D. 1987: *Radical Hermeneutics: Repetition, Deconstruction, and the Hermeneutic Project*, Bloomington: Indiana University Press.
Coles, R. 1991: *The Spiritual Life of Children*, New York: Houghton Mifflin.
Ermine, W. 1995: Aboriginal epistemology. In M. Battiste and J. Barman (eds), *First Nations Education in Canada; The Circle Unfolds*, Vancouver: University of British Columbia Press, 101–12.

Evans, D. 1993: *Spirituality and Human Nature*, Albany: State University of New York Press.

Hay, D. with Nye, R. 1998: *The Spirit of the Child*, London: Fount Books.

Heshusius, L. 1994: Freeing ourselves from objectivity: Managing subjectivity or turning towards a participatory mode of consciousness? *Educational Researcher* 23, 15–22.

Hillman, J. 1996: *The Soul's Code: In Search of Character and Calling*, New York: Time Warner Books.

Kovel, J. 1991: *History and Spirit: An Inquiry into the Philosophy of Liberation*, Boston: Beacon Press.

Longxi, Z. 1992: *The Tao and the Logos: Literary Hermeneutics, East and West*, Durham and London: Duke University Press.

May, G. 1982: *Will and Spirit: A Contemplative Psychology*, San Francisco: Harper & Row Publishers.

Ó Murchú, D. 1998: *Reclaiming Spirituality*, New York: The Crossroad Publishing Company.

Otto, R. 1936: *The Idea of the Holy* (trans. J. Harvey) London: Oxford University Press.

Robinson, E. 1983: *The Original Vision*, New York: The Seabury Press.

Sanders, S. R. 1997: The Most Human Art: Ten reasons why we'll always need a good story, *Utne Reader*, Sept.–Oct., 54–6.

Scott, D. G. 1998: A reconsideration of spirituality and education: Reconceptualizing spirituality. In J. Anderson (ed.), *Connections '98*, University of Victoria, Victoria, BC, 87–98.

—— 1998a: Spirituality, Education, Narraturgy: From Wells of Living, Writing, Reading, Unpublished doctoral dissertation, University of Victoria: Victoria, BC.

Tappan, M. B. 1991: Narrative, authorship, and the development of moral authority, *New Directions for Child Development* 34, 5–25.

Torrance, R. M. 1994: *The Spiritual Quest: Transcendence in Myth, Religion, and Science*, Berkeley, Los Angeles, London: University of California Press.

Chapter 10

Religious Nurture and Young People's Spirituality: Reflections on Research at the University of Warwick

Eleanor Nesbitt

———————

ETHNOGRAPHIC research from 1983 in the Warwick Religions and Education Research Unit (WRERU) at the Institute of Education, University of Warwick shows "religious experience", including experience of *bhakti* (religious devotion, the soul's yearning for God), to be integral to the spiritual development of young people. By referring to Mina and Alice (young women of Gujarati Hindu and English Quaker background respectively) I shall raise the following methodological issues: ethnographic sensitivity, the value given to young people's verbal skills, the importance of a longitudinal approach and the implications of reflexivity.

The Educational Context: Discussions of Spirituality

My conception of spirituality is informed by scholars' definitions such as Wright's "the developing relationship of the individual, within community and tradition, to that which is – or is perceived to be – of ultimate concern, ultimate value and ultimate truth" (1999: 33) and Hay's and Nye's "awareness sensing, mystery sensing and value sensing" (Hay and Nye 1996; Nye and Hay 1996). Checklists and definitions appearing in educational policy documents in England and Wales also provide clues – for example, "the search for meaning and purpose in life and for values by which to live" (NCC 1993: 2). At the same time I am haunted by Priestley's image for attempting to define the spiritual of sending a child to "collect wind in a jar so that it can be examined" (1996: 69).

Focus on Religiously Aligned Young People

This chapter assumes that, given (1) the historically evident relationship between concepts of spirituality and religion, and (2) that some of our pupils are (a) nurtured in particular communities of faith and (b) affirm their distinctive religious allegiances, the wider study of children's spirituality requires us to take seriously data arising from studies of these young people. Implicit in the concept of spiritual *development* is the possibility of actively, consciously developing or nurturing spirituality. It is appropriate to investigate whether some young people's experience of explicit religious nurture, through, for example, Sunday school or corporate worship, has implications for schools' strategies of spiritual development. The focus on religious nurture links this chapter with studies including Fletcher and Ota (1997), although in the WRERU studies young people's spirituality emerged in a context of sustained participant observation.

The Warwick Research

Successive WRERU studies (of eight-year-old to fourteen-year-old Christians, Hindus, Jews, Muslims and Sikhs) have looked at religion in the experience of children and young people. Religious nurture was the primary analytic concern, with spirituality being held in view throughout (see Jackson 1997 for details). A study of 22 young Hindus aged sixteen to twenty-three provided follow-up (Nesbitt 1998). As fieldworker I have interviewed on several occasions 50 Christians, 33 Hindus, 45 Sikhs and 14 Valmikis/Ravidasis (two Punjabi communities problematizing any supposed Sikh/Hindu divide).

Nurture, Religious Experience and *Bhakti*

Following James (1960), Robinson (1977), Hardy (1991) and Hay (1990), the term *bhakti* here refers to the dreams, visions, conversion experiences and memorable sensations understood by the individual concerned as encounters with the divine or with angels, as well as – less dramatically – for what is ordinary experienced in depth. This religious experience is sometimes subsumed in spirituality (Hay and Nye 1996: 6).

Related as it is to their nurturing (Klingberg 1959: 211; Straus 1981), the cultural particularity of children's reported religious experience is unmistakable from our data. To take the eight-year-old to fourteen-year-old Christians, there were continuities between reported religious experience and denominational conditioning: no Protestant Pentecostals were healed by saints, although a Greek Orthodox boy had been, and no Quakers were "born again". At the same time, some experiences were less denominationally specific, with talking to God and hearing God speak to them and dreaming of heaven reported more widely.

Also relevant to planning for spiritual development in schools is acknowledgement of the swift, dramatic nature of the experience that some styles of nurture appear to induce. An eleven-year-old Baptist girl's description of "asking Jesus into her life" began with her account of a Spring Harvest camp that had been organized with the intention of precipitating conversions. Her account discloses the influence of Bible study, of "literature" of an Evangelical kind, of the leaders' suggestion and invitation and the pressure from the crowd on an impressionable young person:

> I felt all shaking and I decided there was something there telling me that was what I wanted to do, so I went to see one of the leaders afterwards with my friend and he gave us some literature about . . . becoming Christian, about Holy Spirit . . . but then later on, after two days, I think it was, I actually stood up when they said if the Holy Spirit had touched us in any way.

Rather different is Alice's profoundly affirming experience, but this too is perhaps best understood in relation to her upbringing, involving as it did weekly attendance at the Meeting for Worship:

> Sometimes you just get a warm glow inside you and you just feel that everybody loves you and you love everybody. (Interview 1990, age fourteen)

How can such experience (and the pupils' articulation of it) connect with schools' checklists for spiritual development? At the very least there needs to be accommodation by teachers of some pupils' nurture-related, or nurture-induced, religious experience as "transcendent" (Woods 1996). Moreover the possibility must be reckoned with that curricular activities in school, for example the exploration of Buddhist meditation suggested by Ogden (2000: 158–9) may impact deeply on individual pupils.

Testimonies by eight-year-old to fourteen-year-old Sikhs and Hindus to the calming or empowering effect of reciting a mantra, and descriptions of the religious devotion of older relatives, are perhaps closer to Alice's experience reported above than are the Christians' experiences of being born again or having visions. For example, an eleven-year-old Sikh boy had found that repeating "Vahiguru" (a name for God) morning and night "keeps me calm". Mridula's grandmother's *seva* (devoted service) to the infant Krishna impacted memorably on her (Jackson and Nesbitt 1993: 116). Such devotion (*bhakti*) is a central concept in Hindu and Sikh discourse on the spiritual path.

Discussion of the relevance of religious nurture to spiritual development more widely needs to engage cross-culturally with different paradigms of spirituality. These may include decisive landmark experiences such as conversion or "asking Jesus into my life" as well as recurrent and continuous states of mind, for example as a result of meditating on a *mala* (prayer beads). What is needed is full recognition of the experience of pupils from diverse religio-cultural backgrounds.

Two Young People's Spirituality

A holistic approach to spirituality suggests the possible value of presenting two young people "in the round". The need to recognize the significance – for their spirituality as adults – of children's spirituality and nurture provides the justification for including their voices aged twenty/twenty-one as well as during their secondary-school education. Both Alice at fourteen and Mina at twenty/twenty-one articulated periods of heightened awareness/religious experience. What follows suggests how such experience connects with their religious nurture and indicates their spiritual development over time.

Mina, the Gujarati, was part of both the 1986–7 Hindu Nurture in *Coventry Project* and the 1995–7 *Longitudinal Study of Young British Hindus' Perceptions of their Religious Tradition*. Interviews with her at the ages of twelve and twenty-one convey her delight in life, her strong social concerns and her intellectual engagement with religious teaching. Alice (quoted earlier) was the daughter of English Quaker parents and had become a member of the Religious Society of Friends (Quakers) (see Punshon 1984) in her own right before her interview aged fourteen during the *Religious Education and Ethnography Project*. A report which Alice wrote at the age of twenty-one provides insights into her spirituality seven years on (Morning Star 1997).

At the age of twelve, Mina was, like her parents and elder sister, deeply involved in the activities of the local devotees of Sathya Sai Baba (see Haraldsson 1987). From infancy Mina participated in the weekly Sai *satsangs* (devotional gatherings) in her home. Accompanying herself on the harmonium she often led the congregation in singing praise to Sai Baba in which he was equated with Jesus, the Buddha and Hindu deities. From an early age Mina had also been a keen member of the weekly Bal Vikas (literally "child development") classes for children. The curriculum included using a *mala* (string of beads) to recite a mantra invoking Sathya Sai Baba plus "silent sitting" (sitting in line, eyes closed, physically still and mentally focused on something beautiful), as well as stories and role play concerned with the "human values" of truth, love, peace, right conduct and non-violence, plus learning to sing *bhajan*s (devotional hymns) and performing *arati* (circling the lamp reverently in front of Sathya Sai Baba's garlanded portrait). This ritual-ized devotion, focused on Sathya Sai Baba, is of a piece with the *bhakti*, which is integral to spirituality in Hindu (and Sikh) tradition more widely.

My fieldnotes record Mina's zest for life: performing traditional dances for community functions, enthusiastic recitation of the prayer before meals in which God (Hari) is identified as the giver, the consumer and the food itself. This zest permeates the "diary" which Mina kept during the first research period – for instance her excitement at finding out the meaning of the syllable that was familiar and precious to her through daily devotional recitation: "*om* . . . the first primal sound from that came all other creation". She elsewhere reported:

> In Bal Vikas we learn about Religions, God and other Spiritual things, we sing songs have games learn new prayers in different languages. It's real good fun. (21 November 1986)

As a twelve year old she eagerly lapped up her teaching on Sai beliefs and practices. Regarding values, her interviews convey reflection on a case of cheating in relation to *karma* (although she did not use this term), and her reticence about coming top in her class as well as her uneasiness about caste distinctions and about applying pressure to God through prayer.

Interviewed again when she was twenty and twenty-one, as a psychology student in London, Mina spoke freely about spirituality. Having herself introduced a distinction between "spiritual" and "religious" she elucidated:

> I myself don't practise a religion – any single religion – but I believe in spirituality: I believe in God . . . I believe that everyone has got a different point of view and that is why I don't necessarily believe in individual religions . . .

Asked if her views had shifted since she was twelve she responded:

> I have always believed more in the fact that every religion should be seen as one anyway, so I don't think I have changed that much . . . except before . . . I would be practising my religion much more because my father would tell me to, but now by choice I don't actually practise any religion, I just

believe in Sai Baba or whatever he teaches . . . I don't see the point of having to follow a single pathway when, by following a more universal way, I can reach the same destination.

Later she acknowledged that the Sai emblem, incorporating as it does symbols of "all faiths", "has had a big effect on me . . . so I would consider myself as more of a Sai devotee than a religious person". In other words she perceived her primary devotion to Sathya Sai Baba as more universal and encompassing than a primarily Hindu allegiance would be.

Her subsequent reflections provide insight into her attempts to differentiate between prayer, meditation and contemplation, all of them meaningful terms from her own experience:

> I'd say prayers in my own words more likely than not. But sometimes I use the main *sloks* [Sanskrit verses] if I meditate. I sometimes use *om* because I like meditating because I think it is really sort of calming. Meditation is almost a form of prayer because it brings you closer to God – well brings you closer to higher consciousness . . . Prayer is quite selfish . . .

Moreover, Mina explained in detail a "candle meditation", which is intended to make the meditator "become one with the light".

When asked whether she had had any religious experience Mina made it clear that she had "had spiritual experience", elaborating that she "didn't have that sudden picture of a God or an image, it is more of a feeling of total peace". This she had experienced both at Prashanti Nilayam, Sathya Sai Baba's centre in India and once when she "went into a church with my friend at home and I felt just as calm as I did when I was at Prashanti".

In reflections such as these, the continuities with earlier nurture in Bal Vikas – and in a staunchly Sai family – are apparent: Mina's experience of changed states of consciousness, and of a greater capacity for calm, stemmed from meditation techniques and inspirational places, which refer back to her childhood nurture. The Sanskrit *sloks*, the syllable *om*, the candle (which she had – in a film – seen Baba use in this way) and her visits to Prashanti – all integral to her religious nurture – illustrate how this has been internalized and activated. Social engagement too had been a strong feature of her Bal Vikas training, and the twenty year old Mina was still "pretty strong on issues!"

We now turn from Mina to Alice. Sunday by Sunday, from earliest infancy, her parents had brought her to Quaker Meeting for Worship. Her spirituality had been nurtured not only in the Meeting for Worship itself but also in the sessions run for young people during the last forty-five minutes of weekly Meeting for Worship. Recent activities had, she said, included role-play and discussion of prejudice, for example, racism in the media. Three times a year, at Junior Young Friend (eleven-eighteen year-olds) weekends, she would hear speakers on issues like vegetarianism or apartheid:

> Friday night Saturday night we have epilogue about ten ... Everyone sits round in a circle usually and we usually have candles in the middle and switch off the lights ... and sometimes we all hold hands with each other.

Quaker insights likewise informed her family life, so "before meals sometimes we have a quiet – we just sit round the table and it's a bit like a small Quaker meeting". Alice's weekday activities included Woodcraft Folk, which she described as a "co-operative" and "demo-cratic" organization. She recognized that, though non-religious as compared with Guides or the Girls' Brigade, Woodcraft shared its emphases on "co-operation and friendship" with Quakers. Similarly, "silence is kind of part of my religion" and this connected with the requirement for one Woodcraft badge:

> to go and sit in a wood or something for an hour and not talk to anybody ... just be aware of where you are and what's around you.

At fourteen Alice, like Mina at twenty, was making clear distinctions and expressing universalism in her reluctance to identify narrowly and unquestioningly as, for example, British or Quaker. So, when asked how she would identify herself she had stated, "I don't like labels in general but I'm a citizen of the world." She proceeded to explain:

> I think of myself as a Quaker first and I'm not sure whether I'm a Christian or not ... I think maybe I believe in Christ like he was a very good person and he was kind ... and that was a good way to live, but I don't believe everything it says in the Bible.

By the age of twenty-one Alice had replaced her family surname with "Morning Star", and under this name her report of the Friends World Committee for Consultation Triennial appeared (Morning Star 1997). Regarding her spiritual affinity with the environment she writes:

> Right relations with the whole world is so deeply part of my spirituality ("Living in the Wisdom of Creation" – George Fox) that I can barely articulate the link between them. (1997: 4)

She refers to "godde", clearly inclusive of God and Goddess, and states that she has become "more comfortable with" Goddess language: "Christianity is not generally the system or language in which I experi-ence my spirituality."

Commonalities

In each case a spirituality with its own "signature" (Hay with Nye 1998: 99) emerged, consistent with the experience and language of Alice's and Mina's nurture in childhood. Both young women were eloquent, analytical and exploratory: Mina at twenty/twenty-one is making distinctions between religion and spirituality, between being a Sai devotee and a Hindu, and Alice at fourteen was concerned with the relationship between being Quaker and Christian. Their interviews show the hallmarks suggested by Hay and Nye (1998) – an intense awareness (of issues, for example) that is also relational. This relationality is articulated by both young women in terms of ethical imperatives: environmental and social concern (for example, Alice at fourteen voiced her pacifism which she found at odds with peers' and teachers' assumptions during the Gulf War, Mina at twelve criticized people's emphasis of caste.) Their intellectual and emotional intensity resonate with Wright's "ultimate concern, ultimate value and ultimate truth" (1999: 33). In each case the longitudinal approach discloses continuities and developments – Mina opting not to practise Hindu (or even Sai) rituals, Alice moving from a God to Goddess framework.

While Mina's nurture was characterized by *bhakti*, a loving devotion for the living master/*avatar* (incarnation of God), Sathya Sai Baba, Alice's Quaker upbringing had its roots in English Protestant Christian dissent. Yet the Sai devotees' diet of silent sitting and attention to human values matches strikingly with the silent Meeting for Worship and Friends' foregrounding of social issues – although the guidance which Sai gurus provide for silent sitting differs from Quaker reference to being open to the Spirit, and justice is probably more highly profiled by Quakers whereas *ahimsa* (non-violence to all creatures, not only humans) is stronger in the Sai schema. (In practice both Mina and Alice were keen advocates of vegetarianism.) Sai devotees explicitly venerate Sathya Sai Baba in a way which is culturally and theologically alien to Quakerism, yet both Sai devotees and Quakers endorse affirmation of diverse religious paths, so freeing their young people from exclusive sectarian allegiance.

An intended future phase of our research at Warwick is a study of schools' spiritual development programmes associated with particular religious communities. These include the Sathya Sai Education in Human Values programme (www.sathyasaiehv.org). This extension of WRERU's research is for the future: to date our studies suggest four methodological issues for researchers of religion and spirituality in young people's experience: ethnographic sensitivity, verbalization, longitudinal study and reflexivity.

Methodological Issues

Ethnographic Sensitivity.   One twelve-year-old Hindu boy described religion as "the most private thing". Like religion, spirituality is a sensitive topic, demanding sensitivity from the researcher (Nesbitt 2000). This requires not only empathy with the child concerned but also a critical distancing from each. A sensitive rapport, that facilitates conversation about religious experience, is eased by prior participant observation in the child's home/ community and the place of congregational worship. Ethnographic sensitivity entails an attentive listening not only during interviews but also when reviewing the tape recordings and transcripts. It is a listening not only for words but also for silences and for emotions such as excitement and anger.

Verbalization.   This listening implies that spirituality is primarily verbal. Here is one of the dilemmas for both the researcher and the educationist, since spirituality is concerned with what "lie[s] beyond anything expressible in rationally articulable discourse" (Carr 1996a: 462), yet is identified through verbal communication. Jane Erricker rightly affirmed that "verbalization is a part of the process of the child's self-understanding" (2000) and Wright goes so far as to regard the ability to use language effectively as central to spirituality (1999). But this suggests that the verbally less able (including children with "special educational needs") are less capable of spiritual maturity. The relationship between verbal discourse and spirituality is contested, with Hay following Vygotsky in striving to uncover a spirituality that is prior to verbal expression, though also arguing that "children need to develop an understanding of the role of language and metaphor in focusing and interpreting our experience of life" (Hay 1990: 107). What is clear from the Warwick data is that both Mina and Alice are unusually articulate, and that there is the risk of over-valuing linguistic fluency and intellectual skills in the pursuit and nurture of spirituality. Written expression (Mina's diary and – in adulthood – Alice's article) valuably supplement interview data, but once again identification of spirituality is complicated by academic factors inherent in literary competence.

Longitudinal Study.   While the evident continuity and consistency in Mina's account cannot be taken to demonstrate a generalizable causal connection between nurture and adult outlook, and other factors need to be taken into account, it is evident that longitudinal data of this sort can usefully add to cross-cultural attempts to map patterns of spiritual development. Alice's article (aged twenty-one) and Mina's follow-up interviews at twenty/twenty-one, point to the value of future ethnographic studies that are longitudinal in design. Research would track the same individuals – perhaps at each Key Stage, or at longer intervals, from early childhood to young adulthood. By showing young people transcripts (or playing recordings) of their interviews years before one can elicit responses of surprise and affirmation. Their reflections on their earlier insights (as in Mina's most recent interview) can help to map their spiritual development. It is through encounter with the adult's world view and priorities that the influence of religious nurture becomes clear. Clearly, longitudinal studies with the same individuals as children and as adults would make a valuable addition to research on spiritual development that reports adults' retrospectives on child-hood (Robinson 1977) or which look only at children at a particular stage.

Reflexivity. At this point it is salutary to recall recent methodolog-ical discussions of reflexivity and – more particularly – of the insider/outsider dilemma in the study of religions. Hay with Nye rightly remind us of Gadamer's statement that "it is no good any researcher in the social sciences claiming to embrace a superficially neutral, open position" (1998: 82–3). As a Quaker researcher, with a particular autobiography, I need to challenge my decision to look to a Sai devotee and a Quaker in particular for pointers to strategies for spiri-tual development in school (Nesbitt 1999). Has this involvement in the Society of Friends not stemmed from and strengthened a predisposition for Alice's and Mina's concern for ethical issues and an empathy with Alice's "warm glow" and Mina's experience of "silent sitting" rather than, say, conversion or glossolalia? In analysing transcripts am I not allowing my own conditioning free rein? Clive and Jane Erricker are right to remind us that our own definitions might betray different sectarian interests (1999: 139).

However, rather than invalidate what the ethnographer draws from particular data, this illustrates the nature of the interactive process inherent both in ethnographic research and in spiritual development. The choice of research focus, the way in which questions are framed, the mode of analysis and the subsequent interpretation of the data will be influenced by the ethnographer's experience and personality. The ethnographer's responsibility is to be as transparent as possible so that readers can recognize and critique the research's intrinsically inter-active nature as well as becoming increasingly aware of their own conditioning.

In the case of young people's spirituality their insights become a part of the fieldworker's own journey while the interview becomes (however minimally) part of the young person's spiritual journey. Moreover, the fact of being interviewed by a researcher can affect a young person's atti-tude to his/her faith. One Gujarati commented on his greater interest in Hinduism as a result of involvement in the study when he was eleven.

The fact that (in Hay and Nye's view – for example, Hay 1990; Hay with Nye 1998) talk of spirituality is generally taboo makes the interviewer's affirmation of this dimension the more significant for the interviewee. The ethnographer's receptive listening is itself a catalyst – and listening is "the heart of spiritual and moral education" (Erricker and Erricker 1999: 139).

Conclusion

The Warwick data supports: (1) the value of drawing upon ethnographic study of religious children's experience when formulating definitions of spiritual development and strategies for enhancing it; (2) the importance of encompassing the diversity of faiths, including NRMs, with their promotion of spirituality; and (3) the need for longitudinal studies, e.g., in primary, secondary and early adulthood, to plot continuities and change and to provide insight into children's spirituality in the context of lifelong development.

To expand (2) further, this inclusiveness problematizes not only definitions honed by Christian traditions of spirituality, but also, possibly, the secular definitions deployed in mainstream UK education. Here I am thinking of the implications for education (which prioritizes critical alertness) of taking seriously the Hindu apprehension of *bhakti* with its emphasis on unquestioning devotion.

Recognition of children's diverse experiences of faith may imply (as Wright 1997a: 16f assumes) that children bring with them to the classroom a specific (Jewish etc.) tradition which needs recognizing and nurturing. But, even more significantly, our data indicates children individually may already have an internally diverse, evolving and plurally influenced spirituality. Wright commends the Warwick project for relating the "emergent world view of the children back to their faith tradition" (1997b: 211). But this is to assume that children's experience – and the Warwick RE Project – are locked in a world religions paradigm of discrete faith traditions (see Jackson 1997; Geaves 1998). It is only on the basis of such misconceptions of lived reality that Halstead (1995) and Carr can suggest even the possibility of schools providing "different sorts of initial spiritual education" that corresponds to children's "rival traditions" (1996b: 176).

Ethnographically based reflection on spirituality must rather be grounded in an understanding of "faiths", and of the experience of those individuals who are variously associated with them, as fluid, internally complex and changing. Unlike the world religions paradigm we need a framework which includes unpejoratively the so-called New Religious Movements (such as devotion to Sathya Sai Baba) as potentially valid partners, rather than as marginalized phenomena – future WRERU studies will open up this school–NRM interface in approaching pupils' spiritual development.

Acknowledgments

Thank you Alice, Mina and all who contributed to the research; to the Economic and Social Research Council (Project no R00232489) for funding Religious Education and Ethnography and to the Leverhulme Trust for funding Hindu Nurture in Coventry, Punjabi Hindu Nurture and the Longitudinal Study of Young British Hindus' Perceptions of their Religious Tradition.

References

Carr, D. 1996a: Songs of Immanence and Transcendence: A Rejoinder to Blake, *Oxford Review of Education* 22(4), 457–63.

—— 1996b: Rival Conceptions of Spiritual Education, *Journal of Philosophy of Education* 30(2), 159–78.

Erricker, C. and Erricker, J. 1999: Spiritual and Moral Development: A Suitable Case for Treatment. In A. Thatcher (ed.), *Spirituality and the Curriculum*, London: Cassell, 124–41.

Erricker, J. 2000: A Collaborative Approach to Researching Teacher Work in Developing Spiritual and Moral Education. In R. Best (ed.), *Education for Spiritual, Moral, Social and Cultural Development*, London: Continuum, 187–98.

Fletcher, M. and Ota, C. 1997: Religious Identity and Children's Worldviews. In C. Erricker *et al.*, *The Education of the Whole Child*, London: Cassell, 114–31.

Geaves, R. 1998: The Borders between Religions: A Challenge to the World Religions Approach to Religious Education, *British Journal of Religious Education* 21(1).

Halstead, M. 1995: Voluntary Apartheid? Problems of Schooling for Religious and Other Minorities in Democratic Societies, *Journal of Philosophy of Education* 29(2).

Haraldsson, E. 1987: *"Miracles are my Visiting Cards": An Investigative Report on the Psychic Phenomena Associated with Sathya Sai Baba*, London: Century.

Hardy, A. 1991: *The Spriritual Nature of Man*, Oxford: Alistair Hardy Research Centre.

Hay, D. 1990: *Religious Experience Today: Studying the Facts*, London: Mowbray.

Hay, D. and Nye, R. 1996: Investigating Spirituality: The Need for a Fruitful Hypothesis, *The International Journal of Children's Spirituality* 1(1), 6–16.

—— 1998: *The Spirit of the Child*, London: Fount.

Jackson, R. 1997: *Religious Education: An Interpretive Approach*, London: Hodder and Stoughton.

Jackson, R. and Nesbitt, E. 1993: *Hindu Children in Britain*, Stoke on Trent: Trentham.

James, W. 1960: *The Varieties of Religious Experience*, London: Fontana.

Klingberg, G. 1959: A Study of Religious Experience in Children from 9 to 13 Years of Age, *Religious Education* 54(3), 211–16.

Morning Star, A. 1997: Points of View, *The Friend*, 29 August, 4.

National Curriculum Council [NCC] 1993: *Spiritual and Moral Development – A Discussion Paper*, York: National Curriculum Council.

Nesbitt, E. 1998: British, Asian and Hindu: Identity, Self-Narration and the Ethnographic Interview, *Journal of Beliefs and Values* 19(2), 189–200.

—— 1999: Friend in the Field: A Reflexive Approach to Being a Quaker Ethnographer, *Journal of Quaker Studies* 4(2), 82–112.

—— 2000: Researching 8 to 13-year-olds' Perspectives on their Experience of Religion. In A. Lewis and G. Lindsay (eds), *Researching Children's Perspectives*, Buckingham: Open University Press, 135–49.

Nye, R. and Hay, D. 1996: Identifying Children's Spirituality: How Do You Start without a Starting Point? *British Journal of Religious Education* 18(3), 144–54.

Ogden, V. 2000: Cultural Development: Its Relationship to School Improvement and the Role of Religious Education. In R. Best (ed.), *Education for Spiritual, Moral, Social and Cultural Development*, London: Continuum, 155–63.

Priestley, J. 1996: Review, *International Journal of Children's Spirituality* 1(1), 69.

Punshon, J. 1984: *Portrait in Grey*, London: Quaker Home Service.

Robinson, E. 1977: *The Original Vision: A Study of Religious Experience in Childhood*, Oxford: The Alistair Hardy Research Centre.

Straus, R. A. 1981: The Social-Psychology of Religious Experience: A Naturalistic Approach, *Sociological Analysis* 42, 57–67.

Woods, G. 1996: Poor Relation or Honoured Guest? The Place of the Transcendent in a State Education System that Seeks to Promote Spiritual Development, *International Journal of Children's Spirituality* 1(1), 31–43.

Wright, A. 1997a: Embodied Spirituality: The Place of Culture and Tradition in Contemporary Educational Discourse on Spirituality, *International Journal of Children's Spirituality* 1(2), 8–20.

—— 1997b: Hermeneutics and Religious Understanding – Part 1: The Hermeneutics of Modern Religious Education, *Journal of Beliefs and Values* 18(2), 203–16.

—— 1999: *Discerning the Spirit: Teaching Spirituality in the Religious Education Classroom*, Abingdon: Culham College Institute.

Chapter 11

The Corruption of Innocence and the Spirituality of Dissent: Postcolonial Perspectives on Spirituality in a World of Violence

Liam Gearon

T HIS chapter explores the implications of the disruptive force of social, political and cultural violence for children's spirituality. Taking the child as the most vulnerable and potentially defenceless member of a global – and increasingly globalized – society, the chapter explores how struggles for territorial and cultural domination infringe the rights of children and their place in the world. I shall make an analogy between this vulnerability and the historical moments of colonialism and postcoloniality and contest that foundational writings of postcolonial criticism – from Fanon and Césaire to Said – provide a model of personal and social development for both the exploited individual person and the political state. It is argued that a spirituality of dissent – often at the extremes of threatened individual and political survival – provides here a model of spirituality as existential limit and that this limit provides an ultimate, existential context for understanding spirituality.

The Corruption of Innocence: Culture and Violence

The incorporation of religious and secular understandings of spirituality as a quest for ultimate, existential meaning has been explored by a number of authors (Gearon 1997; cf. Bigger and Brown 1999; Coles 1995; Copley 1997; 2000; Carr 1996; Erricker 1998; Priestley 1996; Wright 1998; 1999). Here, I want to examine the *temporal* and *contingent* relationship between spirituality and state politics, with particular reference to children's rights in a world of violence. I argue that politics, and in particular the political history of nations and global society, are too often neglected when considering children's spirituality, that political dimensions concerning spirituality are often consciously or unconsciously ignored.

This is most painfully obvious – and strange – when we look at spirituality in education. It is strange because spirituality in education is always going to be "political" and it is painful because the political and historical accounts which *are* presented are clearly so done in the light of a questionable history and politics. Thus, even in a most recent treatment of such history (Copley 2000), a history of spirituality in educational context, critical examination of the political dimension of spirituality is presented, in an otherwise excellent book, as if English education owes everything to imperial cultural process. For example, Copley positively reviews the place of Matthew Arnold in the development of a supposedly liberal education system in Victorian England. Yet he neglects entirely the broader context of expanding Empire to which Matthew Arnold in the nineteenth century was integral. Copley neglects too the control of non-Western culture (indeed its subjugation) during the same period and in particular overlooks the part figures like Matthew Arnold played in this actual (historical, political) colonial subjugation of non-western culture – Arnold's famous *Culture and Anarchy*, for instance, defined western culture as *self-evidently* superior.

Such neglect within education is surprising because in the expansion of empires there has often been an historical relationship between theology and imperialism (Hastings 1999; cf Harlow and Carter 1999) and more widely between culture and imperialism (Said 1994; 1995) – issues seemingly ignored by discussions of spirituality in education to date. The inevitable effect of such neglect is to make discussions both ahistorical and apolitical – indeed Copley's approach is distinctive because it brings both to bear in the field but does so in a way which leaves both politics and history open to question. As will become clear, there *is* a greater need for the inclusion of both history and politics in talking about the spiritual; indeed, arguably, discussions of the latter are meaningless without them, if for no other reason than that structures of ultimate meaning, as the postmodernists tell us (for instance, Rorty 1989), are always to some degree contingent. Here I want to open up debate by examining more closely and critically the historical and contemporary political contexts which inevitably surround spirituality in education. And I want to do this with aid of the growing – and within education surprisingly neglected – body of postcolonial theory and criticism.

Both postcolonial theory and postcolonial criticism examine the power structures which are present between states whose interaction historically involved a colonizer/ colonized relationship. From the outset there is something here worth noting about the distinction in postcolonial theory and criticism between postcoloniali*ty*, as historical and political state of the post-colonial, and postcolonial*ism*, the theory of postcoloniality within and beyond the academy. Gandhi's *Postcolonial Theory* (1998) provides the most accessible discussion of such issues. She provides an overview of an emerging assumption within the field that a distinction needs to be made between postcolonial *theory*, as cultural *commentary* on power imbalances between the colonized and colonizer, and postcolonial *criticism*, as more (actively) political and *engaged involvement in overcoming such power imbalances*.

The above is best illustrated by distinguishing between distinctive key texts, say, between the postcolonial *criticism* of Fanon's ([1961] 1997) *The Wretched of the Earth*, and the postcolonial *theory* of Said's ([1979] 1995) *Orientalism*. Both centre concerns around power imbalances and the oppressive use of such power for domination – territorial gain, cultural and political imperialism – but the two have differences of emphasis and approach. It is possible here to postulate a scale dependent upon the emphasis placed upon either an "engaged" stance or more "detached" cultural criticism position. Such a scale might be described as ranging from a politically engaged anti-imperial nationalism (postcolonial criticism) to cultural commentary (postcolonial theory). Comparing Fanon and Said, it is the difference between the postcolonial *criticism* of Fanon's revolutionary stance against colonialism in *The Wretched of the Earth* and the postcolonial *theory* of Said's cultural analysis of *Orientalism*, a position further exemplified, even typified, by *Culture and Imperialism* (1995). Some scholars, of course, (for instance, Moore-Gilbert, Stanton and Maley 1997), argue that such a distinction between postcolonial *theory* and *criticism* is an oversimplification.

But I have talked from the outset of *violence*. And I want to outline two models: first, physical violence – and by way of example I take the case of the impact of children in armed conflict; second, a more subtle interpretation of violence as cultural. One could take these as two key elements of politics and history which preoccupy both postcolonial theory and criticism: that empires are made not simply by the expansion of military might but are created, and as importantly sustained, by cultural means. In one way or another both could be summed up in the notion not simply of a culture of violence (which would be too simple) but of a more subtle and often reciprocal relationship between culture and violence.

Let me deal – simply and brutally – with the first model, of physical violence. The United Nations Convention on the Rights of the Child (adopted in 1989) promised a number of things (Franklin 1996 contains a wide-ranging review). The Convention established a number of principles about the treatment, nurture and protection of children within nation states. Article 2, for instance, declares that "States Parties shall respect and ensure the rights set forth in the present Convention to each child within their jurisdiction without discrimination of any kind, irrespective of the child's or his or her parent's or legal guardian's race, colour, sex, language, religion, political or other opinion, national, ethnic or social origin, poverty, disability, birth or other status" (cited Franklin 1996: xi). Article 4 declares that "States Parties shall undertake all appropriate legislative, administrative and other measures for the implementation of the rights recognized in this Convention" and that with regard to economic, social and cultural rights "States Parties shall undertake such measures to the maximum extent of their available resources and, where needed, within the framework of international cooperation" (cited Franklin, 1996: xi). Article 6, crucially for our present purposes, declares, at a most fundamental level, that "States Parties shall ensure to the maximum extent possible the survival and development of the child" (cited Franklin 1996: x). These are laudable and high ideals indeed.

Yet literally only a few years later the Secretary General of the United Nations was calling for an expert report on the impact of armed conflict on children. A United nations briefing paper suggests that armed conflict "more than any other force, has transformed the lives of millions of children and women" and that far from simply being caught in the crossfire, many women and children are actually being targeted specifically. Here, the Report chillingly suggests, "Nothing is spared, held sacred or protected":

> It is the singular characteristic of armed conflict in our time that children suffer most . . . In the past decade alone, an estimated 2 million children have been killed in armed conflict. Three times as many have been seriously injured or permanently disabled. Countless others have been forced to witness or even take part in horrifying acts of violence. These statistics are shocking enough, but more chilling is the conclusion to be drawn from them: more and more of the world is being sucked into a desolate moral vacuum, a space devoid of the most basic human values, a space in which children are slaughtered, raped and maimed, where children are exploited as soldiers, starved and exposed to extreme brutality. (United Nations 2000: 2)

As a result of a recommendation of the United Nations Committee on the Rights of the Child, the General Assembly in 1993 requested the Secretary General to appoint an authority to study the impact of armed conflict on children. Graca Machel, the Secretary General's expert on the subject and a former Minister for Education in Mozambique, submitted a report, *The Impact of Armed Conflict on Children* to the 1996 session of the General Assembly (United Nations 2000). The underlying premise of the report is that children should have no part in warfare and should be protected from its effects. The Report shows the full extent of children's involvement in armed conflicts raging around the world, and "sets out findings and recommendations aimed at Governments, entities of the United Nations system, intergovernmental and regional bodies, civil society organizations and individuals" (United Nations, 2000: 2). The Report headings are indicative of the range of issues affecting children in this context and priorities for international action:

> Impact of Armed Conflict on Child Development
> Health and Nutrition
> Promoting psychological recovery and social reintegration
> Education: Investing in the future of children
>
> SPECIAL CONCERNS
> Child soldiers: An affront to humanity
> Children in flight: Refugee and internally displaced children
> Gender-based violence: A Weapon of War
> The devastation of landmines and unexploded ordnance
> Adolescents: A neglected group
>
> PROMOTING THE HUMAN RIGHTS OF CHILDREN
> International law and the protection of children in armed conflict
> The protection of children: A priority for the international peace and security agenda
> Advocating for children rights: Actions for everyone

In its conclusions, the Report suggested the following:

> The lack of control and the sense of dislocation and chaos that characterize contemporary armed conflict can be attributed to many factors, such as political upheavals and struggles for control in the face of widespread poverty and economic disarray. The callousness of modern warfare may be a natural outcome of the social revolutions that have torn traditional societies apart. But whatever the causes, the time has come to call a halt. The international community must proclaim attacks on children for what they are – intolerable and unacceptable. (United Nations 2000: 2)

The high ideals of the United Nations Convention on the Rights of the Child are hardly a reality.

Indeed, five years after the conclusion of the World Conference on Human Rights (1993) at Vienna, which resulted in the Vienna Declaration and Plan of Action, the High Commissioner commented that:

> The international community must conclude that five years after Vienna, a wide gap continues to exist between the promise of human rights and their reality in the lives of people throughout the world. At the beginning of the twenty-first century, making all human rights a reality for all remains not only our fundamental challenge but our solemn responsibility. (United Nations [1998] 2000a: para 104)

If the entirety of the world's troubles cannot be placed at the feet of past empires, postcolonial theory and criticism presents some savage claims that the global community is as it is *because* of the history of imperialism and colonialism originating from the West. If we are to understand children's spirituality, we need to take into account these extremes of political and historical reality; and what it does or might do to children's development in this sphere.

In the more subtle context of culture's potential for violence, it is undoubtedly Said (1994; 1995) who has done most towards developing a contemporary understanding of how culture is a crucial adjunct in the interplay of power relations between peoples, societies and cultures. And all of such is of direct reference to our present considerations on spirituality, since the latter fall always within the remit of the cultural and the contingent, doubly so when placed in educational context (Gearon 2001). Historically the terms of colonialism and imperialism have been applied to these processes – but it is a premise of both postcolonial theory and criticism that cultural representation was (and arguably is) a key to, indeed integral with, the growth of empire. Thus in *Culture and Imperialism*, Said claims that educational and other considerations of "culture" have been dissociated from the power structures that underpin them:

> It is difficult to connect these different realms, to show the involvements of culture with expanding empires, to make observations about art that preserve its unique endowments and at the same time map its affiliations, but, I submit, we must attempt this, and set art in the earthly, global context. Territory and possessions are at stake, geography and power. Everything about human history is rooted in the earth, which means we must think about habitation, but it has also meant that people have planned to have more territory and therefore must do something about its indigenous residents. At some very basic level, imperialism means thinking about, settling on, controlling land that you do not possess, that is distant, that is lived on and owned by others. For all kinds of reasons it attracts some people and involves others in untold misery. (Said 1994: 67)

Colonialism and imperialism involves, then, the possession of territory by an external political/ military force *as well as the consolidation of such domination by means of cultural representation*. But by implication the territory controlled is equally metaphysical, existential; the territory controlled is that of self-definition and meaning. That said, by its very nature, education must always corrupt innocence; it does so by introducing the child to the world as those who control this vision wish it to be seen. The process is imbued with an implicit or explicit violence by the degree to which such vision is enforced or imposed. This may be by or through forces that are internal or external to the state. *"Internally"*, governments – for example, a totalitarian regime – may inflict such violence on its own people. Powerful *"external"* states may seek either to control territory which is not their own (a classical colonialism increasingly unacceptable). More subtle "invasions" of another's territory are also arguably evidenced by the medium of cultural representation, by economic control, by the manipulation of new technologies – these amongst new imperialisms that we see outlined by Said.

Definitions of ultimate meaning – as important for understanding spirituality as for understanding lived experience in religious or secular terms (Gearon 1997) – are thus crucially linked to the *context* in which the terms of the spiritual are allowed to arise and develop. If temporal and contingent factors naturally impinge on the social and the cultural, the spiritual and the religious, development will invariably be dependent upon the power structures that control the representation and definition of the spiritual life. As vulnerable members of nation states and global society, with rights but less power than adults to ensure their fulfilment, children are potentially subject to even greater physical and cultural force, which I have termed violence. Further, though, I contend that all of our present considerations risk furthering a pattern of historical alienation by the perpetuation of models of the spiritual which originate in control, and even subjugation, *through violence*, of one sort or another.

A Spirit of Resistance – Postcolonial Perspectives: Anti-Colonialism, Nationalism and Global Transnationalism

I want now to make certain parallels between the development of postcolonial thinking which discussions around spirituality in education may find useful to consider. I want to suggest that there are three stages in postcolonial thinking of relevance to this topic of spirituality and state politics. These, I argue, are especially important in the light they throw upon the violence (physical and cultural) which permeates the world, and which becomes accentuated through the lives of the vulnerable, particularly in lives of children. Three overlapping, developmental phases might include the following: first, the radical anti-colonial – especially anti-European and anti-American – rhetoric of Césaire's

([1955] 1997) *Discourse on Colonialism*; second, the radical nationalism of
Frantz Fanon's *The Wretched of the Earth* ([1961] 1997); third, Said's
transnational postcolonial theory from *Orientalism* ([1978] 1995) to
Culture and Imperialism (1994). I want to develop this comparison
through a series of extended and representative readings from Césaire,
Fanon and Said, and then draw some conclusions about their possible
relation to spirituality in education.

Césaire's Discourse on Colonialism

Writing in the 1950s, Césaire sees economic imperialism at the root of
all colonizing, "the baleful projected form of a civilization which, at a
certain point in its history, finds itself obliged, for internal reasons, to
extend to a world scale the competition of antagonistic economies"
(Césaire 1997:75). What Césaire calls the "hypocrisy" of the cultural
justification of conquest, especially notions of cultural superiority, he
claims to be "of a recent date", and that such justification came *after*
prevailing economic interests. He argues that earlier imperialists like
Cortez would not have made claims to be "the harbinger of a superior
order", that "the slavering apologists came later" (Césaire 1997: 75).

Césaire is arguably most devastating in his critique when highlighting the dehumanising effects of colonization upon the colonizer:

> how colonization works to decivilize the colonizer, to brutalize . . . in the
> true sense of the word . . . we must show that every time a head is cut off
> or an eye put out in Vietnam and in France they accept the fact, each time
> a little girl is raped and in France they accept the fact, each time a
> Madagascan is tortured and they accept the fact, civilization acquires
> another's dead weight, a universal regression takes place, a gangrene sets
> in, a centre of infection begins to spread; and that at the end of all these
> treaties that have been violated, all these lies that have been propagated,
> all these punitive expeditions that have been tolerated, all these prisoners
> who have been tied up and "interrogated", all those patriots who have
> been tortured, at the end of all the racial pride that has been encouraged,
> all the boastfulness that has been displayed, a poison has been instilled in
> the veins of Europe and, slowly but surely, the continent proceeds
> towards savagery.
>
> And then one fine day the bourgeoisie is awakened by a terrific reverse
> shock: the Gestapo are busy, the prisons fill up, the torturers around the
> racks invent, refine, discuss.
>
> People are surprised, they become indignant. They say: "How strange!
> But never mind – it's Nazism, it will pass!" And they wait, and they hope;
> and they hide the truth from themselves, that it is barbarism, but the
> supreme barbarism, the crowning barbarism that sums up all daily
> barbarisms; that is Nazism, yes, but that before they were its victims, they
> were its accomplices; that they tolerated Nazism before it was inflicted on

them, that they absolved it, shut their eyes to it, legitimized it, because, until then, it had been applied only to non-European peoples; that they had cultivated Nazism, that they are responsible for it . . . (Césaire 1997: 76–7).

We must here acknowledge, I think, along with Césaire, that Nazism was permeated with a highly cultured and strongly nationalistic spiritual identity, the nation-state providing for ultimate, heroic meaning.

Again, spirituality cannot be seen in either ahistorical or apolitical terms. More contentiously, in a United Kingdom context at least, it is arguable that the 1944 Education Act which called for the education system to be underpinned by spiritual development was enacted at a time not only of allied struggle against Nazism but in the context of the political, historical and *imperial* realities of British Empire. In essence, what can we say about a state that encouraged spiritual development in its schools while retaining an empire abroad?

Frantz Fanon's The Wretched of the Earth

If Fanon's foundational text of postcolonial criticism is more structured than Césaire's, as I have already commented, Fanon – like Césaire a native of French-dominated Martinique – was also Marxist-influenced, with a concern for a proletariat especially disenfranchised by colonialism. Fanon increasingly foresees, though, indeed first conceptualizes (as Said will after him) the importance of culture not only as a tool in the armoury of the oppressor but as a potential weapon in the arsenal of the native struggling for liberation. Fanon identifies three phases in this, and I take Fanon's consideration of the native writer by way of example of indigenous resistance. In the first phase, "the native intellectual['s] . . . inspiration is European and we can easily link up these works with definite trends in the literature of the mother country", the period of "unqualified assimilation", and in the second we find the native disturbed, " . . . childhood . . . memory . . . old legends will be reinterpreted in the light of a borrowed aestheticism and of a conception of the world which was discovered under other skies":

> Finally, in the third phase, which is called the fighting phase, the native . . . will on the contrary shake the people . . . [and] hence comes a fighting literature, a revolutionary literature, and a national literature. During this phase a great many men and women who up till then would never have thought of producing a literary work, now that they find themselves in exceptional circumstances – in prison . . . on the eve of their execution – feel the need to speak to their nation, to compose the sentence which expresses the heart of the people and to become the mouthpiece of a new reality in action. (Fanon 1997: 101–2)

What is distinctive of both Césaire and Fanon is in the legitimation of political violence in the struggle to overcome imperialism as well as the use of a national culture as a means of resistance to colonial oppression.

Edward Said's Culture and Imperialism

Said's work, already alluded to, moves substantially beyond Fanon's and Césaire's. In advocating a *trans*-national understanding of power relations rather than direct political action (though Said as a Palestinian American *has* been involved in direct political comment over a number of decades), Said has even been criticized for indirectly supporting the structures of colonialism itself (Ahmad 1997). Said's position is made clear in the following passage from his *Culture and Imperialism*:

> Much but by no means all of the resistance to imperialism was conducted in the broad context of nationalism. "Nationalism" is a word that still signifies all sorts of undifferentiated things, but it serves me quite adequately to identify the mobilizing force that coalesced into resistance against an alien and occupying empire on the part of peoples possessing a common history, religion, and language. Yet for all its success – indeed because of its success – in ridding many territories of colonial overlords, nationalism remained a deeply problematic enterprise. When it got people out on the streets to march against the white master, nationalism was often led by lawyers, doctors and writers who were partly formed and to some degree produced by the colonial power. The national bourgeoisies and their specialized elites, of which Fanon speaks so ominously, in effect tended to replace the colonial force with a new class-based and ultimately exploitative one, which replicated the old colonial structures in new terms. (Said 1994: 269)

Said's recognition of the subtle transformations of imperialism were necessarily collaborative, "that the cultural horizons of nationalism may be fatally limited by the common history it presumes of colonizer and colonized". Importantly, such transformed determinations of imperialism as "a co-operative venture" have as a "salient trait" the claim to be "an educational movement" which clearly sets out "quite consciously to modernize, develop, instruct, and civilize" (Said 1994: 269).

If Césaire's relevance is in recognizing the barbarity of colonialism and its utterly destructive effects upon non-European cultures and societies, and the importance of Fanon lies in the perceived need for organized *political* and *cultural* resistance, Said presents a way to recognize the destructiveness of imperial injustice *and* seek positive political reconstruction: "Instead of the partial analysis offered by the various national . . . schools, I have been proposing the contrapuntal lines of a global analysis, in which texts and world institutions are seen as working together" (Said 1994: 341).

Yet – and this is where political complacency is to be avoided as much as political naivety is to be exposed – it is a world in which imperialism has been transformed rather than eradicated, a world in which new imperialisms are ever-manifest. Imperialism, after all, Said argues, did not end "once decolonization had set in motion the dismantling of the classical empires". New forms of imperialism "could have as easily been applied to the classical empires during their heyday" and some of these "have an extraordinary dispiriting inevitability, a kind of galloping, engulfing, impersonal, and deterministic quality":

> Accumulation on a world scale; the world capitalist system; the development of underdevelopment; imperialism and dependency, or the structure of dependence; poverty and imperialism: the repertory is well known in economic, political science, history and sociology . . . (Said 1994: 341–2)

It is here that one might contend that only by a consciousness of politics and history that spirituality can begin to facilitate consideration of frameworks of metaphysical meaning from whose contingent roots it can never be fully dissociated. Discussions of spirituality in education today remain in large part both ahistorical and apolitical. Drawing upon related work (Gearon 2001), I suggest a radical agenda: the historical and political as a grounding for the metaphysical and the transcendental – a spirituality of dissent.

A Spirituality of Dissent

The child – and it is always upon children that our adult considerations ultimately impinge – is always the most vulnerable and potentially defenceless member of a global and increasingly globalized society. The historical struggles for territorial and cultural domination infringe the rights of children and, particularly, their place in the world. The vulnerability of the child in developing his or her sense of being is obvious when one considered the wider implications of political instability within the nation states. In any quest, in any spiritual life, the child's sense of meaning – a key element in religious or "secular" spirituality – is dependent upon those who have power to control such development. But any search for meaning is thus also dependent upon other structures – cultural, economic, political – which can facilitate or hamper such a search. Here, inevitably, some voices are naturally more empowered than others in the definition and construction of identity, some cultures have more access to the means of representation – education, mass media, information and communications technology, and so forth. A spirituality of dissent resists easy assimilation into the systems of inequitable cultural representation – locally, nationally and globally – and always presents a challenge to the systems that control such representation; a voice, prophetic if necessary, for the voiceless.

Even more crucially, in a global context, and in greater extremes of personal and political survival, a spirituality of dissent will often have heightened necessity and greater urgency. Thus war, poverty and starvation all mock the prevalence of self-indulgent models of cultural and spiritual development in western educational contexts – the glib reiteration of "awe and wonder", the preoccupation with "self-development" at the expense of community, the occasionally vacuous emphasis on "creativity" (SCAA 1995). Postcolonial theory and criticism both provide insights into the power structures that historically have underpinned and continue to underpin such political realities. Thus, if a spirituality of dissent recognizes political realities as integral to spiritual insight, it does so in the light of and as a challenge to the politics of injustice.

Children, then, as always the most vulnerable members of a globalized community, live in a world permeated with suffering and violence; and, most savagely, it is a pattern of suffering and violence in which adults increasingly co-opt children themselves. If we simply say that suffering and violence are an inevitable part of contingent, historical and political realities, a spiritual of dissent *uses* such "limit situations" to investigate a consciousness of human fragility itself. A spirituality of dissent thus provides a model of spirituality as existential and metaphysical limit – and the quest for meaning within such. Arguably, this limit provides the final context for understanding spirituality. Within these "limit situations", children remain the quintessential symptom of such vulnerability. On the scale of states, postcolonial theory and criticism provide models for understanding such vulnerability in the world community. Postcolonial *theory* provides the framework for developing a consciousness of such conditions, postcolonial *criticism* moves towards an examination of structures that would transform the same conditions.

Yet a spirituality of dissent recognizes too that within an earthly context there can never be a final move to any secure haven. There is no final security. As all religious traditions recognize, this life is a passing show. As Alan Watts (1974) once commented, apart from pain, there is a certain wisdom in insecurity. Nevertheless, in the context of human suffering – particularly the suffering of children – we might be advised to avoid complacency, or worse, a cynical indifference. Educationally we are presented with some fundamental challenges: how does spirituality deal with – and respond to – cultural and political violence, the multiple denial of basic human rights, and how might it appropriate answers from the prophetic traditions that have historically dealt with such questions of social justice?

References

Ahmad, A. 1997: *In Theory: Classes, Nations, Literatures*. In B. Moore-Gilbert, G. Stanton and W. Maley (eds), *Postcolonial Criticism*, London: Longman, 248–72.

Bigger, S. and Brown, E. (eds) 1999: *Spiritual, Moral, Social and Cultural Education: Exploring Values in the Curriculum*, London: David Fulton.

Carr, D. 1996: Rival Conceptions of Spiritual Education, *Journal of the Philosophy of Education* 30 (2), 159–78.

Césaire, A. 1997: Discourse on Colonialism, in B. Moore-Gilbert, G. Stanton and W. Maley (eds), *Postcolonial Criticism*, London: Longman, 73–91.

Coles, R. 1995: *The Spiritual Life of Children*, London: Harper Collins.

Copley, T. 1997: *Teaching Religion: Fifty Years of Religious Education in England and Wales*, Exeter: Exeter University Press.

—— (2000) *Spiritual Development in the State School*, Exeter, Exeter University Press.

Erricker, C. 1998: Spiritual Confusion: a critique of current educational policy in England and Wales, *International Journal of Children's Spirituality* 3 (1), 51–63.

Fanon, F. [1967] 1997:The Wretched of the Earth, in B. Moore-Gilbert, G. Stanton and W. Maley (eds) *Postcolonial Criticism*, London: Longman, 91–111.

Gandhi, L. 1997: *Postcolonial Theory*, New York: Columbia University Press.

Gearon, L. 1997: What's the Story?: Spirituality and Writing, *International Journal of Children's Spirituality* 2 (2), 41–52.

—— 2001, forthcoming: A Spirituality of Dissent: Religion, Culture and Postcolonial Criticism, *International Journal of Children's Spirituality*.

Harlow, B. and Carter, M. (eds) 1999: *Imperialism and Orientalism: A Documentary Sourcebook*, Oxford: Blackwell.

Hastings, A. (ed.) 1999: *A World History of Christianity*, London: Cassell.

Moore-Gilbert, B. Stanton, G. and Maley, W. (eds) 1997: *Postcolonial Criticism*, London: Longman.

Priestley, J. 1996: Hockerill Foundation Lecture. London.

Rorty, R. 1989: *Contingency, Irony and Solidarity*, Cambridge: Cambridge University Press.

Said, E. 1994: *Culture and Imperialism*, London: Vintage.

—— [1978] 1995: *Orientalism: Western Conceptions of the Orient*, Harmondsworth: Penguin.

SCAA (1995) *Spiritual and Moral Development*, London: SCAA.

United Nations 2000 [1996]: *Impact of Armed Conflict on Children, Report of Graca Machel, Expert of the Secretary-General of the United Nations*, Geneva: United Nations.

United Nations 2000a [1998]: *Report of the United Nations High Commissioner for Human Rights*, Geneva: United Nations.

Watts, A. 1974: *The Wisdom of Insecurity*, London: Rider.

Wright, A. 1998: *Spirituality Pedagogy: A Survey, Critique and Reconstruction of Contemporary Spiritual Education in England and Wales*, Oxford: Culham.

—— 1999: *Discerning the Spirit: Teaching Spirituality in the Religious Education Classroom*, Oxford: Culham.

Chapter 12

"Theory of mind" or "Theory of the soul?" The Role of Spirituality in Children's Understanding of Minds and Emotions

SANDRA LEANNE BOSACKI

THE holistic perspective recognizes that human development occurs in at least two spheres: the personal, and the spiritual or universal. Such a perspective envisions the child as a human, intentional being where "earners are not only minds or knowers but bundles of affects, individuals, personalities, earners of livings . . . possessors of private lives" (Schwab 1969: 9). During the past decade, the inner world of the child has become of great interest to both psychologists and educators. Although the concept of spirituality consists of both the inner or mental world and the outer, or social, the two fields of developmental psychology and holistic education remain surprisingly separate. Although schooling is a moral enterprise, theories of sociomoral development still emphasize the cognitive rather than the experiential or spiritual. Cognitivism remains valued as the "truth" whereas we are not encouraged to trust our spiritual selves that include our intuition and emotions (Torevell 2000).

This chapter discusses ways in which to address this lack of communication between the fields of developmental cognitive science and holistic education. Building on the Japanese proverb that states "an idea is a sound from the heart" (Barbieri 1995), this chapter explores how educators and psychologists can learn from each other to promote children's spiritual well-being. As mainstream education in both Europe and North America continues to be driven by increasingly cognitive and neuropsychological models, how can we help to reform the educational system to address all needs of the child – including the emotional and the spiritual? How can spirituality serve as a web that interconnects educational initiatives such as student values, moral and socioemotional development, experiential education, health and wellness, and community service? In this chapter I will attempt to answer such questions within the context of "theory of mind" research (the study of children's understanding of mental states in both self and others).

Thus, my goals are twofold: (1) to address the lack of communication between developmental psychologists and holistic educators within the framework of ongoing sociocognitive research with Canadian pre-adolescents; and (2) to bridge the gap between theory and practice with educational strategies that can be used to nourish the child's mind, body and soul. Borrowing from arts and language education, I also consider the educational implications of a spiritual education. I conclude with a challenge for educators: How can schools nourish children's minds and souls? How can schools foster and develop students' appetites for learning, for life in general? Why do some children lose their appetite for learning and perhaps life, what aspects of schooling deaden this appetite?

Cognitive Psychology (Theory of Mind) and Spirituality (Theory of Soul)

What does it mean to have a spirit, or to have a spiritual experience? Like Hardy (1966), in this chapter I do not attempt to define the term spirituality. The majority of research suggests that the term deals with connections and relations to ourselves, others, and the world around us. It refers to both a sense of interiority or an inner reality and a sense of being connected beyond one's own self, connected to something "greater" (Watson 2000). Moreover, in line with other holistic thinkers, I do not define spiritual in terms of any faith tradition, I mean, "the ancient and abiding human quest for connectedness with something larger and more trustworthy than our egos – with our own souls, with one another, with the worlds of history and nature, with the invisible winds of the spirit, with the mystery of being alive" (Palmer 1999: 6).

According to Paley (1999) the spiritual event is the act itself, the story, and the response of the listener. All spiritual events share the common notions of a victory for goodness, for connectedness to others and a new perspective gained in the struggle to overcome loneliness. God does not have to be mentioned. Although spirituality can contain a religious element, religion is not necessary and is often not found within people's subjective definitions. Spirituality can stand for our lifelong search for meaningfulness and purpose in the world. In short, it refers to how we make sense of our selves and the universe (Hutchison 1998). Thus spirituality and stories about our self are one and the same. As Paley states, "Like a child, without a story I cannot explain myself" (1999: 4).

The storying theme of spirituality also highlights the fundamental relational nature of spirituality. Working from this relational notion of spirituality, I suggest that a sense of self and spiritual awareness are one and the same. Spirituality is the feeling of genuine *connectedness*, not only with others and nature/universe, but also with *oneself* (see, for example, Miller 1993). Whether the spiritual dimension is contained within us, or whether it transcends us, is irrelevant. A spiritual dimension includes an awareness of the "genuine" or the kindness and goodness in ourselves and others (Paley 1999; Plunkett 1990). In turn, this awareness enables us to open our hearts and minds to spiritual insight and gives us grounds for hope and fulfilment. In Paley's search for the meaning of a spiritual event, she ponders that if she experiences a "moment of truth" (1999 27) or a glimpse into the nature of human expectations – is this a spiritual event, or simply a deeply emotionally moving, human event? She continues to wonder whether a spiritual experience may be akin to offering new life to a wandering soul. Perhaps this may help to explain why many writers claim that young "children have a natural sense of the self and the spiritual in that they are more connected to the genuine" in themselves and others (e.g., Coles 1990; Donaldson 1992; Hay and Nye 1998). Findings from my own research support Paley's observation that children may be more wise about the nature of kindness than we think they are (for example see Bosacki 1998a, b).

Spirituality in Preadolescents

Both educators and researchers are becoming increasingly interested in exploring the question of whether or not Canadian adolescents are lacking in spiritual awareness. If they are, when does this disconnection occur and why? How can we study this and subsequently intervene to create programmes that foster a spiritual dimension? How can we as educators and researchers, concerned with the spiritual growth of children, prevent such attitudes from developing in the first place? Why does conventional schooling encourage children to be silent about their "hunches" and hide their inner life? How can we as educators truly believe that this will foster a sense of well-being and fulfilment later on in life?

To answer the question of how schooling, teachers and books have become separated or disengaged from spiritual awareness, a fruitful area includes a focus on preadolescents. Researchers could then explore the question of what happens to a child's sense of the genuine and spiritual between young childhood and adolescence. From a psychological perspective, early adolescence (nine/ten – twelve/ thirteen years) is recognized as a pivotal time in all aspects of development, including cognitive reflexivity (e.g., Piaget 1963), self-concept formation (e.g., Harter 1999) and interpersonal relations (e.g., Rosenberg 1989; Selman 1980). Despite recognition of this complex and multifaceted developmental milestone, a holistic approach to exploring the links between self and social understanding, and the development of spirituality, remains to be taken. Thus, research needs to explore children's and adolescents' perspectives of complex concepts such as sense of self and spirituality. Although I did not assess children's perceptions of spirituality directly, given that spirituality and self are inextricably intertwined, my past and ongoing research involves listening to preadolescents' voices on aspects of the self, including their thoughts and emotions. In the sections below I describe this research, followed by how my findings may have implications for holistic education.

Research on the Connection between Cognition and Emotion: Preadolescents' Perceptions

The complex nexus among spirituality, morality and language/literacy are surprisingly understudied, despite the fact that such interconnections have immense implications for all aspects of preadolescent development. Few studies have investigated directly preadolescents' perceptions of spirituality and their spiritual understanding. From a psychological perspective, past research on children's religious and spiritual understanding has focused mainly on the *cognitive* understanding of the concepts (e.g. Barrett in press; Long, Elkind and Spilka 1967; Goldman 1964). Recent research has shown that preschool-aged children are not able to understand the concept of prayer or God's ability to perceive things (Barrett and Newman 1999; Phelps and Woolley 1999). It is not until the age of four or five that children claim to know what it means to pray and have done so themselves. At this age, children are beginning to understand the mentalistic nature of prayer, specifically that knowledge of God and thinking are essential elements of prayer.

Given that the concept of prayer involves mentalistic elements of thought and belief, the studies on children's understanding of religion are in line with other "Theory of Mind" research. Studies from this burgeoning field of child social–cognitive development document that by three to five years of age children clearly differentiate between mental and physical entities, and fantasy and reality (e.g., Wellman and

D. Estes 1986; Woolley and Wellman 1993). Similarly, false belief tasks demonstrate that young children have the ability to attribute mental states to self and others. That is, by age five children are able to understand that other people have mental states such as beliefs and intentions that influence our behaviour (e.g., see Wellman 1990).

In addition to studying the process and development of religious and spiritual concepts in children, researchers have recently begun to study the influence of parental religious beliefs on children's pretend play and fantasy life. More specifically, Taylor and Carlson's (2000) gleaned empirical evidence shows how religion-based attitudes influence adults' understanding of children's imaginary companions. Based on cross-cultural ethnographic evidence, Taylor and Carlson found that religious ideology contributes to substantial variation in adult reaction to and interpretation of childhood fantasy activities. In general, Taylor and Carlson found that there was a tendency to emphasize negative interpretations of fantasy behaviour based on religious beliefs. Such findings suggest that further systematic investigation is needed to explore how parents' religious beliefs may influence their children's sociomoral and affective development.

Some of my own research may also help to shed light on the connections between concepts of self and spirituality. In one of my recent studies, to better understand how Canadian preadolescents perceive themselves and understand self-knowledge, I interviewed 128 preadolescent girls and boys (64 girls, 64 boys aged between eleven and twelve years) on various issues including their perceived sense of self-worth. During individual interviews, I asked them to explain what was the "main reason" why they said particular self-judgements (see Bosacki 1998a, b; 1997; Bosacki and Astington 1999).

One specific question may be especially relevant to the notion of spirituality and an awareness of the genuine. To assess an overall "global sense of self-worth" or general sense of happiness and well-being, students were asked if they were happy being the way that they were, or if they wished they were different? Although the majority of students claimed that they were happy with the way that they were and did not wish to be someone else, many could not articulate *why* they were happy (51 per cent of the children). The most common responses included, "I don't know why I am happy – I just am"; or "I just wish that I was someone else." The second most common response (25 per cent) referred to a social aspect of their lives (e.g., "I'm happy because I have lots of friends" or "I wish that I had more friends and was more popular.")

From a developmental perspective, it is interesting to note that despite the fact these students had the *metacognitive* ability to reflect on their statements, the majority of them were unable to articulate or reflect on their self-statements. Does the *affective* dimension of learning and thought play a hindering role? Would the children have had the same level of difficulty if they had been asked to explain why they chose their particular answers on the standard academic tasks? In relation to the different types of knowledge (objective and subjective) and the link to spirituality, these findings suggest that perhaps the quality of meta-cognition may differ according to how personal the topic is. That is, perhaps it is more difficult to reflect on your own thinking about *your-self* as opposed to thinking about others or inanimate subjects. Could it be that too much reflection (i.e., over-reflection) can impoverish rather than enrich spiritual and self development?

Future Research Directions

In sum, a great more needs to be known about children's understanding of a "spiritual self". Multidisciplinary studies could permit fruitful investigation into the links between cognitive and emotional develop-ment, and how this plays a role in a preadolescent's developing spiritual awareness. Further systematic research is needed on not only the growth of spiritual awareness during preadolescence, we also need to explore its connections with other aspects of psychological under-standing (i.e. self-knowledge) and what it is influenced by (antecedents and consequences).

Spirituality and Education

According to John Dewey, education, growth and inquiry are synony-mous, each is identified as "a constant reorganizing or restructuring of experience" (Dewey 1916: 82). Dewy further claims, "when it is said that education is development, everything depends upon how development is conceived" (Dewey 1916: 54). Educators and researchers interested in the link between scholarship and spirituality need to examine, analyze and reflect upon such issues as: (1) how developmental psychology relates to teaching and learning; (2) the interconnections between culture, mind, self, and education; (3) the process of "schooling minds" in relation to specific school curricula. In addition, educators need to examine how the process of human development involves the whole child in a dynamically changing set of cultural contexts (including the spiritual, socioemotional and moral aspects). Spirituality in education, needs to go beyond knowledge acquisition and enter the realms of personal meaning and purpose.

Nourishment for the Soul: Creating a Spiritual School Culture

Before educators can implement, in a true authentic manner, holistic, educational activities, they first need to examine and reflect upon their own personal philosophies and connections. To address the issue of spirituality in education, educators need to approach education from a holistic perspective. Such a perspective includes the study of both the cognitive (e.g., perspective taking, emotional understanding) and affective/moral/spiritual (e.g., self-concept, emotional experience). Furthermore, teaching and learning is viewed as a transformational process, one that is co-collaborative, and cyclic.

Given the notion that learning and teaching are transformational experiences, education can be viewed as a learning journey or an adventure, within which students will act as "co-travelling partners". As educators, we need to act as mentors and role models for our students. We need to invite students to challenge both themselves and others as they become actively engaged with the school curricula and transform themselves and the world with their new knowledge. Although the educator's role is to provide direction, resources and educational formats to facilitate student learning, ultimately it will be the children's own commitment to their learning that will determine their success.

In addition to developing their own "living educational theories" (Whitehead 2000), educators need to reflect upon and share their stories about instances in which they have experienced spiritual moments in their classes (Laurence 1999). As Pope John Paul II claims, "without wonder, humans would lapse into deadening routine and little by little would become incapable of a life which is genuinely personal" (1998: 7). To further develop an understanding of the connections between spirituality and scholarship, educators need to reflect upon the moments of meaning in their own learning and teaching. As Paley (1999) claims in her observations of her kindergarten classroom, the spiritual event is the act itself, the story, and the response of the listener. All spiritual events share the common notions of a victory for goodness, for connectedness to others and a new perspective is gained on the struggle to overcome loneliness.

As educators engage in this ongoing journey of self-reflection and contemplation, they can create an inviting, nourishing learning environment in their classroom. Such an environment will encourage children to feel comfortable as part of a "learning community" and thus promote feeling of connection with others. In line with Goldberger et al. (1996), educators need to create an inviting, "connected classroom", one in which students feel psychologically secure enough to let their authentic or spiritual voices be heard.

Schools need to become sacred places that offer possibilities for wonder, enchantment, caring and compassion. Conceived as a sanctuary for learning (Klein 2000), such classrooms can invite the use of imagination and fantasy and focus on renewal and transformation. Sacred classrooms are psychologically safe, where children can feel secure and trust in the teacher who is fully present in the moment or "mindful". Through means of critical reflection, awareness and renewal, students will be encouraged to engage in meaningful dialogue with both self and others concerning the complex issues of the links between mind, heart, soul and education.

Practices in Holistic Education: Educational Strategies to Reconnect the Mind, Body, Spirit and Earth

Holistic education cannot be reduced to any single technique. It is the art of cultivating meaningful human relationships; it is a dialectic between teachers and learners within a caring community. The focus is on authenticity, dialogue, connection and the mutual co-creation. Thus, as educators who wish to promote spiritual education, we must begin with openness, open up to ourselves, feel our experience, and explore the inner landscape of our lives. Although openness begins as an inner, personal discipline, it has the potential to evolve into a dynamic, interactive experience. Our own openness can collapse or dissolve boundaries between ourselves, others and the world. By sharing with our students this quality of openness or "presence", we can play a crucial role in combatting the materialism of contemporary culture. Within learning communities, educators can model the practices of openness, awareness, tolerance, respect and kindness. To bridge the divide between theory and practice, below I outline some ideas for holistic educational activities based on promoting the connection between self (mind/body; emotion/cognition, rational/intuitive), community (social relations), and earth/universe.

Self-Connections

Researchers and educators have become increasingly interested in the role that caring and affect play in children's learning. According to Goldstein (1997), teaching with love involves the ability to teach with joy and wonder, from the heart as well as the mind. The ability of the teacher to remain in wonder and constantly learn from the child is what distinguishes the concept of "education" from "schooling".

Borrowing from Nodding's (1984) definition of caring as the ability to step out of one's own personal perspective and into the other's, Goldstein defines loving teaching as the marriage between care, connection and concern. However, despite the strong theoretical claims linking a caring teacher–student relationship to school experience, there has been a lack of systematic research within the context of early childhood education.

Given that teaching with love appears to be at the heart of holistic or transformative education, it was surprising to find few references to educational programs that embrace the principles of holism and spirituality (e.g., Miller 1993). For example, Montessori Schools provide a model of "loving education" by advocating the concept of a "school home" rather than a "school house". Similarly, we also need to draw on Rudolph Steiner's Waldorf schools that promote the aspect of wonder and mystery in learning. Steiner (1976) rejected the notion of the mind/body dualism and emphasized that physical and psychological growth are integrated and mutually complementary processes. Waldorf education (Steiner 1976) provides an explicit example of an educational programme that balances notions of spirituality and teacherly love with an intellectually rigorous curriculum.

Building on the notion that a "spiritual voice" reflects the ability to speak all of one's mind with all of one's heart (Bosacki 1998a), the use of a language arts-based program including personal story-telling, mythology and self-narration (i.e., journal writing) can be a valuable vehicle for self and spiritual development in children. For example, Drake's (1992) Story Model represents a interdisciplinary approach by providing a "generic curriculum" that can be used to study a particular theme in its life context. Once a theme has been chosen by the students (e.g., food), the story model is used to co-create a new story by incorporating the student's and the teacher's personal, cultural, and global or universal story. With Drake's Story Model stories can help children to create a personal guide/muse or inner curriculum to foster personal integration and cultural connection.

The use of language is not the only method to inject spirituality in the classroom. In particular, some emotional and spiritual experiences may become distorted, or misinterpreted through writing and/or verbalization (Sunderland and Engleheart 1993; Wierzbicka 1989). In contrast, more accurate representations of one's inner landscape may be obtained non-verbally through the use of images and/or movement. Holistic educational activities that aim to promote spiritual development non-verbally may also foster children's ability to self-comfort and learn to respect and trust themselves, including relaxation techniques, visualization, art therapy, play therapy, psychodrama and mask-making, etc. For example, to strengthen self-connections, guided imagery and group/classroom meditation can be used to promote the concept of mindfulness or the ability to be aware in the present (Goleman 1995; Miller 1993).

Social Connections

Social connections can be further strengthened by adapting the ecological, spiritual and global perspective towards the self and education. An ecological approach emphasizes our communality with all living things and encourages children to see themselves as part of the "bigger picture" and as an integral part of the global family (e.g., Hutchison 1998). Regarding community connections, children can take part in helping out in preschools, hospitals for sick children, retirement homes. Such connections would foster an understanding of compassion and kindness that transcends the stereotypes of "age".

The integration of indigenous people's literature such as the indigenous concept of the medicine wheel (e.g., Shilling 1986) could provide the basis for various discussions on other "cultural stories" (Drake 1992). Exposure to such stories can help to develop the notion of "spiritual literacy" and can assist children in creating and adapting their own, new personal stories by recognizing the numerous global stories. For example, during a group discussion on North America's obsession with aesthetic perfection, children can question why disordered eating is rarely found in underdeveloped or Third World countries.

Children in today's society may be especially susceptible to this biased way of thinking through their constant exposure to conflicting sociocultural messages. They are exposed to the paradox of school's overemphasis on intellect and society's obsession with the physical body and material objects. For example, a syndrome of self-concept disorders – including anxiety, depression, and disordered eating (anxious somatic depression) – has recently been argued to be the result of the "cost of competence" in young women who aspire to achieve academically in a society that values woman's bodies over their minds (Silverstine and Perlick 1995). Accordingly, programmes based on holistic and transformative educational principles that emphasize personal integration and sociocultural and ecological awareness need to be implemented in elementary school to promote body/mind unity.

Ecological and Universal Connections

An ecological approach to education that emphasizes a "world core curriculum" can be used to encourage children and adolescents to foster and maintain a respect and caring for the earth and natural events that are beyond the realm of the earth (universe). To help young adolescents see themselves as an integral part of the world and universe, physical and creative activities that deal with nature and the environment can be introduced. For example, young adolescents can care for a garden and grow their own organic vegetables. The food can be used in creative cooking classes in the classroom. In addition to caring for plants and gardens, adolescents can care for animals as well. For instance, classrooms can have a class pet (as so often done with primary school children), or adopt a pet at the local humane society and monitor its development.

In sum, the activities mentioned above may encourage children to challenge, question and redefine cultural stereotypes and expectations. Such activities may encourage learners to replace dualistic thinking with a more spiritual, global, holistic perspective that views life as a web or a story, where learning is dependent upon collaborative participation (Vygotsky 1978; Noddings 1984).

Conclusions

Given the problem of spirituality in education, how can schools nourish children's minds and souls? How do we prevent schools from over-intellectualization, which imprisons spirituality? How can we instil that magic, that feeling or experience of wonder and appetite for learning in our classrooms (and in ourselves)? If connectedness is a crucial aspect of spirituality, then what spirituality threatens most is the inherent fragmentation in our educational structures (Laurence 1999). Thus, an educational approach that embraces holism must be paramount.

In short, spirituality in education is about the connection among souls. Authentic, holistic education occurs only when there is a connection among humans as whole beings – both hearts and minds. We need to "awaken" children's spiritual awareness and their appetite for learning and life. We cannot allow them to become "disengaged" from others around them. Psychological isolation is the most terrifying experience that humans can endure. Educational programmes and educators that promote "spiritual literacy" provide the best coping strategies we can offer that will help to protect our children from becoming psychological isolates. Such holistic programs can thus help to ensure that children develop into resilient adults.

As cautioned by other holistic educators (Glazer 1999; Kessler 2000), in the midst of this technological boom, we cannot forget that our purpose as educators is to assist in the formation of better people and the connection among souls, not higher achievement scores. The enrichment of the human spirit is something that cannot be measured by a computer or test score. As we embark upon the twenty-first century, the need is great for educators to co-create a "curriculum of hope" that teaches children to learn to listen, love and accept not only themselves, but also life itself. To conclude, the ultimate goal of all holistic educators should be to foster spiritual literacy within the context of self-fulfilment. By acknowledging the spiritual aspect of education, educators can stimulate and satisfy both their own and their students' appetite for learning and life.

References

Barbeiri, M. 1995: *Sounds from the heart: Learning to listen to girls*, Portsmouth, NH: Hernemann.

Barrett, J. in press: Do children experience God like adults? Retracing the development of god concepts. In: J. Andresen (ed.), *Keeping religion in mind: Cognitive perspectives on religious experience*, Cambridge: Cambridge University Press.

Barrett, J. and Newman, R. 1999: Knowing what God knows: Understanding the importance of background knowledge for interpreting static and active visual displays, Poster presented at the *First Annual Meeting for the Cognitive Development Society*, Chapel Hill, N C.

Bosacki, S. 1998a: Is silence really golden? The role of spiritual voice in folk pedagogy and folk psychology, *International Journal of Children's Spirituality* 3, 109–21.

—— 1998b: *Theory of mind in preadolescence: Connections among social understanding, self-concept, and social relations*, unpublished doctoral dissertation, University of Toronto.

—— 1997: Reconnecting the brain and the body: Holistic education for preadolescents, *Holistic Education Review* 10, 53–60.

Bosacki, S. and Astington, J. 1999: Theory of mind and in preadolescence: Relations between social understanding and social competence, *Social Development* 8, 237–55.

Bruner, J 1996: *The Culture of Education*, Cambridge, MA: Harvard University Press.

Coles, R. 1990: *The Spiritual Life of Children*, Boston, MA: Houghton Mifflin Company.

—— 1997: *The Moral Intelligence of Children: How To Raise a Moral Child*, New York: Plume.

Dewey, J. 1916: *Democracy and education: An introduction to the philosophy of education*, New York: Collier Books.

Donaldson, M. 1992: *Human Minds: An Exploration*, Harmondsworth, UK: Allen Lane.

Drake, S. 1992: A novel approach to integrated curriculum, *Orbit* 23, 5–7.

Glazer, S. (ed.) 1999: *The Heart of Learning: Spirituality in Education*, New York, NY: Penguin Putnam.

Goldberger, N., Tarule, J., Clinchy, B. and Belenky, M. 1996: *Knowledge,*

Differences, and Powers: Essays Inspired by Women's Ways of Knowing, New York: Basic Books.

Goldman, R. 1964: *Religious Thinking from Childhood to Adolescence*, London: Routledge & Kegan Paul.

Goldson, B. 1997: "Childhood": An Introduction to Historical and Theoretical Analyses. In: P. Scranton (ed.), *"Childhood" in "Crisis"?* London, UCL Press, 1–27.

Goldstein, L. 1997: *Teaching with Love: A Feminist Approach to Early Childhood*, New York, NY: Peter Lang.

Goleman, D. 1995: *Emotional Intelligence*, New York: Bantam.

Harter, S. 1985: *Manual for the Self-Perception Profile for Children (SPPC)*, Denver, CO: University of Denver.

Harter, S. 1999: *The Construction of the Self: A Developmental Perspective*, New York, NY: Guilford Press.

Hardy, A. 1966: *The Divine Flame*, London: Collins.

Hay, D. with Nye, R. 1998: *The Spirit of the Child*, London: Fount.

Hutchison, D. 1998: *Growing up Green: Education for Ecological Renewal*, New York: Teachers College Press.

John Paul II 1998: *Faith and Reason*, London: Catholic Truth Society.

Kessler, R. 2000: *The Soul of Education: Helping Students Find Connection, Compassion, and Character at School*, Alexandria, VA: ASCD.

Klein, S. 2000: Curriculum as Sacred Space, *Encounter* 13, 5–10.

Laurence, P. 1999: Can Religion and Spirituality Find a Place in Higher Education? *About Campus* 6, Nov.–Dec.

Long, D., Elkind, D. and Spilka, B. 1967: The Child's Conception of Prayer, *Journal for the Scientific Study of Religion* 6, 101–9.

Miller, J. 1993: *The Holistic Curriculum*, Toronto, ON: OISE Press.

Noddings, N. 1984: *Caring: A Feminine Approach to Ethics and Moral Education*, Berkeley, CA: University of California Press.

Paley, V. 1999: *The Kindness of Children*, Cambridge, MA: Harvard University Press.

Palmer, P. 1999: Evoking the Spirit, *Educational Leadership*, January, 6–11.

Phelps, K. and Woolley, J. 1999: Connections Between Mind and Matter: Young Children's Understanding of Prayer, Poster presented at the *Biennial Meeting of the Society for Research in Child Development*, April, Albuquerque, NM.

Piaget, J. 1963: *The Origins of Intelligence in Children*, New York, NY: Norton.

Plunkett, D. 1990: *Secular and Spiritual Values: Grounds for Hope in Education*, London: Routledge.

Priestley, J. 2000: Moral and Spiritual Growth. In: J. Mills, and R. Mills (eds), *Childhood Studies: A Reader in Perspectives of Childhood*, London: Routledge, 113–28.

Rosenberg, M. 1989: *Society and the Adolescent Self-Image* (revised edn), Middletown, CT: Wesleyan University Press.

Schwab, J. 1969: The Practical: A Language for Curriculum, *School Review* 78, 1–23.

Selman, R. 1980: *The Growth of Interpersonal Understanding*, New York: Academic Press.

Shilling, A. 1986: *The Ojibway Dream*, Montreal: Tundra.

Silverstein, B. and Perlick, D. 1995: *The Cost of Competence: Why Inequality Causes Depression, Eating Disorders, and Illness in Women*, New York: Oxford University Press.

Steiner, R. 1976: *Education of the Child in the Light of Anthroposophy*, (trans. G. Adams and M. Adams), London: Rudolph Steiner Press.

Sunderland, M. and Engleheart, P. 1993: *Draw on Your Emotions: Creative Ways to Explore, Express, and Understand Important Feelings*, UK: Winslow Press.

Taylor, M. and Carlson, S. 2000: The Influence of Religious Beliefs on Parental Attitudes About Children's Fantasy Behaviour. In: K. Rosengren, C. Johnson and P. Harris (eds), *Imagining the Impossible: The Development of Magical Scientific, and Religious Thinking in Contemporary Society*, Cambridge: Cambridge University Press, 247–68.

Torevell, D. 2000: Acting Out of Affections: Embodiment, Morality and (Post) Modernity, *International Journal of Children's Spirituality* 5, 27–36.

Vygotsky, L. 1978: *Mind in Society*, Cambridge, MA: Harvard University Press.

Watson, J. 2000: Whose model of spirituality should be used in the spiritual development of school children? *International Journal of Children's Spirituality* 5, 91–101.

Whitehead, J. 2000: How Do I Improve My Practice? Creating and Legitimating an Epistemology of Practice, *Reflective Practice* 1, 91–104.

Wierzbicka, A.: 1989: Soul and Mind: Linguistic Evidence for Ethnopsychology and Cultural History, *American Anthropologist* 91, 41–58.

Wellman, H. 1990: *The Child's Theory of Mind*, Cambridge, MA: MIT Press.

Wellman, H. and Estes, D. 1986: Early Understanding of Mental Entities: A Re-examination of Childhood Realism, *Child Development* 57, 910–23.

Woolley, J. and Wellman, H. 1993: Origin and Truth: Young Children's Understanding of Imaginary Mental Representations, *Child Development* 64, 1–17.

Chapter 13

The Prospects of Spirituality in a Globalized, Technologized World

WONG PING HO

IT has often been observed that spirituality is becoming increasingly prominent as one of popular culture's preoccupations. At the same time the topic of spirituality has also featured more conspicuously in academic discourse. What does this strong interest in spirituality signify? Are more people now enjoying spiritual enlightenment? This chapter takes the contrary view that this increased concern for spirituality is not due to the robustness of people's spiritual health, but rather indicates that the spiritual situation is in such an unsatisfactory state that people are forced to take note of it. If this view is at least partially valid, the question then is to describe and make sense of this unsatisfactory spiritual state of contemporary society.

Categories of Spiritual Sensitivity

Despite the caution that "attempted definition [of the spiritual] is not only futile but totally counter-productive" because "it is a characteristic of spirit and the spiritual that it is dynamic" (Priestley 1985: 114), discussion would be difficult without certain definite indications of what "spirituality" is taken to mean for the present purposes. The characterization of spirituality I adopt, which I readily recognize from my own felt experience, and which I hope will be similarly recognizable by my readers, is Hay's "categories of spiritual sensitivity": awareness sensing, mystery sensing and value sensing (Hay 1995; Hay with Nye 1998). Awareness sensing refers to a meta-awareness, "being aware of one's awareness" (Hay with Nye 1998: 60), and is "characterized by a sharply focused attention to the here-and-now of one's experience" (Hay 1995: 19). Hay provides the following examples of such a heightened awareness as labelled by different writers (Hay with Nye 1998):

1   **The here-and-now experience**: a complete immersion into the experience of the present moment, being intensely committed to the immediacy of the here-and-now in its full concreteness;
2   **Tuning**: a complete "resonance" or "being in tune" with something outside of oneself, such as a musical performance or nature;
3   **Flow**: a total absorption in the performance of a task, with the feeling that the activity, rather than the performer, is managing itself;
4   **Focusing**: the "bodily felt sense" of any experience (Hay 1995: 19), an expression of the wisdom of the body.

Mystery sensing involves the "awareness of aspects of our life experience that are *in principle* incomprehensible" (Hay with Nye 1998: 66; italics in original). Such mysteries transcend our everyday experience which is concerned with those aspects of reality that are within our comprehension and possibly our control (or so we think). They arouse in us the feelings of wonder and awe. Since they are beyond the known, obvious and comprehended aspects of reality, their conception and investigation require imagination.

Value sensing is the direct perception of value, accompanied by intense emotions, before any intellectual appraisal of the pros and cons. In this sense, value and emotion are one. As extremes on the emotional spectrum, delight and despair are often associated with value sensing. Two other "dimensions of value sensing" mentioned by Hay are the sense of ultimate goodness, that everything is all right, and the sense of meaning.

Hay and Nye highlight the theme of "raised awareness" across all three categories of spiritual sensitivity, and the transcendence of ordinary experience this raised awareness implies (Hay with Nye 1998: 74). Based on her conversations with ordinary school children, Nye further concluded "that 'relational consciousness' is a common thread" tying together their spirituality (Hay with Nye 1998: 118). Such relational consciousness encompasses child–God consciousness, child–people consciousness, child–world consciousness, and child–self consciousness. In the following discussion, I will take the spiritual sensitivities and relational consciousness described by Hay and Nye as unproblematic and reflect on how some of these fare in contemporary social life. I admit that these reflections are speculative, and are subject to disconfirmation by empirical evidence.

Perpetual Distractions

In my childhood, I used to gaze at the sky, feeling strongly its unfathomable depth. It looked as if the sky would go on forever into the
distance. But when I thought about it, it seemed that nothing could go
on forever in space. It must stop somewhere. But then there must also
be something beyond where it stopped. And so on, ad infinitum.
Neither case seemed plausible. That was the time when I had not yet
heard of television.

You could imagine my joy when, some years later, I read that Popper,
in his own childhood:

> could neither imagine that space was finite (for what, then, was outside
> it?) nor that it was infinite . . . The problem is, of course, part (the spatial
> part) of Kant's first antinomy, and it is (especially if the temporal part is
> added) a serious and still unsolved philosophical problem . . . (Popper
> 1976: 15–16)

Further, I found that Kant once declared: "Two things fill the mind
with ever new and increasing admiration and reverence, the more often
and more steadily one reflects on them: *the starry heavens above me and
the moral law within me*" (Kant 1997: 133; italics in original). I wondered
if Kant had not stumbled upon his first antinomy while gazing at the
starry heavens, just as I had done in my own childish way. In my childhood idleness I also troubled (literally) myself with thoughts of life and
death, identity, dreaming and wakefulness, and time, and similar cases
of finding like-minded company through reading occurred more than
once.

By recalling this I do not mean to boast of my precocity. Despite an
undeniable ego-boosting element to these experiences, they were at the
same time humbling, showing that these "mystery sensing", "metaphysical" thoughts were common. Surely the starry heavens above and
the moral law within have continued to fill people's minds with wonder
and awe, to nurture our spirituality, then as now? However, we need to
consider the condition necessary for this to happen as indicated in
Kant's remark: to experience and to renew this wonder and awe, we
need to reflect on these two things (and other things that he did not
mention[1]) often and steadily. Whether we do so depends on whether we
have the time, and given the time, whether we have the necessary
mindset, to engage in these reflections.

As a start, we may note that "Most people say that their spiritual
awareness occurs typically when they are alone" (Hay with Nye 1998:
16). Storr suggests that, to foster children's imagination (a dimension of
mystery sensing), "we should ensure that our children, when they are

old enough to enjoy it, are given time and opportunity for solitude" (1997: 17). He believes that the capacity to be alone is a valuable resource which facilitates "the maintenance of contact with the inner world of the imagination" (1997: 202). Relevant to what Nye calls child–world consciousness, he notes that "Many creative adults have left accounts of childhood feelings of mystical union with Nature", and such moments occur "chiefly when the child is on its own" (1997: 17). We could presume the state of solitude is also in a sense a largely idle state. Thus solitude and silence are related states. Marcandonatou observes that silence has been a very common practice throughout history and across the world "as an aid to worship and/or a method of understanding the working of one's mind" (1998: 310). He explains, "The most important aspect of silence is . . . a listening with one's heart, one's whole being. By listening in this way, one opens to the mystery and meaning of personal existence" (1998: 310). The themes arising from his research into people's experience of being silent closely echo Hay and Nye's dimensions of spiritual sensitivity.

Do people today have the room and the necessary mental disposition for solitude, idleness and silence? In Hong Kong, a common sight in public places is people talking on their mobile phone. Often the first thing a bus passenger does after settling down is to make a telephone call. My observation is that often such calls are not made out of necessity but just to kill time, because people loathe being idle. A famous Chinese scholar-official, Ouyang Xiu, once confessed that inspiration mostly came while he was on his pillow, on the horseback, and in the toilet. Today more efficient means of transport have replaced horses, and mobile phones keep people in touch while travelling. I wonder what they would do to Ouyang Xiu's literary achievement if he lived today. On the other hand, conversations can no doubt produce fine thoughts. Furthermore, do conversations not promote relational consciousness? The question is whether conversations in public, over the mobile phone, while one is on the move, mostly about insignificant matters, are likely to be deep and involving enough to generate fine thoughts and stimulate relational consciousness. I doubt it.

Not every one in Hong Kong possesses a mobile phone, yet. However, for those who do, there seems to be a reluctance not to use it, leaving no room for solitude and silence. Partly this may reflect people's preoccupation with efficiency, with doing as many things as quickly as possible, and hence the tendency towards multi-tasking. People may thus engage in such self-deluding actions as bringing along their mobile phones for their leisure activities, and getting the satisfaction that they are enjoying their leisure time while also handling all sorts of businesses, major and minor, in a most timely manner: having their cake and eating it too. With modern technology, there is no more need for waiting, whereas it can conceivably be argued that the ability to be patient and wait is a spiritual virtue.

If you are one of those who do not yet possess a mobile phone, there are other things in store for you. Recently a local radio station arranged to have its programmes broadcast on the upper-deck of some buses, invading passengers' psychological space. A few newspaper columnists lamented the junk talk they endured during travels, but the practice will likely spread, because it boosts audience ratings. For those who do not wish to enjoy the broadcast, maybe the most natural thing to do is to plug their ears with headphones playing music from their Discman (or whatever machine that is "in"). But that does not help them regain the psychological space needed for the spirit to thrive. Perhaps even without the radio broadcast, their Discmans will any way provide continuous sound to fill up any vacant psychological space, obviating the need for active exercise of the imagination.

The danger is that we may not be able to take charge of the machines. I do not mean the danger of intelligent machines enslaving humans. It is rather that "Human inventiveness has created problems because *human judgment and humanity's ability to deal with the consequences of its creations lags behind its ability to create.*" As a result, "There is now a mismatch between the human mind and the world people inhabit" (Ornstein and Ehrlich 1989: 10; italics in original). There may have been very good evolutionary reasons why humans are "programmed" to seek and respond to conversations, and more generally, external stim-ulations. Such social and physical stimulations may have been far and between in the setting where our ancestors evolved, and when such stimulations did occur, they usually signalled something important that demanded immediate attention. In other words, our neural "hardware" has not evolved to deal with a world in which machines readily provide constant, and even multiple, stimulations. We may be in an analogous predicament to that faced by those rats allowed to electrically stimulate the "pleasure centre" in their brain. In such experiments, "Rats have shocked themselves at the rate of 500 to 5000 times per hour and often at the expense of their true needs. Hungry animals stimulate themselves rather than eat" (Walker *et al.* 1994: 137). These experiments raise some interesting questions. Did the rats stimulate themselves voluntarily or involuntarily (supposing the concept of voluntariness is applicable to rats), or did they in a sense voluntarily act involuntarily? What consti-tuted the rats' "true needs"? Similarly, has natural selection predisposed us to being "hooked" on to the mobile phone? What are our true needs?

The last question cannot even begin to be addressed here, and we must remain satisfied with the assertion that humans have important spiritual needs. As for the question of whether we are in a sense "held hostage" by some new technologies, the answer is rather clear. Comments on the tendency for children and adults alike to be glued to the television set are a platitude, and television's efficient baby-sitting function worries educators a lot. Although it has been argued "that Generation X has evolved beyond the passive viewer syndrome assisted by the invention of the remote control" (Hill 1999: 13), passivity is only slightly reduced: armed with the remote control, today's viewers are involuntarily glued to the television set more actively. Similarly, with the proliferation of entertainments of a similar nature, such as computer games, people are involuntarily hooked on to these entertainments more voluntarily. The point I wish to make is simply that, had television been popular in my childhood, I might not have had the idle time to gaze at the sky and the space in my mind for all those idle thoughts to appear.

There are other aspects of the general problem symbolized by the mobile phone that are worth pursuing. Consider the tendency towards "multi-tasking" – just as I am doing now, writing with my computer, with new e-mail alerts appearing now and then on the screen (not to mention the telephone on my table), which invariably tempt me to open and read the e-mail, thus interrupting my writing. It is doubtful such practice is conducive to the experience of flow rather than fragmentation and superficiality. I am aware that fragmentation and the "surface" have been applauded by some as liberating features of postmodern society, not without good reasons, and my whole stance may seem ultra-conservative. More mundanely, my apparent ingratitude towards technological achievements makes me sound like a hypocritical Luddite, since I am enjoying all the benefits of technology, highlighted by the fact that e-mails and air travel had enabled me to attend the conference leading to this chapter. However, I would not pursue this issue any further, and instead return to other thoughts triggered by Kant's reference to the starry heavens.

Disenchantment of the World

I have argued above that people nowadays have much less time to gaze at and reflect on the starry heavens owing to other more immediately attractive preoccupations forced upon them by new technologies. But even if people had the time, are the starry heavens there to greet them?

The starry heavens are now quite substantially hidden from Hong Kong children. First, everyday activities are mostly conducted indoors. People often spend their weekends inside shopping malls. Mobility is taken care of by public transport, one prominent form of which is the underground train. Buildings in the town centres are connected by covered or even enclosed pedestrian walks. Secondly, most urban residential areas consist of high-rise blocks crowding closely together. One has to raise one's head high to get a glimpse of a small corner of the sky. Few stars are visible, because of the glare of city lights and atmospheric pollution. They also make the sky look much lower and thus fail to trigger the feeling of unfathomable depth I had had as a child. And it is ironic that, short of a trip to the remote countryside, which however does not even then guarantee that all conditions will happen to be right to offer a good view of the starry heavens, we can only enjoy a clear view of the starry night sky through its high-tech simulation in a planetarium. The sky show is reliable and sanitized, not susceptible to uncertainties of the weather. It is also comfortable, with the audience lying in seats so adjusted as to provide the best possible view. The movements of stars are accelerated to make them efficiently visible, so you do not need the time and patience required of a real star-gazer.

The spectacle in the planetarium may inspire wonder (but perhaps not awe?), but at a reduced level and for only a short instant, and not so much at nature as at the achievements of technology. The spectators know that the spectacle is engineered by agents similar to themselves, therefore they rest assured that there are ready explanations for its workings, which are in principle understandable by them. There is much less mystery here than in nature, whose "understandability" can less readily be taken for granted. Something similar can also be said about the simulated "desktop environment" of the computer screen. People just take it for granted that such technological marvels as icons obeying mouse commands are in principle understandable because they are products of the human mind, and this "taken-for-grantedness" might actually fail to stimulate any effort at finding out and understanding. The situation when we are directly faced with nature and its secrets is different, although as explained by Weber, with science and rational modes of thought displacing explanations of natural phenomena provided by beliefs in magic, miracles and the supernatural, even the natural world has to a great extent been disenchanted (Berman 1981). The fact that science can account for many aspects of the world leads many to the comfortable expectation that everything is in principle explainable in scientific terms, thus much diluting the sense of mystery. However, even supposing science can explain everything, yet it cannot explain its own effectiveness. But then what carries psychological force is the feeling of disenchantment rather than argument. Similarly, the artificial, engineered environment now pervading everyday life increases disenchantment. The lesser "pseudo-mystery" of the man-made environment and gadgets diverts our attention further from the most basic mystery of the brute existence and workings of the world.

Fragmented, Shallow Selves

Reference has been made to the trend towards multi-tasking. If we believe that a person is constituted by his or her personal history, material circumstances and actions, then the being of the person in general and his/her spirituality in particular should be affected by the practice of multi-tasking. Each task in its own small way contributes towards the definition of the person and becomes in a sense part of that person. Thus each task deserves commitment. To speak in metaphorical language, a task carried out in dedication, adds depth to the person. Many tasks performed at the same time result in a fragmented and superficial self. This view is contrary to the Cartesian conception of the disembodied self. In this latter conception, since the self is separate from the material world, it is also separate from the tasks it carries out. Tasks can be taken up and shelved freely, in the same way as clothes are put on and taken off, without affecting the personal self.

An apparently different but in fact convergent belief is that the self can be freely deconstructed and reconstructed, a prominent theme in postmodernism. Tradition is to provide resources for the project of self-construction, to be picked up freely without imposing any constraint on the individual. It is assumed that there is no limit to deconstruction and reconstruction. This assumption is actually the same as the belief in the disembodied self, and can be found to lie behind diverse social phenomena. For example, the globalized economy is driven by incessant consumption. In the past, it was not uncommon for family and personal items to serve successive generations. They were both part of, and witnesses to, the family and personal history. But now everything is disposable. To fuel the economic engine, obsolescence is designed into goods. Promotional activities to establish new product trends form an important part of the economy. A paradox can be discerned here. People are enslaved by fashionable products often because they are concerned about their image in others' eyes. This seems to reflect a belief in the definition of the self by one's possessions. Yet at the same time these possessions are readily disposable, therefore they in fact do not define the self (or should we say meta-self).

I hold that there are indeed limits to the extent to which we can deconstruct ourselves, and well before we reach that limit, things already fall apart. In my own experience, the three buildings which provided successive residences for my family until I was 26 have all now disappeared. I would say that in consequence some very significant parts of myself are dead, and my spirit is diminished. This sounds sentimental and nostalgic. But the person is to a large extent constituted by his or her memory, and memories rely very much on material reminders as

crutches. If we accept that person–self relational consciousness is a
significant part of spiritual awareness, the paucity of personal material
"anchors" or "memorabilia" and the consequent diminished memory of
concrete life events would leave an abstract self which the person can
find difficult to relate to. Furthermore, I would suggest that there is a
historical dimension to relational consciousness, which, for want of
a better label, might be called person-predecessor consciousness.[2] This
dimension of the relational consciousness would be particularly strong
in traditional Chinese culture which stressed ancestor worship. This
consciousness would rely heavily on enduring artefacts. When we see
a museum display of, say, a Paleolithic artefact, we feel a strong bond
across time with the unknown yet intimate maker of the miraculously
preserved artefact. In this regard, it is a great pity that in the name of
economic development, old buildings and even entire communities in
Hong Kong are ruthlessly demolished. Few enduring landmarks
remain. Society as a whole becomes rootless and weakened in spirit.
Other expressions of the same underlying trend include frequent
changes of residence, even from one country to another, and of jobs,
especially in this age of cost cutting and downsizing. In addition to the
negative effect on relational consciousness, the fragmentation consequent upon such social developments is also unconducive to the sense
of personal meaning and a coherent life.

Concerning the point that a casual attitude towards old objects is inju-
rious of the development of a "deep", rich self, and does not support
relational consciousness, in particular its historical dimension, the
counter-argument can be made that modern technology has enabled us
to record personal history through photographs and video-recordings,
and this more than compensates for the disposal of old artefacts. This
point is undeniable; however, there is an irony in this. Take the case of
sightseeing tours. Photo-taking or video-recording often blocks whole-
hearted immersion into the sightseeing experience. Tuning would be
impossible when one is preoccupied with taking photos to prove to
others and oneself that one has visited the place. Taking photos is too
easy. It damages our sensitivity, deluding us into believing that the
possession of photographs is the same as the internal experience itself.
In Fromm's (1978) terms, "to have" eclipses "to be". In order to produce
the dead record, we hurt the lively experience; and without any deep,
lively experience to recall in the first place, photographs lose their
meaning.

Another dimension of relational consciousness is person–people
consciousness. Direct face-to-face encounter between two embodied
selves has the strongest impact. However, at the present stage of
development of electronic communication, the feeling of disembodied
self is encouraged by the use of e-mails. The self in the e-mail is almost

equivalent to its thoughts as expressed through the words, and what personal quality that remains to help reveal what sort of person the writer is, is the "style" of writing. Handwriting, which conveys a sense of personal presence and which some would believe to be a reliable mark of the person because it is idiosyncratic, is rendered obsolete, to be standardized by computer fonts. This promotes the sense of the disembodied self whose essence is its thought. In the absence of the full-blooded sensory cues exchanged during a personal encounter, the sense of person–people relationality may be seriously weakened. The general trend for telecommunications to at least partially replace personal encounters has its negative aspects. According to Lorenz (1996), the sensory cues accompanying a personal encounter trigger innate mechanisms that help to restrain the killing of fellow human beings. However, with the use of modern remote-control weapons, "The man who presses the releasing button is so completely screened against seeing, hearing or otherwise emotionally realizing the consequences of his action, that he can commit it with impunity" (1996: 208). We might conclude that humanity is diminished if we do not see each other face to face, because human feelings are not triggered. To further complicate the situation, in the age of virtual reality computer games, the line between virtual and "real" reality may no longer be distinct. Children used to spraying indiscriminate shots at computer characters may do the same to their schoolmates. The "game-player" does not feel a strong sense of connectedness with the human victims. Returning to the issue of the reduction of human communication to abstract exchange of disembodied symbols and images, the resultant weakened person–people consciousness not only means a stunted spirituality, but can even be said to diminish the humanity of both parties within the communication process.

The Demise of Tradition

More generally, the embodiment of spirituality implies that human practice and hence tradition are important to its cultivation. Thus Hay points out that:

> a spirituality that is alienated from the language and culture of a great religion like Christianity, is likely to be naïve, simplistic and intellectually impoverished. To the extent that it has genuinely followed its vocation, the Christian community has reflected intensely for two thousand years on the intellectual, social, cultural and political implications of human spirituality. By analogy, it is like the scientific community which maintains a body of interpretation of physical reality without which our understanding of the material world [would] be primitive and naïve. The

essence of a secular culture is not so much that [it] denies our spirituality
(for in a sense that is undeniable) but that it offers no coherent context of
reflection that permits us to integrate it with the rest of life. (1995: 18)

However, owing to increasing technologization and globalization,
many well-trodden religious paths that had in their own time facilitated
the spiritual quest of many, do not seem inviting any more in the new
and ever-changing cultural landscape. Spirituality is thus impoverished
in this quest without path. Of course any quest itself will be "path-
breaking", and indeed this seems to be the only way out, considering
the impossibility of returning to old paths that may now have become
dead ends (though the new track(s) blazed will likely cross the old ones
at numerous points). However, just as the slow natural evolutionary
process is outpaced by changes of our own making, leaving us with a
maladapted mind in a maladapted body, so the building up of an effective and benign tradition also requires time, but society is changing so
fast that no tradition can get off the ground in the first place. A balance
between tradition and innovation is needed. There had been many
groundbreaking innovations in the past, and they had the time to get
slowly digested and elaborated by culture, and tradition evolved corres-
pondingly. Today such time is lacking, and tradition simply breaks
down instead of evolving. To return to Hay's point, in the absence of a
mature, nourishing tradition, spirituality is likely to be "naïve,
simplistic and intellectually impoverished".

The situation is complicated by globalization. More and more parts
of the world are being pulled into the global economic system, and
invariably non-capitalist countries are defeated by capitalist countries
in the international economic contest. The only way to survive the
onslaught of capitalist businesses is to adopt their practices. This in itself
dismantles the traditional cultural scaffolding for the cultivation of
spirituality. In addition, capitalism as it has evolved in the West is an
integral part of the whole package of Western culture and its value
system. When the capitalist system is adopted in a desperate survival
effort by other cultures, there is the danger that only the profit motive
which stands out as the most conspicuous and relevant aspect of the
package will be transplanted, and indeed it is the easiest to transplant
because it is relatively superficial. What will be missing are the other
elements, including spiritual ones, in Western culture that help to
counterbalance the profit motive. Lorenz makes the following general
point about the interaction of cultures:

The balanced interaction between all the single norms of social behaviour
characteristic of a culture accounts for the fact that it usually proves highly
dangerous to mix cultures. To kill a culture it is often sufficient to bring it

into contact with another, particularly if the latter is higher, or is at least regarded as higher, as the culture of a conquering nation usually is . . . As the system of social norms and rites characteristic of a culture is always adapted, in many particular ways, to the special conditions of its environment, this unquestioning acceptance of foreign customs almost invariably leads to maladaptation . . . Even in the less tragic case of rather closely related and roughly equivalent cultures mixing there usually are some undesirable results, because each finds it easier to imitate the most superficial, least valuable customs of the other. (1996: 225–6)

By quoting this I do not mean to imply that the cultures "invaded" by the profit motive are necessarily "lower" than that of the West, whatever "higher" and "lower" mean in this context. I just want to lend support to the point that the profit motive is transplanted without the concomitant restraints and is thus likely to develop malignantly like cancer cells in its newly found hosts, to the detriment of spirituality. I suggest that this is the case in Hong Kong. People are constantly being bombarded by the message that getting rich fast by almost whatever means is admirable and even necessary. Taking chances and taking shortcuts are preferable to diligence and earning one's worth. Without a dedication to meaningful work which helps define one's identity, the possibility of a profound sense of meaning, a hallmark of spirituality, is seriously compromised.

As globalization progresses, the "countries of origin" of capitalism themselves are not immune to the havoc Mammon plays with societies that adopt capitalism second-hand, probably partly as a result of a negative global feedback loop. Speaking of the West, Hull observes that "Money has become the god of our culture . . . It is because children and young people come to have faith in money as being the power of life that we can speak of a content-displacement between the transcendent absolute of religious faith and money as the object of ultimate concern" (1999: 243, 246). In other words, children and young people (and society at large) have an idolatrous reliance on money. And idolatry, because of its fixation on something finite rather than infinite, is spiritually constricting.

Conclusion

In this chapter I have tried to describe the ways in which conditions of contemporary social life do not seem to bode well for spirituality. The analysis is necessarily one-sided, determined by the very nature of an attempt to pin down the contingent, constituted aspect of spirituality. In the process, the dynamic, transcendent aspect of spirituality is bracketed. My excuse is that an understanding of its own predicament is essential for the human spirit to transcend the predicament. Despite the apparently pessimistic tone of much of what is said above, hope lies in the fact that concern for spirituality is increasing, the more so if my conjecture that such concern arises out of unease with present circumstances is on the mark.

Notes

1 See Hick (1999) for an enumeration of the various "windows on the transcendent": windows in the physical sciences, social sciences, natural world, and human life.

2 A person might also experience a person–descendant consciousness that can help prevent the person from leaving behind an uninhabitable world that threatens the survival of future generations. However, since the future is not yet represented in the present by any of its elements and is therefore abstract, the chance of a person–descendant consciousness being experienced may be lower. Another point is that the terms "predecessor" and "descendant" might not be entirely appropriate ones to use here, as the relation can conceivably be with something in history or the future other than people.

References

Berman, M. 1981: *The Re-enchantment of the World*, Ithaca, NY: Cornell University Press.

Fromm, E. 1978: *To Have or to Be?*, London: Jonathan Cape.

Hay, D. 1995: The validity of the experiential approach to religious education, *Hong Kong Journal of Religious Education* 7, 14–26.

Hay, D. with Nye, R. 1998: *The Spirit of the Child*, London: HarperCollins Religious.

Hick, J. 1999: *The Fifth Dimension: an exploration of the spiritual realm*, Oxford: Oneworld Publications.

Hill, B. 1999: Should the fourth "R" for "Generation X" be "S"?, The religious education of youth in the global village, *Journal of Education and Christian Belief* 3(1), 9–21.

Hull, J. M. 1999: Bargaining with God: religious development and economic socialization, *Journal of Psychology and Theology* 27(3), 241–9.

Kant, I. 1997: *Critique of Practical Reason*, translated and edited by M. Gregor, Cambridge: Cambridge University Press.

Lorenz, K. 1996: *On Aggression*, translated by M. Latzke, London: Routledge.

Marcandonatou, O. 1998: The Experience of Being Silent. In R. Valle (ed.), *Phenomenological Inquiry in Psychology: existential and transpersonal dimensions*, New York, NY: Plenum Press, 309–20.

Ornstein, R. and Ehrlich, P. 1989: *New World New Mind: moving towards conscious evolution*, New York, NY: Doubleday.

Popper, K. R. 1976: *Unended Quest: an intellectual autobiography*, London: Fontana.

Priestley, J. G. 1985: Towards finding the hidden curriculum: a consideration of the spiritual dimension of experience in curriculum planning, *British Journal of Religious Education* 7(3), 112–19.

Storr, A. 1997: *Solitude*, London: HarperCollins Publishers.

Walker, M., Burnham, D. and Borland, R. 1994: *Psychology*, 2nd edition, New York, NY: John Wiley and Sons.

Chapter 14

The Experience of Religious Varieties: William James and the Postmodern Age

JACK PRIESTLEY

IT was in the Spring of the year 1900 that William James settled down to write the Gifford Lectures which he was to deliver at the University of Edinburgh during the Academic Year 1901–2. They were published immediately afterwards as *The Varieties of Religious Experience* and have remained more or less continuously in print throughout the ensuing century. *(All references in this chapter are to the 1982 Collins Fount paperback edition.)*

Almost exactly a hundred years later, in the closing year of that same century A. N. Wilson (1999) published *God's Funeral* in which he traces the decline of religion and the growth of secularism and atheism from the publication of David Hume's *Dialogues Concerning Natural Religion* in 1779 up to the present day. But it is with William James that Wilson concludes his study even though, chronologically, he precedes other twentieth-century figures. For it is James's work which enables Wilson, despite his funereal narrative, to end on something approaching a note of religious optimism. William James's had "bid a definite goodbye to dogmatic theology" (1982: 430) near the end of his lectures but the parting has been somewhat drawn out. Not that James was entirely alone. He stands with a small number of others who have managed to ignore or stand outside of the mainstream philosophical and theological approaches to religion over the two hundred year period since the Enlightenment and instead, have concentrated on their own and other peoples' spiritual experiences. My aim in this chapter is to place the work of William James within that thin line of resistance. My contention is that a book written to influence the twentieth century stands ready to come into its own to point the way forward for the twenty-first.

James's Purpose

William James never claimed to have had a religious experience of any definitive sort for himself. However, like his brother Henry, he lived his early life, well into adulthood, in the shadow of their father's over-whelming experience one May night in 1844 while the family was staying in Windsor Great Park. William was just two years old. As Wilson comments:

> we cannot doubt that it was the experience of Henry senior in Frogmore Cottage which was the primary factor in guiding William's thoughts about this subject in his philosophical maturity. (1999: 408)

Nevertheless, William James prepared his Gifford Lectures from his own rational and self-conscious base whilst describing his task, in a letter to Frances Morse written on 13 April 1900, as "*my* religious act". He saw this task as two-fold. First, it was, "to defend experience against philosophy as being the backbone of the world's religious life", acknowledging as he did so that this was "against all the prejudices of my class". Secondly, it was to convince his listeners that, "although all the world's manifestations of religion may have been absurd yet the life of it as a whole is mankind's most important function" (James, H. Jnr. 1969: 127).

Commenting on these statements Richard Niebuhr (1997: 218) emphasizes the need constantly to acknowledge that James was both a psychologist and a philosopher. As the former he describes what in this context James himself had called "the religious propensities". These are feeling and impulses which, in his lectures, are "recorded in literature produced by articulate and fully self conscious men (sic.) in works of piety and autobiography" (James 1982: 26).

But James himself acknowledged in his very first lecture (1982: 27) that this is an entirely different order of question from that of value which belongs to philosophy. Furthermore, he refers to it as a "spiritual judgement". The significance of this cannot be overstated. It is reminiscent of Carl Jung's pithy comment, "only the psyche can observe the psyche" (Jung 1982:3). Moreover, it was Jung himself who, a page later, added, "a very widespread view conceives the spirit as a higher and psyche as a lower principle of activity".

In short what is being suggested here is that the process of interpretation inevitably contains a strong subjective element; it cannot be otherwise, for

> we must have already in our mind some sort of general theory as to what the peculiarities of a thing should be which give it value for purposes of

revelation: and this theory would be what I call a spiritual judgement.
(James 1982: 28)

The significance of this for us is that William James was not following
the obsession with objectivity which characterized the "higher
criticism" behind nineteenth-century Biblical and historical scholarship
and which was to continue well into the twentieth. It was just such a
method which, in James's eyes, had de-spiritualized the very phenomenon with which he was dealing. He simply ignores this approach and
focuses on what he terms the "religious geniuses" or "pattern setters"
of the past.

This acknowledgement of the validity of the subjective is what separates him from his own period. In terms of the philosophical fashion of
the time it made him appear premodernist. A century later it raises the
possibility of categorizing him as an early postmodernist. But did he
stand alone? Or is it possible to link him with other thinkers in the two
hundred year period between the dawn of the Enlightenment and our
present day thought world?

Fellow Travellers

It was Samuel Taylor Coleridge, the philosopher poet, who distinguished between the rational, as that which could be demonstrated to
be the case, and the reasonable, as that which could not be demonstrated
not to be the case. Religious faith, therefore, he regarded as reasonable.
Coleridge was one of the few Englishmen of his time who could speak
German and he studied for a year at Tübingen at just the time when the
new Biblical scholarship was just beginning to take hold. Coleridge was
impressed by the scholarship but unmoved by its implications for belief.
Poetry, with its deep understanding of metaphor, imagery and rhythm
– "the right words in the right order" – was more aptly the language of
the spirit than was the language of science. Or, as Alec Vidler,
commented, about him:

> The divinity of Scripture rested not in the letter but in the spirit: not in the
> infallibility of its statements, but in the power to evoke faith and penitence
> and hope and adoration. (1961: 81)

Basil Willey (1973, 1980) has shown Coleridge's enormous influence
in Britain on other key figures who between them, can now be seen as
an alternative culture to the dominance of mainstream theological
(Christian) scholarship through the nineteenth and twentieth centuries.
These include Thomas Arnold, whose ideas on character formation
transformed English educational theory for a century or more, and his
son Matthew who became the first Chief Inspector for what now must

be called the state school sector. Recently Terence Copley (2000) has written of Matthew Arnold's abhorrence of "absurd dogmas" and of "idolaters of a Bible fetish" and of his making a "unique contribution to the values debate about the curriculum and the place of the spiritual within it" (Copley 2000: 39).

To these must be added the names of some prominent churchmen such as John Henry Newman and John Keble, established academics who simply abandoned university life to emerge themselves in pastoral work and to express their spirituality in the form of poetry, hymnology and the general pursuit of the religious life.

But perhaps the most significant nineteenth-century rebel against Enlightenment-based theological method was one of whom James was destined to remain ignorant. Søren Kierkegaard's writings were only translated from Danish into English at Princeton during the 1940s, by which time William James had been dead for over thirty years. They show one whom many regarded as a crank and a misfit – like many others in James's sample – but who can increasingly be seen as the great prophet of the Enlightenment insofar as he was rebelling against the very notion of introducing the new scientific, objective methodologies into both theology and philosophy. With Coleridge and Kierkegaard we have the founding of two counter movements, Romanticism and Existentialism, both of which rejected the dehumanizing influences of modernity but both of which, in the very *isms* attributed to them, were themselves turned into the very systematic abstractions they sought to deny.

To proceed beyond James's own lifetime is to mention such names as Rudolf Otto whose *Idea of the Holy* ([1917] 1928) stressed the significance of the non-rational as distinct from both the rational and the irrational and Alfred North Whitehead, James's successor at Harvard, whose *Religion in the Making* (1927) concentrated on the priority of the affective over the cognitive in the formation of all religions.

But perhaps the most surprising twentieth-century academic admirer of William James was Ludwig Wittgenstein whose friend Drury records,

> He was early influenced by William James's *Varieties of Religious Experience*. This book, he told me, helped him greatly. And, if I am not mistaken the category of *Varieties* continued to play an important part in his thinking. (Drury 1984: 93)

Furthermore, he continues by showing Wittgenstein's own commitment to James's form of categorization, quoting Wittgenstein as saying:

> The ways in which people have had to express their religious beliefs differ enormously. All genuine expressions of religion are wonderful, even those of the most savage peoples.

And that, "none of them was making a mistake except where he was putting forward a theory".

Such insights may well go a long way to explaining Wittgenstein's own concept of *spracht speil* or language games and to demonstrating the way in which so much of his own work has been wrongly interpreted as positivistic. But they also serve to point up the significance and validity of William James's approach to religion by one of the twentieth century's most highly recognized thinkers.

William James and the Nature of Spiritual Experience

After this somewhat lengthy introduction we can now turn to the content of James's work and attempt some direct assessment of why it is of as great a value today as it was when it was first published and why it is particularly relevant to the modern debate about the notion of a spiritual dimension of education.

James's search was for what he termed "the original experiences which were the pattern-setters for the mass of suggested feeling and imitated conduct" (1982: 29) which has resulted in institutional religion.

His sole interest in the phenomenon we term "religious" was that psychological experience which comes in the form of an individual personal vision. Institutional religion can only ever be, at best, a second-order activity. At its worst it becomes not just a substitute for, but a means of actually destroying, the primary experience which provides its very *raison d'etre*. It is when an individual succeeds in communicating such an experience to others, through a language which can only be metaphorical and wins adherents thereby, that institutional religions come into existence.[1]

At that point the primary process goes into reverse. What James terms "metaphysical monsters" and "absolutely worthless inventions of the scholarly mind" replace the power of the original vision[2] as later adherents attempt to recapture it via a cognitive process centred on creeds and doctrines. Churches live at second hand upon tradition but "the founders of every church owed their power originally to the fact of their direct personal communion with the divine" (1982: 49).

Nevertheless, although James clearly regards both philosophical and theological formulas as secondary products, "like translations from a foreign tongue", he still accepts that they have some role to play. It is always reasonable that human beings should attempt to process their emotions through their intellects but the danger comes when the intellectual models become substitutes for the original experience. At that point an entirely different psychological process comes into play. It is this reversal of the original process which makes this issue one of fundamental importance.

David Hay (1982, 1998) is among those who have more recently maintained that what James is drawing attention to here is no less than the germ which lies at the very heart of our civilization and to the fact that an educational system which cannot encompass this area within its vocabulary is in danger of destroying its seed corn. To James it seemed all too self apparent that the civilized, educated Western version of *Homo sapiens* which had found ways of translating experience into language superior to almost any other culture in history, was set on destroying its own genius. Instead of ending with words in attempting to describe experience we were becoming in danger of starting with words out of which we hoped to create constructs from which others might gain experience. But these constructs are nothing more than words about words when initially they were words about direct, deeply felt emotional experience.[3] Moreover, they also constitute a formula for those who wish to control rather than liberate the individual.

The very fact that there is variety, argues James, suggests that logical reason alone cannot construct religious objects. For all the high status we afford it, our logical reasoning acts in religion exactly as it does in so many other areas of life such as love, patriotism and politics. Rationality may find arguments for the convictions to which we have become emotionally attached but it cannot of itself provide the grounds of those convictions in the first place, a point absolutely central to the work of Rudolf Otto and the end point of Wittgenstein's *Tractatus* (1961, originally 1921). It is that to which we ascribe the term "mystical".

But what characterizes the mystical? What form does it take? Silence, was the response that Wittgenstein was to give in the first instance but James had previously suggested four possible qualities, whilst adding the very strong proviso that in no way did they constitute a system. A metaphysical system, he argued, was a contradiction in terms. It purported to set up an alternative to the inner life by constructing something in the form of a reified object totally outside and separated from ourselves which could only be grasped by a process of intellectual conceptualization. This was the great sin against which Kierkegaard (1941) had railed in his *Concluding Unscientific Postscript*, first published in 1846 but not translated into English until a century later.

William James and the Four Characteristics of the Mystical

At the risk of oversimplification I shall try to summarize James's four descriptions as briefly as possible. The mystical, he argued, is:

Ineffable. It is symptomatic of those who lay claim to some sort of mystical encounter that they claim to be lost for words – hence the Wittgensteinian silence. But while silence may be one legitimate response another is that of indirect, as opposed to direct, communication. The language used must be that of simile and metaphor because the experience is ultimately rooted in the emotions and not the intellect and, as in other cases, such as falling in love, direct description is impossible. Another avenue of expression must be that of non-verbal communication, forms of which predominate in religious worship. What is dangerous is attempted literalism of which, as we now know, the twentieth century was to see a huge growth.

Noetic. Those who undergo *noetic* experiences often claim that while they came from the feelings they resulted in absolute intellectual certainty. Often people will assert that they were never more sure of anything in their lives and even that, from that moment on, their lives were in some way changed. Robinson (1984) gives many examples of this from adults reflecting back to experiences of childhood which have affected their subsequent lives. Moreover, the things about which we are most sure are those upon which we try to act. They become part of our being. Consequently the line between religion and morality often appears to become blurred. While it is perfectly possible to be moral without being religious the opposite is not the case. Mystical experience must, in some way or other, show itself. Or, as Wittgenstein was to say towards the end of the *Tractatus*, (proposition 6.552), "there are indeed things which cannot be put into words. They *make themselves manifest"* (his italics).

Transient. The mystical state cannot be retained. It can only be held in the memory and there is no way of proving that the memory is correct. It is, perhaps, akin to the experience of remaining in a concert hall after the close of a moving performance. The dramatic moment has gone forever and can never be fully replicated. What can be said, however, is that there are countless descriptions of this experience, perhaps none more poignant than Wordsworth's accounts in two of his greatest poems, *The Prelude* and his *Ode on the Intimations of Immortality*. The inability to hold the moment results in a certain melancholy, a common characteristic of the mystical temperament.

Passive. It is a common feature of any sort of mystical experience for there to be an accompanying sense of being taken over. The ascribing of any sort of identity to such a power is itself dependent not on the individual so much as on the community of which he or she is a part. (For Wordsworth is was simply a "power that disturbs".) The individual memory is that of a feeling which was accompanied by a profound sense of being important. But it is the community memory which possesses a history, a narrative and/or a collection of symbols and images which gives identity and explanation to the experience. It is here that the theologian comes into play, seeking greater understanding by clarifying these community-based images. But for William James, far from enhancing the experience, such efforts eventually destroy it.

in the theologians' hands . . . verbality has stepped into the place of vision, professionalism into that of life . . . Did such a conglomeration of abstract terms give really the gist of our knowledge of the deity schools of theology might indeed continue to flourish but religion, vital religion, would have taken flight from the world. (1982: 428)

The wheel has turned full circle. To begin to discuss passivity is to return to the question of ineffability. The more we attempt to give verbal clarification to the images the more we become removed from the reality of the experiences themselves. James's work is based on attempting to capture immediacy and the only way in which he can come near to that end is by recording variety. In short, he allows each individual case the freedom of expressing his or her experience in its own narrative. It is this abandoning of the grand narrative into which individuals must fit their experiences and its replacement by a variety of individual stories which makes William James a forerunner of the postmodern movement.

Implications for a New Century

What then are the implications of all this for the future, especially as they may relate to education? I would suggest four areas for greater reflection.

First, certainly as far as British attitudes to education are concerned, there has, in recent years, been a marked trend away from all aspects of indirect communication in terms of the arts and the humanities and towards the direct language associated with strictly scientific assumptions about knowledge. Teaching as telling has been reasserted. Child centeredness has become a term of official disapproval. Teaching and learning have come to be regarded as the only worthwhile verbs in the educational vocabulary. Education has become synonymous with curriculum in much of public discussion. However, there are signs that a counter-revolution is beginning to re-emerge with a dawning realization that a civilized society needs rounded educated individuals possessing creativity and imagination as well as the ability to serve the economy. Whilst moves to centralize the curriculum, even in religious education, continue there are hints of change and recently books such as Clive and Jane Erricker's *Reconstructing Religious, Spiritual and Moral Education* (2000) have begun to introduce a line of development which closely mirrors William James's approach to knowledge.

Secondly, it has to be recognized that we live in a much more diverse society than a century ago when James delivered his lectures in Edinburgh to audiences which were predominantly Protestant Christian. But the importance of James's work surely lies in its opening up of the wide range of individual experience and interpretation within what purports to be the same tradition. Ironically, it may well prove to be the case that there are greater similarities of experience across traditions than sometimes exist within them. A classic example of this would be Thomas Merton's experience. A Trappist monk in a remote Kentucky monastery for over a quarter of a century, Merton found on his Asian journey an affinity with certain Buddhist monks, particularly in Sri Lanka, closer than any association he had had with most of his fellow Christians. The search for harmony in a multi-cultural, multi-religious society is unlikely to be as successful via theological enquiry into comparative belief systems as at the individual level into personal experiences communicated in different symbolic forms.

Thirdly, I would suggest that we need to give significance to the fact that James's raw material consists of narrative; it comes as story, not as proposition. That emphasis is very much the idiom of a postmodern age. Despite a modernist assumption that story is essentially for children, who grow out of it as they move towards adulthood – an assumption made meaningless by the popularity of the soap opera – the fascination with stories is as great as ever. What may be of concern is the depth or the shallowness of the stories which predominate in a culture at any particular time. The ephemeral is all around us while the deep myths which have been the foundation stories of European culture for generations have supposedly been exploded because they are "not true".

There is nothing in James's work which encourages us to abandon the traditional stories of the world's religions in education. The problem lies not in the stories themselves but rather in the adult tendency to add interpretation to narration so that children are left with nothing to explore for themselves. Interestingly, it has been certain avowed atheists who have made the most telling points on this issue. It was the former Poet Laureate, Ted Hughes (1995), who saw in the Christ Story a huge potential for stimulating children's imaginations but he also saw in it the foundation story for a whole culture insofar that those who had no knowledge of it were in a very real sense, "not one of us". (It is perhaps necessary to add here that my own experiences of teaching British Muslim students soon persuaded me that most knew the Christian story far better than the "Christians" of the majority but this is often the case among any religious and cultural minorities.) To know is not necessarily to believe in any religious sense.

It was another atheist, Ludwig Wittgenstein, who drove that point home:

> queer as it sounds the historical accounts of the gospels might, historically speaking, be demonstrably false and yet belief would lose nothing by this:

not, however, because it concerns "universal truths of reason"! Rather, because historical proof (the historical proof game) is irrelevant to belief.

Among other things we have here support for James's view that a certain type of narrative, whilst not itself subject to rational investigation, forms the basis of our rationality – a position going back to the Platonic Dialogues where the point is made again and again that when we have gone as far as *logos* can take us we must resort to *mythos* – a point which modernity has always failed to take on board.

Finally, a consideration of James's work should encourage us once again to consider that the need of education is not factual knowledge so much as self-knowledge. The basic assumption behind his whole investigation was that the highest value lies in the subjective rather than in the reified objectivity of scientific analysis of the human condition. The more educated we become the greater our individual differences will be. When the masses think alike most are not thinking at all. That which has the highest value for us as individuals, the truths for which we are most prepared to suffer, are essentially subjective truths.

The process of human development and of education is not from the centre outwards towards some system but from the periphery of my vision towards the centre. Thinkers, not systems, provide the unity by which thought is held together. James's concern was primarily with religious beliefs and the primary foundation upon which they were built and developed. But the process is never completed; systems in the world of human affairs are never finished. Again, it was Kierkegaard who snarled that, "an unfinished system is merely another hypothesis".

William James wanted to bid a definite goodbye to dogmatic theology with its "worthless-invention-of-the-humanmind-God" but his work, while closing those doors, opens a million others. For, as A. N. Wilson concludes:

> instead of using the tired, clapped-out old weapons of philosophy to justify religious belief, he used the fresh lens of experimental psychology to observe actual religious experience. And instead of using the harsh new scientific method (in itself as intolerant as the old theology) to tell men and women what they could and could not believe, he used every fibre of his intellectual energy to defend and justify freedom of the will and, in his phrase, "the right to believe". (1999: 430)

At the very end of his lectures William James recognized (1982: 497) that "the current of thought in academic circles runs against me", but that "what I now say sufficiently indicates to the philosophic reader where I belong". He was, I would suggest, a thinker ahead of his time and that where he belonged was not the opening years of the twentieth century but here and now at the beginning of the twenty-first.

Notes

1 Alfred North Whitehead, William James's later successor at Harvard, developed this idea in his 1926 Lowell Lectures, later published as, *Religion in the Making*. See the References below.
2 Edward Robinson drew on Edwin Muir's use of this phrase for the title to his own collection of experiences of childhood. See the References below.
3 So, for example, commentators like Janik and Toulman see in the total and sudden collapse of the Austro-Hungarian Empire the motivation for Wittgenstein's attempts to rediscover the integrity of language.

References

Copley, T. 2000: *Spiritual Development in the State School*, Exeter: Exeter University Press.
Drury, M. O'C. 1984: Some Notes on Conversations with Wittgenstein. In R. Rhees (ed.), *Recollections of Wittgenstein*, Oxford: Oxford University Press
Erricker, C. and J. 2000: *Reconstructing Religious, Spiritual and Moral Education*, London and New York: Routledge Falmer.
Hay, D. 1982: *Exploring Inner Space: Scientists and Religious Experience*, London.
Hay, D. with Nye, R. 1998: *The Spirit of the Child*, London: Fount.
Hughes, T. 1995 [1970]: Myth and Education. In G. Fox (ed.) *Celebrating Children's Literature in Education*, London: Hodder.
Janik, A. and Toulman, S. 1973: *Wittgenstein's Vienna*, New York: Simon and Schuster.
James, H. Jnr. 1969: *The Letters of William James*, Boston: Atlantic Monthly Press.
James, W. 1982 [1902]: *The Varieties of Religious Experience*, Glasgow: Collins Fount.
Jung, C. 1982 [1945]: The Phenomenology of the Spirit in Fairy Tales. In J. Campbell (ed.), *Papers From The Eranus Yearbooks, Vol. 1.*, Princeton: Princeton University Press.
Kierkegaard, S. 1941 [1846]: *Concluding Unscientific Postscript*, London: Oxford University Press.
Niebuhr, R. 1997: William James on Religious Experience. In R. A. Putnam (ed.), *The Cambridge Companion To William James*, Cambridge: Cambridge University Press.
Otto, R. 1928 [1917]: *The Idea of the Holy*, London: Oxford University Press.
Robinson, E. 1984 [1977]: *The Original Vision*, New York: Seabury.
Vidler, A. 1961: *The Church in an Age of Revolution: 1789 to the Present Day*, London: Penguin.
Whitehead, A. N. 1927: *Religion in the Making*, Cambridge: Cambridge University Press.
Willey, B. 1973: *Nineteenth Century Studies*, London: Penguin.
—— 1980: *More Nineteenth Century Studies: A Group of Honest Doubters*, Cambridge: Cambridge University Press.
Wilson, A. N. 1999: *God's Funeral*, London: Abacus.
Wittgenstein, L. 1961 [1921]: *Tractatus Logico-Philosophicus*, London: Routledge.

Pedagogical Approaches

PEDAGOGY provides the link between theory and practice, research and teaching. Pedagogy can provide a strategy for change or for stasis. Hence, lying behind any pedagogical approach lie the values it seeks to espouse, and within the approach are the practical means for its effectiveness in promoting those values.

It follows that "spiritual education" is always framed in a particular conception of values. The following chapters make this clear by drawing attention to the values that underpin their arguments and analyses, conflicts of values within their research focus, and values that they are opposing on the basis of their judgements. The chapters in Part III indicate that the consideration of spiritual education necessarily involves political controversy and a challenge to many accepted perceptions of education and of the capabilities of those whom we seek to educate.

Jane Erricker is concerned with how "spirituality" should influence the notion of citizenship in education as it is developed within the National Curriculum provision in England and Wales. She advances a vision of spiritual education that is separate from religious education, that focuses on the investigations and reflections of children and is linked to their experiences. Her constructivist model allows for the notion of fluid, changing and self-styled identities which, she argues, we must help children to construct through a dialogic process. Here she refers to developing the skills of relationship in the context of emotional literacy, understood as an aspect of holistic education. Turning to the neurologist Oliver Sacks and his account of Rebecca, a young girl who was cognitively defective but "came alive in narrative", she argues that we must concentrate on the qualities children possess and not on their perceived deficits. This she places at the heart of citizenship education.

Paul Yates places in opposition the modernist practice of schooling and the spiritual needs and realities of students. His chapter focuses on the relationship between education and identity. Beginning with a discussion on the nature of identity for the individual in late modernity he states that it is characterized by an emphasis on individualism, in its liberal and postmodern forms. Following Giddens he introduces the notion that "shame derives from a failure to live up to expectations built into the ego-ideal" that predominates. He relates this, institutionally, to the varieties of targeting used in schools to "maximize cognitive production". Pursuing a critique of this method of education he argues that the institutional identity imposed by schools conflicts with the dynamic and differentiated cultural milieus experienced by students. The "myopic-monoculturalism" of the former, reflecting the modernist state, fails to take account of the fluidity of students' identities and cultural experiences. In conclusion he locates the idea of the spiritual through analogy with poets and artists who, quoting Deleuze and Guattari, "tear open the firmament . . . to let in a bit of free and windy chaos and to frame in sudden light a vision that appears through the rent".

Tony Eaude's contribution is based on his research into how teachers of young children understand spiritual development and he argues that teacher's views are the necessary starting point for considering curriculum development. After examining the "curiously English" legislation on spiritual development he considers the international context in which it can be understood. Considering a range of research into the subject he introduces his own. In his findings he emphasizes the willing, albeit diffident, responses of teachers, and their openness to change in their perceptions and views. He suggests that developing a teacher's understanding of the spiritual may be best effected by enabling discussion; a strategy that our present educational culture might find "alarmingly subversive". Constructing his own working definition of the spiritual, which highlights its universality and "ordinariness", he argues that teachers must be helped to understand the spiritual in this way and apply it by being attentive to children.

Laura Morris asks how notions of spirituality impinge on the experiences of autistic children. Her enquiry attempts to provide a spiritual context in which to understand autism; detect autistic expressions of spiritual awareness; and identify how spiritual language and practice might help people with disability. Drawing on mystics from different religious traditions and concluding that spiritual experiences are characterized by a process of relating, she asks where this leaves the autistic child for whom relating is so difficult. On the basis of the findings of research into autism she finds a correlation between neurological activity in autistic children and that which is found in altered states of consciousness. She argues that autistic children may well possess a capacity for insight that requires sensitivity to detect and, as a consequence, using spiritual practices that do not depend on normal cognitive skills could provide a way forward in addressing the spiritual education of autistic children.

Wim Westerman begins by relating spiritual education to rites of passage and children's understandings of time. Providing historical comparisons of Chinese, Jewish and Christian examples he identifies how stages of development are understood in relation to these rites. He then questions this relationship on the basis of whether age and development can be equated in such a demonstrable fashion in contemporary societies. He also illustrates how religious rites and symbols are being replaced by those of commercial interests in a globalizing society. He asks how we are to address a "deep pedagogical unrest" resulting from the demise of traditional rites and developmental expectations, which previously identified the spiritual characteristics of childhood and youth, whilst accepting increasing social and cultural diversity and acknowledging the increasing commercial shaping of childhood.

Cathy Ota presents her research findings into nurture in Catholic schools. She contextualizes this by identifying that they continue to thrive on the basis of a reputation for providing a moral ethos, good results, an holistic approach to learning, and Catholic nurture. In practice her research reveals problems with the notion of Catholic identity and how it is related to spiritual and religious education, significant variations in the concept of nurture in relation to that of catechesis, and distinctive differences in perception between students and staff. She argues that progress in spiritual education in Catholic schools depends upon attending to the quality of relationships between teachers and students, the balance of power between the same, and the valuing of individuals. She identifies disparity between the mission statements of schools and how they are, or are not, put into practice. In conclusion she reflects on the implications of this study for other denominational schools and pedagogic practice generally.

Clive Erricker's chapter examines a crisis in Muslim faith education. In a study of the debate within the Khoja Shi'a Ithnasheeri tradition of Islam he considers what would constitute an appropriate approach to the spiritual education of their youth. In a diasporic situation, in which the more plural and diverse cultures within which the young are situated is significantly different to that experienced by their elders, he advocates the importance of seeking to understand and converse with the youth and address issues of concern and identity. He also suggests that attending solely to moral matters will not satisfy their spiritual needs and relational requirements. Instead, he advocates a metaphoric model based on the Islamic understanding of *tawaf*, the circumambulation of the Khaaba, acting as a symbolic recognition of coming closer to Allah. He applies this to the way in which pedagogy in the *medrassas* is pursued, within which the teachers need to engage with matters of existential concern to their students.

Chapter 15

Spirituality and the Notion of Citizenship in Education

JANE ERRICKER

I N this chapter I shall address the place of spirituality and spiritual education in the revised version of the National Curriculum in England. I will ask questions about the possibility of actually carrying out spiritual education, and will suggest what that spiritual education might look like. To conclude, I shall discuss the relationship of spiritual education to the new subject of citizenship that is about to be introduced in schools in England and Wales.

Spirituality has always occupied a tenuous and ill-defined position in the curriculum in Britain. It has been given a particular status because of the overarching statement at the beginning of the National Curriculum document, and it was highlighted in legislation by the 1988 Education Reform Act and again in Circular 1/94, another government publication. The first paragraph of the circular provides the context for the curriculum in relation to the aim of education:

> The Education Reform Act 1988 sets out as the central aim for the school curriculum that it should promote the spiritual, moral, cultural, mental and physical development of pupils and society, and prepare pupils for the opportunities, responsibilities and experiences of adult life. (DfE 1994: 9)

This statement has proved to be a hostage to fortune because while the promotion of cultural, mental and physical development are fairly easily demonstrated in the subject-based curriculum, and moral development, though more difficult to pin down, is certainly there within the culture of the school and in Religious Education, there is a problem with spiritual development. Spiritual development is not only difficult to define but was impossible to measure (and we all know how important it is nowadays to be able to measure children's achievements!). I think we all thought, and still do think, that spiritual development in children *is* sometimes taking place, but we aren't sure if it is because of what happens in school or in spite of it. So it is difficult to talk about spiritual *education*, because that implies that educational institutions might have a role in the process, or at least not actively hinder it and I am not sure that this is the case.

So we find ourselves in a difficult position. The writers of the original National Curriculum obviously felt that spirituality was important, and I personally feel it is very important, but in the twelve years since the 1988 Education Reform Act we have not clearly defined what we mean by it and it has been marginalized in the curriculum. This has been particularly true in the primary curriculum since the drive for standards and the advent of literacy and numeracy hours have taken up so much time in the school day. Those teachers and educators who believe that spirituality, and therefore spiritual education, is important, believe it to be so because we think that addressing that aspect of a person affects all other aspects, including the ability to learn and to become a happy and useful member of society. If we could convince policy-makers that spiritually nurtured children achieve higher standards, and are less likely to become football hooligans or single parents or whatever the latest obsession of the politicians is, then maybe we could raise its status in the curriculum. But there are many of us who firmly believe that spiritual education can be another way of saying the education of the whole child, and that such a holistic vision of education is what is missing from today's fragmented, standards-driven schooling.

Let me develop this vision of spiritual education. First I would like to look at the connection of spirituality with religion. I want to disconnect spirituality and spiritual education from religion and religious education. In other words I would like to say that spirituality is not necessarily religious in nature. This is not to say that it often *isn't* religious in nature, but that it doesn't *have* to be. I think that this disconnection is essential, particularly for young children, even if the connection between religion and spirituality is remade later on. Young children do not understand religion. Children can be told about religion, but they do not necessarily understand it until they can understand their own feelings. As constructivist theory in science suggests, we must start from children's own ideas and allow these ideas to be challenged by experience, and reconstructed as a result of that experience. Working from any other premise there is a danger that children will never have ownership of the explanations and justifications of human existence that religion provides. To use a metaphor that Cathy Ota has developed (Ota 1998: 215ff), if we provide children with a ready-made jumper of meaning to wear, with the pattern already decided, then how can they claim that they are accurately represented by that demonstration to the outside world. I would prefer to knit my own jumper, to demonstrate who I am myself, providing, of course, I know who that self is. Later on, I shall have the chance to find out whether the Christian jumper or the Buddhist jumper does in fact represent me well and I will wear it. But I would rather that it wasn't given to me before I've had a chance to work things out for myself, and that I was expected to be comfortable in something that wasn't mine.

Children must be allowed to investigate and reflect on their experiences and they must be allowed to interpret and judge their own feelings and those of others before we can put to them the complexities and subtleties of a faith. How can they appreciate the reasons for a faith, the necessity for an explanation that goes beyond their experience or the experience of any human being, until they have examined their own meaning making? Spirituality is essentially human. If spirituality is understood to reach a pinnacle in the connection of the human with the divine, that is an understanding arrived at on the basis of individual experience and choice. But it should not be allowed to be the criterion by which *all* human spirituality is judged, particularly not in young people who are striving hard to make sense of themselves and their lives.

So, if we disconnect spirituality and spiritual education from religion and religious education, at least for the time being, how does that develop the vision of spirituality and spiritual education that I am proposing? Well, if children need to understand themselves and their own meaning making before they can decide about a faith, then perhaps spiritual education can be just that. It can be the nurturing of all children towards a fuller understanding of their own emotional and aesthetic potential and the development of the skills required. I would argue that these are practised first of all in reflection on their own relationships. The best thing about this way of looking at spirituality is the way in which it brings together spirituality, morality, emotional literacy and citizenship.

We need to allow children to develop their own identity. We need to allow them to examine the existential problems they encounter and to work out how they will address them. They need to work out "Who am I and how do I feel about these issues? How do I want to behave and how do I want other people to behave?" Developing personal identity needs to take place in a supportive environment. That it should be done in the home goes without saying. Indeed most education should be done in the home. But we have allowed schools to take responsibility for rectifying the deficiencies of parents since the original notion of compulsory education and spiritual education should not be excluded from this. Children need professional help, as well as familial encouragement, in exploring who they are.

There is a lovely quote from Morris West in his book *The Ambassadors*:

Identity! That was the word. That was the key to the whole human problem. Unless a man understood, however dimly, what he was and how he was linked with his fellows and with the cosmos, he could not survive. Put him in a padded cell, separate him from the sight, sound and touch of the world, and you would in a short time reduce him to madness and physical disorder. (West 1965: 75)

The question is "How can we understand our identity? Is that identity something we must discover? Like a modernist view of knowledge, is our identity there and hidden from us, an essential truth that will be revealed to us partially and gradually? Or is it something we construct, is it even something that has no fixed nature, but is ephemeral, contingent? Is it a Sartrian role that we can put on and take off, like Cathy's jumper?"

Susan Hekman describes a person, or a "discursive subject", which is

neither relational, feminist, postmodern, nor a product of theories of race and ethnicity, yet it borrows from each of these discourses . . . [Its] identity is [not] disembodied, given, transcendent . . . It is [not] what the subject "discovers" as he "finds" himself. For the discursive subject, by contrast, identity is constituted, multiple, and fluctuating. The subject is a work of art, fashioned from the discursive tools at the disposal of the situated subject. (Hekman 1995: 109)

If Hekman's description of a person is correct then we can choose who we want to be and we can be someone different at different times. Problematic enough for an adult, it is a much more difficult task for a child seeking to know who they are. It is important for a child to know that they might feel like a different person at different times. Gary Younge explained this in an article in the *Guardian* when he talked about what it was like to be British, but with roots in Barbados, and to be asked about his identity:

We would pick and mix, and the answer we gave depended partly on what we thought the motivation for the question was, partly on the fact that nobody gave us the option of being both (Bajan and British) at the same time, and partly on what we perceived our interests to be at any given moment. When it became apparent to me that there was more to racial identity than nationality and that, in any case, I didn't have to cement myself in one identity and stay there for the duration of an entire conversation, let alone my whole life, it was a great relief. (Younge 1999)

Mick Cooper and John Rowan explain this view in more detail when they explain the plight of the postmodern individual, as he or she

turns and turns to face the onslaughts of an ever-fragmenting social world, so the notion of a unified, monolithic self appears increasingly untenable. Within a modernist world, characterized by "one man, one job" – along with such "grand narratives" as linear development, progress, and the scientific search for truth – the notion of an autonomous, singular self moving towards its ownmost future seems deeply credible, to the point of being transparent. But in a world characterized by multi-fragmented social positionings and the deconstruction of absolute truths, the notion of a unified self begins to stand out like a relic from a bygone era. (Rowan and Cooper 1999: 1)

If children, if people, construct their identities, their fluid, contingent identities, how do they do it? We need to know this if we are to help children in the process of identity construction. Carol Gilligan says that we all do it by examining ourselves as reflected in others. In other words, we look at ourselves and construct ourselves in relationship to other people.

> We know ourselves as separate only insofar as we live in connection with others, and that we experience relationships only insofar as we differ-entiate other from self. (Gilligan 1982: 63)

And I have said more simplistically: "who you are depends on what happens to you, who you talk to and how you talk . . . The dialogic process constructs the self and because of this the self is necessarily fluid, changing, contingent, responsive." (Erricker and Erricker 2000: 112).

Children need to be allowed the opportunity to carry out this process of identity construction, and, more than that, they need to be nurtured in the skills that they need to do it. If identity is constructed in relationship, then the skills of relationship are what are needed. This could be seen to be the new and fashionable emotional literacy; it is part of holistic education, which I strongly advocate. I have identified the skills of emotional literacy elsewhere. They include:

1   reflection on one's own emotions,
2   self-knowledge (understanding *why* one does something),
3   understanding of consequences,
4   self-criticism (according to one's own recognised principles),
5   self-control,
6   reflection on the emotions of others,
7   empathy,
8   criticism of others (according to one's own recognized principles),
9   understanding why others do things,
10 recognition of relationship,
11 recognition of difference, and
12 recognition of the complexity of social discourse.

(Erricker, J. 1999: 386)

These skills incorporate ones which might be said to be part of "morality" – the understanding of consequences, for example; and others that might be more comfortably located in "spirituality" – e.g., reflection on one's own emotions. I have called them skills of emotional literacy because I hope to avoid some of the issues and connotations of "spiritual" and "moral" and I believe that the terms, although not synonymous, do overlap to a large degree. In this respect we might regard "emotional literacy" as paying due attention to the balance between rational and affective domains in the discourse of educational development.

We have found in our research with primary aged children that they address these skills best in narrative form (C. Erricker *et al.* 1997). This does not mean fictional stories, but the sharing of their own life histories. When we "interview" children we give them permission to use us as listeners for their own stories, the ones by which they are making sense of what has happened to them. They are saying, "This is what's happened to me. This is how I have made sense of it all. This is *me*." When children tell their stories they are actually carrying out the process of identity construction. It may well be that it is only the identity of the moment, but we have already acknowledged that identity can be multiple and contingent. The importance of the narrative process is just that – the process of the construction rather than some essential and unchanging product.

Our research has shown us that children have abilities that are never made visible, never acknowledged, never praised, never nurtured within a school system that values knowledge that can be tested (C. Erricker *et al.* 1997). These are their abilities, identified above, to empathize, to understand other people's situations, to feel compassion, to judge how best to help; these abilities are demonstrated in the conversations we have had with children. These are the attributes of the whole person, not the partial, cognitively judged person. We know only too well from the experiences of developmental psychologists that tests, for example intelligence tests, tell us how good someone is at doing the tests. It is very dangerous to make overarching judgements about a child's worth based on test results. So if a child does well in Key Stage 2 mathematics Standard Assessment Tasks (SATs), then we know that she is very good at doing the kind of mathematics that white, middle-class, Western people value. We don't necessarily know how good she is at being happy, fulfilled or a valued member of society.

Oliver Sacks tells the story of Rebecca in his wonderful book *The Man Who Mistook His Wife For A Hat* (Sacks 1985: 169). This young girl was cognitively very defective but came alive in narrative. She had "gross perceptual and spatio-temporal problems, and gross impairments in every schematic capacity – she could not count change, the simplest calculations defeated her, she could not learn to read or write, and she would average sixty or less in I.Q. tests". But she loved stories. Her grandmother said that she had a hunger for stories. Sacks says that "This seemed to be a deep need or hunger in Rebecca – a necessary form of nourishment, of reality for her mind." Sacks saw her when she was sitting gazing at the April foliage and appreciating a beautiful spring day. Here she appeared composed and together, a picture that contrasted starkly with the de-composed person who had done so badly in the psychological and neurological tests that she had been given. Sacks describes these tests as designed "not merely to uncover, to bring out deficits, but to decompose her into functions and deficits". (It is relevant to ask how these compare with the tests and assessments that we give children in school.)

Rebecca was given treatment that consisted of workshops and classes as part of what the psychologists call developmental and cognitive drive, but they didn't work for Rebecca. Sacks thinks that it was not the right thing to do, "because what we did was to drive them (the patients) full-tilt upon their limitations". He thought that "we paid far too much attention to the defects of our patients . . . and far too little to what was intact or preserved. Rebecca made clear, by concrete illustrations, by her own self, the two wholly different, wholly separate, forms of thought and mind, 'paradigmatic' and 'narrative' (in Bruner's terminology). And though equally natural and native to the expanding human mind, the narrative comes first, has spiritual priority. Very young children love and demand stories, and can understand complex matters presented as stories." Sack's Rebecca used a metaphor, describing herself as "a living carpet. I need a pattern, a design like you have on that carpet. I come apart, I unravel, unless there's a design". She found her place in a theatre group, where, when she was on stage, her deficiencies became undetectable.

Sacks uses this story to show how narrative can be the means by which someone holds themselves together as a complete entity, rather than seeing themselves as made up of separate, disparate and in the case of Rebecca, deficient, parts. Sacks seems to mean narrative as fiction, but I'm not sure how much he would subscribe to the differentiation between fact and fiction here. How much more powerful must personal narrative based on individual experience be in providing the integration that makes a person whole, and in their wholeness so much more than the sum of their measurable parts? And therefore how important it is to allow space for children to tell their own stories, and to listen carefully and respectfully to those stories.

If children need to tell their stories, and we need to make space for them to do so, where can this happen? I would like to think that at one time children told these stories in their own homes, in response to other

members of the family telling theirs. But perhaps I have a romantic idea
of the family in the past. Suffice to say that, from what children have
said to us in the course of our research, there are many children for
whom the family does not offer such opportunities. However, if this is
an important part of children's development, in particular their spiritual and moral development, then it should be part of schooling. But
where in the curriculum could it take place? The curriculum is already
very overcrowded.

In Britain, the new curriculum for 2000 introduced a new subject, citizenship. This is to be a completely new subject in the secondary
curriculum, and within personal, social and health education in primary
schools. It was to include spiritual and moral education. When I heard
about this I was full of hope. Before one can be a citizen, I thought, one
has to have an identity of one's own. Here was the opportunity to argue
for a space in the school day for children to investigate their own identities. As it is we don't allow children to investigate and then celebrate
who they are as individuals. We worry about self-esteem but it can take
the form of unconnected praise, not a facilitation of a personal investigation into one's own values and beliefs, and into the way as an
individual we relate to others. Before one can be moral, one has to
develop the self that is moral. Before one can understand the complexities of the wide social relationships that citizenship requires, one must
be able to handle and understand the relationships in the narrower
sphere of one's family and friends. This is the progression of learning
that I feel children should be guided and nurtured through.

The new subject of citizenship could be an opportunity for
addressing the whole person: a place for spirituality and morality to
come together in the expression of who we are, through what is
important to us. A chance for children to ask themselves, "How do I
want to live?" and, "How do I think other people should live?" The new
subject represents an opportunity to open up a space in the curriculum
where children can be valued for who they are rather than what they
can do. There are some statements within the citizenship curriculum
that we can take to refer to spirituality, though the word is mentioned
just briefly in the Key Stage 3 and 4 guidelines. Apart from that, aspects
of what we might define as spirituality are divided and shared among
Religious Education (R.E.), Personal, Social and Health Education
(PSHE) and citizenship. With this division the essential aspect of spirituality – its holistic nature, its integrative function – is lost. Here we'll
talk about your relationship with God, there we'll mention your
relationships with other people, somewhere else we'll talk about what
it means to be a member of society. And given the small amount of space
in Citizenship to address children's own views and experiences, it will
be hard for teachers to find the space to do this in the school day. I know

this from the work we have done with teachers in primary schools, where they expressed not only the difficulty in finding the time to hear children's narratives, but the guilt they experienced when they "neglected" a core curriculum subject to attend to the individual child's need to speak. A teacher illustrates this point:

> *Teacher G*: I then asked myself . . . why feel guilty about going with the mood and needs of the group and abandoning a core subject!! (Erricker, J. 1999: 387)

The temptation will be to address in citizenship those things that can be measured and assessed most easily, because that is what teachers have to do these days. It would be terrible if the chance was lost because it is so difficult to "objectively" measure more elusive things, while it is so much easier to teach and assess civics – knowledge of how our country's government works.

The difficult task of nurturing a whole person will disappear from the list of priorities, and that whole person, a person who can take his or her place in society knowingly, meaningfully and with integrity, an educated person rather than someone who just knows things – *a spiritual person* – will be lost under a heap of assessments and certificates.

References

Department of Education 1994: *Religious Education And Collective Worship: Circular 1/94*, London: DfE.
Erricker, C., Erricker, J., Ota, C., Sullivan, D. and Fletcher, M. 1997: *The Education of the Whole Child*, London: Cassell.
Erricker, J. 1999: Teachers Developing Spiritual and Moral Education, *Teacher Development*,3(3), 383–96.
Erricker, J. and Erricker, C. 2000: *Reconstructing Religious and Spiritual and Moral Education*, London: Routledge.
Gilligan, C. 1982: *In a Different Voice*, Cambridge, MA: Harvard University Press.
Hekman, S. 1995: *Moral Voices, Moral Selves*, Cambridge: Polity Press.
Ota, C. 1998: *The Place of Religious Education in the Development of Children's World Views*, unpublished Ph.D. thesis, University College Chichester, UK.
Rowan, J. and Cooper, M. 1999: *The Plural Self*, London: Sage.
Sacks, O. 1985: *The Man Who Mistook His Wife for A Hat*, London: Picador.
West, M. 1965 *The Ambassadors*, London: N.E.L.
Younge, G. 1999: Are My Roots Showing? *Observer*, 12 September 1999.

Chapter 16

Postmodernism, Spirituality and Education in Late Modernity

PAUL YATES

THIS chapter explores education and identity, or knowledge of the self. I have argued elsewhere that spirituality in school is reconstituted and represented within the dominant bureaucratic culture (Yates 1999). In this essay I suggest that identity is the territory that in late modernity covers the issues of being and knowing which the discourses of spirituality traditionally described. Foucault notes that early Christianity was centrally concerned with knowledge and truth and that in establishing a Christian identity it not only requires adherence to a set of precepts but also "importantly involves knowing who one is: 'that is to try to know what is happening inside him, to acknowledge faults, to recognize temptations, to locate desires' . . . " (Barker 1998: 80).

I begin with a discussion of the nature of identity and the individual in late modernity. This is followed by a critique of schooling and knowledge that are reflections of the culture of the bureaucratic state and remain resolutely rooted in modernity. This creates a dissonance between the multiple cultures of late modernity and the monoculture of school. Finally, I argue for a schooling that attempts to reflect the identity of young people through recognizing the legitimacy of new knowledges of the world and of the self.

The Late Modern Self

The problem with discussing identity is not that the concept and the reality have changed, which would attract broad agreement, but that the extent, and most particularly the significance, of change is contested and difficult to empirically establish within the positivist Anglophone culture of social and educational policy (Mullard and Spicker 1998). Much of the current discourse of identity is built on particular theoretical orientations of Marxism or materialism (Isin and Wood 1999), structuration theory (Giddens 1991), the more traditional cultural psychological framework of Bruner (1999), and the radical commentary from postmodernism (McGuigan 1999).

In the last half century identity has become politicized, first in America and more latterly in Europe. Ethnicity, race, gender and sex, as well as locality, region and community are not only elements in the shifting tectonic plates of late modern identity but they also tend to be group as well as individual identities with a concern for rights of expression and legal recognition and more local forms of empowerment. The discourse of the individual, however, will inevitably predominate, for a while it may be the case that new types of collective identity are being formed by larger numbers of people; individualism in its old liberal and new postmodern forms is a basic aspect of Western society.

Bruner's (1999) discourse draws firmly on modernist sources in his critique of schooling and identity. He argues from a liberal humanist position where the experience of the individual is understood as a universal human essential and as the proper subject of education. For Bruner (1999: 172), "perhaps the single most universal thing about human experience is the phenomenon of 'Self', and we know that education is crucial to its formation". Bruner also argues for autonomous agency against both radical constructivists and behaviourists in order to link the self to esteem that is derived from our reflective evaluation of our performances in the light of our goals. While this is not seen as part of the essential self it is nonetheless "a ubiquitous feature of selfhood . . . this mix of agentive efficacy and self-evaluation" (1999: 173). Giddens (1991: 68) similarly suggests that self-referential shame now characterizes moral evaluation in late modern society where "shame derives from a failure to live up to expectations built into the ego-ideal". One can see this as the necessary dynamic of the widespread use of varieties of targeting in schools to maximize cognitive production and perhaps of the increasing interest in the use of formative assessment.

Bruner (1999: 174) argues that agency and esteem are central to the construction and maintenance of self in which case "the ordinary practices of school need to be examined with a view to what contribution they make to these two crucial ingredients of personhood". Within postmodern models of the self, the notion of a universal or essential self is challenged by new models that stress plasticity and flux. While the concept of structure itself may be universally applied, how each individual constructs herself locally will be determined by the cultural contexts she defines herself within; and the plurality of narratives she draws upon.

Bruner also makes a distinction between "logical-scientific thinking" and "narrative thinking" which he again confidently asserts are universal: "no culture is without both of them though different cultures privilege them differently" (1999: 174). Both Bruner and Giddens point to the role of narrative in relation to self-construction and maintenance. Bruner rather gently makes the point that "it has been the convention of most schools to treat the arts of narrative – song, drama, fiction, theatre, whatever – as more 'decoration' than necessity, something to grace leisure" (1999: 175). More particularly because schools are driven by instrumental rationality, with an intense focus on ends, they are unable to value the expression of the narrative self of pupils because to do so would transgress the boundaries of the bureaucratic self, the subject of controlled production in school.

The Abrahamic religions and with them Mediterranean culture are founded on a shared set of narratives which continue to inspire and inform social practice. More generally, as Bruner suggests, we use story to generate self-understanding: "our immediate experience, what happened yesterday or the day before, is framed in the same storied way. Even more striking we represent our lives (to ourselves as well as to others) in the form of narrative" (1999: 175). It is a bizarre distortion of modernity's privileging of the subject's individual genius in the concept of the author that "creative writing", which could be an authentic medium of self-production or self-knowledge through the development of an individual's voice, is subjected in school to regulated conformity and abstracted external assessment.

A generalized model of the western Abrahamic sense of self would be of an essential, inherent and relatively stable identity transcendentally authenticated by God. This contrasts with the model of self that Giddens suggests typifies late modernity. Giddens (1991: 75) draws on the therapeutic uses of narrative to construct his notion of the self as a reflexive project on a trajectory from the past to an anticipated, but essentially uncontrollable, future for which the individual feels responsible. This level of responsibility for self-construction is contrasted with a "traditional" society where the nature of the person was determined by fixed points of kinship and gender identity, locality and inherited social status, none of which have the power to sustain self-identity in late modernity and all of which are impermanent in themselves to some degree. For much of the nineteenth and twentieth centuries the life trajectory of people in a settled industrial state was to an extent foreseeable and reliable and involved limited choice. However, currently in English male adolescent culture the decision to be a lad, a Goth, a crusty or a boff(in) represent lifestyle choices that are possibly short term, and may have equally transient implications for gender identity and attitudes towards, and patterns of, consumption.

It is perhaps in the notion of narrative that we can dissolve the distinction between actual and invented selves, that a bridge can be seen between the traditional conception of self and the postmodern critique. McGuigan (1999: 80) talks of "fractured identities", that is to say the story of self may be more complex and multifaceted than a single linear narrative. Haraway's myth of the cyborg, the entity that is both human and machine, is quoted as a model for the dissolution of traditional boundaries of being. In the cyborg the human/animal distinction is blurred. (This can also be seen in the extension of "human" rights to animals and the, sometimes violent, political activity around this idea.) Two other boundaries are breached in the conception of the cyborg. First, that between the organic entity and the machine which echoes the way in which "smart machines have increasingly put the distinctiveness of human mental and physical capacities into question, and, indeed have also extended such capacities" (1999: 82). Secondly, in the combination of micro-technology and human person the virtual and the actual do not separately signify but are indistinguishable. The cyborg is also devoid of essence and mirrors the fractured identity of postmodernity where "there are no essential identities of class, ethnicity, gender or sexuality: everything is potentially fluid and transformable into something else" (1999: 83). McGuigan quotes Hall (1996) attempting to come to a synthetic and positive sense of identity that avoids the potential alienation of some postmodern critiques:

> I use "identity" to refer to the meeting point, the point of *suture*, between on the one hand the discourse and practices which attempt to interpolate, speak to us or hail us into place as the social subjects and particular discourses, and on the other hand, the processes which produce subjectivities, which construct us as subjects which can be "spoken". (1999: 87)

For McGuigan (1999: 103) identity can be understood as "a multi-accentual concept, mediating self and history in many complex ways". The signal contribution of postmodern thinking to our understanding is the challenge to essentialist thinking about class, race, ethnicity, gender and sexuality. The human subject is "constantly in process of becoming and increasingly hybrid" (1999: 103). There is no transcendentally guaranteed essential subject; indeed, in order to avoid even the hint of a metaphysical validation of our identity Foucault denies the theological, the Cartesian and the essentialist view of our selves. Barker succinctly renders his position: "it is as material beings in the world that we interrogate our relation between the world and our existence in it, and this interrogation can only be undertaken from where we find ourself located at a specific historical and cultural juncture" (1998: 76). This is unexceptional in itself but for Foucault the relationship we have with the world provides no sure ground of truth of being but what we achieve is a series of coherences "on which relations with ourselves and others are elaborated" and which "emerge from the encounters with the cultural milieu in which we find ourselves" (1998: 78). It is in this way that our subjectivity is constructed within the discourses of the human sciences: "it is the elaboration of oneself in relation to a series of new master/experts – psychiatrists, psychologists, psychoanalysts, social workers – that constitutes who we are today, a subject that is completely subjected not in a negative sense but in terms of a multiplicity of positivities" (1998: 81). This model of self compares with Giddens's late modern person who constructs her own life trajectory partly through recourse to expert knowledges that constitute a set of constraining contexts and discourses. However, in contrast to Foucault, within Giddens's general model of structuration knowledgeable creative agency characterizes the subject who self-creates within the recursive interplay between individual and social structure. For Foucault we seem to be in thrall to the discursive practices that represent our selves to our selves, whereas for Giddens we actively and reflexively participate in our own self-construction.

Epistemology and School

The current knowledge map can be understood as composed of three elements in different combinations, and with different emphases, in different times and places; they are revelation, rationality and relativism. The first, and possibly the oldest, is revelation, the idea that knowledge has a transcendental origin and guarantee of truth or validity; what Berger termed the "sacred canopy". The notion that knowledge in some sense pre-exists the knower is still basic to many religious communities, for example, in Islam, biblicist Christian groups, and the Roman Catholic and Orthodox churches. The externality of knowledge is also implicit in the notion of scientific objectivity and the concept of natural laws or regularities that are pre-existent and merely need to be discovered. However, most often in natural science our being and our knowledge of the world are immanently expressed, but not exclusively so, as we now have non-rational creation science.

The second epistemological frame is rationality. Within the transcendental paradigm Augustine had already typified humans as the "rational animal". An effect of the European Enlightenment was to remove God in favour of an essential *man* and to elevate rationality to the place previously occupied by God as ultimate guarantor of the truth of knowledge. The assumption among Western rational intellectuals until relatively recently was that religion would wither away in the face of rational understanding of our nature and grounds of being, most especially within natural science. Critically within the classical natural science paradigm knowledge in some sense pre-exists and inheres in the nature of the object. Thus, the argument that scientific knowledge exists independently of the knower and is beyond culture continues to have currency. All these conceptions more or less depend upon a correspondence model of language, that there is an independent reality and that what language does is mirror or map that reality. Upon this mapping the truth value of modern thought ultimately depends.

It is in the wake of the fundamental shift in linguistics, most often associated with de Saussure, that the epistemologies of modernity begin to look less secure. The significance of de Saussure's model of language is that it denies the connection between language and its objects in favour of a system of signs that creates meaning through its internal regulation. Thus, the world of knowledge becomes a system of representations, language pictures of a possible reality, which like language itself only exists from moment to moment and changes with each utterance. The benign version of the epistemological implications of de Saussure's model is relativism. This has many variations but a basic tenet is that knowledge is a function of language and is produced in real social contexts and its truth-value is defined by those contexts. Thus, Western rationality loses its universal and essential character and with it the power to validate objective independent and universal truth. The debates on relativism brought with them many issues of enduring concern to education that cannot be pursued here (Hollis and Lukes 1982).

The postmodern critique of language, especially that of Derrida, pushes de Saussure's ideas a little further than relativism in a complex and innovative view of language and truth. Pertinent to my purposes is the general notion that what language does is play over our world of experience and that meaning, that is our ultimate trust in language to represent the world, is fugitive. The notion of play suggests a constant movement, like dappled light on stained glass, where we participate in the multi-layered games of language which are no more nor less than that. The subject is created and recreated within the flow of discourse and language is detached from its objects. Meaning is continually deferred because it looks forward to be qualified by the next utterance. Absent language, what is not spoken, is as powerful as presence. Meaning is like desire, always potential never fully or finally achieved (Barthes 1975). These radical conceptions of language have been intellectual currency for decades but they do not inform school language which exclusively reflects bureaucratic culture (Yates 2000a). In school only Apple's "official knowledge" may penetrate (Ainley 1999: 169).

The Fantasy Curriculum and the Real Person

Ranson raises a series of critical questions occasioned by the current conditions of late modernity.

> The economic, social and political transformations of our time are fundamentally altering the structure of experience: the capacities each person needs to flourish, what it is to live in society, the nature of work and the form taken by polity. The changes raise deep questions for the government of education and for the polity in general about: *what is it to be a person?* (1998: 96)

School is rooted in modernity and implicit in schooling is an essential or natural self "a pre-existent subject expressing itself in the words made available to it by language" (Usher and Edwards 1994: 67). Essentialism in relation to knowledge of the self acts in much the same way as revelation or a transcendentally legitimated social order in that it puts the subject somehow beyond history and so beyond critical engagement. If our nature is a universal given then insofar as relationship implies a dynamic element and the possibility of change then we can have no effective relationship with our selves. This is reflected in school where the school person that is promoted by the organization and social practices of the institution is that of a strongly individuated entity instrumentally engaged in cognitive production. School does not recognize the possibility of a dynamic interiority of social being, nor difference, nor the individual voice. The model of the school person is strongly boundaried and excludes the affective dimension in favour of a limited bureaucratic person recognized and judged in terms of conformity of performance. This has wider social significance and is in turn central to the external legitimation of school, that is its licensing through conformity to inspection criteria, where failure to conform can ultimately mean dissolution. Thus, education seems to be increasingly a self-referential system inured to the changing world in which it is set.

In considering schooling and identity there is also an issue of power over defining what is real. In school this is achieved through screening out the external world and the cultures that pupils embody through the rituals of conformity and constant policing through measurement. The latest version of the National Curriculum continues to construct knowledge as an emptied out Enlightenment map that would be recognizable to D'Alembert or Locke. This compares with the process of colonialization as understood by Said (1985) where the colonized understand themselves in the categories of otherness devised by the coloniser. What this means in relation to identity and schooling is the appropriation of the pupil's voice by a reductive functional bureaucracy which denies the active agency of the pupil in creating the narratives within which she represents herself. This is achieved pedagogically and organizationally through the maintenance of the boundaries of the maps of knowledge and of the self and their presentation as external to the subject. The exclusion of the subject, and the denial of a social or negotiated model of knowledge, is necessary to the process of social control via conformity. If the dynamic and constructivist nature of new knowledge, including knowledge of the self, were admitted into school then its social control effect would be lessened and enforced conformity through inspection would become unreliable. In short school would be radically altered as an agent of the bureaucratic culture of the state.

This disjunction between school and its cultural contexts can be understood through the textual metaphor. Morgan (1999: 247) contrasts the traditional text that I am constructing now with "hypertext" where the reader approaches the text by "creating links between one segment and another, one phrase or concept or argument to another, as your imagination, memory or participation suggest. Give the text different colours, fonts, formats. Add pictures, sound, movies". As Morgan suggests, "this digitised, hypermedia text-world is increasingly the home environment of young people across the globe" (1999: 247). This is reiterated by Ainley's discussion of learning policy that has been subject to rapid shifts in recent times, so that flux replaces stasis as the background to students' experience where "these transformations are accepted as normal by those who are born into them" (1999: 209).

This different type of text from the traditional static book invites a more participative relationship between subject and text. This in turn implies a constructivist rather than a transmission model of knowledge because it is through the particular interaction that the text becomes part of the production of knowledge. The content and nature of that knowledge is not entirely predisposed by the text and so cannot be safely predicted, and could theoretically be highly variable. The locus of validation of socially constructed knowledge is within the relationships between the knowledge producers and within its use value. Such knowledge would not easily be subject to standardized testing.

It is arguable that while a more relativist epistemology now characterizes social knowledge and this can accommodate the essentially positivist epistemologies of school the reverse is not the case. School as currently constituted is unable to include and legitimate knowledge as a social construction because it is based on a view of the text as authority within one dimension unaffected by its real contexts of time and place.

The static authority of traditional text is not confined to the relationship between teacher and taught but perhaps more critically is built into the surveillance systems of government agency control of the teacher through prescribed curriculum and pedagogy and through the instrument of the inspection report. These texts are aimed at the achievement of a centrally defined bureaucratic reality and have no necessary relationship with anything outside the text. For example, in order to achieve this desired result the Qualifications and Curriculum Authority's voluminous advice on citizenship education is predicated on a fantasy model of society as a static entity with a largely uncontested meaning. It is permeated by the protestant work ethic, the confusion of morality with conformity and a strong social control agenda aimed at both teachers and their pupils (Yates 2000b). The role of the teacher is here reduced to conformity with the text and their work "has become a daily struggle at least to appear to comply with the latest demands of central government in order to secure their own positions against growing insecurity and proletarianization" (Ainley 1999: 199). The removal of the professional autonomy of teachers and their recreation as bureaucratic functionaries has an inevitable effect on teachers' practice. Ainley suggests that the increasing emphasis on the end of education as certification has brought about a "growing alienation from and instrumentalism towards institutionalised learning on the part of both staff and students" (1999: 199).

On the social control agenda implicit in current social practices in school Ainley (1999) quotes Lave and Wenger who question the notion that learning is what motivates much educational practice:

> the focus of attention shifts from co-participation in practice to acting on the person-to-be-changed. Such a shift is typical of situations such as schooling in which pedagogically structured content organizes learning activities [so that] the identity of learners becomes an explicit object of change where there is no cultural identity encompassing the activity . . . The commoditization (sic) of learning engenders a fundamental contradiction between the use and exchange values of the outcome of learning, which manifests itself in conflicts between learning to know and learning to display knowledge for evaluation . . . Test taking then becomes a new parasitic practice, the goal of which is to increase the exchange value of learning independently of its use value. (Ainley 1999, quoting Lave and Wenger 1994: 112)

School imposes an institutional identity through its particular emphases in social practice. School certificates become a competitively acquired commodity, which are valued because they can be exchanged for social goods rather than because the knowledge can be integrated into constructive social performance. As Ainley suggests, "this process of commodification of learning means that less and less of any real worth is being learnt at any level of education"

(1999: 199). Indeed one might say that learning in school is quite literally useless.

Thus, the issue of identity can be understood as, first, one of dissonance between the cultures of schooling and the more general trends in knowledge production in society at large, including knowledge of the self constructed within the dynamic and differentiated cultural milieus of students. Secondly, and more specifically, the forms of school knowledge, embedded in its social practice, tend towards an individuated and alienated experience that undermines both the social nature of knowledge and knowledge of the self. The question of what knowledge is for is not addressed apart from its being an object of competition and a measurement of self-worth via testing. This last is evidenced by renewed concern with pupils' self-esteem.

Visions and Versions

In this essay I have tried to provide a critical explanatory framework for understanding identity as an equivalent discourse to that of spirituality in school. I have located the issue within the relationship between school and society as realized in the implicit models of the social that inform educational practice. While school reflects a mono-cultural neo-liberal world dominated by market models of social practice, the world outside of school is characterized by the features of late modernity, that is to say pluralism, relativism and the global economy (Cohen and Kennedy 2000). Robertson (1992) argues that globalization is not an alternative to modernity and the image of nation-based economies it is simply another layer. Similarly, Foucault (1976) suggests that we should think of postmodernism not as an epoch but as a mood, a mode of thought. It is not the case that the postmodern, despite the temporal nature of the term, has replaced modernity but that they simultaneously exist. The sticking points in regard to education are the nature of pluralism and relativism, both of which are strongly represented in the social worlds of pupils and both of which are denied in a schooling that only reflects the modernist state.

This myopic mono-culturalism fails to recognize the nature or importance of lived and expressed difference. For example, there are at least three different models of the individual in circulation. First, there is the neo-liberal individual that is embedded in the texts of the National Curriculum and the Qualifications and Curriculum Agency. This individual has an essential self-identity whose dominant characteristics are autonomy, self-reliance and a belief in the market and the enterprise culture. This individual has no affective dimensions and the original model may well be male. Secondly, there is the late modern individual of Giddens's (1991) structuration theory. This individual can conceive of self as a future oriented project and work towards desired identities through the commodification of lifestyle. This individual has practical consciousness that gives the subject an active agency within Giddens' recursive loop between individual and social structure. This capacity of the subject to act freely may be lost in the third variant, the postmodern individual. For Foucault (1970) the subject is decentred and is constituted in the confluence of discourse and practice, and of power and knowledge. This individual is fluid and exists from moment to moment with the flow of discursive production.

There is an intimate connection between being, our conception of ontology and knowing who we are. However, there is no recognition of this in the pupils' experience of schooling. School can be seen as an antique technology and is rooted in the values and attitudes of a nostalgic modernity (Ball 1994). School knowledge refers to a fantasy domain; it lacks use value. The question of what learning is, and what it is for, are not easy to clearly formulate in the current state of education. For example, Ainley claims, "most academics and many teachers have become so confused between learning and its assessment that it is very difficult for them to begin to address the basic question of what it is to learn" (1999: 199).

For example, there is a recent emphasis on raising standards that is seen as a disassociated good in itself. Bureaucratically justified standards may be vaguely attached to the notion that success in school improves life chances now just as it did for working-class grammar school boys after the Second World War. There is a current emphasis on "thinking skills". Leaving aside the question of whether the phrase has any meaningful referent, the rationale is in terms of acquiring such skills in order to accelerate the production of cognitive performances rather than any contribution to the development of critical autonomy (McGuiness 1999). The National Literacy Strategy is aimed at improving literacy that, as the fundamental meta-skill of learning, will in its turn improve everything else. But the process of achieving this literacy has to be seen as an isolated competitively acquired cognitive skill. This is legitimated not by any judgements about its worth and potential for active learning, but by measurement and so becomes just another item of decontextualized performance in a school life too often characterized by frenetic preparation, on the part of both pupils and teachers, for some ultimately meaningless external judgement.

There is a set of unresolved, indeed largely unformulated issues around the affective curriculum, and the capacity of school to recognize more dimensions of the person than the cognitive, that would need to be addressed if school knowledge were to contribute to students' purposeful sense of self and agency, rather than purvey a fantasy of self and society. The differentiated realities of the social need to permeate the fantasy world of school. This requires a reassessment of how school relates to the prevailing models not only of the person but also of the economy, including global capitalism as well as the developing global technologies because these have political implications for the nature of the social world that pupils will have to continually locate and re-locate themselves within. In order that education is not experienced as irrelevant or even disabling, the unengaging official model of the person as a conformist, modernist apparatchik might be supplemented with an awareness of the nature and implications of pluralism and life politics; of postmodernism and new knowledges and ways of knowing the self. The relevance of school to life would be improved by entering the real world of risk (Giddens 1991).

On Chaos

Imagine who we might become if school were predicated on the following brief exposition. Deleuze and Guattari are translated as using the word opinion where we might put values, the point of which is to keep chaos at bay; we "do not perceive the present without imposing on it a conformity with the past. This is all that we ask for in order to *make an opinion* for ourselves, like a sort of umbrella that protects us from chaos" (1994: 202). They argue that the world of ideas "art, science and philosophy requires more: they cast planes over the chaos" (1994: 202). This organization of ideas is in some sense natural; "there would not be a little order in ideas if there was not also a little order in things or states of affairs, like an objective antichaos" (1994: 202). Pursuing the metaphor they argue, "people are constantly putting up an umbrella that shelters them and on the underside of which they draw a firmament and write their conventions and opinions. But poets, artists, make a slit in the umbrella, they tear open the firmament itself, to let in a bit of free and windy chaos and to frame in sudden light a vision that appears through the rent" (1994: 203).

References

Ainley, P. 1999: *Learning Policy, Towards the Certified Society*, Basingstoke: Macmillan.
Ball, S. J. 1994: *Education Reform: A critical and post-structural approach*, Buckingham: Open University Press.
Barker, P. 1998: *Michel Foucault: An Introduction*, Edinburgh, Edinburgh University Press.
Barthes, R. 1975: (trans) Miller, R. *The Pleasure of the Text*, New York: Hill and Wang.

Bruner, J. 1999: Culture, Mind and Education. In B. Moon and P. Murphy (eds), *Curriculum in Context*, London: Paul Chapman / The Open University Press, 148–78.

Cohen, R. and Kennedy, P. 2000: *Global Sociology*, London: Macmillan.

Deleuze, G. and Guattari F. 1994: (trans) Tomlinson, H. and Burchell, G. *What is Philosophy?* New York: Columbia University Press.

Foucault, M. 1970: *The Order of Things*, London: Tavistock.

—— [1976] 1990: *The Will to Knowledge: The History of Sexuality: vol. I*, London: Penguin.

Giddens, A. 1991: *Modernity and Self-Identity, Self and Society in the Late Modern Age*, Cambridge: Polity Press / Basil Blackwell.

Hall, S. 1996: Who needs "identity"? In S. Hall and P. du Gay (eds), *Questions of Cultural Identity*, London: Sage.

Hollis, M. and Lukes, S. (eds) 1982: *Rationality and Relativism*, Oxford: Basil Blackwell.

Isin, E. S. and Wood P. K. 1999: *Citizenship and Identity*, London: Sage.

Lave, J. and Wenger, E. 1994: *Situated Learning, Legitimate Peripheral Participation*, Cambridge: Cambridge University Press.

McGuigan, J. 1999: *Modernity and Postmodern Culture*, Buckingham: Open University Press.

McGuiness, C. 1999: *From Thinking Skills to Thinking Classrooms: a review and evaluation of approaches for developing pupils' thinking*, Norwich: Department for Education and Employment/HMSO.

Morgan, W. 1999: Postmodern Classrooms on the Borders? In J. Leach and B. Moon (eds), *Curriculum in Context*, London: Paul Chapman / The Open University Press, 247–64.

Mullard, M. and Spicker, P. 1998: *Social Policy in a Changing Society*, London: Routledge.

Ranson, S. (ed.) 1998: *Inside the Learning Society*, London: Cassell.

Robertson. R, 1992: *Globalization: Social Theory and Global Culture*, London: Sage.

Said, E. [1978] 1985: *Orientalism*, Harmondsworth: Penguin.

Usher, R. and Edwards, R. 1994: *Postmodernism and Education*, London: Routledge.

Yates, P. 1999: The Bureaucratization of Spirituality, *International Journal of Children's Spirituality* 4(2), 179–93.

—— 2000a: Legitimating the Moral Curriculum. In R. Gardner, J. Cairns and D. Lawton (eds), *Education for Values: Morals, Ethics and Citizenship in Contemporary Teaching*, London: Kogan Page, 79–95.

—— 2000b: The Spirit and the Empty Matrix: The construction of spiritual, moral, social and cultural education. In R. Best (ed.), *Education for Spiritual, Moral, Social and Cultural Development*, London: Cassell, 22–36.

Chapter 17

Searching for the Spirit

TONY EAUDE

THIS chapter results from a research study (Eaude 1999) into how teachers of young children in English primary schools understand spiritual development. After summaries of the research background and methodology adopted, I describe the findings and explore the emerging issues. I argue that the basis for a "universal" spirituality lies in the search for personal identity and that an important route to understanding young children's spirituality is through psychology and learning theory. My own background is as a teacher and headteacher in primary schools. In the end, successful curriculum development needs to take account of, and start from, teachers' views, especially in an area so elusive and contentious as the spiritual. Just as any good lesson must build on children's prior understandings, we must know what teachers understand by spiritual development if we are to help them to make better provision.

The Context of Legislation, Guidance and Curriculum

A brief summary of how legislation, policy and curriculum guidance has approached "spiritual development" may provide a historical context for my work and highlight the ambivalence both in legislation and the resulting guidance to teachers. The debate about spiritual development has been a curiously English one, both because of distinctive legislation and the powerful influence of the established Church. However, this debate has a wider international, and indeed universal, application.

The 1944 Education Act in England and Wales asserted the importance of the spiritual development of children. What this meant was never developed, and little discussed, in the next forty-five years. The lack of definition and discussion about its meaning suggests that there was an implicit consensus, or that it was in everyone's interests to make of it what they wished. The assumption appeared to be, at least until the 1960s, that schools would prepare pupils for their place within a Christian society and that attendance at collective worship and the teaching of religious ideas were desirable.

The 1988 Education Reform Act introduced sweeping changes in almost every area of the curriculum. Yet the spiritual retained its primacy as schools were required to promote "the spiritual, moral, cultural, mental and physical development of pupils at the school and of society" (DES 1988: S.1 (2) a.). There was still no explanation of what this meant. Little seemed to have changed.

Debate on what is meant by the spiritual was fuelled primarily by the 1992 Education Act, which set up a system of school inspection with public reporting. Among the four main areas on which the Office for Standards in Education Handbook for the Inspection of Schools required inspectors to make a judgement was the "spiritual, moral, social and cultural development of pupils" (Ofsted 1993: Section 2.1). Suddenly, the need for discussion of what spiritual development entails, and of criteria on the basis of which it can be described and reported, became a matter of pressing urgency.

The last ten years has seen a succession of guidance and documentation from Government agencies such as the National Curriculum Council (1993), Ofsted (1994), the School Curriculum and Assessment Authority (1995, 1996) and the Qualifications and Curriculum Authority (1997). This debate has helped the search for a common language to describe what spiritual development might "look like". Understandably, this guidance tends to concentrate on what is observable (and demonstrable) rather than on implicit and unseen qualities. Certain phrases, such as "awe and wonder", have been widely adopted. However, teachers and inspectors remain unclear about what is meant by spiritual development, with inspectors' views often seen as dependent on personal judgement.

During the same period, curriculum change came with the regularity, it seemed, of the passing seasons. Teachers were presented with a succession of new curriculum documentation, of assessment procedures, of planning models, culminating in the introduction of the National Literacy Strategy in 1998 and the National Numeracy Strategy in 1999. Most teachers were so busy that the spiritual, as such, hardly entered their thinking. At best, the criteria by which the success of pupil, teacher and school were to be judged, and the strategies recommended to achieve this, seemed to grate with suggestions that teachers should encourage opportunities for "a sense of awe, wonder and mystery" (SCAA 1995). The National Curriculum documents of 1995 (DfE 1995) or 1999 (DfEE 1999) laid no emphasis on this aspect.

The Wider Social and Cultural Context

It is puzzling how little the legislation seemed to recognize the difficulties and, probably, the opportunities of spiritual development retaining this pre-eminence. From the 1960s onwards, considerable social changes impacted on society, and on education, undermining many of the certainties and complacencies of the preceding years. Among these were:

- more social and geographical mobility, often accompanied by family dispersal or breakdown;
- the greater disruption among communities, with the decline of heavy industry, the casualization of work, and the impact of globalization;
- a growing level of wealth and of consumerism, often fuelled by powerful messages from increasingly sophisticated and powerful mass media;
- the decline of the influence of organized religion and reduced levels of attendance at church; and
- the arrival and entry, especially in big cities, into many communities and schools of large numbers of families who attend places of worship outside the Christian tradition.

Naturally, some of these changes impacted much more heavily on some areas and schools than on others. But, even at the level of the teacher of young children, wider social considerations undermined, or questioned, much that had been previously taken for granted – such as the place of religion, the security of the family, the messages from outside affecting the child. Old certainties have become much more tenuous.

Considering Previous Research

Any discussion of young children's spirituality must take account of the wider philosophical debates about spiritual development. Until the 1990s much of the research into young children's religious and moral development adopted a broadly Piagetian view, or extrapolated back from studies of adolescents or adults. But the last ten years have seen a greater interest in research explicitly into young children's spirituality. There has been a growing interest in observing, and understanding, young children's experience, and the role of the spiritual within it, rather than taking a preconceived idea of the spiritual and trying to relate it to young children. It has been important to take young children's experiences seriously in exploring how they think and talk.

Although studies such as that of Hay and Nye (Hay with Nye 1998) and the Children and Worldviews Project (Erricker *et al.* 1997) are time-consuming and encounter methodological dilemmas, they start from the child's perspective and are attentive to the child's view of the world. Hay and Nye's idea of "relational consciousness" places the relationships that the child makes with other people and the world around as central to spiritual experience. This position asserts that the spiritual is open to all and is located within everyday experience. Although the word "consciousness" implies that spiritual development occurs only, or primarily, at the conscious level, much of our most important learning occurs at an un- or extra-conscious level. The authors in the Children and Worldviews Project describe young children as engaged upon the telling and re-telling of "personal narrative". In this, they highlight the integrating quality of narrative, and its importance for the child in making sense of diverse, and often puzzling, experiences. Especially significant is their emphasis on the place of narrative in helping children to cope with loss, and the fear of loss, and with resolving conflict. Stories give shape, structure and meaning to our lives in profound ways.

These developments are in marked contrast to a much more limited, and limiting, academic debate. Carr (1994, 1995, 1996) claims that the search for a "secular", or universal, spirituality is at best confused and at worst misguided. He argues that, since spirituality has always been located within religious traditions, it is a misuse of the word to imagine that it can be successfully transferred outside them and that it is a concept only applicable to religious, and to some extent creative, traditions. Spiritual truths and beliefs can be accessed only within such a tradition, just as we can learn language only by learning a specific language.

This would be an abstruse and largely irrelevant academic argument if it did not impact on work such as that of Wright (1998, 1999), who relates this debate to the task of the teacher. He offers a definition that "spirituality is the developing relationship of the individual within community and tradition to that which is – or which is perceived to be – of ultimate concern, ultimate value and ultimate truth" (1988: 88). Surely, we might expect, this implies that any activity which leads us to question what it is that is fundamental to human existence falls within the spiritual domain; the position of those like Hay with Nye (1998) and myself that this search is a universal one, implicit in the human condition and open to all.

Yet Wright asserts, following Carr, that such a search requires acceptance of the traditions of a faith community. While exploration of the spiritual does require involvement in community and tradition, the argument that such community and tradition cannot exist outside a faith community seems to me simply unproven. While I would not wish to lose the insight of traditions of spirituality, it is important to search for ways of making spiritual experience accessible to all.

Two different approaches argue against the use of the language of spirituality in this context. Blake (1996) suggests that what I am calling spirituality can largely be reduced to the moral domain and that its use by the forces of reaction should warn us against adopting it. Conroy (1999) argues that the word "spirituality" means so many different things to different people that we should simply abandon its use, and find other words to describe what we mean. While this has a superficial appeal, modern, secular discourse about spirituality would be the poorer if it did not benefit from the insights of traditions of spirituality. More pragmatically, the legislation demands that teachers provide for children's spiritual "development". However unsatisfactory a term, an issue discussed below, we have little alternative but to live with it.

Lewis (2000) has trenchantly argued against the narrow exclusivity of Carr, which restricts spirituality to those (ever fewer) within a faith tradition and the limitations of Blake's model – both of which serve to place severe restrictions on any redefinition, or re-description, of the spiritual and deny the possibility of a universal spirituality. Lewis goes on to provide an interesting framework for describing young children's spirituality based on recent research into brain function and the cognitive work of those such as Donaldson (1984, 1993) who demonstrate the limitations of Piaget's theory in describing young children's affective learning.

Developing My Research Question and Method

I wanted to consider in some depth how teachers understand the idea of spiritual development. This directed me away from the questionnaire approach towards longer interviews. While Davies' (1998) findings from a survey of the attitudes of headteachers in Wales are of interest, the use of statistics in an area such as this is largely spurious unless the respondents share a common view of what the categories and words mean. In an area such as the spiritual this is inherently improbable, if not impossible. If we are to understand what, and how, teachers think about the spiritual, we need to do more than ask them to put statements into an order of importance. We must probe more deeply into the underlying meanings they ascribe to language. It may not be useful or sensible to draw any statistical conclusions from a small sample such as mine. Such patterns as do emerge may be little more than anecdotal. But the interpretive tradition would argue that "thick" data offers far better chances of understanding underlying, often paradoxical, meanings than the simple certainties of numbers.

As a result of my reflections on young children's learning, and more simply because research tends to focus on older children and their teachers, I wanted to look at teachers with children at the younger end of primary school. My research was based in schools within the City of Oxford, both for geographical convenience and because of my own interest and experience in urban primary schools with issues such as ethnic and religious diversity, impacting particularly strongly on city schools.

Any small-scale study inevitably runs into the difficulty of knowing how typical the sample will be of the wider population (of schools and of teachers). In determining which schools to visit, I was keen to choose a variety of types of school and teacher likely to include a wide range of view. I included two schools serving a multi-ethnic catchment area, two schools of an Anglican foundation, and one of a Roman Catholic foundation. Given the limitations of time, and my wish to identify teachers prepared to discuss the subject, I restricted myself to those schools considered within an Ofsted inspection report to make provision for spiritual development that was good (or better) than average. My further research, currently in progress, considers a wider range of schools, with teachers in a slightly younger age group.

My research question was:

> To examine the understandings of teachers of young children (between five and seven years old) in four urban English primary schools of the spirituality of children of that age, and how they seek to enable it to develop and enhance it through suitable activities within the classroom and the wider school environment.

Given that I undertook in one school a full pilot study broadly similar, both in method and outcome, this paper considers both the pilot and the main study together.

Description of Method

I interviewed three teachers in each school, the headteacher and two other teachers of children between five and seven years of age. I asked the headteacher to nominate two teachers likely to want to take part, recognizing that some teachers, because of factors such as ill-health, pressure or newness at the school might not be appropriate. This resulted, almost certainly, in the sample being skewed towards more experienced teachers who had given the matter some thought. Certainly there was an over-representation of older teachers and only two in their first two years of teaching.

The approach adopted was to conduct semi-structured interviews, most of which lasted around thirty minutes, which I tape-recorded and transcribed. I offered complete confidentiality and was very clear that I was seeking to describe and to understand, rather than make an evaluative judgement about their views. I offered in most classes to go in briefly beforehand, partly to offer something in return for their involvement, partly to give me a context if there was nothing to say. In practice, a few teachers steered me away from this, and a few really tried to make use of me, but for most I suspect that my presence was no great help, and in fact somewhat of an imposition.

The range of questions I set out to explore was:

- what the teacher understands by the term "spiritual development";
- school policies on spiritual development;
- aspects of school life which help to develop spiritual awareness;
- what the teacher thinks inspectors are looking for;
- which subject areas, if any are most, and least, suitable for spiritual development;
- the relationship to religious faith;
- the attributes of a spiritually aware child;
- any patterns of groups of children who are especially aware spiritually;
- a particular incident which led to a child or group of children's spirituality being developed; and
- the teacher's best moment in teaching recently.

Reflections on the Process

Maybe the most remarkable finding was how willing, and even keen, almost all the teachers were to talk about personal, and in some cases difficult, issues. With possibly two exceptions, the teachers were thoughtful, open and willing to explore what was for them an area which they had not discussed in depth with another individual. Even those two who were less open provided considerable insights, despite my feeling that they were never entirely comfortable with their involvement. On more than one occasion, I was humbled by the simplicity with which an interviewee captured in a few words what I had found, and still find, elusive. That teachers, especially those of young children, do not talk much about the spiritual, does not mean that they cannot do so, or offer significant insights.

This said the majority of the teachers were somewhat diffident about their views, especially at the start of the discussion. While this may have been no more than an initial nervousness, it tended to indicate that they were unused to talking very much about the spiritual, even in schools where the spiritual was deemed to be good. Two articulate headteachers commented that they had little idea why their school had been commended for its approach to spiritual development.

It was interesting how those teachers who made clear assertions early on tended to modify them as the discussion continued. For example, one teacher who said that it was to do with encouraging religious faith ended the discussion by saying that during the course of the discussion he had changed his mind. There were few teachers whose emphasis did not change significantly during the course of the interview. The process of thinking through the complexity seemed to help teachers realize that the spiritual is both elusive and capable of description. The most effective way of developing teachers' understanding of the spiritual may simply be to enable discussion. The forthcoming debate on citizenship may provide an important forum for this to happen. Yet our present culture would seem to find such an activity alarmingly subversive.

Looking for Patterns of Response and Categories of Understanding

The detail of my findings can be found in the thesis itself (Eaude: 1999). As one might expect, the more experienced the teacher, the more likely they were to give a fluent account of their views. Too few men were involved for any conclusions on the basis of gender to be made. While the teacher's subject background seemed to make little difference, many teachers initially emphasized the possibilities of their areas of interest or particular ability as fertile ground for the spiritual. But most came to the view that the spiritual could be located within (almost) any subject, and that approach and teaching style mattered more than content. Most surprising to me was that the personal religious faith of the teachers seemed to influence their view of the spiritual needs of their children remarkably little.

By far the most obvious pattern emerging was the similarity of colleagues within the same school. Whether this reflected an underlying ethos within the school, a particular culture and tradition or the personality of the headteacher, I cannot judge. But it was very clear that the sort of factors mentioned were common to schools far more than to other categories. It may be that each group adopted a "party-line". But my sense was that how staff related to each other and to children was by far the most powerful factor in their responses.

A revealing sideline emerged from the question about policies –

maybe more a comment on policies than on the spiritual. Although no school had a specific policy as such for the spiritual, most non-headteachers were fairly sure that there was one. And all the headteachers, except one, were somewhat apologetic that there was not one. The exception, in musing why not, concluded that it was so embedded in the school that a policy would have been too limiting.

One question which was revealing, especially with those who were not fluent in their views, was that about the spiritually aware child. Without exception, the teachers were able to describe a particular child and what led them to that description, the most common qualities being generosity, sensitivity and awareness of others. This reinforces the point that description is both easier, and arguably more productive, than attempts at definition.

The question most people found hardest to answer was that of patterns, or factors, which tend to lead to spiritual awareness or maturity. This may reflect wariness about making generalizations in an area so fraught with uncertainties, and where criteria for making such a judgement are personal. The two factors mentioned – though not very widely – were the influence of the family and those who attended the local church. This might suggest, tentatively, that emotional security and involvement in a reflective tradition are thought to be necessary foundations for spiritual awareness, without being in any way guarantors.

Without exception, the teachers thought that spiritual development was something much wider than religious development. This was a surprise to me. In some schools, especially the one with a Roman Catholic foundation, the development of religious faith was thought to be profoundly important. But religion was seen as only a part of the spiritual, both for those who are regular worshippers within a faith tradition and those who are not. This seemed to go beyond the obvious point that many children would be excluded if spirituality were to be located only within religion, to a deeper sense that religion is only one way of responding to universal questions.

One further surprising strand to emerge, in three of the five schools, was how often loss, tragedy, or severe illness was identified as a time when the school as a whole had been affected, and strengthened. The death of a pupil, the very severe illness of another, the response of a child to her parents' disability were all cited as occasions when the children were enabled to grow spiritually. Where such events had occurred they had made a considerable impact. It would seem that how such issues were handled was both a reflection of, and a contribution to, the ability of the school to deal with difficult and painful issues appropriately and sensitively.

Underlying almost all the responses was the importance of relationships within the school. Most teachers were quite explicit about this. Some used the language of relationship more implicitly. This will be of little surprise to those with a knowledge of primary schools, but the constant return to ethos, to caring for each other, to empathy within and beyond the school was very marked. The link with Hay and Nye's (1998) idea of relational consciousness could hardly be clearer.

Towards a More Coherent Language for the Spiritual

The notion of spirituality, and of spiritual development, is elusive and crosses all sorts of boundaries. While most people would regard the spiritual domain as incorporating aspects of moral, emotional, aesthetic or religious experience, the boundaries remain not only unclear, but inherently so. We can describe the spiritual without difficulty, once we have overcome emotional or cultural unwillingness to engage in this activity. But, while there is considerable commonality of what is meant by the spiritual, no definition can capture exactly what is distinctive about the spiritual. Following Wittgenstein's notion of family resemblances, we see underlying similarities and patterns, just as in a family, without quite being able to say what they are. While we may know it when we see it, we struggle to pin down the necessary and sufficient conditions to state quite what spirituality is.

Priestley (1996, 1999) has raised a more underlying difficulty with the idea of "spiritual development". He argues, coherently and convincingly, that the idea of development has connotations of aspects of learning, such as the cognitive and growth, such as the physical, but that spirituality works unevenly, without there being some end-point of arrival, without there being even implicitly an epiphany of unfolding. Priestley's diagnosis seems to me broadly correct.

We need different words which avoid the idea of linear progression towards an end-point. The word "development" brings with it a sense of consecutive stages within a Piagetian viewpoint. The metaphors are flawed. And since the spiritual is so elusive, the underlying metaphors implicit in the language we use are especially important. The adjective "spiritual" is flexible and useful, but I tend to avoid the noun "spirituality" in relation to young children, as I cannot dissociate it from the underlying metaphor of something exotic, distant and difficult. But spiritual experience is everyday, near-at hand and natural for those who have not learnt otherwise.

The elusiveness of the spiritual means that any alternative terminology will have flaws. The metaphor of growth is attractive but it has the implication of either a successful outcome, or failure of growth leading to death. Within it is embedded the idea of a progression from seed to fruition and the present state of growth being always related to some ideal end-point. I do not think that spiritual experience is like that. The spiritual is simultaneously quite normal and quite remarkable for young children, as for all of us, embedded in how we make sense of the everyday.

The alternative metaphor – of a spiritual journey – seems better, but is still fraught with some difficulties. Its strength is the implication of exploration rather than arrival, of uncertainty and possible false turnings rather than the safety – and the atrophy – of a final position. But the underlying metaphor is still linear, and suggestive of only one point of arrival. Routes of spiritual development may be very uneven and personal. My sense is that the very young, and the very old, are often especially open to the possibilities of spiritual experience. I prefer the notion of "spiritual health", which Fisher (1998) has suggested. Within this, the individual constantly moves within a spectrum, and there is no suggestion of a perfect end-point. There is the possibility of prevention, of active encouragement, and of remediation. As with growth, there is an emphasis on the environment of the individual and the need for nurturing and for attention.

Although legislation leaves us stuck, for now, with the notion of spiritual "development", to recognize its limitations and learning to play with other metaphors and conceptions of the spiritual is a necessary part of understanding the richness of this domain.

Future Paths in Relation to Young Children's Spirituality

Hull (1998), writing in 1972, argued that "Piaget's theory of the unfolding of intelligence is not adequate for religious growth. But from what source can Piaget be supplemented? We must look to psychoanalysis and to learning theory . . . ". If true of religious growth, how much more so of the spiritual? Yet there has been very little take-up of Hull's insightful recognition that the debate about young children's spirituality cannot be separate from that about learning itself.

It is encouraging that research is now focusing more on young children, rather than extrapolating back from adult experience. The research of cognitive psychologists such as Vygotsky (1978), Bruner (1996) and Donaldson (1984, 1993) provides fertile ground for seeing how children make meaning from all experience. For instance, the role of culture and context is increasingly recognized. We know that learning is both personal and only possible within culture and tradition. And although emphasis on learning through the symbolic mode remains dominant in our thinking, it seems likely that the enactive and iconic modes are especially important in learning at the most profound level.

Explorations of how young children learn and make sense of experience need to consider work on infant development such as that of
Bowlby (1965) and Winnicott (1984) and the new neurological and
psychological research into brain function. For example, how habit-
uation affects the physical development of the brain in early childhood
and Goleman's (1995) work on emotional intelligence must inform how
we look at all affective learning. Secure attachment and emotional
security provide the foundation. Having the space to question and to
learn through exploration and play helps children to move away from
an egocentric standpoint and to see the world from differing perspectives. Spiritual maturity (or health), at any age, requires this ability to be
curious, to be playful, and so to see the world afresh. Yet we tend to
trivialize play, and to regard playfulness with some suspicion.

The spiritual domain is simultaneously very complicated and
terribly simple. Some of the complications are obvious, and the
language we use often serves only to make them worse. In essence,
the spiritual seems to be the search for answers to the "why, where
and who?" questions, those which explore purpose, location and
identity. Yet we understand ourselves as individuals only in relationship to others; we know what makes us different only in relation to what
makes us the same.

I have mentioned the difficulties of any definition, but I value
"working" definitions – recognizing them as both necessary and necessarily inadequate. So I offer my own:

> spiritual experiences and episodes are those which enable the individual,
> through aspects of experience beyond direct sensory experience, to
> explore and understand his or her purpose, location (in relation to both
> space and time) and identity (in relation to other people and to the
> environment).

Such a definition is as open to criticism as others. But I would argue
passionately for its emphasis on the universality and the ordinariness
of the spiritual, even though spiritual experience is usually individual
and may often be remarkable. Any search for a "universal" approach to
the spiritual needs such a "wide" definition, rather than a narrow or
exclusive one.

Teachers do not talk much about the spiritual, for many reasons; such
as uncertainty, the pressure of other activities and embarrassment. But
my research suggests that, when enabled to explore their own view,
many teachers have an understanding at some deep level of the spiritual very like my own definition. If we are attentive to teachers, we can
help them to be attentive to children. And it is only when teachers learn
to attend to children that they provide the security necessary to prevent
them being, in the words of one teacher, "unanchored ships".

References

Blake, N. 1996: Against Spiritual Education, *Oxford Review of Education* 22(4), 443–56.

Bowlby, J. 1965: *Child Care and the Growth of Love*, London: Penguin.

Bruner, J. 1996: *The Culture of Education*. Cambridge, Mass.: Harvard University Press.

Carr, D. 1994: Knowledge and Truth in Religious Education, *Journal of Philosophy of Education* 28(2), 221–37.

—— 1995: Towards a Distinctive Conception of Spiritual Education, *Oxford Review of Education* 21(1), 83–98.

—— 1996: Rival conceptions of spiritual education, *Journal of Philosophy of Education* 30(2), 159–77.

Conroy, J. 1999: Personal and group discussions at the 6th Conference on Education, Spirituality and the Whole Child, Roehampton Institute.

Davies, G. 1998: What is Spiritual Development? Primary Headteachers' Views, *International Journal of Children's Spirituality* 3(2), 123–34.

DES (Department of Education and Science) 1988: *Education Reform Act*, London: HMSO.

DfE (Department for Education) 1995: *The National Curriculum*, London: HMSO.

DfEE (Department for Education and Employment) 1999: (jointly with QCA) *The National Curriculum*, London: DfEE/QCA.

Donaldson, M. 1984: *Children's Minds*, London: Flamingo.

—— 1993: *Human Minds: An Exploration*, London: Penguin.

Eaude, D. A. 1999: *Searching for the Spirit*, Unpublished M.Sc. Thesis: University of Oxford.

Erricker, C., Erricker, J., Sullivan, D., Ota, C. and Fletcher M. 1997: *The Education of the Whole Child*, London: Cassell.

Fisher, J. 1998: *Helps and Hindrances to Fostering Students' Spiritual Health*, Unpublished paper at the 5th Conference on Education, Spirituality and the Whole Child, Roehampton Institute.

Goleman, D. 1995: Emotional Intelligence – why it can matter more than IQ, New York: Bantam Books

Hay, D. with Nye, R. (1998): *The Spirit of the Child*, London: Fount.

Hull, J. 1998: *Utopian Whispers – Moral, Religious and Spiritual Values in Schools*, Norwich: Religious and Moral Education Press.

Lewis, J. 2000: Spiritual Education as the Cultivation of Qualities of the Heart and Mind: A Reply to Blake and Carr, *Oxford Review of Education* 26(2), 263–83.

National Curriculum Council 1993: *Spiritual and Moral Development*, York: NCC.

Ofsted 1993: *The Handbook for the Inspection of Schools* (as amended by insert 1994), London: DfE.

—— 1994: *Spiritual, Moral, Social and Cultural Development*, London: DfE.

Priestley, J. 1996: *Spirituality in the Curriculum*, Frinton-on-Sea: Hockerill Educational Foundation.

—— 1999: Moral and Spiritual Growth. In J. Mills and R. Mills (eds), *Childhood Studies – A Reader in Perspectives of Childhood*, London: Routledge.

QCA (Qualifications and Curriculum Authority) 1997: *The promotion of pupils' spiritual, moral, social and cultural development*, London: QCA.

SCAA (School Curriculum and Assessment Authority) 1995: *Spiritual and Moral Development*, SCAA Discussion Papers No. 3, London: SCAA (reissue of NCC 1993).

—— 1996: *Education for Adult Life: the Spiritual and Moral Development of Young People*, SCAA Discussion Papers No. 6, London: SCAA.

Vygotsky, L. 1978: *Mind in society: the development of higher psychological processes*, Cambridge, MA: Harvard University Press.

Winnicott, D. 1984: *The Child, the Family and the Outside World*, Harmondsworth: Pelican.

Wright, A. 1998: *Spiritual Pedagogy*, Abingdon: Culham College Institute.

—— 1999: *Discerning the Spirit – Teaching Spirituality in the Religious Education Classroom*, Abingdon: Culham College Institute.

Chapter 18

Autism and Childhood Spirituality

LAURA MORRIS

Descend lower, descend only into the world of perpetual solitude,
world not world, but that which is not world.

T. S. Eliot, *Burnt Norton*

*T*HE *Oxford Handbook of Clinical Specialities*, a key reference book to
the British medical profession, gives a definition of what constitutes mental health. Featured on the checklist of criteria is the
following: "efficient contact with reality: not too little, not too much. (As
T. S. Eliot said, 'humanity cannot bear very much reality')" (Collier,
Longmore and Brown 1999: 314). This same medical reference book
says of autism: "this neuro-developmental disorder is, if severe, the
antithesis of all that defines mental health" (1999: 402).

Autism is a developmental disorder of the brain that affects half a
million people in Britain or approximately one percent of the population. Almost one-quarter of sufferers are children. The disability is
diagnosed solely by examination of behaviour and there are five key
symptoms said to manifest themselves before the age of three. These are:
impaired social relationships; impaired communication, including use
of language; impaired make-believe play; a preference for repetitive
rituals; and a peculiar pattern of intellectual habits (Frith 1989). The
exact causes of autism are as yet unknown and it is variously suggested
that a genetic predisposition or a problematic birth, the Mumps, Measles
and Rubella vaccine or other environmental factors could be implicated.

The difficulty in isolating the causes and core features of the disability
lies in the fact that autism is rarely "pure", it is often accompanied by
other learning disabilities and it also presents itself in varying degrees.
Autism can be severely debilitating, leaving a child mute and also incapable of the most basic personal care. However, for people with

higher functioning autism, or Asperger's Syndrome, a poor social intelligence is paradoxically combined with high intelligence in other areas, including the ability to use language. There is also the possibility of "slight autism" with autistic traits such as withdrawal, but an otherwise seemingly normative pattern of development (Durig 1996). In sum, a child who falls within the vast "autistic spectrum" cannot bear too much shared reality. He or she makes a descent into the perpetual solitude that T. S. Eliot described as "not world".

This chapter presents a theoretical consideration of the spirituality of children with autism and seeks to attain three main objectives: first, to provide a spiritual context within which to understand autism; secondly, to detect autistic expressions of spiritual awareness; and thirdly, to look at ways in which spiritual language and practice might help people with the disability. The focus here is on childhood autism, although the discussion is also relevant to adults with autism and their spirituality too. Children with autism do grow up and whilst they may make progress, they do not often develop out of their disability.

The Spiritual as "Relational Consciousness"

According to the sociologist Alexander Durig:

> A society that does not appreciate meaningful perception will not be able to appreciate Autistic perception. In a society undergoing a crisis of meaning, people with Autistic perception will be misunderstood. (1996: xiii)

Equally, in a society struggling to define what is spiritually meaningful, autistic spirituality may be misunderstood. One way of defining spirituality is by means of the study of spiritual experience, which is detected to be at the heart of all religions. This is an experience which may vary its approach according to religion, culture, age or ability, but which ultimately does approach all. As David Hay and Rebecca Nye put it, this is a "biologically natural experience" (1998: 9–14).

For the purposes of their research into the spirituality of non-disabled children, Hay and Nye defined the spiritual experience as having three general features: awareness sensing, mystery sensing and value sensing. This heightened state of consciousness is experienced in its essence to be distinctly other than ordinary experience, although it can be experienced in any ordinary everyday situation. As a result of interviewing thirty-eight primary school children, this higher state of consciousness was redefined as a "relational consciousness", for the inter- and intra-personal relationships of the children seemed inextricably linked to their understanding of spiritual meaning.

The "relational consciousness" expressed in the language, symbols and stories of the children interviewed has been similarly articulated in the language of adult theologians and mystics adhering to various world faiths. Martin Buber of the Jewish tradition understood the religious life in terms of the "I–Thou relationship", a relationship between humanity and God which acknowledges the tension of separation, but which leads people to always strive to relate more (Buber [1958] 1959). In the Islamic tradition the Sufi Ibn Arabi spoke in a similar language of humankind's spiritual journey. According to Ibn Arabi this involves balancing the duality of God's distance (*tanzih*) and nearness (*tashbih*) from the world, whilst living in the knowledge that in the ultimate relationship, God and humankind are in union (*tawhid*) (Chittick 1989). In the Christian tradition St Teresa of Avila echoes this belief that the spiritual experience is ultimately a movement towards the intimate relation of union, the perception that "all things are seen and contained in God" (James [1902] 1977).

Within Indic religions there are similar expressions of belief in a relational experience as spiritually meaningful. Ramanuja's Hindu theology proclaims that a dialectical relationship between humankind and the Godhead Brahman ultimately ends in the bliss of intimate relation. Whereas in the Hindu monism expounded by Sankara the relationship between the many aspects of the one reaches its climax in unity rather than union (Lipner 1993). For the Mahayanan Buddhist, realization of *anatman* (no-self) ends the differentiation that is *Samsara* and reveals that all human beings are related in sharing the Buddha-nature (Harvey 1996).

It would reduce the particular truth claims of each believer or tradition represented here to propose that they are all synonymous. However, the common ground is that each does express a world view for which the capacity to relate is at the heart. If across many religious traditions spiritually meaningful experiences are characterized by a process of relating, where does this leave an autistic child for whom inter-personal relationships can be a struggle? To answer this question is difficult because of the nature of autism. When considering children who, at the extreme end of the autistic spectrum, are unable to articulate and communicate the most simple of their life experiences, it can feel impossible to detect (and thus it perhaps becomes tempting to project) an autistic spiritual awareness. Psychological theories of autism and rare and valuable autobiographies by more able adults with the disability compensate by providing an insight into how children with autism perceive the world. Below I shall consider various definitions of autism and, with reference to a relational articulation of spiritual experience, discuss the autistic potential for meaningful spiritual perception. The reflections given might better relate to the higher functioning or slightly autistic child, since the resources available have made it easier to consider the spirituality of people with autism of this kind. It is hoped that the conclusions will also enrich understanding of spiritual experience and development across a wider range of ages and abilities.

Autism as a Cognitive Deficit

One understanding of autism portrays it as primarily a cognitive deficit explained in terms of a lack of a "theory of mind". A "theory of mind" is the awareness of the presence of other minds, an awareness that involves the ability to "mind-read" or to make rational inferences about other people's states of mind. Typically, an autistic child will be able to understand literal and mechanical events, but may find it difficult to understand other people's thoughts in relation to those events. Exponents of the theory of mind approach to autism propose that this cognitive deficit explains the autistic struggle with interpersonal relationships and imaginative play (Frith 1999).

Whilst the capacity for abstract thought and the ability to infer other people's beliefs and intentions may provide a greater *cognitive* understanding of spirituality, it would seem that their development is not required in order that young children engage with "the spiritual". However, without the ability to participate in imaginative play, which as Jerome Berryman has shown is an effective means of childhood religious education (Berryman 1995), young children with autism could be challenged in their spiritual development. Julie Donnelly, the mother of a young adult with the disability, encourages us to consider that there are alternative ways in which a child with autism may discover and express spiritual awareness:

> There are so many myths about people with autism. That they don't care about people, that they can't think abstractly, that they couldn't possibly understand religion. And yet I find great inspiration in their thoughts and words. Perhaps it is that they have something to teach us about spirituality. (1999)

Autism as an Emotional Deficit

R. Peter Hobson's research at the Tavistock Clinic, London, was vital in introducing an alternative understanding of autism to that of the cognitive, "theory of mind" approaches (Hobson 1993). His studies involved monitoring the autistic failure to give attention to and appropriately use facial gestures, eye contact and intonation of speech. Hobson concluded that such inability points to an emotional and not just a cognitive deficit:

the autistic child has difficulty reading the most basic gestures aimed at interpersonal engagement, gestures which seem to be based upon emotional reflex and intuition rather than upon cognition in the ordinary sense. On the basis of this research into autism, Hobson proposed a new theory of normal cognitive development, which included the acknowledgement that "perception is relational: in the early stages of personal relatedness perceiving has intrinsic connections with feeling and acting" (1993: 187).

Temple Grandin is a university lecturer on animal sciences who has higher functioning autism. In sympathy with Hobson's articulations Grandin explains her typically autistic difficulty with everyday social encounters in terms of a weak emotional intuition of how appropriately to interact. The distance she feels from other people is aptly conveyed when she describes herself as feeling like "an anthropologist on Mars" (Sacks 1995). Although Grandin struggles to relate to other human beings, she claims to have a strong capacity for empathy with animals. This may seem a paradoxical statement for someone who designs slaughter houses – one-third of all cattle and hogs in the USA are handled using equipment that Grandin has designed – but Grandin professes to have devoted her life to designing slaughterhouses that are "humane".

According to Grandin "for many people with [higher functioning] autism, religion is an intellectual rather than an emotional activity" (1996: 191). However, whilst attempting to find the most gentle way to hold a cow when sending it to slaughter, Grandin had what she calls a "religious experience"; an experience characterized not by intellect, but by the feeling of intimate relation. The following description of the experience suggests that an emotive spiritual encounter *is* possible for people with higher functioning autism:

> When the animal remained completely calm I felt an overwhelming feeling of peacefulness, as if God had touched me . . . For the first time in my life logic had been completely overwhelmed with feelings I did not know I had. (1996: 205)

The Autistic "Weak-Central Coherence"

Underlying the cognitive and affective deficits that define autistic behaviour is a perceptual style of "weak central coherence" or "local information processing"(e.g., Happé 1994, 1999). A weak central co-herence perceives and directs attention towards the details of experience, focusing on parts rather than wholes, and thus causing a highly fragmentary perception of reality. At the extreme, this height-ened sensitivity to detail translates as a multi-sensory *hyper*sensitivity;

vision and sound may be incomprehensibly jumbled, clothes can feel unbearable as they touch the skin. Emotional outbursts or a passive withdrawal from the world are typical autistic reactions to what one psychoanalyst has called "a body centred, sensation dominated state" (Tustin 1981: 3). Some children with autism are thus very in touch with their physical and emotional world, but in such cases it can be an intense and unmanageable experience.[1]

Autism and Creativity

According to both Franceseca Happé of the Kings Institute of Psychiatry, University of London, and Allan Snyder of the Centre for the Mind, Australian National University, Canberra, a processing style that focuses on detail, accounts not only for autistic deficits, but also for the autistic *assets* that are savant skills. Savant skills include heightened creativity, a skill of memory, mathematics or computing – in Grandin's case a creative and mathematical genius conducive to engineering her slaughterhouse designs. Half of all savants are autistic and one in ten children and adults with autism have savant skills. Although nine out of ten children with autism are not savants the relationship between creativity and spirituality in this context begs to be explored.

Happé's view is that autistic perception is completely different to normal perception: when non-autistic people read a story they automatically go for the gist, thereby demonstrating "global information processing" or "strong central coherence". They do not have the ability to remember "as a list" every single word that makes up the story (Happé 1999). Allan Snyder on the other hand, proposes that the autistic perceptual style is an early stage of information processing to which we all once had access. Non-autistic people also initially perceive and absorb every detailed iota of information via the five sense faculties. In the later stages of information processing these raw facts are assembled into meaningful concepts, objects and ideas, by what Snyder calls our "mindsets" (1998, 1999a).

A mindset is a mental paradigm moulded by culture and past experiences, which provides the conceptual tools for the interpretation and classification of present and future experiences. Snyder claims that autistic perception is without mindsets: an autistic child has not yet developed the filtration system of later information processing and, according to Snyder, it is precisely this lack of conceptual integration that allows for savant skills. Nadia, a three-year-old autistic savant who draws like Leonardo Da Vinci, begins her drawing at any random point on the paper, piecing together the detail of her subject without any obvious assessment of the perspective or an aim at integration.

According to Snyder, this focus on detail means that the she brings no general preconception to the creative process and thus can perceive salient features that might otherwise have gone undetected (1998).

Oliver Sacks, who has also worked with autistic savant children, appears to have similar thoughts on the creative processes involved in savant skills. Steven Wiltshire was nine years old when he first met Sacks in the late 1980s, astounding him with his effortless and yet detailed and accurate drawings of his favourite city scenes. Sacks asserts, much like Snyder, that savants do not need to break down conceptual barriers to creativity, precisely because "on many levels from the neural to the cultural", they have not yet made these constructs. Sacks says of Steven, "his vision is valuable it seems to me precisely because it conveys a wonderfully direct unconceptualized view of the world" (Sacks 1995: 232).

Snyder notes that Nadia "lost" her savant skills as soon as she developed the ability to use language (1998: 7). Does language weigh us down, obstructing a clear and creative perception of the world? Both the works of Snyder and Sacks stimulate epistemological questions that have long puzzled scholars of mysticism and religious experience: is it possible to have a direct, pre-linguistic, pre-conceptual experience? If we could step outside of our cultural context, our social conditioning or "our mindsets", would we experience the Real *an sich* (in itself)?

The constructivist position of psychologist Jerome Bruner is that there is no such thing as the real in itself, or what he calls an "aboriginal reality": we construct worlds, always basing them upon some prior constructed world that is taken as given (Bruner 1986). Similarly, the postmodern philosophical position as expressed by non-realist theologian Don Cupitt is that there is no pure pre-linguistic spiritual experience. Spirituality is a relative human creation. Language and thus interpretation "go all the way down" (Cupitt 1998).

Is silence to be defined only as relational to language, as gaps between words that are primary (thus rendering everything in our experience as "secondary")? Or is there a silence prior to and distinctly other than language that can be accessed and experienced outside of the process of its articulation? A study of autism necessarily encounters such philosophical questions. However, it is not within the scope of this chapter to attempt an answer (if indeed it were possible that an answer could ever be found).

Autism and Resonance

Donna Williams is an artist from Australia who has higher functioning autism. With a challenge to the postmodern position on language,

Williams claims the autistic experience to be pre-conceptual. According to Williams, we all enter the world at a stage of undifferentiated unity with no distinction between self and other and people with autism are either "stuck" at, or retain close access to, this stage of development. Williams values this early stage of development as an egalitarian place without ego and its desire for "comparison, reflection and the competition and hierarchy born of it" (1999: 30). Describing this experience as "like knowing 'God'" (1999: 58), she seems to be suggesting that children with autism know what it means to be "where we are before we are", in a mystical union or unity prior to differentiation and the development of mindsets and language. She calls this an experience of "resonance", claiming that it involves openness to a psychic sense perception that provides "the ability to feel not just for someone or something, but as someone or something" (1999: 118).

Oliver Sacks also talks of the young artistic savant Stephen Wiltshire as having an ability to "resonate". However, Sacks explains this skill in terms of an act of "mimesis", defined as a pre-linguistic "power of mind, a way of representing reality with one's body and senses, a uniquely human capacity no less important than symbol or language" (Sacks 1995: 229). It has elsewhere been claimed that this was once humankind's main method of communication and that this capacity for mimesis is still open to us all early in life. As one psychologist puts it: "language skates on the surface of a mimetic culture".[2] In addition to verbal language and regular body language, this mimetic language perhaps also provides a means of meaningful spiritual relating. If Williams's personal experiences are typical for all people with the disability, children with autism might experience connection to a wider reality through an early capacity for resonance or mimesis. However, whether this resonance has the psychic quality that Williams suggests may well be impossible to assess.

Autism and the Right-Brain Hemisphere

According to Snyder the neurological foundation of autistic perception is damage to the left-brain hemisphere.[3] Snyder follows the view that the two cerebral hemispheres of the human brain represent a dual mode of human consciousness. The left-brain hemisphere is said to be dominant in the formation of language, logic and reason, providing us with our "mindsets". The right-brain hemisphere, the dominant hemisphere in children with autism, is considered to control visual and spatial awareness, musical and creative flair (1999b).

In the psychology of religion the possibility has been discussed that the spiritual experience is primarily a right-hemisphere phenomenon, the left-brain hemisphere controlling the articulation of that experience (Beit-Hallahmi and Argyle 1997: 93). This is not to reduce spiritual experience to mere neurological activity; the source and fruits of the experiences may indeed reach far beyond the brain. If meditation, like the autistic experience, has been found to involve more right hemisphere activity, could the silent one-pointed focus of the autistic child be similar to the meditative state? Temple Grandin says that after her spiritual experience at the slaughterhouse:

> I thought about the similarities between the wonderful trance like feeling I had had while gently holding the cattle in the chute and the spaced-out feeling I had as a child when I concentrated on dribbling sand through my fingers at the beach. During both experiences all other sensation was blocked. Maybe the monks who chant and meditate are kind of autistic. I have observed that there is great similarity between certain chanting and praying rituals and the rocking of an autistic child. I feel there has to be more to this than just getting high on my own endorphins. (1996: 205)

Donna Williams describes an occasion when as a child she "curled up in a ball and rocked for three days" (1992: 131) and like Temple Grandin she notes the parallels to traditional spiritual techniques of sense-withdrawal and self-withdrawal. According to Williams, her actions were coping strategies of great value and meaning: in her chaotic world of sense bombardment, repetition helped by focusing the attention onto actions that were predictable and reliable. In this way Williams says that she would seek to lose all sense of self and other, undergoing a process of depersonalization and derealization:

> People think of reality as some sort of guarantee they can rely on. Yet from earliest I can remember I found my only dependable security was in losing all awareness of the things usually considered real. In doing this, I was able to lose all sense of self. Yet this is a strategy said to be the highest stage of meditation, indulged in to achieve inner peace and tranquillity. Why should it not be interpreted as such for Autistic people? (1992: 206)

Spiritual practice, particularly that of certain mystical traditions, can involve social isolation and rituals which aim for stimulus deprivation and self-withdrawal. A Hindu *sadhu* will retreat to an isolated mountain cave away from social interaction, engaging only in meditation intent on reaching *moksha* or liberation from his worldly self. In his meditative state of *samadhi*, the *sadhu* may use minimal speech and have a far away look in his eyes (Durig 1996: 94). He may also be experiencing equivalent brain activity. However, these are perhaps solely surface similarities. In answer to Williams's question, autistic behaviour is normally distinguished from "the highest stages of meditation" because whilst the accomplished meditator attempts an ascent beyond the limitations of language and self, the autistic child withdraws in a descent prior to their sufficient development.

The Spiritual Value of Language and Personal Identity

John Rowan, a transpersonal psychologist, has pointed to a problem with the left- and right-brain hemisphere distinction in the context of spiritual experience:

> this puts in one place two things which are very different – the pre-personal (which has not yet got to the position of formal logic, or which finds it too hard and denies it), and the transpersonal (which goes beyond the ordinary categories of thought and finds them insufficient or inappropriate for its work). (1993: 11)

The autistic experience of union, as perhaps found through an act of resonance and the autistic experience of no-self, as perhaps encountered in repetitive rocking, are what transpersonal psychologists might call pre-personal rather than trans-personal experiences. A child with autism may withdraw from the world and people's habits of thought or meddling mindsets. A child with autism may enter a state of being and perceiving that is highly aware, empathetic and creative; this could possibly even lead to an expression of self-less spiritual devotion (Durig 1996: 113). However, as noted by Abraham H. Maslow, a founder of the Transpersonal School of psychology:

> Precisely those persons who have the clearest and strongest identity are exactly the ones who are most able to transcend the ego or the self and to become selfless, who are at least relatively selfless and egoless. (1970: 176)

Whilst the creative autistic savant Steven Wiltshire could instantly "resonate to the holy atmosphere" of a monastery and communicate this in a wonderful drawing, Oliver Sacks notes that Steven did "not have any religious sense of his own" (1995: 222). Steven had yet to fully engage with language and other tools that facilitate the process of inter-personal communication, a process through which individual self-identity is developed.

Whilst children with autism do have a unique, non-autistic dimension to their self-identity or personality, this can become engulfed by the autistic disability and confused by a boundary-less experience of the "other". The possible autistic ability to "resonate" could thus be a hindrance to the stability of self-identity that is needed for spiritual growth; perhaps it is even dangerous to depersonalize yourself and de-realize your reality before developing a healthy articulation of who and where you are. There is possibly also an imbalance to a style of spiritual perception that is characterized by excessive introversion and privitization.

In his poem *Burnt Norton*, T. S. Eliot says, "words, after speech, reach into the silence". Whilst language may introduce differentiation and thus separation, it also provides a shared means to relate and communicate, as individual selves, the most personal of spiritual experiences. The spiritual style that is natural to autistic perception needs balance: silence in equal measure with language, right-brain activity accompanied with the left, heightened awareness with an interpretation system that facilitates meaningful communication. Hence Allan Snyder distinguishes the creativity of autistic savants from a "higher order creativity" that does not *deny* mindsets, but which rather actively engages with and attempts to understand as many mindsets, or as many interpretations of experience as possible. It can be added that with openness to many "mindsets" and able to communicate with many spiritual language systems, humankind's capacity for spiritually meaningful speech or expression is more fully realized. In the process of articulating this speech there is found a "higher order" spirituality which allows the theist to appreciate the intimate silence of union, or the monist the blissful silence of unity, anew. It is with this relational end vision clearly in sight that isolated experiences of spiritual awareness are drawn together and the spiritual life provided with a "strong central coherence".

Conclusion

Tito is a remarkable eleven-year-old autistic boy from South India. To borrow the title of his book, Tito has gone *Beyond the Silence* (this could be understood as the pre-personal, rather than the trans-personal place of silence) and has gathered his thoughts in a collection of poetry and prose. In the following song he sings the desire of all autistic children for the integration of individual self and an integrated experience of other:

> The fragmented world needed unification.
> Fragmented world of fear and pieces,
> Beyond "our" understanding and reaches,
> Broken into bits and parts,
> With the cause of our escaping hearts!
> (Mukhopadhyay 2000: 56)

Autism is a disability that involves an impairment of psychological connection and affective engagement with other people. These are the cognitive and affective capacities for interpersonal engagement that lie at the heart of a normal childhood relational consciousness. Also at the heart of the relational consciousness is the movement of the heart itself, expanding to reach its full capacity to love. In Tito's poem we find that the heart of an autistic child does yearn to relate, even if perhaps the means to fully realize this desire are not yet developed.

Certain spiritual practices and techniques that do not depend on normal cognitive skills could help children with autism to engage spiritually and to better contribute to the world. Through involvement in religious activity that is in accordance with his or her ability – for example, performing simple and repetitive rituals in religious prayer or service – a child with autism might better understand the value of religious participation. Research in progress suggests that a more able child with autism might also find meditation valuable in assisting with emotional management and the development of self-esteem (Fawcett 2000). Music therapy has also been found to be a useful technique in this respect (Trevarthen *et al.* 1998); Temple Grandin found specifically religious organ music valuable in arousing what she called "religious feeling"(1996: 191). Intimate spiritual communities might also provide a supportive, meaningful and manageable environment for people with the disability (Durig 1996: 106).

Spiritual "languages" or "modes of communication" – whether in the form of words, gesture, movement, music or mime – could provide a common discourse through which children with autism further experience, interpret and communicate spiritual awareness. T. S. Eliot could be right: it may be that none of us can bear too much reality – but sharing through language and most crucially, with love, makes reality all the more bearable. Although for those with this biological disorder, the ability to relate may not be such a biologically natural trait, a holistic spirituality might help redress that balance. Paul Naussbaum, a young adult who has autism, encourages hope:

> Spirituality . . . I've had to find that to balance myself in all the many challenges I've had and in dealing with this disability. For me . . . one of the things that has helped me to survive was searching for that faith. (Donnelley 1999)

Notes

1   Regrettably, there is not the opportunity here to further explore the psychoanalytical approach to autism and its potential contribution to understanding autistic spirituality. Recommended reading on psychoanalytical approaches includes Tustin 1981 and Alvarez and Reide 1999. For a psychoanalytical articulation of "autistic" spiritual styles within adult religious belief and practice see the work of Paul Pruyser (ed. Maloney 1991).

2   Merlin Donald of Queens University in Kingston, Ontario (quoted in Spinney 2000).

3   Other neuro-biological accounts of autism propose that damage to other areas of the brain, a different brain chemistry or a metabolic disorder could rather be implicated (e.g., Shattock and Savery 2000).

References

Alvarez, A. and Reid, S. (eds) 1999: *Autism and Personality: Findings from the Tavistock Autism Workshop*, London: Routledge.

Beit-Hallahmi, B. and Argyle, M. 1997: *The Psychology of Behaviour, Belief and Experience*, London: Routledge.

Berryman, J. W. 1995: *Godly Play: An Imaginative Approach to Religious Education*, Minneapolis: Augsburg Fortress.

Bruner, J. 1986: *Actual Minds, Possible Worlds*, Cambridge, MA: Harvard University Press.

Buber, M. [1958] 1959: *I and Thou* (trans. Ronald Gregor Smith.), Edinburgh: Clark.

Chittick, W. 1989: Ibn al-'Arabi: *The Sufi Path of Knowledge*, New York: State University of New York.

Collier, J., Longmore, M. and Brown, T. D. 1999: *The Oxford Handbook of Clinical Specialities*, Oxford: Oxford University Press Medical Publisher, 5th edition.

Cupitt, D. 1998: *The Religion of Being*, London: SCM Press.

Donnelley, J. 1999: Speaking for Themselves: The Thoughts and Words of Individuals With Autism, Paper presented at *Autism 99 Web Conference*: *www.autism99.org/html/Papers*

Durig, A. 1996: *Autism and the Crisis of Meaning*, New York: State University of New York Press.

Eliot, T. S. [1944] 1949: Burnt Norton. In *Four Quartets*, London: Faber and Faber.

Fawcett, M. 2000: Using Meditative Methodology to help Students with Complex Special Needs Experience Spiritual Awareness, Paper presented at the *First International Conference on Children's Spirituality*, 12 July 2000, University College Chichester, UK.

Frith, U. [1989] 1999: *Autism: Explaining the Enigma*, Oxford: Blackwell Publishers.

Grandin, T. 1996: *Thinking in Pictures, and Other Reports from My Life with Autism*, New York: Vintage Books.

Happé, F. 1994: *Autism: An Introduction to Psychological Theory*, London: UCL Press.

—— 1999: Autism: Cognitive Deficit or Cognitive Style? Paper presented at *Autism 99 Web conference: www.autism99.org/html/Papers*

Harvey, P. 1996: *An Introduction to Buddhism*, Cambridge: Cambridge University Press.

Hay, D. with Nye, R. 1998: *The Spirit of the Child*, London: Fount Paperbacks.

Hobson, R. P. 1993: *Autism and The Development of Mind*, Hove: Psychology Press.

James, W. [1902] 1977: *The Varieties of Religious Experience: A Study in Human Nature*, London: Fontana.

Lipner, J. J. 1993: *Hindus*, London: Routledge.

Maloney, H. N. and Spilka, B. 1991: *Religion in Psychodynamic Perspective: The*

Contributions of Paul W. Pruyser, New York and Oxford: Oxford University Press.

Maslow, A. H. 1970: Religious Aspects of Peak Experiences. In W. A. Sadler (ed.), *Personality and Religion: The Role of Religion in Personality Development*, London: SCM Press, 168–179.

Mukhopadhyay, T. R. 2000: *Beyond The Silence: My Life, the World and Autism*, London: The National Autistic Society.

Rowan, J. 1993: *The Transpersonal: Psychotherapy and Counselling*, London: Routledge.

Sacks, O. 1995: *An Anthropologist on Mars*, London: Picador.

Spinney, L. 2000: Bodytalk, *New Scientist*, 8 April 2000, 2233, 30–3.

Snyder, A. 1998: Breaking Mindset, *Mind and Language* 13(1), March 1998, 1–10.

—— 1999a: Game, Mindset and Match, *The Weekend Australian*, 4–5 December, 1999, No. 10,947. See website: *www.edime.com.au/mind/main.htm*

—— 1999b: Breakthroughs Come From Way Out in the Left Field. Paper presented at the *Adelaide Festival of Ideas*, Elders Hall, Adelaide, Australia, 10 July 1999b. See website: *www.edime.com.au/mind/main.htm*

Tustin, F. 1981: *Autistic States in Children*, London: Routledge & Kegan Paul.

Trevarthen, C., Aitken, K., Papoudi, D. and Robarts, J. 1998: *Children With Autism: Diagnosis and Intervention to Meet Their Needs*, London: Jessica Kingsley Publishers, Second Edition.

Williams, D. 1992: *Nobody Nowhere*, New York: Pantheon.

—— 1999: *Autism and Sensing: The Unlost Instinct*, London: Jessica Kingsley Publishers.

Chapter 19

Youth and Adulthood in Children's and Adults' Perspectives

WIM WESTERMAN

R ECENTLY a Dutch newspaper had the screaming headline: "The day with tears". The newspaper portrayed girls and boys at the age of twelve during their last days in primary school. The end of a period of eight years, leaving behind a well-known and secure situation and having the prospect of the uncertainty of a new school with new classmates, teachers and rules. Such thresholds in time are critical periods and show emotions. Tears well up easily.

As part of a research project on children's perspectives on life stages I invited ten and eleven year olds to draw pictures as they see themselves now and at a younger age and how they expect to be when they are adults. At the invitation to write their names and ages on the drawings Tim asked what to do. "Now I'm still ten, but in eighteen days I'm eleven." So the boy implicitly asked me to consider him as not too young. And a twelve-year-old boy told me he would go to a secondary school after the school holidays. His twin sister would be joining him. "But she is younger than I am, because I'm some minutes older", he said.

Obviously it is important for children to be a few minutes older than their twin and to know they will become a year older in eighteen days from now. It is also clear that ages, departures from former situations and the entrance to the future are emotional themes. Age, coming of age, birthdays and official permission to do activities for the very first time are emotional moments in children's and youngster's spiritual lives. Such thresholds are connected with beliefs, values and norms, and have legal, social, educational and psychological significance. Sometimes there are even religious connotations. Children who feel themselves safe and sound want to be older. As soon as they are aware of their own and other's ages they are in a hurry to grow older and to cross thresholds which bring permission for new activities. So, at a certain threshold in time a child goes to school for learning reading and writing. At a later age she or he is permitted to come home late and is longing for the far off moment when driving lessons begin.

Such new perspectives for the young generation can worry parents and other responsible adults, as was illustrated in a motorbike advertisement in an Indian newspaper. It showed a boy shouting, "Eighteen! At last! Ready for a bike!" But his worried parents hesitated, "Eighteen? Already? Ready for a bike?" And of course the advertiser explained that his bikes are safe, even for eighteen-year-old boys (Explorer Advertisement 1986). Such examples show that the crossing of age borders is not a neutral but an emotional step. A step interwoven with likes and dislikes, values and norms, experiences and sometimes concerns and perspectives for the future. Ages and age borders can never be seen separated from the developing children's or youngsters' spirituality. Every concept of age has for children moral, religious, pedagogical, psychological, juridical, cultural and social components.

Rites of Passage

So it is not a coincidence that the crossing of age thresholds is often connected with rituals. The ethnographer Van Gennep pointed this out in his study *The Rites of Passage*. He collected, compared and classified examples of rites. He focused mainly on rites related to individuals entering a group, with the course of life through pregnancy and child-birth, childhood, initiation rites, marriages and funerals.

One of his examples concerned the traditional Chinese ceremony of the departure from childhood. At this rite it was believed that a boy leaves childhood at sixteen to enter the stage of adolescence. And that, at the same age, a girl becomes a woman. Once the ceremony had been completed, the "Mother-goddess of children" ceased to have the children in her keeping, and the individuals fell under the authority of the gods in general. That is why this ceremony was called "Thanking the Mother" (Van Gennep 1960: 59). This ceremony was one of the last ceremonies in a row of rites connected with child development in the old Chinese Taoistic–Confucianistic cultural tradition. Other age-connected rites were, for example, the "Ritual of the Third Day" when red-dyed eggs were sent by the maternal grandmother to the newborn's family as a gift celebrating the birth. And the "Ritual of a Hundred Days" when the child was called "a child of one hundred days". One hundred days symbolizes longevity (Than 1989: 45ff). A special category of child development rites was connected with learning. So the classical *Book of Rites* presented an explicit phasing for learning:

> At six children learn to count and they learn the points of the compass . . .
> At nine they learn the lunar phases as well as the cycle of sixty. Boys leave
> their homes when they are ten and then they are instructed by teachers.
> They learn how to write, to calculate and are instructed in the "li" [good
> behaviour]. When they are thirteen they learn music, singing, shao-
> dancing, etc. (Wei 1993: 180)

All beginnings in the Chinese tradition of learning had their own rites (Ting 1990). Tan Kok Seng, who went to school in Singapore at the end of the first half of the twentieth century, gave some examples in his auto-biography:

> On that first day in class I was terribly nervous and uncomfortable. Early
> next morning my mother cooked many delicious things for me, including
> spring onions, leaks, pork, liver, eggs and other things, saying: "On the
> first day children go to school they should eat these things to make them
> clever, first of all 'ts'ung' (spring onion) with the head and the tail cut off
> to leave a hole through it, meaning you will quickly see the point of things;
> then 'suan' (leek) which means you will be quick at counting" . . . And so
> it went on. (Seng 1972: 19–22)

Ts'ung was associated with understanding, because of a resemblance of the sounds for "spring onion" and the sounds of the words for "clever" and "intelligent".

In the 1940s the young Tan Kok Seng already protested against his mother's superstitious ideas on rites and schooling. Now most of the traditional Chinese age rituals have disappeared. The Chinese cultural traditions inside the Chinese mainland and overseas Chinese communities dissociated themselves more and more from these kinds of age rites. This was because of a worldwide loss of traditional rituals and an increasing general secularisation, and also because of fierce anti-religious programmes in the first decades of the People's Republic of China. For example, the Third Plenary Session of the Eleventh Party Congress in 1979 decided that all worship directed to mysterious super-natural powers be called superstition. "Religion is superstition, but not all superstitions are religion." Various feudal superstitions were not seen as religious, but "all religions are illusory, erroneous reflections created by humans who experience fear and helplessness when faced by the forces of nature and society" (MacInnis 1989: 32f).

Such attacks on superstitions and religions, however, did not abolish all rituals connected with age. The Chinese Communist Party even introduced new rites for children reaching certain stages in their development, and in some Chinese communities, overseas as well as in

China itself, rudimentary forms of centuries-old rituals survived. Since the Great Teacher of China, Confucius, often accused by the Chinese Communist Party of conservatism, is more or less rehabilitated it is not uncommon to observe a mother bringing a young child to a temple. There the child can creep around a statue of Confucius or that of any other learned person, with the expectation that the child will take on at least some of the learned wisdom before he or she goes to school.

Rites of passage not only connect the stages in children's and youngsters' development but are also connected with pedagogical ideas about their development. For example, in the traditional Japanese culture, at the age of seven, rites of passage clearly marked a fundamental change in pedagogical approaches towards the children. The traditional Japanese view of young children was revealed in the saying "one of the gods until the age of seven". Thus the age of seven was seen as a significant milestone for the children. Before that age children were seen as weak. Younger children could die easily from sickness and so return to the world of gods and buddhas at any time. They were believed to be creatures close to the supernatural forces, they were also thought to possess the power to transmit the will of the gods and often played the role of a medium between gods and the people. For this reason they were allowed to act as they wished, free from the rules and restrictions of society.

Once a child had reached the age of seven she or he began to work. As "children who are at the stage prior to adulthood, they began slowly to learn the lifestyle and profession of the adults" (Kumon Children's Research Institute 1998: 10f). And it was because of this age of seven that every year at the Star Festival, on the seventh day of the seventh month, prayers were said for the improvement of performing skills such as reading and writing. The number seven and the age of seven had clear meanings for the education of the children. At that age parental authority was handed over from the gods to the one who raised the child. So it was obvious that the seventh birthday needed to be marked with special rituals. The seventh birthday marked also the start of the learning to read process.

Marcus describes in his book *Rituals of Childhood* another interesting example of rites of passage connected with the beginning of "official learning" (1996: 16f). He explains how Jewish boys living in medieval Germany or France began with formal schooling by participating in a special initiation ceremony, and how in this rite Judaic and Christian influences interacted. Living apart and yet together in Latin Christendom, Jews and Christians celebrated their religious cultures in public ceremonies which the members of the other observed and which helped to shape their own way of making sense of the world. According to Marcus, Ashkenazi Jews adopted from the Christian majority the idea of having a marked moment in the development of children when they officially start to learn at school. In this way a "child's school initiation rite" originated. It took place at Shavuot when the revelation of the Torah at Mount Sinai was celebrated. In this rite a boy ate sweet honey cake Hebrew letters. The letters represented the Torah as in the prophet Ezekiel's metaphorical vision of eating God's words being "as sweet as honey" (Ezekiel 3: 1–5). The food the child ate was traditionally equated with the Torah: milk and honey, flour and oil. The child was placed on the lap of the teacher, and the teacher was, like Moses, compared to a nurturing mother (Numbers 11:12). At the conclusion of the ceremony the teacher led the boy to a riverbank. Here the metaphor is of the Torah being like life-giving water (see Psalm 1:3). According to Marcus the symbolic act of ingested sacrificed bread – the honey cake letters, as a symbol for the Torah – was a response to the Christian Eucharistic devotion. The ways the teacher and child were portrayed, the boy sitting on the teacher's lap, make sense especially in the light of the imagery of the Christ Child and the Madonna; the father who brings his son to school competes with the image of the Christ Child in the Eucharist as a sacrifice (Marcus 1996:16f).

When the school entrance ceremony emerged in the Middle Ages it was not at home but in the synagogue. This reflects a shift from domestic to more formal and public events. Initially providing a boy with his religious education was, like circumcision, a father's religious obliga-tion. It could be delegated to the father's agent. So the school initiation rite was also a Jewish response to public Christian initiation ceremonies. Originally Jewish life-cycle ceremonies as circumcision, marriage and mourning the dead were only performed at home. But during the Middle Ages they moved more and more into the public arena, into the community's synagogue. So these ceremonies became shared public celebrations and Christians could no longer accuse Jewish people of secret rites.

Originally, among the Jewish life-cycle events of childhood, no special ritual to mark a person's attainment of religious majority existed. What later was called "bar mitzvah" and referred to the chronological event of boys reaching the age of thirteen years and a day was not marked by a special ceremony. But during the late Middle Ages the Jewish school initiation disappeared and was replaced by the new rite of passage: "bar mitzvah". That reflects not only the development of a new attitude towards children in the Jewish culture but also in the Christian culture. Both cultures swapped new awarenesses of child-hood. And not only new concepts of childhood per se were developed but also visions on the relation between a child's age and consent to his assuming full religious responsibility. In the Christian tradition this was illustrated by leaders of religious communities and synods resisting more and more the practice of oblation, children's incorporation in monasteries (before the ages of twelve for girls and fourteen for boys) (De Jong 1986). This resistance was the Christian equivalent of the Jewish entry, around the age of twelve or thirteen, into the adult religious life of the synagogue community.

In the meantime the Ashkenazi school initiation rite has disappeared. But some Jewish communities still mark the day when a young child receives his of her first humash (Pentateuch) or siddur (prayer book) by handing out honey cakes, candies and other treats. In The Netherlands and other areas of the European continent sweet cake and chocolate letters are still a speciality for young children around the age of six at the St. Nicholas festival in early December. Is this a Jewish artefact within a Roman Catholic tradition?

Stages of Development and Stages under Discussion

The traditional Chinese rites when children started to learn writing, the Japanese ceremonies at the seventh birthday, the former Jewish school initiation rites and many other life-cycle ceremonies, and not only rites in connection with the start of the formal learning process, mark the idea of stages of development in children's lives.

It is a heritage from the classical Romans to discern in childhood three stages of seven years. The *infantia*, the first stage, ends when the milk teeth are changed for permanent teeth. The second period of seven years, the *puertia*, is followed by the *adolescentia*. The magical, or in some religious traditions even holy, number of seven was and is central for many other models of developmental stages. Mediaeval lawyers saw children in the stage of *infantia*, the infants, as not moral responsible for their acts. *Puers* however, who learned reading and thinking, could be held responsible (Van Lieburg 1997: 29f). In today's anthroposophical pedagogy the step from six to seven, when permanent teeth replace the milk teeth, is still seen as the principal step from the playing child towards the learning child (Carlgren 1972). The concept of stages in development and especially the prospects of children at stages was a permanent object of discussion, the Roman lawyer Quintillian wrote in his pedagogical guidelines that reading lessons could start at a much earlier age than at seven (Bonner 1977: 161; Rawson 1992: 170).

Stages in the human life-cycle became a popular theme. So the *Stairs of Ages* was frequently published as cheap print editions for children from the early seventeenth century onwards to the nineteenth century in Germany, The Netherlands and Italy (Van Veen: 101–4). Usually these stairs showed steps of seven or ten years, climbing up from *infantia* towards middle age and then descending to the grave. Each step of these printed presentation of stages in human development had its own characteristics. Infants till seven were portrayed with their dolls and balls, since they were supposed to play. Children at the next stage had their books and pencils, since the learning of reading and writing was the characteristic of that stage. Evidently in those days ideas about life-long playing and learning did not exist.

These popular stairs can be seen as more or less primitive concepts of age and child development. From the eighteenth century onwards, when psychology started its slow development towards an inde-pendent academic discipline, stages in human development became an object of scientific observation. This fitted very well into the paradigm of the Enlightenment; that development could be classified in stages, that each stage has its own characteristics, and that development is a historical process towards higher and qualitatively better levels. (Although criteria for "quality" were seldom clearly identified.)

Through the improvement of psychological methods the under-standing of human developmental processes improved tremendously, indirectly also in the area of children's spiritual development. Cognitive studies of Piaget stimulated Kohlberg to clarify moral development and Goldman to research *Religious Thinking from Childhood to Adolescence* (Kohlberg 1995; Goldman 1964). The influence of such studies, mainly focused on cognitive development, was often so strong that religious and moral educators overlooked the significance of other areas of devel-opment such as in emotionality, spirituality and creativity. They overlooked that religious education, moral or spiritual education has other dimensions than just intellectual instruction (Godin 1971: 111). Another problem with the Piagetian approach to the faculties of the child's development is the denial of cultural biases, or the cultural dependency of certain developments of some theories on child develop-ment (Gardin, Mutter and Kosnitzki 1998; Lloyd 1983). Certainly in a plural culture this is not acceptable. The fundamental problem is a too rigid trust in developmental stages that ignores the broader develop-mental issues, although not many religious or moral educators go as far as Starbuck, who more than hundred years ago calculated average ages for conversion (Starbuck 1901).

It is evidently an advantage to have a rigid belief in clear and well-defined stages possibly marked by transition rites and ceremonies, because it meets the demand for clarity and, since the days of the Enlightenment, the highly valued methodology of classification and nomenclature. It is easy, within the system, to know that a five-year-old plays and a seven-year-old child conquers reading skills, or to celebrate a birthday that gives the legal right to open one's own bank account. It is also the case, within such a system, that a whole society can reach a stage of shock and disorientation when children's behaviour is not in accordance with what could be expected at their age. An extreme example of this was the Bulger case in Britain when two young boys killed a toddler. This case and others illustrate that, more than ever before, the idea of clear developmental stages, marked by ceremonies, has to be open to critical discussion. Our newspapers show us daily that the evidence of historical connections between ages and levels of development is being challenged. What is the minimum age for film censorship? What is the minimum age for compulsory education? When is a young hooligan sent to youth court and when not? At what age can young people buy alcohol or cigarettes in France, Britain, Sweden or in Malaysia? What is the age definition of a child soldier in Sierra Leone compared with The Netherlands? What is the maximum age for young-sters to be welcomed as asylum seekers in Holland? And is, when officials think that they report a false age, a radiological scan of their collarbone the right way to prove their real age? Is there a minimum age for membership of the Dutch national Young Investors Association? What is the minimum age for participation in the celebration of the Holy Communion in the distinguished churches? And which arguments are used for answering these "what" questions? With so many age-related questions the uncertainty concerning childhood and the borders between children and adults are vaguer than ever before.

The earlier examples given of Chinese, Japanese and Jewish rites at the start of formal schooling showed that ages and rites have their own histories, developments and were influenced by other cultural or religious traditions. So changes and developments in the interpretations of the developmental ages and related rites are no new phenomena. Yet, it seems as if at this moment the number and sizes of changes is greater than ever before in history. Some authors say that the "myth of child-hood innocence" is wiped out today. We read that "childhood innocence is a cultural myth that has been 'inculcated and enforced' upon children" (Jenkins 1998: 2). A popular explanation for the present multitude of changes is the reference to the postmodern state of global society with a growing plurality, increasing commercialization and new technological opportunities; the inference being that social fragmenta-tion is to blame (see, for example, McDonell 1994). However, other explanations are possible, explanations which at first glance appear rooted in biological developments. For example, the changing of milk teeth for permanent teeth when crossing the border from the stage of *infantia* to the stage of *puertia* looks like an innate biological source of change, but not all children change teeth at seven. Medical biologists have found that the so-called innate developments and stages are heavily influenced by climate, food and other social conditions. It was in 1900 that the Swedish practitioner Axel Key, the husband of Ellen Key, the lady who announced that the twentieth century was the

"Century of Childhood" (Key 1902), wrote that puberty now started at an earlier age and that this was attributable to a fashion for children to spend more hours in sunshine then ever before. This "heliogenic acceleration" was more attributable to a cultural than a biological factor, fashion and not nature stimulated changes in children's dress and playing in the sunshine. This "acceleration" went hand in hand with the making of a children's culture. Children's culture was invented (Kline 1998). The cultural factor and globalization are pivots in the present plurality of concepts of childhood and stages of (spiritual) development. (Western) societies have never been so plural as today. But on the other hand there is a striking growth of conformity. "Coca Cola Culture" or the "McDonaldization of Society" are symbols of this growth (see Ritzer 1996). One of the results is that nowadays commercial logos are better known than old religious symbols. Young people in the cities of the world know the MacDonalds "M" better than religious symbols such as the cross or the crescent. And the commercial world knows that childhood and youth are not only important markets in contemporary society, but also for the future. But that is an old wisdom: "The young generation in your hands means the future in your hands", says a Dutch expression. So it is not surprising that children and youth are often used as the main targets in commercial advertisements. Saving banks present themselves first of all as committed to the future of young people.[1] And for many decades telecommunication firms have explained how they want to introduce "a new type of civilization, of better opportunity for the average man, comfort and convenience that enrich the daily life of all the people".[2] An international chemical company explained two decades ago how to see the future and how to promote that "children understand the multicoloured diversity of the world".[3] But not only commercial advertisers present the future and children in their advertisements. Organizations with idealistic messages, such as the World Wildlife Fund, prophesying the future of the world as a "green earth or a dry desert", also often put children in their messages.[4]

   Opposing cultural globalization we find a slowly growing acceptance of diversity in society and culture. This opens our eyes to divergent traditions of child rearing and a wide diversity of practices and rites connected with age and passages of age thresholds. Today a wide variety of moral practices and cultural, religious and spiritual expressions can be observed next door to each other in Western societies. As a result the majority of adults are confused about the best options for spiritual education and about the right moments and stages for their educational interactions. Traditional arguments that things have to be done because they have always been done do not convince young people any more.

   The boom in information technology is a central catalyst in all these changes. Technologies of information have always stimulated new developments in spiritual life. The invention of printing stimulated the sixteenth-century Reformation, and the need for broad public schooling systems. So it can be understood why reformers such as Luther and Calvin stimulated the founding of schools and colleges (Luke 1989), and how that brought about, in turn, the development of "the era of childhood", with distinct age groups of pre-schoolers, schoolers and post-schoolers (Sommerville 1990).

At this moment it looks as if the introduction of electronic information technology may, in certain respects, invert the stages of youth and adulthood. Most young people know ways on the electronic highways unknown to adults. This can be seen as a threat, especially for parents coming from paternalistic cultural traditions. In reaction some of these parents grow even more paternalistic than they ever were before. This can be one of the explanations for growing conservatism in some spiritual traditions.

Conclusion: Future Enquiries

It is evident that today the rigid stairs of ages from the cheap seventeenth-century prints have lost their clear steps. Not only children under seven play; many children, worldwide, start learning to read and write before the age of seven. Life-long learning, even after *puertia* and *adolescentia*, is becoming more and more a widely accepted concept. Most of the rites at the official start of schooling have disappeared or have been changed. Religious dimensions of learning to read and write are being replaced by technological dimensions. But, at the same time, our present society is zealously searching for new rituals, values and norms, orientations, morals and religious dimensions in combination with a deep pedagogical unrest. This underlines the importance of a further exploration of the concept of stages of development, and especially the underlying spiritual dimensions, and connected rites of passage. That is the aim of a recently started research project. The project gives priority to qualitative research, especially to narrative, historical and comparative methods. Here children are the main sources of information about concepts of childhood, age and developmental levels of spirituality, and connected rites. Which age steps and rites of passage do they identify? Do they, as the commercial advertisement makers do, believe that the future is theirs? Comparisons will be made between the opinions of children from different cultural and ethnic backgrounds to trace influences of globalization and growing plurality, to see if such messages as "having a birthday in a few days' time" or "to be a few minutes older than the twin sister" are important in all cultural traditions; to explore the perspectives of children and youth on childhood and adulthood and, in a complementary way, the ideas of adults, parents, teachers and others on the spiritual characteristics of childhood and youth.

Notes

1 See, for example, a National Savings advertisement showing a grandfather helping (by saving) his granddaughter buy her first flat, *The Independent*, 8 October 1980.
2 See Bell Telephone System advertisement, "This is the telephone's mission", *The National Geographic Magazine*, USA, 1930.
3 See the advertisement "Hoechst research ensures they'll have a future worth living", *Bulletin*, Australia, 31 August 1982.
4 See, for example, W. W. F. for "World Conservation" advertisement in *The Nation*, Bangkok, 21 August 1983.

References

Bonner, S. F. 1977: *Education in Ancient Rome*, London: Methuen.
Carlgren, F. 1972: *Erziehung zum Freiheit*, Stuttgart: Verlag Freies Geistesleben.
De Jong, M. 1986: *Kind en klooster in de vroege Middeleeuwen*, Amsterdam: Historisch Seminarium Universiteit Amsterdam.
Explorer advertisement 1986: "18!", *India Today*, Bombay.
Gardin, H. W., Mutter, J. D. and Kosnitzki, C. 1998: *Lives Across Cultures. Cross-Cultural Human Development*, Boston: Ally and Bacon.
Godin, A. 1971: Some Developmental Tasks in Christian Education. In M. P. Strommen (ed.), *Research on Religious Development*, New York: Hawthorn Books, 109–154.
Goldman, R. 1964: *Religious Thinking from Childhood to Adolescence*, London: Routledge & Kegan Paul.
Jenkins, H. 1998: Childhood Innoncence and Other Modern Myths. In H. Jenkins (ed.), *The Children's Culture Reader*, New York: New York University Press, 1–41.
Key, E. 1902: *Das Jahrhundert des Kindes*, Berlin: Fischer Verlag.
Kline, S. 1998: The Making of Children's Culture. In: H. Jenkins (ed.), *The Children's Culture Reader*, New York: New York University Press, 95–109.
Kohlberg, L. 1995: *Die Psychology der Moralentwicklung*, Frankfurt am Main: Suhrkamp.
Kumon Children's Research Institute 1998: *Children Represented in Ukiyo-e. Japanese Children in the 18th-19th Centuries*, Osaka: Kumon Institute of Education.
Loyd, B. 1983: Cross-Cultural Studies of Piaget's Theory. In S. and C. Modgil and G. Brown (eds), *Jean Piaget. An Interdisciplinary Critique*, London: Routledge & Kegan Paul, 27–41.
Luke, C. 1989: *Pedagogy, Printing, and Protestantism. The Discourse on Childhood*, Albany: State University of New York Press.

MacInnis, D. E. 1989: *Religion in China Today. Policy and Practice*, New York: Maryknoll.

Marcus, I. G. 1996: *Rituals of Childhood. Jewish Acculturation in Medieval Europe*, New Haven: Yale University Press.

McDonell, K. 1994: *Kid Culture. Children and Adults and Popular Culture*, Toronto: Second Story Press.

Rawson, B. 1992: Children in Roman Families. In: B. Rawson (ed.), *The Family in Ancient Rome*, London: Routledge, 170–220.

Ritzer, G. 1996: *The McDonaldization of Society*, Thousands Oaks, CA: Pune Forge Press.

Seng, T. K. 1972: *Son of Singapore*, Kuala Lumpur: Heinemann Educational Books.

Sommerville, C. J. 1990: *The Rise and Fall of Childhood*, New York: Vintage House.

Starbuck, E. D. 1901: *The Psychology of Religion. An Empirical Study to the Growth of Religious Consciousness*, London: Walter Scott.

Than, S. C. 1989: Religion and Modernization. A Study in Changing Rituals Among Singapore's Chinese, *East Asian Cultural Studies*, 23, 45–138.

Ting, J. S-p. 1990: *Children of the Gods. Dress and Symbols in China*, Hong Kong: Urban Council.

Van Gennep, A. 1960: *The Rites of Passage*, London: Routledge & Kegan Paul.

Van Lieburg, M. J. 1997: *De geschiedenis van de kindergeneeskunde in Nederland*, Rotterdam: Erasmus Publishing.

Van Veen, C. F. *Centsprenten. Catchpennyprints. Dutch Popular – and Childrenprints*, Amsterdam: Rijksmuseum.

Wei, Y. 1993: *Das Lehrer-Schüler-Verhältnis bei Rousseau und Konfuzius*, Münster: Waxmann.

Chapter 20

The Conflict between
Pedagogical Effectiveness and
Spiritual Development in
Catholic Schools

CATHY OTA

THIS chapter concerns itself with a complex tension faced by Catholic schools in the UK today: the tension between nurturing pupils within a faith tradition, whilst also seeking to enable and facilitate their spiritual and holistic development. Drawing on my research conducted in church schools, and exploring the nature of children's spirituality, I will explain why I see these two elements as currently creating a tension for Catholic denominational schools.[1]

Catholic Schools in the UK

Catholic schools have been part of the education system of England and Wales since the nineteenth century and although contemporary society may be increasingly secular, church schools generally are highly regarded, occupying a prominent role in the broader educational system (Chadwick 1994: 4). Catholic schools continue to be popular with Catholic and non-Catholic parents alike; it is acknowledged by school admission boards that parents would think nothing of moving house, regularly attending mass and becoming more involved in their parish if it means securing a place for their child at the local school.[2]

Historically, the evolving character and role of Catholic schools in the UK differs from Church of England schools (Chadwick 1997; McLaughlin, O'Keefe and O'Keeffe 1996), reflecting, perhaps, distinct aims and shifting closeness to the state throughout the twentieth century. Representing the established church of the nation Church of England schools are traditionally seen to maintain a balance between a general/inclusive aim to serve the local community and a domestic/inclusive aim to educate the children of its own faith community. In contrast, Catholic schools can be identified as unequivocally favouring a domestic approach (Chadwick 1994: 8), existing in relative isolation and providing a Catholic education for children of Catholic families (McLaughlin, O'Keefe and O'Keeffe 1996: 4ff).

Despite this significant difference in purpose and vision the present theoretical debate about church schools (both Church of England and Catholic) can be seen to centre around the following kinds of questions, as highlighted by Chadwick:

1   How does the Christian school explicitly nurture the faith of its pupils while educating them to be intellectually critical?
2   What should be the relationship between the Christian school and nearby parish communities?
3   In what ways will the ethos of a Christian school be distinguished from a county school?
4   To what extent will that ethos affect the teaching of non-religious subjects and how members of the school relate to each other? (1994: 1f)

There has been much consideration over the last twenty years given to discriminating between the meaning of terms such as nurture, evangelism, instruction, education, indoctrination and catechesis, in addition to addressing the place of such concepts in juxtaposition to RE, the church and the home environment (see, for example, Arthur and Gaine 1996; Astley 1994: BCC 1984; Crump Miller 1990; Day 1996; Groome 1994, 1996; Hastings 1996; Hull 1990; Rossiter 1990). Although there are those who seek a return to exclusivity (for example, Arthur 1995), the theoretical debate in this arena incorporates others who urge a serious reassessment of the notion of nurture and catechesis within the church school environment (for example: BCC 1984; Crump Miller 1990; Day 1996; Hastings 1996; Hull 1990; Phillips 1994; Rossiter 1990; Westerhoff 1994). Rossiter, for example, challenges the way "religious education in Catholic schools has long been regarded primarily as education in faith or more intensively as catechesis". Calling for a "creative divorce" between religious education and catechesis, he is amongst those who suggest, "perhaps Catholic school-based education should be re-conceptualized more along educational than catechetical lines" (Rossiter 1990: 291). Representing the pursuit of an even more critical appraisal, Groome, citing Friere, raises an epistemological consideration in looking for a way forward that incorporates the notion of critical praxis:

> at the bedrock of our Christian education task there is an epistemological question – what does to know mean – and in this case, to know Christ. The pedagogical question is how we should go about enabling others with ourselves to know him . . . I believe that much of our traditional Christian education has been based on . . . a banking concept of education to deposit divine truths in the minds of people . . . Instead I opt for a praxis approach . . . then I believe our educating can be truly liberating and our future will be built on our past and present but not on a reproduction of it. (Groome 1994: 224f)

The distinctive nature and purpose of Catholic education continues to be discussed. What is agreed is that it "is confronting a challenging and uncertain future" (Losito 2000: 59). Among the issues that have to be faced are the demand for a Catholic education by non-Catholic parents, financial crises,[3] a dramatic reduction in priests and other religious present in schools, the composition of the student body and the relationship of the Catholic church to a pluralistic society (Losito 2000; Raddell 2000: 105). Staffing issues, specifically the desire to appoint only practising Catholics as teachers, senior managers and head teachers (Nichols 2000) compounds this situation yet further.

Whilst debate and concern for Catholic education exists, it is never-theless observed that there is a lack of coherence in the way it is being addressed:

> there is no community of Catholic intellectuals pursuing a coherent agenda of inquiry to serve as a significant resource for educational leaders . . . [a] lacuna . . . not gone unnoticed by the broader academic community. (Losito 2000: 59)

The need for further discussion and dialogue is a necessity for the Catholic community, but what kind of discussion and dialogue would be most fruitful and appropriate? Exploring the significance of tradition in Catholic schools, Groome (1996: 117) describes a sharing of "story and vision" that acknowledges a catechetical element and goes beyond "learning about" to "learning from". He elucidates this further in relation to the pupils being "personally influenced and enriched by Catholic faith" (1996: 118). Whilst I suspect Groome and myself have different perspectives on this I would like to reflect on his phrase "personally influenced and enriched". What does it mean? Does what presently exists in Catholic schools serve to achieve this? Groome proposes that for pupils to be personally influenced and enriched Catholic schools should "inform, form and transform their [the pupils] identity and agency – who they are and how they live – with the meaning and ethic of Christian faith" (1996: 118). If such transforma-tions occur in Catholic schools – and indeed it is this kind of vision that many head teachers and governors would claim to be realized in their communities – then can a judgement be made about such changes being either positive or negative for pupils?

Before proceeding to look at how one might go about answering such questions it is perhaps pertinent to consider that what lies at the heart of these questions for Catholic schools is the issue of *identity*, especially their distinct identity within a broader education system. Haldane's comments on the difference between Catholic *experience* and Catholic *identity* are useful here (1996). Speaking of personal experience and ecclesial identity Haldane considers that in Catholic schools the two are often closely intertwined and confused. This is an interesting insight, and one that has relevance for this discussion; for in thinking about the aims and impact of Catholic schools we are, at the same time, reflecting on the experience given to pupils and the "Catholic" identity that is shared with them.

Haldane directs our attention beyond the theoretical to the practical, lived experience of Catholic schools and here I must confess to a startling realization (and one I challenge you to ask of yourself): so far I have talked of Catholic schools but where have I included pupils? I suddenly realize that I have used the term "Catholic schools" as short-hand for staff, management and organization of schools, in essence the adults involved rather than the children and young people. We must consider what the experience of pupils can bring to this discussion of identity. What do they say about Catholic schools and their way forward for the future?

The Pupils' Experience of School

> When one studies children's experiences of school rather than the curriculum, management or teaching styles, some personal and consistent insights emerge . . . indeed one of the most fundamental insights that children have of school is their own powerlessness, their helplessness in the face of a given system. (Cullingford 1999: 195)

Cullingford's analysis of the child's broader experience of school raises searching questions about the possible discrepancy between what schools (and parents) think they're doing versus what is achieved in relation to the children's experience. The following transcript, taken from my own qualitative research in Catholic schools locates these questions within a Catholic school context:

Jonathan: No one really [listens], teachers don't much, well, they say things to you but we're not really kind of like listened to;

Paul: If we know something they never kind of like believe us cos they
             think, I mean I know we are immature and all that but some chil-
             dren aren't and they're really clever and if teachers make mistakes
             and children correct them they don't listen;
Samuel: Children don't have rights really, compared to adults;
Jenni: It's the way adults talk to children.
                                          (Interview, School A, Autumn 1996)

Lucy: [Head teacher B] tells us about the things she believes and the
             things she imagines and like it sort of confuses you because you've
             got your own beliefs and like your own vision of heaven . . . [and]
             she'll tell you hers . . . and you might not like her idea of it, you
             might think well, I don't want to go to heaven if its like that . . .
             [It's important to use you own imagination] because then that
             teaches you to sort of decide whether you want to go somewhere
             or what you want to think . . . and like whether you think heaven's
             a bad place or whether you think its somewhere you might like
             . . . When you read books, like even if there's no pictures at all in
             the books you've got [your imagination] . . . because . . . they're
             just like black and white, but your pictures in your head, you can
             colour them any colour you like and nobody will be able to see
             them.
                          (Interview with Lucy and Kate, School B, Autumn 1996)

Kate: [Head teacher B] goes on about hers . . . and so that makes the
             younger children believe it . . . its nicer to imagine your own, to
             have your own ideas . . . and what you believe in . . . but like they
             don't imagine their own ideas. [If you have your own imagina-
             tion] like it let's you do more things...[its] like when I read books
             . . . I was really interested to see what their imagination was
             compared to mine and it was completely different, I think mine
             was better! . . . Its better, I like that you can imagine.
                          (Interview with Lucy and Kate, School B, Autumn 1996)

These conversations can be set alongside comments given by head
teachers at the same schools:

> At St———'s Catholic school we aspire to sustain enriching relationships
> with ourselves, with others and God by promoting child-centred devel-
> opmental curriculum whose religious dimension enables us to journey
> together with Christ as our guide in faith, respect and dignity. (Head
> teacher A, questionnaire)

> a supportive environment that "shows" love and respect for the unique-
> ness of the individual as well as recognizing the "family" of the school
> who work together and love each other . . . our RE programme has in-built
> quiet circle time for [the] child's own reflections and a personal question
> for them to answer. (Head teacher B, questionnaire)

These interviews come from qualitative research that sought to investigate the place of church school religious education, in its broadest sense, in the development of children's worldviews. Employing a narrative approach the research encouraged children to speak about their experiences of religious education, to tell their stories about who they were, what was important to them and what it was like for them to be part of a church school community. In total I talked with 125 ten and eleven year-old children in small groups of six. Further to this ten children were re-interviewed in pairs. Additional data included children's drawings and questionnaires from the head teachers and class teachers (see Ota 1998).

Underpinning these conversations was a strong commitment to listen to the children and to remain mindful of the restrictions that particular conceptions of childhood, and adult-child relationships, might impose. In exploring the lived experiences of children and listening to their personal stories in a genuinely child-centred way, I was guided by the following considerations:

1   how we engage with the narratives and voices of children;
2   the restrictive sentiments adults may consciously / unconsciously assume and impose;
3   what children are, can do and what age means;
4   the plurality of pathways to maturity, especially in culturally diverse societies like Britain, and what it means to speak of the variety of different childhoods.

The main findings of the inquiry offer some important considerations. For example, the theme of relationship emerges across the data as a key issue – a perceived absence is alluded to by Samuel, Paul, Jonathan and Jenni in the section quoted above. This is in direct contrast with the head teacher comments also quoted, where the adults speak of a child-centred approach that encompasses listening and working together in a close relationship. Closer analysis of the interviews offered a way of gaining a deeper understanding of the relationship between teachers and pupils, and what emerged was a balance of different relational qualities concerning the:

1   degree of *negotiation* within the relationship;
2   way in which *meaning* is provided for the child within the relationship;
3   degree of *security* provided for the child within the relationship;
4   degree of *freedom and independence* (physically, cognitively and spiritually) within the relationship;

5   place of *authority* and *authoritative statements* within the relationship.

These qualities simplify and at the same time lead us into the
complexity of relationship for each individual child and each relationship that child has. The way these five qualities are balanced in any
given relationship at a particular time opens up infinite possibilities of
variation; yet whatever the balance, they work together to form the nuts
and bolts in the machinery of each relationship. Alongside this theme
of relationship is the significance of the *opportunity for narrative response*
(for example, in the time given for classroom discussions).

To relocate this framework of analysis within the schools, what can
be said about nurture and spiritual development? The children's interviews reveal a widespread recognition of authority that resides with
the teachers and head. Arising out of this, for many children, is the
issue of truth; according to the children's understanding the school's
claim to authority enables it to present children with a tight, well-
defined worldview and belief system that is upheld as the truth. This
model of RE, with a strong focus on its own authority seems to be at
the expense of encouraging children to engage in their own meaning construction. In retaining authority for itself the school appears to
be restricted in being able to give permission or foster confidence in
the children so that they are able to speak with their own voice of
authority.

Staying with the dominant role of authority within this model of RE
we can consider how this emphasis limits the qualities of *negotiation,
freedom and independence*. In presenting a contained worldview and
belief system as the truth we may speculate that within the relational
structures of the schools there is little space or perceived need for either
negotiation, freedom or independence: these qualities are not present
or fostered simply because they are not deemed necessary.

Nevertheless, throughout the data there are examples where the children exhibit a high degree of negotiation, freedom and independence in
their discussions about religious concepts. These instances are, however, outside of data which specifically addresses RE, and in them the
children reveal a remarkable capability to engage in their own meaning
construction, displaying a range of skills and abilities that enable them
to reflect and communicate with each other. Thus we have contrasting
data which not only demonstrates the value of negotiation, freedom and
independence within the relational process but also highlights how,
according to the children's experience, such qualities are visibly lacking
within the relational process of RE.

Returning to the issue of truth and the school's presentation of a
contained, well-defined worldview and belief system we can explore

how the qualities of *meaning* and *security* fit within this construct of RE. Examining the data the fairly rigid authoritarian worldview and belief system, as perceived by the children, is both useful and a source of tension. It is useful because:

- it provides a clearly defined sense of identity which, in different instances, the children understand as religious, Christian and/or Catholic. The data suggests that the children see themselves as sharing in this identity to a lesser or greater degree and this provides them with a sense of belonging and *security*;
- in offering such a clearly defined worldview and belief system this model of RE provides *meaning*: it presents the child with concepts and ideas which are either accepted, or assimilated and developed in the child's own meaning construction.

Alongside these two edifying aspects there is data that suggests that this same rigid framework of belief and truth can also create conflict and tension. This is apparent, for example, when the children express difficulty in accepting the truth claims presented in RE or when the concepts presented by the school conflict with their own ideas, reflections or experiences. Assessing the overall balance of qualities of relationship at the school authority is the prevailing feature, and the diminished presence of other qualities is directly related to this emphasis.

If we locate the opportunity for narrative response within RE, this means we will be seeking to determine how and where a given model of RE allows children to consider and express their own reflective understanding. Within a number of children's conversations that do not address RE it is possible to find examples of narrative response: for instance when discussing relationships that provide opportunities for narrative response (with parents or friends) as well as the interview situation itself. There is a stark contrast between these examples and where the children's generally negative, non-engaged comments about formal RE point to a lack of opportunity for narrative response. To probe and evidence this lack of opportunity in this model of RE we can note the ways in which the children comment upon the issues of engagement and involvement:

- there are occasions when the children speak about feeling engaged and involved in RE; for example, when they serve at mass or are involved in assembly;
- these occasions are seen as outside of what normally happens in formal RE (lessons and collective worship) and serve to highlight the children's general understanding of RE where they don't feel engaged or involved in collective worship or lessons.

When the children are encouraged to work from their own experience and be involved they express less estrangement from RE. Equating the issues of engagement and involvement with an opportunity for narrative response, we can say that although formal RE does not allow for narrative response as a matter of course, children welcome its opportunity when it does occur.

Listening to the children alerts us to how the teacher–learner/adult–child relationship exists in their experience. Whilst their shared community story offers security, they also find little relevance of what they are told to their own lives. In his discussion of moral development in Catholic schools Day refers to "a pedagogy of estrangement" (1996: 163ff) and with respect to the children's narratives about school we may surmise that, for them, the "Catholic pedagogy" they experience could certainly be more relevant to their lives, affording greater authority and recognition to them, as well as offering the space and support to genuinely reflect and create meaning out of their own experiences and stories.

This is not to deny the importance of the shared "community" story that the Catholic school can offer. However, Day's thoughts are useful in identifying that unless the child's experience is truly relational (which includes genuine dialogue[4]) the school will be able to offer little more than estrangement – estrangement spiritually, culturally and morally as well as from the Catholic faith.

Children's Spirituality and Pedagogical Effectiveness

Let us be clear then, within Catholic schools there is indeed a tension between what it sets out to achieve for its pupils (for example being child-centred and attending to the development of the whole child) and what in fact is experienced by the children. Such tension is not exclusive to the Christian tradition or church schools (see chapters 21 and 5 by Clive Erricker and Mark Chater in this volume) but in the context of Catholic schools let us look for a way forward.

Jumpers and Worldviews:[5] Identifying the Tension

To appreciate the complexity of the relational process and its role in the development of the whole person I want to introduce the metaphor of knitting a jumper. This is a useful tool by which we may represent the way worldviews and identity form different aspects of the self. Through the process of knitting (relationships) a jumper is created (the self). A jumper has two different sides; that which faces inwards (identity) and that which faces outwards (worldviews) and although these sides are different they are created simultaneously through the one knitting process.

To take this metaphor a step further we can also note that a knitting pattern may or may not be used when knitting a jumper. It is possible to relate this image to the concerns of this chapter; is the jumper (the self, identity and worldviews) made with or without the use of a knitting pattern (the Catholic school and its RE)? Is a pattern helpful (does it enable the development of worldviews) or does it hinder the knitting process (create conflict, for example)?

Kate and Lucy, who spoke earlier, clearly expose tensions in how the school contributes to their worldview development (and by "worldviews" I here include spiritual growth). For them the knitting pattern provided by the school does not work – the jumper it makes for them does not fit and is not one they want to wear, at least not all the time. To extend this metaphor we may conclude that it would be far more beneficial and valuable if the school sat beside the girls and helped them knit – i.e. established the kinds of relationships that shared experiences and engaged with the girls rather than simply delivered a finished product.

The Tension of Common and Individual Stories

[The] Catholic context . . . is deeply in need of co-conspirators in a responsive reading of the text our students bring to us; one already richly alive with moral thought, adventure and intrigue, already ripe for intervention, but only after we have discovered it to be there. Where such a will is lacking . . . the breach is reproduced. Where it is present the words of the tradition may be heard and spoken anew, for they will be seen as part of a common quest that belongs to the parties involved . . . One's own story including its subplots of moral characters, quests and conflicts, has to be received before one can be provoked to re-narratize one's self or the world. (Day 1996: 171f)

As Day suggests, a clearer understanding of relationality and the shared responsibility to live and share a common story perhaps offer us a way forward in this tension. This entails, on a theoretical level, a consideration of the nature and goals of the schools, including, as Crump Miller submits, the more unquantifiable realm of providing tools and methods with which to live meaningfully:

they [children] need the tools, knowledge and methods to live meaningfully in a new kind of world that is faced with almost insuperable problems . . . Rather than outline specific goals in terms of description, what we need are areas in which generalised goals may be established. If

> we take a pluralistic and flexible view of the meaning of religious maturity, we cannot expect results in terms of fixed beliefs or codes of behaviour. If we take seriously the meaning of human freedom responding to a specific and vague stimuli, both human and divine, we may hope to evoke insights but we cannot determine assembly line results. (Crump Miller 1990: 253f and 258)

But is such a shift in focus possible in church schools? Within the current theoretical debate it is clear that an open, dialogic process is advocated and endorsed, but are there those who can also show that it is possible to authentically recast the form of church school RE, whilst, for example, maintaining confidence in a distinctive philosophy and separate identity?

Certainly the inherent difficulties in this situation are not ignored in the contemporary discussion (see British Council of Churches 1984: 39, para 110f; McLaughlin 1994) and concern is expressed for a "clearer differentiation of aims, contexts, processes, methods and expectations for RE" (Rossiter 1990: 299) within the school environment (as distinct from the role and function of the church) (Leahy 1994: 426). Narrating his experiences of implementing a process model of RE, Hastings, head of a RC Secondary School, commends a process model, bluntly signalling the necessity for different goals, despite the difficulties:

> the choice is now between a growth of openness to intellectual challenge and dialogue with the human race, and a continued censored conversation between obedient neophytes . . . knowing and loving being the great activities of life, a school aiming at relationships must pursue intellectual and moral search, involving growth in personhood and relationship. A Catholic school cannot offer a packaged answer about God or the meaning of life, but a hunger for, and determination to find truth and rightness. (1996: 283)

An Ontological Justification – A Way Forward

We have, perhaps, identified a tension that cannot be resolved, although likewise perhaps there will be others, both within and outside of the Catholic community, who will occupy a different position on the matter, depending on the vision and purpose they have for their schools. I propose that this inevitable tension can be used in a creative and constructive way: both for the individual within the school community – staff and pupils – and for the community as a whole.

One way in which this tension can be creative is the degree of theoretical reflection and debate it can stimulate. The need for a grounded and rigorous debate is paramount (as is also recognized by Losito 2000: 67), one that is informed by research and the contribution of education and social theory generally. Beyond this such discussions need opportunities for further dialogue and dissemination. Again we return to the theme of meaningfulness: for the debate to have any meaning it needs to be in dialogue with the reality of church schools as it is experienced by staff and pupils alike, as well as governors, advisers and diocesan boards of education.

Alongside this is the need for awareness raising in the purpose and identity of Catholic schools. Effective staff development is a real challenge (Moore 2000: 94), as is initial / ongoing teacher training and governor training. These are, nevertheless, crucially important (Guerra 2000: 88), particularly the question of what might constitute the distinctive character of Catholic teacher training (McLaughlin 1996: 150). Further to this I would endorse Hyper (1996), Barnes (1996) and Murray (1996) who all call for a coherent educational policy, especially in relation to the issues of race and other faiths.

To return to the classroom and the children we also return to the idea of enabling children to become storytellers within their communities (Erricker and Erricker 2000: 129ff). As my research demonstrates, children, even as young as seven, are not unaware of themselves, the complexities of life, morality and their (plural) identities (Cullingford 1999). They face the same issues of identity and meaning that we as adults face – "how to make new experiences fit" (Cullingford 1999: 267). For Catholic schools to contribute meaningfully and positively to the child's personal growth this requires them to engage with pupils, allowing them to share their stories and contribute to the community's story. Seeking to develop what he terms a "Catholic anthropology" Groome posits three commitments for Catholic education:

- to affirm students' basic goodness, to promote their dignity, to honour their fundamental rights, and to develop their gifts to the fullest – as *God's reflections;*
- to educate people to live responsibly, with God's help, for the fullness of life that God wills for self and others – as *responsible partners;*
- to convince and mould people to live as if their lives are worthwhile and have historical significance, that their every effort advances the well-being of all – as *history makers.* (1996: 111)

"Responsible partners" – for the tension I have highlighted to be truly creative I would contend that that term needs careful unpacking and reconsideration. If Catholic schools seek to really make a difference to the lives of their pupils then the how, what, why and when of relational responsible partnering is a possible way forward.

Conclusions

Like Groome I acknowledge that what I have outlined exists as a future possibility, a future vision for Catholic schools, it is something that is yet to be empirically realized (Groome 1996: 123). My research indicates that anything other than a process based approach has fundamental problems in engaging with children and offering anything that is meaningful and relevant to them.[6] This therefore suggests that however difficult the transition to confronting diversity, accepting ambiguity, complexity and different kinds of belief and unbelief, RE in church schools has to consider not just if a move towards process is *possible* but whether it is in fact *essential* if it wishes to genuinely contribute to children's social, moral, cultural, spiritual development and meaning construction.

It is unfortunate, to say the least, if, despite their sustained efforts and wishes, church schools are not part of this process.[7] This is not to deny that the process may also be "demanding and painful" (McLaughlin 1996: 151) but in highlighting the failure of RE to substantially affect children's worldview development this study urges church schools to reconsider their vision for education and the relationships they foster in their schools. For RE in church schools to be effective, relevant and meaningful this research marks out a way forward that is not characterized by right answers but by dialogue, interdependent relationships and a searching together. Only then will church schools be able to declare with confidence that they have not left children stranded in their quest for meaning construction, but have strengthened their pupils with the courage and ability not just to embrace the world and themselves but to also try and make sense of it in relation to the question of faith.

Notes

1   In addressing these issues I speak not only as a qualitative researcher who has worked in a variety of schools, but also as a parent, as a governor of a local Catholic primary school, and as someone who was educated from the age of five to eighteen in the Catholic school system in England.

2   Before admitting a child many Catholic schools require a copy of a baptism certificate and a Parish Priest's signature. In oversubscribed schools this may still not guarantee a place and further evidence of regular mass attendance and/or having an active part in parish life may be necessary.

3   Catholic parishes currently contribute significant amounts of money towards running Catholic schools. With rising costs and the changing patterns of mass attendance parishes find it harder to support schools and the nature of the school–parish relationship has been brought sharply into focus (Murphy O'Connor 1996).

4   For more on the role of dialogue and relationality in church schools see Ota 1998.

5   For more on how I develop worldviews as a concept see Ota 1998.

6   This replicates findings of research carried out by McClure (1996) and Egan (1988: 141).
7   I was surprised by the degree of irrelevance and ineffectiveness expressed about RE in many narratives, particularly in the light of the nature and depth of meaning construction referred to outside of RE (for example with friends, family and church) and their own existential/ ontological concerns and readiness to engage in discussion about them.

References

Arthur, J. 1995: *The Ebbing Tide – Policy and Principles of Catholic Education,* Herefordshire: Gracewing.

Arthur, J. and Gaine, S. 1996: Catechesis and Religious Education in Catholic Theory and Practice. In L. Francis, W. Kay and W. Campbell (eds) *Research in Religious Education,* Herefordshire: Gracewing and Georgia, USA: Smyth and Helwys, 335–57.

Astley, J. 1994: The Place of Understanding in Christian Education and Education About Christianity. In J. Astley and L. Francis (eds) *Critical Perspectives on Christian Education,* Herefordshire: Gracewing, 105–17.

Barnes, M. 1996: Catholic Schools in a World of Many Faiths: Church Teaching and Theological Perspectives. In McLaughlin, T., J. O'Keefe and B. O'Keeffe (eds), *The Contemporary Catholic School: Context, Identity and Diversity,* London: Falmer Press, 232–8.

British Council of Churches (BCC) 1984: *The Child in the Church,* Reports of the Working Parties on The Child in the Church and Understanding Christian Nurture, London: BCC.

Chadwick, P. 1994: *Schools of Reconciliation – Issues in Joint Roman Catholic-Anglican Education,* London: Cassell.

—— 1997: *Shifting Alliances – Church and State in English Education,* London: Cassell.

Crump Miller, R. 1990: Theology and the Future of Religious Education. In L. Francis and A. Thatcher (eds), *Christian Perspectives for Education,* Herefordshire: Gracewing, 253–63.

Cullingford, C. 1999: *The Human Experience: The Early Years,* Aldershot: Ashgate.

Day, J. M. 1996: Recognition and Responsivity: Unlearning the Pedagogy of Estrangement for a Catholic Moral Education. In McLaughlin, T., J. O'Keefe and B. O'Keeffe (eds), *The Contemporary Catholic School: Context, Identity and Diversity,* London: Falmer Press, 162–73.

Egan, J. 1988 *Opting Out: Catholic Schools Today,* Herefordshire: Fowler Wright Books.

Erricker, C. 2000: True Stories and Other Dreams. In C. Erricker and J. Erricker (eds), *Reconstructing Religious, Spiritual and Moral Education,* London: Routledge, 1–11.

Erricker, C. and Erricker, J. 2000: Narrative Constructions Towards Community. In C. Erricker and J. Erricker (eds), *Reconstructing Religious, Spiritual and Moral Education,* London: Routledge, 107–31.

Erricker, C., Erricker, J., Ota, C., Sullivan, D. and Fletcher, M. 1997: *The Education of the Whole Child,* London: Cassell.

Groome, T. 1994: Shared Christian Praxis: A Possible Theory/Method of Religious Education. In J. Astley and L. Francis (eds), *Critical Perspectives on Christian Education*, Herefordshire: Gracewing, 218–37.

—— 1996: What Makes a School Catholic? In T. McLaughlin, J. O'Keefe and B. O'Keeffe (eds), *The Contemporary Catholic School: Context, Identity and Diversity*, London: Falmer Press, 107–25.

Guerra, M. 2000: Key Issues for the Future of Catholic Schools. In T. Hunt, T. E. Oldenski and T. J. Wallace (eds), *Catholic School Leadership: An Invitation to Lead*, London: The Falmer Press, 79–90.

Haldane, J. 1996: Catholic Education and Catholic Identity. In McLaughlin, T., J. O'Keefe and B. O'Keeffe (eds), *The Contemporary Catholic School: Context, Identity and Diversity*, London: Falmer Press, 126–35.

Hastings, P. 1996: Openness and Intellectual Challenge in Catholic Schools. In T. McLaughlin, J. O'Keefe and B. O'Keeffe (eds), *The Contemporary Catholic School – Context, Identity and Diversity*, London: The Falmer Press, 272–83.

Hull, J. 1990: Christian Nurture and Critical Openness. In L. Francis and A. Thatcher (eds), *Christian Perspectives for Education*, Herefordshire: Gracewing, 306–19.

Hyper, P. 1996: Catholic Schools and Other Faiths. In McLaughlin, T., J. O'Keefe and B. O'Keeffe (eds), *The Contemporary Catholic School: Context, Identity and Diversity*, London: Falmer Press, 216–31.

Leahy, M. 1994: Indoctrination, Evangelisation, Catechesis and Religious Education. In J. Astley and L. Francis (eds), *Critical Perspectives on Christian Education*, Herefordshire: Gracewing, 426–36.

Losito, W. F. 2000: Reclaiming Inquiry in the Catholic Philosophy of Education. In T. Hunt, T. E. Oldenski and T. J. Wallace (eds), *Catholic School Leadership: An Invitation to Lead*, London: Falmer Press, 59–68.

McLaughlin, T. 1994: Parental Rights and the Religious Upbringing of Children. In J. Astley and L. Francis (eds), *Critical Perspectives on Christian Education*, Herefordshire: Gracewing, 171–83.

—— 1996: The Distinctiveness of Catholic Education. In McLaughlin, T., J. O'Keefe and B. O'Keeffe (eds), *The Contemporary Catholic School: Context, Identity and Diversity*, London: Falmer Press, 136–54.

McLaughlin, T., O'Keefe, J. and O'Keeffe, B. 1996: Setting the Scene: Current Realities and Historical Perspectives. In McLaughlin T., J. O'Keefe and B. O'Keeffe (eds), *The Contemporary Catholic School: Context, Identity and Diversity*, London: Falmer Press, 1–22.

McClure, M. 1996: How Children's Faith Develops, *The Way Supplement* 86, 5–13.

Moore, L. 2000: Staff Development in the Catholic School. In T. Hunt, T. E. Oldenski and T. J. Wallace (eds), *Catholic School Leadership: An Invitation to Lead*, London: The Falmer Press, 93–104.

Murphy O'Connor, C. 1996: *The Catholic School – The Church in the World: An Invitation to Dialogue*, Crawley: R. C. Diocese of Arundel and Brighton Schools Commission.

Murray, V. 1996: Other Faiths in Catholic Schools: General Implications of a Case Study. In McLaughlin, T., J. O'Keefe and B. O'Keeffe (eds), *The Contemporary Catholic School: Context, Identity and Diversity*, London: Falmer Press, 239–53.

Nichols, V. 2000: *Memorandum on the Appointment of Teachers to Catholic Schools – A Guide for Governors.* http://www.cesew.demon.co.uk/bpsmemo.html

Ota, C. 1998: *The Place of Religious Education in the Development of Children's Worldviews,* Unpublished Ph.D. thesis, University College Chichester, University of Southampton.

Phillips, D. Z. 1994: Philosophy and Religious Education. In J. Astley and L. Francis (eds), *Critical Perspectives on Christian Education,* Herefordshire: Gracewing, 439–52.

Rossiter, G. 1990: The Need For A "Creative Divorce" Between Catechesis and Religious Education in Catholic Schools. In L. Francis and A. Thatcher (eds), *Christian Perspectives for Education,* Leominster: Gracewing, Fowler Wright, 291–305.

Raddell, W. J. 2000: The Challenge of Teaching Religion in Catholic Schools. In T. Hunt, T. E. Oldenski and T. J. Wallace (eds), *Catholic School Leadership: An Invitation to Lead,* London: Falmer Press, 105–12.

Chapter 21

The Spiritual Education of Khoja Shi'a Ithnasheeri (KSI) Youth: The Challenges of Diaspora

CLIVE ERRICKER

"My father says I am free to express myself to him. But I can't because our culture dictates that young people do not assert themselves before their elders", says Hussain. "Heavy metal is my only outlet. All my pent up energy is released when I listen to it." (del Nevo 1992: 3)

HUSSAIN, from Lahore in Pakistan, is a 19-year-old urban, middle-class boy with a desire to be a journalist. He further remarks, "In the West a boy of my age can make his own choices . . . He can talk to girls, drink, listen to any type of music. We don't necessarily want to indulge in these things. But we do want the freedom to choose. And our parents don't understand – they feel threatened" (1992: 3).

Globalization presents new opportunities, new threats and new challenges, especially across generations and to established cultures and traditions. Hussain's society is Islamic, though he is most probably not Khoja. Nevertheless, his voice is not untypical of the tensions experienced by Khoja youth. These tensions are endemic to a situation within which secularity and increasing opportunity for the young, if well educated, confront tradition and conformity to religious values. This chapter seeks to investigate how this situation is being addressed within the context of the Khoja Shi'a Ithnasheeri (KSI) community, not in Pakistan but in the West, and in Britain in particular.

A Brief History of the Khoja Shi'a Ithnasheeri

Khojas hail from India, in the Sind region around Bombay. Originally Thakkers, prosperous landowners within the Hindu caste system, they

converted to an uncertain form of Islam through the influence of Pir
Sadruddin. From him they gained the title Khwaja, Khoja being a
phonetic corruption of this term. Their occupation became trading and,
in particular, plying the trade route between the Western Indian and
East African coast during the eighteenth and nineteenth centuries, by
which time they were recognizably a part of the Ismaili Nizari tradition
under the leadership of the Aga Khan.

In dispute with the Aga Khan, when he migrated to India from Iran,
and under threat of religious persecution, some Khojas left for East
Africa, and in particular Zanzibar. From here they plied their trade the
other way and, during the period of dispute and subsequently, they
became established as a branch of the Shi'a Ithnasheeri tradition
(Ithnasheeri meaning those who follow the twelve Imams). Zanzibar
became a conducive environment for the KSI, being Islamic. Those who
settled elsewhere in East Africa, for example in Kenya and Uganda,
were already in diaspora in the sense that these countries were not
Muslim. In the 1960s and '70s the situation changed dramatically with
the end of colonial rule.

In 1964 revolution took place in Zanzibar. In 1972 "Asians" were
expelled from Uganda under Idi Amin. Forced to leave suddenly,
Khojas migrated to the West where they could take up new nationali-
ties. In Britain, for example, they could take advantage of their previous
colonial status. It is from this point that they had to determine how to
reconstruct their previous identity given that the organizational infrastructure that maintained their faith and communities previously was
absent; that the West consisted, by and large, of countries that
were significantly secularized; and that a Muslim and especially Shi'a
presence was minor if not, in some locations, entirely absent.[1]

The Internal Debate:
Tradition, Change and Controversy

The contention among many in the KSI is that the institutions have failed
the youth (Rahim 1994: 7). Rahim speaks specifically of those aged
between fifteen and twenty-five, whilst others cited later are concerned
with younger Khojas below this age. Rahim also acknowledges, in
passing, that younger Khojas are subjected to parental and community
pressure to attend *majalis* (religious gatherings) and that the later result,
once free of this pressure, is to opt out (1994: 7). Thus, we may surmise
that the problem of disaffection starts earlier. Disaffection and disinterest
may be understood as a normal teenage response, and some community
members interpret in this way and see less to worry about; others think
differently. This leads us to a consideration of the internal debate.

There is a cultural domestication which separates off young Khojas from their generational elders. It is this distinction that lies at the heart of the existing tensions. As a result, young Khojas will have different expectations to those that older generations require or may deem suitable, for example, with regard to dress, manners and relationships. These differences exist not just on the basis of ignorance of religious teachings, though this may be the case with respect to the lack of nurture in some homes, but more importantly they exist because conceptually and experientially Western-born Khoja Shi'as live in a different world.

For Khojas a high level of education is paramount. This ensures the qualities required by the community continue to be forthcoming. Intellectual and economic capability creates an articulate and financially stable network of centres that are able to attend to their own professional, political and spiritual needs and debate and resolve the issues confronted by them. Here there are certain similarities with the Jewish Diaspora experience.

In their recent study of Jewish continuity in the USA, *The Next Generation: Jewish Children and Adolescents* (Keysar, Kosmin and Scheckner 2000), the authors comment that:

> Involvement in Jewish life and the organized community generally requires significant sums of money . . . Given a parental commitment to Jewish socialization, children in households with a higher per capita income not only are given more options to enrich their life, but also more opportunity to develop, bond, and connect with their heritage, and become more involved with the Jewish community. (2000: 32)

They also cite Winter's observation that:

> The decision of whether or not to affiliate to a synagogue . . . is not solely a consequence of family income. (It) is apt to be dependent both on family income . . . and on the degree of Jewish identity or commitment. (Winter 1989: 149; 2000: 33)

Relating the analysis of Jewish community to the Khoja Shi'as we can identify three important factors in ensuring continuity. A high level of secular education of the youth to equip them for professional employment or self-employment, which will perpetuate future sufficient household per capita income to maintain and develop organized community life; effective religious or faith education to perpetuate commitment to religious identity; and marriage relations, since unsuccessful marriage results in lower income for one-parent families (2000: 26–32), and thus limits the options available, and marriage outside the Khoja, Shi'a, or wider Muslim community will weaken commitment.

As with the Jewish situation, faith nurture within the family is the most significant factor in ensuring religious commitment. Without this, there is the tendency to adopt a purely secular and possibly materialist lifestyle. In the Khoja situation the intervening period between migration and the setting up of religious and community centres created a hiatus within which assimilation to the secular culture of the host country had already started to develop. Thus the distinctive family environment of a Khoja Shi'a household had, in many cases, lost the faith influence of the Shi'a religion, without which being Khoja was no more than an ethnic designation entailing cultural difference. The effect of this tendency was and still is felt within the *medrassas*, subsequently established, since young Khojas may come having no acquaintance with their religion and no motivation to study and practice it. Also, the effect of success within secular education without faith education for young adults can manifest itself in lucrative ambition for its own sake.

As with both Jewish and Roman Catholic communities previously the need for "revitalizing and intensifying religious education through greater investment by the community and parents" (2000: 9) has been recognized by the Khojas. The success of this initiative, however, depends upon two factors. The first is the organization of an appropriate curriculum, but the second, without which the venture will surely fail, is an educational process that engages the learner. In short, what is required is good pedagogy. To have the former without the later can amount to a form of religious instruction but it is not spiritual education. My argument from this point on is to distinguish what spiritual education, as opposed to religious instruction, would mean in this context. In outline, my distinction relates to the differing sociological terms "identity" and "identification". In the Jewish context they have been differentiated as follows: "Jewish identity is one's sense of self with regard to being Jewish", but "Jewish identification is the process of thinking and acting in a manner that indicates involvement with and attachment to Jewish life" (Himmelfarb 1982: 32; Liebman 1973 quoted in Keysar et al. 2000: 1). The distinction between the two terms implies that whereas identification can be observed as evidence of belonging, identity implies an ownership of the world view at a deeper level of self-understanding. My contention is that religious instruction can result in forms of identification but that spiritual education consists, at least in its prime aspiration, in the ownership of a particular identity.

Shifts in Authority and Identity

Having outlined the problem and indicated something of the complexity of the issue to be addressed we have to ask whether the KSI has the resolve and resources to tackle it. Traditionally, the spiritual direction and vision in a *Jamaat* (religious centre) is provided by the *mulla* or *dhakir*. He or they communicate the relevance of the teachings to those present at the *majalis*. At this practical level there are significant difficulties.

Putting it bluntly, Anis Somani asks:

> Look around yourselves next time you attend a *majalis*. You will no doubt see in attendance kids, teens, young adults, mid-aged and seniors, men and women; and sitting on a pulpit will be an Aalim reciting a *majalis* . . . How many times have you and I come out of *majalis* as if nothing was gained. Ask yourselves. Be honest. (Somani 1994: 69)

Her point is that the topic covered contains nothing new and the *majalis* does not address the needs of the gathering. A consequence of this, and especially so given the amount of travel often required within a dispersed community, is that, as Salim Sachedina points out, "most of the time our children do not want to accompany us. They say they have better things to do. And perhaps they are right!" (Sachedina 1994: 160). For Sachedina, the problems question the contemporary relevance of the gatherings in a number of fundamental ways. These are not simply about adjustments to present procedures but a lack of understanding of the needs of the community by its leaders. For her it is as if the latter occupy a different reality, misplaced in space and time, within which a lack of respect for the community and its youth is endemic.

> You wonder, in this day and age, in the West, why do you have to sit on the hard floor for hours listening to a *Mulla* who is sitting in comfort over the pulpit (*mimbar*) and who is not respectful of your time and discomfort. You wonder why is this Mulla talking about the superiority of Shi'a Islam, as compared to Sunni, to a Shi'a congregation. We do not need any convincing. Does he not know that we are Shi'a and thus already convinced? Why doesn't he go to a Sunni congregation and try to convince them that they are on the wrong path and see if he can come out of it alive?
>
> So my generation, the one preceding and the one following, have been raised to believe that attending majalis is a blissful act – Sawaab. Our children will not buy such nonsense. And to conduct our *majalis* in, say, English will not change anything . . . because they understand how nonsensical the whole process is. It is analogous to somebody who is blind from birth, gaining his eyesight only to see, in living colour, at first hand the ills and sufferings of life around him. (1994: 160–1)

Here issues of authority and identity collide. The issues often deemed of importance to leaders with traditional views do not match with those of significance to younger generations. Furthermore, the mechanisms and procedures required for change and adaptation clash with the traditional values relating to the authority given to religious leaders and even parents. For, example notions of leadership and obedience are conceived of in different ways, but to question across these different conceptions is perceived as questioning the efficacy of Islamic values in themselves. In effect, this lack of communication amounts to a refusal to listen and a compulsion to instruct in the face of the fear of secular indoctrination from the wider society and the belief that all that is required is maintaining traditional ways and teachings. The complexity of the situation remains unacknowledged as long as the problem is located outside the community rather than within it. Medievalizing the situation by constructing a fortress of Islam fails to take account of the trade in interests, ideas and values already passing through the gates. Whilst, in the *medrassa* (faith school), Khoja Shi'a youth are asking the question "Why?" the teachers are answering the question "What?" Conceptions of authority that worked in another, more conducively Islamic time and place, as Merali and Aslam observe, lose their relevance and collapse into authoritarianism:

> Parents of the immigrant generation are often accustomed through their own backgrounds to their role being both authoritative and authoritarian. As children grow up in a Western society, parents now find that their experiences become increasingly less relevant. As they try to guide their children in matters of behaviour, choice of friends, careers and most significantly marriage, parents often find themselves being authoritarian because they can no longer be authoritative. (Merali and Aslam 1998: 372–3)

If we ask why this is the case we find ourselves at the heart of the matter. Authority depends on the resonance of advice and guidance given with the dilemmas experienced by those who are within a situation of ambiguity or irresolution. To deny the tensions inherent in such a situation, by recourse to instruction that ignores its ambivalence, is to be authoritarian but not to be worthy of the title authoritative. In other words, respect is lost because understanding is not evident.

The Broader Picture: Post-colonial Identity within Postmodernity

An alternative approach for the community is to take the spirituality of the young much more seriously. By this I mean recognizing and negotiating issues of identity as they are experienced by Khoja Shi'a youth. In order to do this we first have to gain some impression of the broader context within which the youth find themselves, to gain some psychological understanding of the complexity of establishing a notion of identity. With respect to this, the analyses of Homi Bhabha on post-colonial identity are applicable. Bhabha quotes Walter Benjamin as stating, "The state of emergency in which we live is not the exception but the rule" (Bhabha 1994: 41; Benjamin 1968: 257). Benjamin's comment is made as an observation on Western industrialized capitalist culture in its development within the late nineteenth and the first half of the twentieth century. Bhabha comments on this by further observing "the state of emergency is also always a state of emergence" (Bhabha 1994: 41). Benjamin's state of emergency can be traced in the utterances of the educational and social commentators referred to above and their desire to eliminate it with a return to the imposition of traditional ways and the reconstruction of traditional institutions; it can also be identified in the comments made on the religious leaders and gatherings in the Khoja community. Both cases are attempts to deny what Bhabha refers to as emergence. Emergence we can apply to the critical voices calling for change. The denial of emergence by those in authority admits of no negotiation over what are perceived as timeless truths threatened by chaos (the fragmentation of social cohesion). It is as if we have two diasporas merging together. The diaspora of postmodernity in which, in the West and within globalization, traditional "civilizing" structures start to decay, and the diaspora of the Khoja Shi'as, as a political and geographical event, with its concomitant collapse of the infrastructure supporting traditional religious and cultural forms. This is the psychological site within which young Khoja Shi'as find themselves.

The difficulty then becomes communication, in a number of ways, since the constructions of identity within the various groups and institutions affecting the lives of young Khoja Shi'as are multifarious. Whereas their parents and other generational elders, especially those in the third generation, such as grandparents, may have experienced a sense of homogeneous culture, first-generation British-born Khoja Shi'as experience one of heterogeneity, as understood by Bakhtin, for example (Bakhtin: 1986: 19). Thus, we can apply to their situation specifically different spiritual needs in the sense that Bhabha describes in quoting Goethe, "What of the more complex cultural situation where 'previously unrecognized spiritual and intellectual needs' emerge from the imposition of 'foreign' ideas, cultural representations, and structures of power" (1994: 11–12; Springarn 1921: 98–9). Whilst Goethe was referring to the effect of the Napoleonic wars, within which the idea of foreignness was readily identifiable, for the young Khojas what is foreign resides often ambiguously in their consciousness. For example, whereas Shi'a teachings may be part of the cultural and religious life histories of older members of the community, they may be absent from or peripheral to their own. This may especially be the case if the teachings are clothed in traditional forms that pre-date the youth and convey certain alien messages, for example in relation to gender and authority.

The articulation of difference, for young Khojas, is fraught with difficulty in the face of instructional requirements. If the categories of interpretation do not match, that is what requires attention; however, reflection on experiences that are difficult to articulate to older generations are resolved more by a sense of "how to go on" than by inheriting a precept from the past that has not yet found its place in the context of their experience.

The Khoja Shi'a situation can usefully be conceptualized, using Bhabha's term, as an interstices where "the overlap and displacement of domains of difference" occur and where "the intersubjective and collective experiences of *nationness* (and we may substitute identity), community interest, or cultural value are negotiated" (1994: 2). The critical activity is that of negotiation, what forms it can take and what limits proscribe it. Within this activity there is a need for "reciprocal recognitions" (Fanon 1986: 218; Bhabha 1994: 8) and an awareness that the boundary with the past created by the diaspora experience is not just, in Heidegger's words, "that at which something stops but . . . that from which *something begins its presencing*" (Heidegger 1971: 152; Bhabha 1994: 1). This presencing is to be found in the voices of the Khoja youth, to which I return in the last section of this chapter.

Spiritual and Moral Education in the KSI Context: The Implications

When we seek to attend to the difference between the spiritual and moral education of the youth we are required to consider the metaphoric significance of events in Islam, as interpreted within the Shi'a tradition. Datoo provides us with some interesting, helpful, but somewhat confusing observations on the relationship and distinctions between spiritual, moral, ritual and philosophical understanding. He argues:

> The primary objective that *majalis* sought to accomplish in East Africa was spiritual . . . By contrast, the overriding function of *majalis* in western societies must be moral . . . The need for this change in emphasis, as it relates to our broader responsibilities, can be demonstrated with reference to the epic tragedy of Kerbala. While we refer to it as martyrdom, our treatment of it smacks of homicide . . . The distinction between homicide and martyrdom is very important because the implications of each are vastly different. When a homicide occurs, we feel a person's life has needlessly been wasted . . . But Imam Hussain engaged in a conscious confrontation, offered courageous resistance to a ruthless ruler. He showed by action . . . how to stand up to oppression. Therefore it was martyrdom. But martyrdom must arouse more than sorrow and

compassion; it must generate commitment to sacred causes. (Datoo 1994: 40–1)

Datoo also comments further on his understanding of the spiritual as paying homage to *Ahlul-Baith* and gaining understanding of the status of the Prophet. This, he concludes, was sufficient in itself and an un-questioned assumption as to the purpose of *majalis* in the East African context. This aim had its own ritual sufficiency as a time of uplift and edification for the community. In the West, the situation is different and the young do not readily accept the traditional ritual and cultural relevance of such gatherings. Datoo suggests they need to be given a philosophical underpinning or reasoning for their Islamic way of life which is symbolically intelligible and has, as a result, an existential relevance. Thus he uses the following example:

> The essence of symbolism is that there is a deeper, profound meaning in the acts. *Tawaf* and sa'y have been likened to struggles of the soul and the body respectively. *Tawaf* signifies the movement of getting ever closer to Allah (S. W. T.) who should be the centre (the *"kabaah"*) of our existence. The motion is circular, with the same beginning and end . . . *Sa'y* denotes the search for material well being . . . the motion is linear, with one begin-ning (starting point) and a different end (final destination). It captures the joys of living and the necessity for participation in this world . . . Islam disproves of the dichotomy between religious and secular obligations . . . Life is a sum, is a combination of *tawaf* and . . . *sa'y*. (1994: 42)

Tawaf is the circumambulation of the *kabaah, sa'y* is the walk between the mountains of Safa and Marwa. Both these rituals, completed on *hajj*, symbolize the struggles of Ibrahim and his wife Hajar, and their son, Ismail. Datoo's intention, in invoking this symbolism, is to distance the philosophical from the ritual understanding (1994: 41–2). Datoo appears to be equating moral and philosophical, as reasoned understandings, and separating them of from the other half of his equation, spiritual and ritual, which he regards as sufficient only within a traditionally Islamic society. His philosophical/ ritual distinction is provided to ensure that culturally traditional practices are clearly demarcated from "Islamic practices" or faith teachings. At the same time he advocates an emphasis on moral application in the Western environment rather than spiritual understanding (insofar as it is based on the emulation of examples of historically elevated figures in the *Ahlul Bait* – family of the Prophet – and the Prophet himself without question). His distinctions have some merit, in that he appears to suggest that a requirement to follow previous example has no significance for the young if it has no moral relevance to their lives today.

At the same time, however, his notion of philosophical under-

standing implies something more than reasoned acceptance and introduces a different understanding of the notion of the spiritual and
spiritual education. It implies reconceiving of an Islamic way of life for
those whose enculturation in the secular west implicitly denies such a
conception. In investigating this issue, we may locate the complexity at
the heart of the KSI dilemma. Datoo is concerned to emphasize how this
change in cultural location, from East Africa to the west, requires a
change in the function and content of *majalis*, but his analysis is equally
applicable to and in part addresses the role of both the *imambara* and the
medrassa. The young being brought up in the west (and bearing in mind
the effects of global communication and the influence of popular culture
his analysis is applicable beyond that) do not readily accept their Islamic
heritage and attendant religious and cultural practices without
question. There are peer and educational influences that reflect a
different sociocultural conditioning and cause the young to critically
challenge the value of traditional views and beliefs for their own lives.

Datoo's solution is to orient the young to a moral and philosophical
understanding of Islam, but his use of these terms requires some investigation. Moral, as it is used in relation to the distinction between
martyrdom and homicide, is inadequate. It appears that the understanding he wishes the young to acquire is the significance of witnessing
(as in the case of Imam Hussein) to the truth, i.e. the conviction that
living Islamically (being a good Muslim) requires sacrifice and resistance. This is different to an understanding of the event merely as an act
of homicide. The distinction between the two understandings is not one
of two different moral understandings but a distinction between a moral
judgement (homicide) and a witness to one's identity in relation to one's
convictions; a matter of *jihad* (struggle) against *shirk* (forgetfulness).
Such conviction arises not from an inculcation of normative ethical
codes of behaviour but from the piety exemplified in Datoo's metaphorical reference to *tawaf*, spiritually speaking seeking to come closer to
Allah. Sa'y, the living out of one's life in this world, in society, is then
informed by the spiritual purpose that proceeds from *tawaf*. The result
is an ownership of Muslim identity rather than just Muslim identification. The danger inherent in Datoo's analysis lies in confusion over
the meaning of terms. In arguing that what is required is a reasoned
acceptance of Islamic values Datoo falls into the trap of Western
thinking. The latter consists in the idea that rationalism is a sufficient
foundation for knowledge. As a consequence, it rejects the spiritual
insofar as it does not conform to this model. To the contrary, I would
argue that within Datoo's metaphoric illustration of *tawaf* we find a
spiritual aspiration that goes beyond his notion of rational faith and
moral understanding. In his example of martyrdom and witness we
have more than moral commitment, hence my reference to piety.

In summary, my argument is that prioritizing the moral and rational over the spiritual, whilst theoretically being an acknowledgement
that instruction of itself is not sufficient, will not enjoin young Khojas
to take on Shi'a identity. Ownership of a faith identity goes beyond
rational justification and a commitment to certain moral values,
though it will include these. Ownership resides in the existential conviction of a relational experience with that which is at the heart of the
faith – thus the spiritual significance of *tawaf*. Without this the possibility of identification without identity is still very real, as is the
likelihood of simplifying the pedagogical process such that it becomes
a means of instilling traditional moral understandings without
taking account of the cultural context which young Khoja Shi'as are
experiencing.

Voices from the Next Generation

I conclude with an example of how ownership of Islamic identity can
operate within the lives of specific individuals among the Khoja youth
but does so by choice. This example focuses on the wearing of *hijab*.
Hijab, for female Shi'as, identifies them as different from their peers by
appearance, thus it becomes a means of identification. The following
illustration is taken from an interview in which I am seeking to determine to what extent wearing *hijab* also represents an ownership of
Islamic identity.

> T: In my school there are loads of Muslims . . . In my form there are three
> . . . (but) There's like five Shi'as in the whole school. And, like, in RE classes
> we'll be discussing something and they'll say "You wear *hijab*, how come
> she doesn't?" Some people wear it just because of their parents, so they
> don't wear it properly in school, and they (non-Muslim students) say,
> "Well, what is the point of doing that?"
> M: You've got to understand. If it doesn't make sense to us then there is
>   no point in doing it. If it didn't make sense, we wouldn't do it.
> T: In schools, if you have self-respect people will respect you as well. If
>   you value yourself other people will value you as well . . . If we were to
>   lose our religion we would lose our moral values, our community, we
>   would lose everything about us and have no identity . . . we would feel
>   really lost and out of place, not knowing where to go and what to do.

This response indicates that these two girls have worked through the
connection between adopting a Muslim appearance and relating that to
their own convictions. In their articulation of this, there is recognition
of why this needs to be the case in relation to self-worth and respect
across difference accorded by their non-Muslim peers. If *medrassa*
education is to be of any worth it needs to take the message these young

Shi'as are articulating seriously. It needs to be concerned with that which matters in terms of self-identity, which means taking the experiences of Khoja youth seriously. Metaphorically speaking, encouraging them to wish to continue circling the *kabaah, tawaf,* will not be achieved by teaching them *sa'y* in a manner that takes no account of social and cultural change. To do that would ensure that the circling loses its momentum.

Equally, we might say that in its configuration spiritual education in the *medrassa* should be less like *sa'y* in design, a linear experience or instructional in nature, and more like *tawaf,* guidance that encourages the motivation for continuing momentum. Understood in this sense faith education can be an aid to, or support for, the ownership of Shi'a identity rather than *the* means of its inculcation.

Note

1   The history of the KSI is little documented and relies mostly on publications produced within the community itself. The following give more detailed accounts: Jaffer, Asgharali M. M. (undated): *An Outline History of the Khoja Shia Ithnaasheri in East Africa.* Harefield, Middlesex: Dar al Tableegh; C. Erricker 2001: The Diaspora of the Khoja Shia Ithnasheeries. In C. Erricker and J. Erricker (eds), *Contemporary Spiritualities: religious and social contexts.* London/New York: Cassell. Also transliteration of terms varies across different works, there has been no standardization in KSI literature. In this essay I have not changed the forms used, thus they vary in the quotations included, and are not necessarily in the standard form used in academic literature.

References

Bakhtin M. M. 1986: *Speech, Genres and Other Late Essays.* In C. Emerson and M. Holquist (eds), V. W. McGee (trans.), Austin, TX: University of Texas Press.

Benjamin, W. 1968: Theses on the philosophy of History. In *Illuminations,* New York: Schocken Books.

Bhabha, Homi K. 1994: *The Location of Culture,* London/New York: Routledge.

Datoo, B. A. 1994: Redefinition of the Institution of Majalis. In J. Alloo, M. Noormohamed and M. Datoo (eds), *The Role of Imambaras and Majalis in Modern Times,* London: Marble Press.

del Nevo, M. 1992: Letter from Lahore: Ozzy and Hussain, *The New Internationalist* 238, December.

Erricker, C. 2001: The Diaspora of the Khoja Shia Ithnasheeries. In C. Erricker and J. Erricker (eds), *Contemporary Spiritualities: religious and social contexts,* London/New York: Cassell.

Fanon, F. 1986: *Black Skin, White Masks,* London: Pluto.

Heidegger, M. 1971: Building, Dwelling, Thinking. In *Poetry, Language, Thought,* New York: Harper and Row.

Himmelfarb, H. 1982: Research on American Jewish Identity and Identification:

Progress, Pitfalls and Progress. In *Understanding American Jewry*, New Brunswick, NJ: Transaction Books.

Jaffer, Asgharali M. M. (undated): *An Outline History of the Khoja Shia Ithnaasheri in East Africa*, Harefield, Middlesex: Dar al Tableegh.

Keysar, A. Kosmin, B. and Scheckner, J. 2000: *The Next Generation: Jewish Children and Adolescents*, Albany: State University of New York Press.

Merali, S. and Aslam, S. 1998: On Marriage Ways – Norms of a By-gone Era. In S. Kurji, F. Alloo, M. Sumar and M. Datoo (eds), *Our Marriage Ways Will They Survive the Next Millenium*, Birmingham, Birmingham Jamaat.

Rahim, Mohammed Sadiq Hussein 1994: The Youth and the Imambaras. In J. Alloo, M. Noormohamed and M. Datoo. (eds), *The Role of Imambaras and Majalis in Modern Times*, London: Marble Press.

Sachedina, S. 1994: Majalis Contents for the Future. In J. Alloo, M. Noormohamed, M. Datoo (eds), *The Role of Imambaras and Majalis in Modern Times*, London: Marble Press.

Somani, A. 1994: Traditional Majalis-Valid in Modern Times? In J. Alloo, M. Noormohamed and M. Datoo (eds), *The Role of Imambaras and Majalis in Modern Times*, London: Marble Press.

Springarn, J. E. (ed.) 1921: *Goethe's Literary Essays*, New York: Harcourt, Brace.

Winter, Jerry A. 1989: Income, Identity and Involvement in the Jewish Community: A Test of an Estimate of the Affordability of Living Jewishly, *Journal of Jewish Communal Service* 66 (2), 149–56.

Conclusion

If the "warp" of this book's design is the different disciplinary approaches to spiritual education, the "weft" of the pattern lies in the connections across contributions from different disciplines and the issues highlighted when these connections are observed. Below we have identified issues which have emerged as being of obvious significance.

Religious Language and Spiritual Experience

Hay, for example, is clearly concerned that religious language should not disappear as a medium for spiritual expression, but cautions against literacy being the measure of spiritual development. The latter point is echoed in both Berryman's and Morris's contributions but argued differently. The former is present in Tacey's and Chater's searches for a renewed theology consistent with the spiritual searching of the young. In a different context, Clive Erricker identifies the importance of Islamic religious metaphor as a basis for constructing pedagogic practice within that faith. Elsewhere, however, other contributors also stress the need to ensure that religious and spiritual are not terms to be equated.

The Cultivation of Relationship

This is a key theme running through the contributions and is related to notions of identity, enculturation and nurture, community and the importance of listening. With respect to this Westerman, Yates, Chater, Priestley and Wong Ping Ho point to a spiritual poverty in modernism. Gearon further politicizes this by advocating a spirituality of dissent. Nesbitt emphasizes the importance of the influence of the nurturing environment on the individual. Champagne identifies that listening is an active, responsive and analytic activity. Hay disabuses us of the idea that spirituality is developed in solitude. Alexander and Ben-Peretz criticize the idea that curriculum is epistemologically based rather than values based. Dixon speaks of the centrality of a nurturing relationship and the need to rediscover it. Eaude suggests that conversation and attentiveness are key activities at the heart of spiritual education.

The Importance of Narration and the Empowerment of Children and Young People

These are themes intimately linked to the one above. Storytelling and narrative are recognized as being powerful tools and important processes in the construction of identity and relationship. In particular Scott emphaizes how personal narrative may perform a number of functions and that the teller may feel embarrassed to express her or himself so intimately for fear of ridicule. Sasso speaks of stories being important as vehicles for spiritual questioning. Narration for many of the contributors is the key to accessing understanding of the spiritual and for engaging in spiritual education. This is clear in the contributions of Scott, Ota, Hay, Champagne and Dixon amongst others.

The Importance of Affective or Holistic Education

This is centrally addressed in Bosacki's contribution where she seeks to find a meeting point for cognitive psychology and emotional development. It is also addressed by Jane Erricker when she speaks of children's emotional and aesthetic potential. Allusion to this theme is found also threading through the majority of contributions in different ways in speaking of the whole person, addressing questions of identity, or seeking to ground education in experience.

The significance of the above considerations for pedagogy is without doubt. But, whilst there are practical skills identified as important within the contributions, it is emphasized that they cannot be acquired and utilized without a vision of what the educator is seeking to achieve overall, and how that fits with a conception of education related to social values and what it means to be a person, as opposed to just a child, consumer, worker or other identity label that is simply functional in nature. In Westerman's phrase, we have to address "a deep pedagogical unrest".

The overall value of this collection of research into children's spirituality and spiritual education amounts to more than the sum of its parts. It provides a severe criticism of modern education and the shallow conceptions on which it is based. This can be seen to apply generally, whether speaking of it taking place in a religious faith environment or a state or "secular" one (which is not to say one cannot find "examples of good practice"). It also presents very clear indicators as to what is required to transform educational provision and social well-being. In doing so it affirms spiritual education as not just a subject in a curriculum or something addressed across a curriculum. It is what is required, as a conception of education, before a curriculum can be properly constructed or any educational venture embarked upon.

The Contributors

Hanan A. Alexander teaches philosophy of education at the University of Haifa where he heads the Centre for Jewish Education and the Ethics and Education Project. He previously served as Vice President for Academic Affairs at the University of Judaism, as Lecturer in Education at the University of California Los Angeles, and as Editor of *Religious Education: An Interfaith Journal of Spirituality, Transformation, and Growth*. His book *Reclaiming Goodness: Education and the Spiritual Quest* (2001) charts a middle course between New Age spirituality and neo-Marxist critical theory on the left and fundamentalism on the right.

Jerome Berryman is an Episcopal priest who founded and directs the Centre for the Theology of Childhood in Houston, Texas, USA. He served for a decade as Canon Educator at Christ Church Cathedral in Houston and a decade in the Texas Medical Centre in Houston teaching medical ethics and developing paediatric pastoral care as well as many years in various school and parish settings. His training includes Princeton Theological Seminary and Tulsa University Law School, and his publications include some 30 articles, 10 chapters in books, and four books, among which is *Godly Play* (1991).

Sandra Leanne Bosacki is an Assistant Professor in the Graduate and Undergraduate Department of the Faculty of Education at Brock University, St. Catharines, Ontario, Canada. Her research interests include sociocognitive and spiritual/emotional development, gender issues, and resulting educational and cultural implications. She is currently a contributing associate editor of the *International Journal of Children's Spirituality* and has published in both psychology and education journals including the *Journal of Educational Psychology* and the *Journal of Early Adolescence*.

Elaine Champagne is Chaplain at the Montreal Children's Hospital of the McGill University Health Centre where she offers emotional and spiritual support to children and families dealing with serious illness or accidents. She is also a Ph.D. candidate at the Faculty of Theology of University of Montreal, Québec, Canada. Her research focuses on young children's spirituality in daily life.

Mark Chater is senior lecturer and subject leader in Religious Studies at Bishop Grosseteste College, a Church of England College of Higher Education in Lincoln, UK. His teaching and research covers theology, spirituality, educational management and church management.

Cynthia Dixon, a graduate of Aberdeen University, has a background of teaching, clinical psychology and religious education. Her interest in child development, particularly religious development, led to her doctoral studies at Murdoch University, Western Australia on the subject of the development of religious commitment in adolescents. Heading up a new Religious Studies Department at Edith Cowan University she has lectured for over twenty years in educational psychology, religious education and pastoral care seeking to make psychological insights available to the practical expression of the Christian faith. Linking academic interest with community involvement is expressed in projects such as volunteer religious instruction and chaplaincy in state schools and the role of the church in the issue of domestic violence. Retiring as Associate Dean of the Faculty of Arts she now holds an honorary position of Senior Fellow at Edith Cowan University.

Tony Eaude was previously headteacher of SS. Mary and John First School, Oxford and is currently studying for a D.Phil. (exploring how teachers of young children understand the notion of spiritual development) and working as a freelance consultant.

Clive Erricker is Reader in Religious Education at University College Chichester. He is co-director of the Children and Worldviews Project and co-editor of the *International Journal of Children's Spirituality*. His recent publications include joint authorship of *The Education of the Whole Child* (1997) and co-authorship of *Reconstructing Religious, Spiritual and Moral Education* (2000). He is also co-editor of and contributor to *Contemporary Spiritualities* (2001) and *Meditation in Education: Calmer Classrooms, Clearer Minds* (2001). He lives in Lee on Solent, Hampshire, UK with Jane and his four children: Katy, Sam, Polly and Tana.

Jane Erricker is a Principal Lecturer in Education at King Alfred's College Winchester, where she teaches Science Education and Spiritual and Moral Education and Citizenship. She co-directs the Children and Worldviews Project with Clive Erricker, and co-edits the *International*

Journal of Children's Spirituality. She is a member of the management committee of Antidote, an organization promoting Emotional Literacy. Her publications include *The Education of the Whole Child* and *Reconstructing Religious, Spiritual and Moral Education*.

Liam Gearon is a Reader in the Faculty of Education, University of Surrey Roehampton. He is joint editor of *Contemporary Catholic Theology: A Reader* (1999), editor of *English Literature, Theology and the Curriculum* (1999) and has recently also edited *Religion and Human Rights: A Reader* (Brighton and Portland: Sussex Academic Press 2002).

David Hay is a zoologist who worked for several years at the Religious Experience Research Unit in Oxford on the biology of religious experience. In 1985 he was appointed director of the Unit, and remained in that post until 1990. Latterly he was appointed Reader in Spiritual Education at the University of Nottingham, a position from which he retired in the summer of 2000. His most recent book *The Spirit of the Child*, written with Rebecca Nye, was published in 1998. Currently he is writing a book about his latest research into the spirituality of adults who have no formal religion.

Laura Morris was educated at Cambridge University, where she graduated with a BA Hons in Theology and Religious Studies. Laura is at present training to teach Secondary/High School pupils Religious Education at Exeter University. Her interest in Autism began with the diagnosis of her godson, Jack. Laura continues to work with children with Aspergers in the Autism unit at her first school placement in Dorset, UK.

Eleanor Nesbitt is Senior Lecturer in Religions and Education at the Institute of Education, University of Warwick. She has conducted ethnographic studies of religious nurture in Christian, Hindu and Sikh communities. Her publications include (with Robert Jackson) *Hindu Children in Britain* (1993), (with Gopinder Kaur) *Guru Nanak* (1999, winner of Shap award for 2000) and *The Religious Lives of Sikh Children: A Coventry-Based Study* (2000).

Cathy Ota is a research fellow for the Children and Worldviews Project which is currently jointly funded by King Alfred's College Winchester and University College Chichester. Having recently completed her doctoral studies on church schools and children's development she continues to work with Jane and Clive Erricker, combining research with editorial duties for the *International Journal of Children's Spirituality*. She lives in Brighton, East Sussex and as well as enjoying her new baby is Chair of Governors at the local Catholic Primary School where her two sons Ben and Nick attend.

Miriam ben Peretz teaches curriculum studies at the University of Haifa where she previously served as Head of the Centre for Jewish Education and Dean of the School of Education. She is a recipient of the Life Time Achievement in Curriculum Studies from the American Educational Research Association. She is also the author of numerous articles and books including *The Teacher–Curriculum Encounter: Freeing teachers from the tyranny of texts* (1990), *Learning from Experience: Memory and the teacher's account of teaching* (1995), and most recently, with Shifra Schonmann, *Behind Closed Doors: Teachers and the role of the teachers' lounge* (2000).

Jack Priestley was Principal of Westhill College of Higher Education, now fully integrated into the University of Birmingham. He has returned as a Research Fellow to his former institution, the School of Education at the University of Exeter. Freed from administration, he has begun to produce a string of papers centred around the notion of the spiritual dimension of education, offering a critique of the business dominated values which he sees as endangering the concepts of education, culture and religion throughout the Western world. He has a particular interest in the prophetic voices of the nineteenth and twentieth centuries such as those of Kierkegaard, Coleridge, William James, Whitehead and Wittgenstein.

Rabbi Sandy Sasso Eisenberg has been the spiritual leader of Congregation Beth-El Zedeck, Indianapolis. Ordained from the Reconstructionist Rabbinical College in 1974 she received her Doctorate of Ministry from Christian Theological Seminary. She is the author of nationally acclaimed children's books including *God's Paintbrush* and *In God's Name*. Publisher's Weekly selected *But God Remembered* and *A Prayer for the Earth* as Best Books of the Year. She is lecturer in Religion and Judaism at Butler University and Christian Theological Seminary. Her essays have appeared in *The Woman's Torah Commentary*, *Falling From Grace* and *Women and Religious Ritual*.

Daniel Scott is an Assistant Professor in the School of Child and Youth Care, University of Victoria, Victoria, BC, with additional teaching responsibilities in the Department of Curriculum and Instruction, Faculty of Education. He is currently collecting narratives of late childhood and early adolescent spiritual experiences as part of a research project that seeks to understand the role of spirituality in the formation of adult values and identity. He is also involved on a team that is developing a handbook on the use of story telling in community building and community development for the World Council of Churches URM network. His publications include "Rites of passage in adolescent development: A re-appreciation", *Child & Youth Care Forum* 27(5), (1998), which was part of a special issue exploring rites of passage that he co-edited.

David Tacey is Associate Professor and Reader in Arts at La Trobe University, Melbourne. He is an author, lecturer, public speaker and journalist who addresses such topics as popular spirituality, youth experience, ecology, Aboriginal reconciliation and contemporary religion. His books include *ReEnchantment: The New Australian Spirituality* (2000), *Remaking Men: Jung, Spirituality, and Social Change* (1997), *Edge of the Sacred: Transformation in Australia* (1995), and *Patrick White, Fiction and the Unconscious* (1988). His new book, *Jung and the New Age*, a study of popular spirituality and the New Age movement, will be published in 2001.

Wim Westerman, born in Indonesia, was trained as a teacher and studied philosophy of education at Amsterdam Free University. He has worked in primary and secondary education, in initial and in-service teacher training, and as an educational consultant for intercultural and religious education. For the last ten years he has been involved in educational projects in developing countries and Eastern Europe. He is secretary of the European Association for World Religions in Education.

Wong Ping Ho is a Senior Lecturer at the Department of Educational Psychology, Counselling and Learning Needs, the Hong Kong Institute of Education, Hong Kong, China. He had been a secondary-school teacher for ten years before moving into teacher education. He studied for his M.Ed. in religious and moral education at the University of Hong Kong. He is now also a Ph.D. student at the University of Hull, working on the issue of spirituality in education.

Paul Yates is an anthropologist lecturing in the Graduate Research Centre for Education in the University of Sussex. His major research interest is in the relationship between school and postmodernity especially as reflected in education policy and its outcomes. Recent publications have focussed on the affective curriculum, particularly the meaning and place of spirituality in school and the proposals for citizenship education.

Index